I. C. S.
REFERENCE LIBRARY

A SERIES OF TEXTBOOKS PREPARED FOR THE STUDENTS OF THE
INTERNATIONAL CORRESPONDENCE SCHOOLS AND CONTAINING
IN PERMANENT FORM THE INSTRUCTION PAPERS,
EXAMINATION QUESTIONS, AND KEYS USED
IN THEIR VARIOUS COURSES

FRENCH GRAMMAR

SCRANTON
INTERNATIONAL TEXTBOOK COMPANY

55

PRESS OF
INTERNATIONAL TEXTBOOK COMPANY
SCRANTON, PA.

26160

CONTENTS

CONTENTS

CONTENTS

CONTENTS

FRENCH GRAMMAR

(PART 1)

INTRODUCTION

1. Historical Element in Language Teaching. — It is well known that memory retains with greater ease and tenacity that which is understood. An abstract grammatical rule, unaccompanied by explanation or illustration and with no apparent reason for existence, is not only perplexing but is quickly forgotten. To be attractive, grammar should account for its rules. Constant appeals to memory, rather than to reason and judgment, render any subject tiresome and uninteresting; in this work, therefore, reference will frequently be made to facts in the origin and evolution of the French language, whenever such facts will aid in accounting for present idioms or present grammatical forms and constructions. It should be stated, however, that no citations will be made from historical grammar that will require a knowledge of the classics for their comprehension.

LANGUAGE AND GRAMMAR

2. Language in General. — In its widest sense, the word *language* includes every means by which thought or feeling may be made known. Thus, we speak of the various languages of nature, and of the language of painting, sculpture, and architecture. Everything in nature, as well as everything that bears marks of the thought and labor of man, speaks, more or less plainly, a language. The world

§ 16

is full of inanimate things that tell of human hope, purpose, and struggle; of achievement, taste, and refinement. Such thought and feeling as the lower animals are capable of, they can make known to us more or less intelligibly. But this dumb and wordless language requires no grammatical treatment, for it makes no use of nouns and verbs, or of words and sentences. It is the language of man alone that is governed by laws, and is, therefore, capable of being reduced to a science.

There are many ways in which man may make his thoughts known to others; as, for example, by grimace, gesture, the signs of the deaf and dumb, symbols, pictorial writing, and pictures. But better than any or all of these, are oral speech and written language. It is chiefly by this faculty of speech that man is distinguished from the lower animals, and this faculty is so far above the power of expression possessed by brutes that many people believe human language to have been a gift of divine origin.

3. Origin of the Word Language. — The word language is derived from the Latin word *lingua*, the tongue; and since this is the chief organ used in speech, the word for *tongue* is employed in many languages to mean oral speech. In the early history of our race, language was spoken but not written. With the advance of civilization, however, came the need for something more lasting than mere verbal utterance. This gave rise to the first attempts to record thought by writing, which, we are told, were at first mere symbols or rude pictures so arranged as to have a meaning more or less plain, and traces of which are said to remain in the letters of our own alphabet. Thus, it is now believed that our letter A has taken its present form from the representation of an *eagle* by the ancient Egyptians; B, from that of a *crane;* C, from the picture of a *throne;* etc.

The word language denoted at first only spoken thought, but its meaning was extended as explained above. For grammatical science, however, the only kinds of language considered are spoken and written.

Definition.—**Language,** *as treated in grammar, is the body of uttered and written signs used by men to express and communicate their thoughts.*

4. Living Languages.—As has been stated, written language is an outgrowth from mere speech; and each language, both spoken and written, continues to grow and to improve as long as the people using it maintain their national existence. Discovery, invention, and changes of every kind are constantly bringing to knowledge many things never before heard of—new articles of manufacture, new processes, new wants, tastes, arts, and sciences. These require exact expression and consequently new words must be devised. On the other hand, old things pass away and the words that named them become useless and are no longer employed; that is, they become *obsolete*. So rapid is this process of change that English as it was written 1,000 years ago is nearly as difficult for us to understand as is Greek, Latin, or German. Letters have acquired new forms, words have changed, both in their form and meaning, or have passed entirely out of use, and the spelling and pronunciation of those that remain are now very different from what they were some hundreds of years ago.

A language, while it is in actual use and is undergoing these additions, losses, and changes, is said to be a *living* language.

5. Dead Languages.—It has often happened in the history of the world that nations have lost their country by war. The people have sometimes been driven out by invaders, reduced to slavery, and gradually destroyed; or, deprived of their political powers and rights, they have been permitted to remain in their country, and by a slow process of absorption, have merged their identity as a people into that of their conquerors. Many examples of such national catastrophes will occur to the student.

The Roman Empire was destroyed in this way by the barbarian ancestors of the people that now inhabit Northern

Europe. The Latin language was soon no longer spoken in its purity, but was mixed with the speech of the conquerors. All that remained of it was what was found in the books that had been written before the fall of the Empire. Many of these have been lost during the long period since, but enough remain to show that at that time these people had the richest literature in the world. But, however great has been the change wrought upon the Latin language by the races that overthrew the people of Rome, many of the books written by great authors of the ruined nation remain unchanged. These still give us, in its purity, the wonderful language of Rome—the language of Livy and Tacitus, of Cicero and Cæsar, of Vergil, Ovid, and Horace. What they wrote nearly 20 centuries ago, remains today exactly as they wrote it; and without doubt it will be studied in the schools for thousands of years to come in the precise form it has at present. It other words, it is a *dead* language. There are many others like it, and the books written in them centuries ago may be read and understood by scholars as well as we read and understand books written in our own language.

HISTORY OF THE FRENCH LANGUAGE

6. Origin of the French Language.—The French language is derived from the Latin. Several other languages spring from the same source, chief among them being the Italian, the Spanish, the Portuguese, and the Wallachian. Together they form the so-called **Romance languages.**

The language and the history of peoples are intimately related. Two great events in the history of France had a vital influence upon her language. Between 58 B. C. and 50 B. C., the Romans conquered the Celts, who were the first historical inhabitants of what is now France; in the 5th century the Franks became masters of her soil. These two events had not, however, the same effect upon the language.

It is a general law of history that when one people is conquered by another and—by the slow processes of amalgamation—the identity of the one people is lost in the identity of the other, the more polished and refined language, whether that of the victors or the vanquished, is adopted as the language of the mixed nation. In obedience to this general law, the Celts abandoned their own tongue for the Latin of their Roman conquerors, and in a later day the rough, unlettered Franks cast off their mixed Teutonic dialects for the incipient French of the steadily mixing Gauls and Romans. They introduced, however, into the newly forming French tongue about 400 words of Teutonic origin.

7. Influence of the Celtic Language.—The Celtic, although abandoned for the nobler Latin of Rome, has nevertheless left its influence upon the French; and this heritage is not limited merely to the material part of the language, to words designating objects, but it has also had a most potent influence over the general process of elocution, over the spirit of grammar. Many words naming animals and plants, many expressions relating to agriculture and mineral substances, and many common words referring to tools, arms, utensils, clothes, and similar things, have a Celtic origin. It should be noticed that most of these words are monosyllabic—a characteristic of all primitive tongues.

Two facts that point out still more clearly the intimate relation existing between the Celtic and the French (and which are the chief grammatical distinction between the French and the Latin) are the use of the article in the French and the suppression of those involved and complicated declensions that form at once the difficulty and the charm of Latin. Although the word *ille, illa, illud,* from which the French article is derived, is a Latin word, the use of the article is a Celtic peculiarity. There were no declensions in the Celtic, and it was but natural that a people whose native tongue did not provide for them should have rejected all declensions when adopting the language of a foreign conqueror.

Even French pronunciation has been influenced by the Celtic. The letters *u*, *è*, and especially the *e* mute, so rare in other languages, and the *j* (having the sound of *sh*, or of *s* in *pleasure*), which was unknown to other European peoples, were all found in the pronunciation of the Celts.

8. Influence of Latin. — When Cæsar conquered the Gauls, he spared neither favor nor promise to win adherents from those whom he had vanquished. The result was that many Gauls renounced their own national customs and were rapidly Romanized. Thenceforth the Latin language, which had already gained a foothold throughout Gaul, was industriously propagated by the Romans through the various agencies of governmental administration, commerce, literature, the theater, and by other means which Rome knew so well how to manipulate to impose her language, manners, and customs upon subject peoples. Perhaps that particular feature of the Roman system which contributed most to the adoption of Latin by the Celts, was the Roman judicial system and the establishment of Latin as the official language of the law courts, so that plaintiff and defendant were both compelled to address the Roman magistrate and to state their cases in Latin.

The poorer classes, and especially those of the country districts, naturally did not adopt the new language so soon as the rich and the powerful, or the inhabitants of cities, who every day heard the polished language of Roman officials and the coarser speech of the Roman soldiery. But as time went on the poor peasants began to imitate the Roman habits and speech of their superiors, until at last Latin had permeated the whole of Gaul. The native tongue rapidly fell into disuse, and in the 4th century Latin was spoken from the mouth of the Seine to Marseilles.

9. Popular and Classical Latin. — The history of a language is very similar to that of the people that use it. Both people and language have each at first substantial unity, neither having any apparent lines of cleavage. Soon, however, the nation separates into well-defined classes, usually two: one of these is made up of the learned, the wealthy, the well-born; the other is composed of the common people — the laboring classes. The language used by each of these classes always partakes of the nature of the people themselves — correct, refined, and finished in the one case; incorrect and devoid of fixed rules in the other. In their extreme development, these two varieties of speech are called **Classical,** and **popular** or **vulgar** (from *vulgus*, the common people).

In Rome, therefore, two varieties of Latin were in daily use: the *popular Latin* of the common people, and the *Classical Latin* of the noble, the learned, and the wealthy. These two, while preserving a close general resemblance, had separated so far that in many cases different words were used to express the same idea. In Classical Latin, for example, *equus* stood for horse, while the popular term was *caballus*.

Classical Latin had a complicated declension composed of six cases, expressing delicate and subtle shades of meaning. These refined variations were too difficult for uncultured peasants, so that in vulgar Latin the cases were reduced to two: the *nominative* for the subject, and the *accusative* for the object. Finally, of these two, only one remained — the accusative — it being the case most frequently used in the sentence. It was this vulgar Latin that the soldiers of Rome carried with them into Gaul. The Celts gradually transformed it, chiefly by altering its pronunciation.

10. Invasion of the Franks. — At the time of the Frank invasion in the 5th century, the Roman Empire fell to pieces. Administration, justice, schools, and scholars largely disappeared; with them went also the Classical Latin, which thus became a dead language. But the vulgar Latin remained and was adopted by the Franks.

It may seem strange, at first sight, that victorious invaders should abandon their own tongue for that of their defeated enemies, but the great numerical superiority of the Gallo-Romans among whom the Franks settled, and the fact that the Franks themselves had no uniform and well-defined language, but spoke various Teutonic dialects, contributed chiefly to this end. Furthermore, not long after their conquest of Gaul, the Franks were converted to Christianity, and their religion then compelled them to understand Latin. But although the Franks were unable to break down the Latin language, they introduced into it many Teutonic words descriptive of the new institutions they brought with them from beyond the Rhine. From these three elements — Celtic, Roman, Teutonic — another tongue sprang up, new, imperfect, and rude, but at least rich in national characteristics.

11. Dialects and Patois. — The confusion attendant upon the fall of the Roman Empire made it impossible for this changing Latin to be uniform throughout the Celtic domain. From the wreck of that Empire there sprang up in France innumerable petty kingdoms and dukedoms, and the independence and partial isolation of these little states resulted in the birth of many **dialects,** which, although having a common origin in the mixed language of the Celts, the Romans, and the Franks, were characterized by radical differences.

In Gaul, two great rival races sprang up, each having its own dialect. The tongue of the northern race, on which the influence of the Franks was greatest, was known as the *Langue d' Oil;* the tongue of the southern race, where the influence of the Romans was greatest, was known as the *Langue d' Oc.* These names were given in accordance with the custom in the middle ages of designating a language by its word for *yes*, the sign of the affirmative.

The language of the north, in its turn, being used by populations of various origin (Normands, Picards, Bourguignons, etc., each of whom pronounced Latin in his own way), was itself subdivided into as many dialects as there were political and racial centers. In Normandy, for example, all official acts and literary writings were composed in the dialect of the province. Normand, Picard, Bourguignon, and Français, the four chief dialects of the north, were about equally distributed. French, Français, was at first merely the dialect of Isle-de-France, a small province with Paris as its capital. Outside this province French was regarded as a foreign dialect; but because of the peculiar situation and consequent augmenting political influence of Isle-de-France, its dialect was destined to become the language of the entire French nation. In the course of time the dukes of Isle-de-France became kings of France, and gradually extended their authority over the whole country. The French dialect followed in the wake of the kings and slowly became the dialect of the conquered provinces. It was a long time, however, before the common people relinquished their own dialects and adopted French.

When the peasants began to write in French, their provincial dialects degenerated into mere *patois*, an idiom not used in written speech and having no recognized standing as a language. It will thus be seen that the patois, which is often erroneously thought to be the corrupt French spoken by the peasants of the provinces, is nothing more than the remains of those dialects that were once the literary languages of medieval provinces.

12. Other Influences. — Many words of foreign origin have been gradually introduced into French by political and scientific influences. Thus, in the 13th century the crusades and the influences incident to an extensive commerce with the East, added some Arabic and Oriental words; in the 16th century, wars with Italy, combined with the sweeping effects of the Renaissance, added about 500 words of Italian origin; in the 17th century, wars with Spain and Germany introduced a few words of Spanish and German origin; and in the century that has just closed, some words relating to sport, commerce, railroads, inventions, and other mechanical, business, and scientific matters were adopted from the English. Many new words required by the development and discoveries of science are also constantly being formed from Classical Greek and Latin words and incorporated into the French vocabulary.

GRAMMAR

13. **The Province of Grammar.** — In order to understand a language, it is necessary to be familiar with the forms and sounds of its letters and with their various combinations in words. Of these words, we must know the forms generally approved by the best authorities, how they are pronounced, and what they mean when united in sentences. If, in consequence of being used in various ways, words undergo changes in form, pronunciation, or meaning, the principles and laws that regulate these changes must be understood. Besides all this, it is necessary to be familiar with the origin of words, with the elementary parts that compose them, and with the meaning of those parts alone and in combination. Then, too, when words are associated in sentences to express thought, the person that speaks or writes, as well as he that hears or reads, must, in order to understand exactly what those sentences mean, be acquainted with the laws that regulate the order, form, and relations of the words in such combinations. Besides, if we would choose words and arrange them in sentences that will be smooth and musical, concise and forcible, easily understood, and in accordance with the best usage, there are many other things with which we must be perfectly familiar. All this knowledge and much more make up, when properly arranged, the science of *grammar*.

Definition. — Grammar *is the science that treats of the principles governing the correct use of language, either oral or written.*

14. **Divisions of Grammar.** — Grammar has been divided into three parts: (1) the study of letters (*phonetics*), (2) the study of words (*lexicology*), (3) the study of sentences (*syntax*).

The first part may also be called the grammar of letters, since it treats of the spelling and pronunciation of words. The other two parts include such principles as are necessary in giving the sentence its approved form and in properly arranging its constituent parts.

THE STUDY OF LETTERS

15. The Alphabet. — The French alphabet is the same as the English. The letters and their names are as follows, the names being pronounced as French words:

a, *ah*	**h,** *ache*	**o,** *o*	**v,** *vé*
b, *bé*	**i,** *i*	**p,** *pé*	**w,** *double vé*
c, *cé*	**j,** *ji*	**q,** *ku*	**x,** *ikse*
d, *dé*	**k,** *kâ*	**r,** *erre*	**y,** *i grec*
e, *é*	**l,** *elle*	**s,** *esse*	**z,** *zède*
f, *effe*	**m,** *emme*	**t,** *té*	
g, *gé*	**n,** *enne*	**u,** *u*	

16. Division of Letters. — The letters of the alphabet are divided into *vowels* (*voyelles*) and *consonants* (*consonnes*), the first having a proper sound by themselves, while the second cannot very well be pronounced without the aid of a vowel. The vowels are *a, e, i, o, u, y*.

17. Division of Words Into Syllables. — (*a*) A consonant belongs to the vowel following, not to the preceding one. Thus,

sa-la-de, a-mi, po-ta-ge, sa-lut, me-nu, ha-ri-cot, ma-la-de.

(*b*) In case of a double consonant, the first belongs to the preceding vowel, the second to the following one. Thus,

cor-don-nier, ex-cel-lent, mar-ché, bal-lon, par-fait.

(*c*) *l* or *r*, following another consonant, form a compound consonant subject to the foregoing rules. Other compound consonants are *st, gn, ch, ph.* Thus,

a-che-ter, ac-com-pa-gner, bi-bli-o-thè-que, cham-bre.

These rules are of the utmost importance in determining the pronunciation of masculine and feminine adjectives.

To form the feminine of adjectives, *e* is usually added to the masculine. Thus,

grand, gran-de; pe-tit, pe-ti-te; brun, bru-ne; vert, ver-te.

The feminine in these cases contains one more syllable than the masculine. The last consonant in the masculine is generally silent, while in the feminine, it is sounded.

18. Tonic Accent.—In most languages, some one syllable in a word is uttered more strongly than are the others. This syllable is said to be **accented.** In French, this accent is slight—hardly observable—still it exists and *falls upon the last syllable of a word.*

But, if the last syllable is mute (ending in *e,* or in the *ent* of the third person plural of a verb), the accent *falls on the preceding syllable.* Thus,

sa-la-de, **par**-lent, mar-**cher,** jou-**er,** par-**ler, mar**-che.

VOWELS

19. a is ordinarily short, like *a* in *fat,* when it has no circumflex accent over it. Thus,

avec, mal, cas, çanapé, bal, rat, salle.

But in syllables containing the tonic accent before a mute syllable, the sound of *a* is a little longer. Thus,

table, salade, voyage, malade, page, rage.

â with a circumflex accent is long, like *a* in *far.* Thus,

bâtir, je bâtis, gâter, nous gâtons, gâteau.

i always has the sound of *ee* in *bee,* but with varying length. It is short in

ami, ici, si, midi, riz, nid, rire, lire.

î is long if it has a circumflex accent or is followed by *e.* Thus,   dîner, je dîne, jolie, je prie, amie.

y between consonants, or alone, sounds like the French *i.* Thus,   y, il y a, style, physique, pyramide.

o is short when it has no circumflex accent. Thus,

Carnot, potage, trop, votre, loto, domino.

ô is long when it has a circumflex accent. Thus,

hôtel, le nôtre, le vôtre, dôme, monôme.

u has no equivalent in English. In pronouncing it, the lips should be shaped as if about to whistle.

Note.—Students who have taken the Conversational French should listen to the following words, as given in Lesson XII: *connu, dû, pu, su, voulu.*

u is lengthened when followed by *e.*   Thus,

> connue, due, voulue, sue, rue, mue, nue.

e without an accent is sounded like *e* in *her*, or like *u* in *fur.*   Thus,

> le, me, ne, te, se, je, revoir, menu, ce, que.

e without an accent is mute at the end of a word.   Thus,

> parle, désire, madame, marche, salle, rame.

In such cases, the preceding consonant is always sounded. When **e** without an accent lies between two sounded consonants, it is not pronounced.   Thus,

> samedi, avenue, boulevard, acheté, promener.

é with an acute accent should be carefully noted.   It has the sound of *a* in *fate.*   Thus,

> parlé, désiré, dîné, mangé, marché, demeuré.

Its sound is heard in *er* when the *r* is mute (as, for example, in the endings of the infinitives of verbs of the first conjugation).   Thus,

> parler, désirer, demeurer, étudier, donner, marcher.

The same sound also occurs in the endings *ez, ied, ieds.* Thus,

> vous parlez, vous désirez, je m'assieds, il s'assied.

è with a grave accent has the sound of *ai* in *air* and is illustrated in the following:

> je me lève, dernière, mène, mère, père, frère.

The same sound occurs in words ending in *er* in which the *r* is sounded.   Thus,

> amer, cher, éther, fer, hier, hiver, fier, mer, ver.

ê with a circumflex accent resembles *è* with the grave accent but is longer in duration.   Thus,

> la tête, même, être, bête, fenêtre, hêtre.

COMPOUND VOWELS

20. ou has the sound of *oo* in pool. It is illustrated in the following words:

> vous, où, Loubet, toujours, nous, oubli, sous.

au, aux, eau, eaux have the broad sound of *o* in *note*. Thus, aussi, canaux, beau, chapeaux, nouveau, taux.

eu, eux, œu, œux have the broad sound of *u* in *fur*. Thus,   peu, seulement, cheveux, vœu, vœux.

In the different forms of *avoir*, *eu* has the sound of the French *u*. Thus,

> J'ai eu, J'eus, Il eut, Nous eûmes, Ils eurent.

ai, ay, ei, ey, ais, and **ait** are pronounced like *è*. When initial or final, as in

> mais, reine, j'aimais, il chantait, jouais, aimable.

When followed by a mute syllable, as in

> Madeleine, reine, plaine, peine, baleine.

When **ai** is final in the past definite or future of a verb, it is sounded like *é*. Thus,

> Je parlai, J'écoutai, Je parlerai, J'écouterai.

VOYELLES NASALES—NASAL VOWELS

21. When *m* or *n* follows any vowel, there are three cases to be considered.

1. *m* or *n* between two vowels belong to the following syllable (see Art. **17**). Thus,

> semaine, dîner, ami, Rome, lune, ami.

2. Double *m* or *n* is pronounced as in English. Thus,

> comment, pomme, année, donne.

3. At the end of a word or before a consonant, *m* or *n* is nasal. There are four nasal sounds in French. They are merely vowel sounds in which the *m* or *n* must not be heard at all.

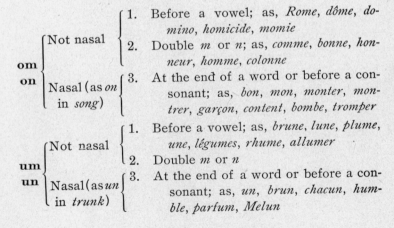

am an em en — Not nasal
1. Before a vowel; as, *ami, semaine, demi*
2. Double *m* or *n*; as, *année, emmener, anneau*

Nasal (as in *aunt*)
3. At the end of a word or before a consonant; as, *devant, ensuite, entrer, empêcher, splendide, enfant, langue*

im in — Not nasal
1. Before a vowel; as, *finir, minute, limite, lime*
2. Double *m* or *n*; as, *inné, immortel*

Nasal (as *an* in *slang*)
3. At the end of a word or before a consonant; as, *médecin, voisin, cousin, inspirer, imprimer, important*

Exceptions. — en preceded by *i* or *y*, is pronounced like *in* when the combination is a diphthong. Thus,

bien, italien, chien, citoyen, moyen, le mien.

But, in most adjectives and nouns, this sequence of letters is not a diphthong, consequently it preserves its natural nasal sound. Thus,

patient, patience, science, impatience.

In foreign nouns, *en* and *em* have the sound of nasal *in*. Thus,

agenda, Benjamin, Bengale, benzine, Européen, examen, mentor.

om on — Not nasal
1. Before a vowel; as, *Rome, dôme, domino, homicide, momie*
2. Double *m* or *n*; as, *comme, bonne, honneur, homme, colonne*

Nasal (as *on* in *song*)
3. At the end of a word or before a consonant; as, *bon, mon, monter, montrer, garçon, content, bombe, tromper*

um un — Not nasal
1. Before a vowel; as, *brune, lune, plume, une, légumes, rhume, allumer*
2. Double *m* or *n*

Nasal (as *un* in *trunk*)
3. At the end of a word or before a consonant; as, *un, brun, chacun, humble, parfum, Melun*

Exception. — **um** sounds like *om* (*m* pronounced) in the following words:

album, rhum, géranium, forum, opium.

22. **y** has the sound of *i*; but when it occurs after a vowel in the body of a word, it has the double sound of two *i*'s, the first being attached to the preceding syllable and the other to the following syllable. Thus, *pays* is pronounced as if it were *pai is; noyer,* as if it were *noi ier; citoyen,* as if *citoi ien.* However, in the following words it retains the sound of *i*:

Bayard, Bayonne, La Haye, Biscaye, Mayence,
La Fayette, mayonnaise.

DIPHTHONGS

23. Certain combinations of two vowels in one syllable are called **diphthongs.** Thus,

ia: fiacre, diable, lia, piano, plia
ié or **ier:** prié, volontiers, pied, scié
io: violon, yole, fiole, carriole
oi: boire, voir, avoir, roi, moi, crois
ui: lui, luire, cuire, induire, conduire
ieu: vieux, Dieu, lieu, mieux
ien: bien, lien, mien, rien, italien
oin: loin, moins, point, soin, foin
uin: juin, suinter, suint, Alcuin
ouen, ouan: Rouen Ecouen, Saint-Ouen, Chouan

24. Concerning a, e, and o. — The **o** is not pronounced in *faon, Laon, paon;* neither is the **a** in *Saône, taon, août;* nor the **e** in *Caen.*

25. Combinations With l and ll. — ll preceded by a vowel other than *i*, is always sounded. Thus,

fallu, allons, aller, salle, balle, barcarolle, colle, nulle.

It is also sounded in *ill* initial. Thus,

illicite, illettré, illustre, illégal, illégitime;

as well as in the following words:

> syllabe, Achille, distiller, Lille, mille, tranquille,
> ville, villa.

ill is generally pronounced like the French long *i* followed by a short sound of the *u* in *fur*, the *ll* being mute. Thus, famille, vanille, Bastille, manille, charmille,

> s'habiller, je m'habille, pupille, mantille, grille.

ail, ails, aille, ailles sound like *i* in the English word *fine* followed by the short sound of the *u* in *fur*, the *ll* being mute. Thus,

> travailler, je travaille, le travail, émail, bataille,
> paille, détail.

eil, eils, eille, eilles have no sound of *l* proper but the sound may be decomposed into *a* as in *fate*, followed by a short sound of *ee* in *bee*, and *u* in *fur*. Thus, merveille, Marseilles, Marseillaise, soleil,

> conseil, bouteilles.

ouil, ouille have a compound sound of *oo* in pool followed by *ee* in *bee* and *u* in *fur*. Thus,

> bouillon, grenouille, bouillir, brouillard.

eil, euille, ueille have a sound that may be resolved into a broad sound of the *u* in *fur* followed by a short sound of *ee* in *bee* and *u* in *fur*. Thus,

> auteuil, veuillez, feuille, deuil, je cueille.

CONSONANTS

26. The French language makes its consonants more prominent in pronunciation and its vowels less prominent than does the English.

B

27. b is more strongly emphasized than in English. It is always pronounced except in *aplomb*, *plomb*, and *Doubs*.

C

28. c is hard, like k, before *a, o, u*, and before consonants. Thus,

> pacte, placard, café, compter, cure, sucre.

c has the sound of soft *s* before *e, i, y;* also before *a, o, u,* when it is written with a cedilla ç. Thus,

> merci, ce, cycle, français, leçon, reçu.

c final is sounded like *k* in

> arc, avec, bec, bloc, bouc, choc, duc, lac, Luc,
> parc, public, pic, roc, sac, sec, suc, zinc.

It is not sounded in

> banc, blanc, clerc, estomac, flanc, franc, porc,
> tabac, tronc.

ct final is pronounced like *kt* in the following words:

> contact, correct, direct, district, intact, tact.

It is not sounded in

> abject, distinct, instinct, respect, suspect;

but is sounded in the derivations of these words. Thus,

> abjection, exactement, respectueux, etc.

ch has the sound of *sh* in English. Thus,

> achat, acheter, charité, chien, chat, acheter.

It has the sound of *k* in words of foreign origin. Thus,

> archange, chaos, chœur, chrétien, choléra, orchestre.

But it is silent in *almanach.*

D

29. **d** final is ordinarily silent. Thus,

> bond, billard, boulevard, canard, quand, etc.

However, it is sounded in *Alfred, David, sud.*

F

30. **f** final is pronounced in

> bœuf, bref, chef, neuf, œuf, soif, vif.

But it is silent in

> bœufs, cerf, clef, chef-d'œuvre, nerf, œufs.

G

31. **g** has the hard sound before *a, o, u.* Thus,

> cigogne, gâteau, gâter, garde, légumes.

Before *e, i, y*, it has the sound of *s* in pleasure. Thus,

> angine, girafe, argent, engagement, obligé.

g final is silent in

> rang, sang, long, legs, vingt.

gu has the hard sound of *g* before *i* and *e*; the *u* is silent, since it serves only to harden the *g*. Thus,

> langue, guide, vague, fatigué, ligue, digue.

ge before *a, o, u* has the *e* silent; it serves only to soften the *g*. Thus,

> nous mangeons, je mangeais, geai, nous protégeons.

gn has two pronunciations:

1. Like *gn* in the English word *ignorant*. Thus,

   > agnostique, diagnostic, ignition, stagnation.

2. In other words, it has the sound of *n* in *onion*. Thus,

   > Boulogne, Espagne, campagne, digne, Champagne, magnifique, signal.

H

32. **h** is always silent in French. There are, however, two uses of the letter:

1. The **aspirated h,** which prohibits the elision of the *e* or the *a* of a preceding *le* or *la*. Thus, *la hache, la Hollande.*

2. The **mute h,** before which the elision of *e* and *a* necessarily occurs. Thus, *l'honneur, l'homme, l'heure.*

Liaison (see Art. **46**) never occurs before an aspirated *h*. There are no rules by which to determine whether *h* is aspirated or mute, but the following are the principal words in which *h* is aspirated:

le hableur, *the boaster*	le harnais, *the harness*
le hachis, *hash*	la harpe, *the harp*
la hache, *the ax*	le hasard, *the hazard*
la hachette, *the hatchet*	la hâte, *haste*
la haie, *the hedge*	hacher, *to chop*
la haine, *the hatred*	hagard, *haggard*
le harem, *the harem*	la halte, *the halt*

le hamac, *the hammock*
le hameau, *the hamlet*
la hardiesse, *boldness*
le hareng, *the herring*
le haricot, *the bean*
le héros, *the hero*
le hêtre, *the beech*
héler, *to hail*
le hibou, *the owl*
haïr, *to hate*
hardi, *bold*
hâter, *to hasten*
la hanche, *the hip*
le hangar, *the shed*
Henri, *Henry*

la hauteur, *the height*
le hors-d'œuvre, *the side dish*
hors, *out*
hideux, *hideous*
le homard, *the lobster*
la Hollande, *Holland*
la honte, *the shame*
le houblon, *the hops*
la houe, *the hoe*
la houille, *the coal*
le Huguenot, *Huguenot*
la hutte, *the hut*
le hurlement, *the howling*
le hussard, *the hussar*
huit, *eight*

The following words are pronounced as if they had an aspirated *h*:

le onze, *the eleventh*
le onzième, *the eleventh*
la ouate, *cotton-wool*
le oui, *yes*

le yacht, *the yacht*
le uhlan, *German lancer*
le yatagan, *the yataghan*
la yole, *the yawl*

J

33. j always has the sound of *s* in the English word *pleasure.* Thus,

je, acajou, jour, toujours, joli, jeu, jeune.

K

34. k has the same sound as in English.

L

35. l final is ordinarily pronounced. Thus,

bal, bol, cil, fil, general, canal, journal, etc.

It is not pronounced in

baril, coutil, fusil, gentil, outil, sourcil.

M

36. m final is generally silent and has a nasal sound. Thus, daim, nom, parfum, renom, faim.

In proper nouns, however, **m** final is sounded.   Thus,

Amsterdam, Cham, Jérusalem, Sem.

m followed by *n* is pronounced in the following:

amnistie, calomnie, hymne, insomnie, indemnité, omnipotent, somnambule.

It is silent in

automne, condamner, damner.

emm and **enn** are pronounced, respectively, as *am* and *an* in English in the following:

ardemment, femme, négligemment, patiemment, prudemment, solennel.

em and **emm** initial are nasal.   Thus,

emmancher, emmagasiner, emménager, emmêler.

N

37.   **n** final is nasal, but is joined to the sound of the next vowel.   Thus,

en‿entrant, un‿an, un‿homme.

P

38.   **p,** followed by *t* or *s*, is ordinarily sounded.   Thus,

abrupt, adapter, adopter, excepté, septembre, Psyché.

But it is silent in the following words:

baptême, compter, compte, dompter, exempt, escompte, prompt, temps, longtemps, sept, sculpter, sculpteur, sculpture.

p final is silent in the following:

beaucoup, champ, camp, drap, galop, loup, sirop, trop;

but it is sounded in *cep*, *cap*, *gap*.

Q

39.   **q** is sounded in *coq, cinq;* but it is silent in *cinq* followed by a word beginning with a consonant.   Thus,

cinq francs, cinq jours, cinq livres.

q in *cinq* is sounded in dates.   Thus,

le cinq mars, le cinq septembre, le cinq avril.

q is always followed by *u* except when final. **Qu** sounds like *k*. Thus,

  qualité, quatre, quand, que, quel, qui, quinze.

However, it is sounded like *kw* in the following words:

  quoi, aquarelle, équateur, quadrupède, équestre.

R

40. The letter **r** must be rolled in French. When final, and preceded by a vowel other than *e*, it is always sounded. Thus,   car, cœur, dormir, dur, finir.

But **r** final in *monsieur* is not sounded.

r is long and strongly emphasized in words ending in **eur, eure.** Thus,

  leur, demeure, beurre, heure, malheur, auteur.

r preceded by *e* is pronounced in the following words:

  cher, hier, amer, cancer, cuiller, fer, enfer,
     Esther, fier (*proud*), hiver, Jupiter, mer,
     revolver, ver.

r final is silent in other nouns, adjectives, and verbs ending in *er*.

Nouns	*Adjectives*	*Verbs*
cocher	altier	chanter
dîner	dernier	désirer
escalier	entier	parler
soulier	premier	demeurer
fermier	singulier	fier (*to trust*).

S

41. s has two sounds:

1. Between two vowels it has the sound of *z*. Thus,

  maison, désire, base, raisin, voisin.

2. It has the hissing sound of *s* in *sister*.

(*a*) When initial. Thus,

  sonner, servir, sortir, sublime.

(*b*) When preceded or followed by a consonant. Thus,

  assortir, descendre, Espagne, asperge.

(*c*)   When placed between two vowels in compound words.
Thus,   Lesage, entresol, contresigner.

s, by exception, sounds like *z* in the following words:
   Alsace, Jersey, Israël, transaction, transatlantique.

s is mute in
   Avesnes, Descartes, Deschamps, Despréaux,
      Rouget-de-l'Isle.

s final is, in general, silent, but is carried over like *z* before
a vowel.   Thus,
   Denis, Judas, Nicolas, Louis, les‿hommes, mes‿amis.

The **s** of the plural is never sounded, but may be carried
over.

s final has the hissing sound in the following words:
   aloès, atlas, bis, blocus, chorus, fils (*the son, l*
      silent), hélas, iris, jadis, gratis, le lis, maïs,
      mars, mérinos, omnibus, rébus, rhinocéros,
      sens, tous (pronoun) vis, Brutus, Minos,
      Ruy-Blas.

sc initial has the sound of *s* hard.   Thus,
   scène, scélérat, science, Scipion, scier.

sc in the body of a word sounds like double *s* hard.   Thus,
   ascension, susciter, incandescence, viscère.

sc followed by *a, o, u* sounds like *sk*.   Thus,
   scalpel, scudéry, sculpter, scolaire, ausculter.

T

42.   **t** followed by *i* in the last syllable of certain nouns,
adjectives, and verbs is pronounced like *s* hard.
   tion: attention, action, addition, nation
   tie: aristocratie, démocratie, prophétie
   tial: initial, nuptial, martial, partial
   tiel: essentiel, partiel, substantiel
   tieux: ambitieux, factieux, facétieux
   tien: patience, patient, quotient
   tier: initier, balbutier, satiété

Exceptions.—t keeps its natural sound in

> altier, entier, partie, volontiers.

When the final syllables *tion* or *tie* are preceded by *s* or *x*, t keeps its sound. Thus,

> question, amnistie, dynastie, modestie.

th sounds like *t* alone. Thus,

> thé, theâtre, théologie, athée, Thomas.

t final is silent in

> appât, avant, aspect, bout, comment, dont,
> défaut, et, est, front, point, rat, prompt,
> respect, souvent, statut, surtout.

t final, followed by a word commencing with a vowel, is united with that word, except in the case of *et* (and), the *t* of which is never carried over. In *Jésus-Christ*, the final *s* and *t* are silent, but in *Christ* alone, both *s* and *t* are sounded.

V AND W

43. v is sounded as in English.

w has ordinarily the sound of *v*, except in *whist* and *whig*, where is has the sound of English *w*.

X

44. x in the initial *ex* followed by a vowel or by *h* mute, sounds like *gz*. Thus,

> examiner, exiler, exemple, exulter, exiger.

ex before a consonant has the sound of *ks*. Thus,

> excepter, excès, expliquer, exclure.

x before final *e*, *er*, *ion* is like *ks*. Thus,

> axe, boxe, luxe, reflexion, fixer.

x has the sound of *ss* in the following:

> Auxerre, Bruxelles, Auxonne, dix, six, soixante.

x final is silent, except in

index, larynx, onyx, préfix, Béatrix, Félix, Dax, Halifax.

Z

45. z is soft, as in English, when initial or medial.
Thus, zèbre, zélande, douzaine, treize.

z final is silent in

assez, chez, nez, avez, entrez.

z sounds like *s* hard in

Alvarez, Metz (*t* silent), Retz.

PRONUNCIATION OF NUMBERS

46. *Cinq*, *six*, *sept*, *huit*, *neuf*, *dix*, have the following peculiarities:

1. At the end of a phrase, their last consonant is sounded.
Thus, Il en a huit, J'en ai cinq, En avez-vous dix?

2. In dates, the last consonant is sounded. Thus,

le cinq mars, le six septembre.

3. Before a vowel, the last consonant is united with the following vowel. Thus,

six‿hommes, cinq‿heures, huit‿œufs.

4. Before a consonant, the final consonant is silent. Thus,

cinq livres, sept chapeaux, huit bœufs.

In *dix*, the *x* has the sound of *z* in *dix-sept*, *dix-huit*, *dix-neuf*.

The *gt* of *vingt*, when *vingt* is used alone or before a consonant, is silent. Thus,

J'en ai vingt, vingt minutes.

The t of *vingt* is united to a following vowel. Thus,

vingt‿arbres, vingt‿œufs.

The t is sounded in *vingt-et-un*, *vingt-deux* . . . to *vingt-neuf*. The t is silent in *quatre-vingt-un*, *quatre-vingt-deux* . . . to *quatre-vingt-dix-neuf*.

LIAISONS

47. Liaisons are the carrying over of the last consonant of one word to the next word when that following word begins with a vowel or *h* mute. Thus,

vous‿avez, les‿hommes, un‿an.

The consonant thus carried over is pronounced as if it belonged to the following word. The liaisons are designed to render the language more harmonious and musical.

48. Important Principles of the Liaison.—The following important principles of the liaison should be carefully noted:

1. *s*, *x*, and *z*, when carried over, have the sound of *z*. Thus,

vous‿avez, je suis‿heureux ici, un choix‿agréable, entrez‿au salon.

2. *d* is carried over with the sound of *t*. Thus,
un grand‿homme, quand‿arrive-t-il?

3. *f*, when carried over, has the sound of *v*. Thus,
neuf‿heures, neuf‿hommes.

4. *g*, carried over has the sound of *k*. Thus,
un long‿espoir, sang‿humain.

49. Remarks on the Liaisons.—1. When a liaison gives a double meaning, it must be avoided. Do not say, *Lourd‿à porter*, *Louis‿a chanté*. In the first case, *lourd* (masculine) would sound like *lourde* (feminine); in the second, *Louis* would sound like *Louise*.

2. When several soft syllables come together, avoid the liaison; it then has the sound of an affectation. Do not say, *ces tasses‿et ces soucoupes‿étaient bleues.*

3. In the words *aspect*, *respect*, *suspect*, *circonspect*, *c* with the sound of *k* is carried over instead of the *t*. Thus,
aspect‿effrayant, respect‿humain.

4. Final *d* or *t* preceded by *r* is not carried over. Do not say: *le sort‿en est jeté.* But *d* final in the third person

singular of a verb followed by a pronoun, is carried over with the sound of *t*. Thus,

Combien perd-il?   Ce chien mord-il?

5. Final *d* is carried over with its usual pronunciation in *Nord-Est, Sud-Est, Nord-Ouest, Sud-Ouest*.

6. Final *p* is not carried over, except with *trop* and *beaucoup*.

7. In words ending in *rd*, *rt*, the *r* is carried over instead of *d* or *t*.

_____

ORTHOGRAPHIC MARKS

50. The **orthographic marks** are the accents (*accents*), the dieresis (*tréma*), the cedilla (*cédille*), the hyphen (*trait d'union*), and the apostrophe (*apostrophe*).

There are three kinds of **accents:** The *acute accent* (l'accent aigu), as in *abbé, café*.

NOTE.—This acute accent often replaces an *s* in the old French; as, *épée* for *espée*, *école* for *escole*, *répondre* for *respondre*.

The *grave accent* (l'accent grave), as in *procès, là*.

The *circumflex accent* (l'accent circonflexe), as in *pâte, apôtre*.

NOTE.—The circumflex accent replaces a letter suppressed from the old French; as, *pâte* for *paste*, *apôtre* for *apostre*.

The **dieresis** (¨) is placed over a vowel that should be pronounced separately from a preceding vowel; as, *Saül, haïr*.

The **cedilla** (ˌ) is placed under *c* before *a, o, u*, to give it the sound of *s*.

NOTE.—Formerly, a small *s* was placed over the *c* to give to this letter the sound of *s*; later, it was placed under the *c*. Subsequently the *s* was replaced by the cedilla.

The **hyphen** is used to connect two or more words; as, *arc-en-ciel, venez-vous?*

The **apostrophe** replaces one of the letters *a, e, i*, before another vowel or *h* mute; as, *l'abeille, d'honneur, s'il vient*.

THE STUDY OF WORDS

CLASSES OF WORDS

51. Parts of Speech. — Words have been divided into classes called *parts of speech*. The class in which a word belongs depends entirely upon the use that is made of it in the sentence. No one can classify a word until its use or function in some sentence structure is determined; for, since a word may be differently used in different sentences, it may belong now to one part of speech, or again to another.

LE NOM—THE NOUN

52. In order to distinguish various objects, men, in the beginning, felt the necessity of giving them names. A very large part of our words are employed to name things that are known by means of our senses, such as *apples, house, tree*, etc. Such *names* are **nouns**, for the two words mean exactly the same thing, except that the one is used in the language of every-day life, while the other is a *technical*, or scientific, term used in grammar. Such words as those given above call up in the mind ideas, or pictures, of *real* things — things with color, size, taste, weight, and other *sensible* qualities. But there are many names that denote things without any such qualities, and we can talk and think of these just as if they were real things. Such words as *distance, loneliness, hatred, liberty, vice*, and *wisdom* are of this kind. While the mental pictures produced by these words are not so distinct nor so easily formed as the ideas of objects having sensible qualities, such words can be used in sentences in precisely the same way as nouns denoting sensible things.

Definition. — *A noun is any word or expression used as the name of something.*

L'ARTICLE—THE ARTICLE

53. The **article** is a part of speech not found in Latin, for it was rendered useless by the various case endings of nouns. It owes its origin in French to the absence of these case endings, and to the consequent need of adding to the function of the noun. Placed before a common noun, it denotes that the object or class of objects named by the noun is particularly referred to or pointed out—is taken in a *determinate* sense.

The article has two forms in the singular—*le* with masculine nouns, and *la* with feminine nouns. The plural has but one form, *les*, for both genders. The article is really a demonstrative adjective in function and was formed from the Latin demonstrative pronoun *il*le (masc.), *il*la (fem.).

Definition.—*The* **article** *is a word placed before a noun for the purpose of particularizing or pointing out distinctly the object named by the noun.*

L'ADJECTIF—THE ADJECTIVE

54. The objects denoted by class names or nouns, as *arbre*, *vent*, *homme*, *maison*, are distinguished from one another by their qualities of color, size, form, etc. In order that persons with whom we converse may know which particular individual or group of individuals we mean, *modifiers* must be joined to the class name. Each modifier narrows, or restricts, the number of objects denoted by the word that is modified, and at the same time indicates more exactly what the thing intended is like. Thus, the *number* of objects denoted by the following decreases in order, but what they are like becomes more exact and definite: *hommes*, **grands** *hommes*, **deux grands** *hommes*, **deux grands** *hommes* **blonds,** etc. Words used in this way to modify the meaning of nouns are **adjectives.**

Definition.—*An* **adjective** *is a word used to modify the meaning of a noun or a pronoun.*

LE PRONOM—THE PRONOUN

55. Pronouns, as the word indicates, are substitutes for nouns (*pro, for,* or *instead of*). They do not, like nouns, name things, but they refer to them in such a way as to make plain what is meant. Without them, our language would be very awkward. A person speaking does not need to mention his own name, or even to know that of the hearer. He uses *Je, moi,* etc., when he means himself, and *il, elle, lui, leur,* etc., when he refers to other persons. The pronoun can do the same work in a sentence that a noun can do; it enables us to talk of anything whatever without naming it more than once.

Definition.—*A pronoun is a word used to denote persons or things without naming them.*

LE VERBE—THE VERB

56. In every language, by far the most important class of words is the **verb;** for, without a verb, no complete thought can be expressed. Every sentence must contain a verb. By using the noun, we name things concerning which we may affirm or deny something; but to express such affirmation or denial in the form of a sentence—and this is the only form in which a thought can be written or spoken—a verb must be used. Thus, *Jean, oiseaux, étoiles,* are names, but they tell us nothing—they are the signs of *ideas,* not of *thoughts.* But when suitable asserting words are joined to them, we have thoughts—sentences. Thus,

    Les étoiles *brillent.*   Les oiseaux *ont chanté.*

    Jean ne *viendra* pas.

Such words as *brillent, ont chanté, viendra,* are *verbs.* So important in the sentence is the office of the verb, that its name means *the word*—that is, *of all words, the verb is of greatest consequence.*

Grammarians say that the verb *predicates* being or action of that which the subject names. This word comes from a Latin verb meaning "to tell" or "speak out" in public. The fact is that there is much need for a word that has all of the following meanings: to *assert*, to *deny*, to *question*, to *command*, to *wish*, to *entreat;* for the verb is the chief word in sentences by which all these forms of thought are expressed. But, of course, the need cannot be met, for there is no such word. The nearest approach to it is, perhaps, the word *predicate;* and if the student will remember what the grammarians would like this word to mean, he will know what the functions of the verb are.

Definition. —*A* **verb** *is a word used to predicate being or action of that which is denoted by a subject.*

LE PARTICIPE—THE PARTICIPLE

57. The **participle** is a form of the verb used as an adjective. It has its origin in the verb but has the function of an adjective.

L'ADVERBE—THE ADVERB

58. The principal use of the **adverb** is to do for the verb just what the adjective does for the noun—*modify its meaning*. With only a few exceptions, the verb, like the noun, denotes classes—not of *objects*, however, but of *actions*. For example, the action expressed by *parler* may be performed in so many different *manners*, at such a variety of *times* and *places*, and under such a multitude of other conditions and circumstances, that it may denote a class of predicated action as extensive as that named by a common noun. This will be clear from the illustration that follows:

$$
\text{Je } parle \begin{cases} \text{lentement, vite, distinctement} \\ \text{souvent, maintenant, fréquemment} \\ \text{ici, là-bas, partout} \end{cases}
$$

The word *adverb* implies that this part of speech is joined directly *to the verb* (*ad*, to). But while this is often the case, the adverb, like the adjective, may often be widely separated from the verb it modifies.

But it is not the meaning of *verbs* alone that adverbs modify; they are frequently used to modify the meaning of *adjectives*, as well as that of other *adverbs*.

Verbs, like nouns, are class words. The same is true of most adjectives and adverbs. Thus, when we say, *Je suis malade*, there are many degrees of the quality expressed by the adjective *malade*, many conditions under which it may exist, and we may wish to indicate some of these differences.

Je suis *malade* { très peu, tout à fait, pas
à la campagne, à la ville, partout, souvent
en été, en hiver

Similarly, in the sentence, *Le temps passe vite*, the adverb denotes many degrees of rapid motion, such as may be indicated by *très*, *tout à fait*, *trop*, *plus*, *moins*, etc.

Definition.—*An* **adverb** *is a word used to modify the meaning of a verb, an adjective, or another adverb.*

LA PRÉPOSITION—THE PREPOSITION

59. Sometimes, ideas may seem to be so widely separated, so unlike, that nothing could ever bring into relation the words denoting them. Yet, they may often be joined by means of a *word bridge* between them. Examples of this are shown below.

Un palais { *près de*
sur
au-dessus de
loin de } la mer

These *word bridges* are called **prepositions.** They are so named because they are nearly always *placed before* the noun or pronoun that they connect with some preceding word. The work done in sentences by prepositions is twofold. (1) they *connect words;* (2) they *bring words into relation.*

Definition.—*A* **preposition** *is a word used to connect words and bring them into relation.*

LA CONJONCTION—THE CONJUNCTION

60. As the word implies, a **conjunction** is (like the preposition) a word used for joining or connecting other sentential elements. There are, however, some differences that are easily seen between these two classes of words. With the conjunction, its *joining* or *uniting* function is the prominent fact; with the preposition, the chief use is to *denote relation*.

Definition. —*A* conjunction *is a word used to connect sentences, or sentential elements that are used alike.*

L'INTERJECTION—THE INTERJECTION

61. The **interjections** are usually regarded as forming another part of speech, but it should be remembered that they have no place in sentential structure. They are *thrown among* (*inter*, among, and *jectus*, thrown) sentences to indicate *emotion* only, not *thought*.

Definition. —*An* interjection *is a word that has no relation to other words in a sentence and is used to express feeling or emotion.*

PARTS OF SPEECH GROUPED

62. The order of parts of speech given is that generally followed in French Grammars. This classification is not made, however, according to their importance. The logical order would be as follows:

1. The Indispensable Parts of Speech. — These are the **verb** and the **noun** or its substitute, the **pronoun.** With the verb and the noun, or the pronoun, a complete sentence may be formed; and these are the only parts of speech with which this can be done.

2. The Auxiliary, or Helping, Parts of Speech. These include the remaining classes of words:

(*a*) The *modifiers* (the article, the adjective, the participle, and the adverb).

(*b*) The *connectives* (the preposition and the conjunction).

(*c*) The *interjection*.

SYNOPSIS

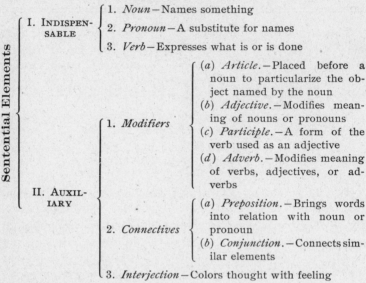

Sentential Elements

I. INDISPENSABLE
1. *Noun* — Names something
2. *Pronoun* — A substitute for names
3. *Verb* — Expresses what is or is done

II. AUXILIARY
1. *Modifiers*
(*a*) *Article.* — Placed before a noun to particularize the object named by the noun
(*b*) *Adjective.* — Modifies meaning of nouns or pronouns
(*c*) *Participle.* — A form of the verb used as an adjective
(*d*) *Adverb.* — Modifies meaning of verbs, adjectives, or adverbs

2. *Connectives*
(*a*) *Preposition.* — Brings words into relation with noun or pronoun
(*b*) *Conjunction.* — Connects similar elements

3. *Interjection* — Colors thought with feeling

The order followed in this work slightly differs from the order just described. The verb, being the most important part of speech, is first treated. The participle follows, on account of its close relation with the verb. Then the article is given, because of its importance in distinguishing the gender of French nouns. The study of the noun and of the adjective is then undertaken; they are associated in treatment on account of the similarity of the rules for forming their feminine and plural. Finally, the pronoun and the auxiliary parts of speech, as classified above, are discussed.

FRENCH GRAMMAR

(PART 2)

LE VERBE—THE VERB

1. What Verbs Express.—We have already learned that in every sentence the verb is the *predicating word*. By this is meant that the verb is the word by means of which it is possible to declare, to question, to command, and to express a wish or an entreaty. In order that the student may understand the real nature of the verb and the reasons for the classifications that are to follow, it is necessary to consider more fully just what this part of speech does in the sentence.

The most important matter with which language can be concerned is *action*—the various changes and movements and doings of things material and immaterial. In the expression of thought many words are required, but the most useful of them all are the "action words." Now, action is of many kinds, and it is sometimes not easy to see that a certain verb really does express action.

Physical action is recognized without difficulty, generally by the aid of the senses. Some verbs that denote this kind of action are *marcher, pousser, écrire, bâtir,* etc.

Mental and emotional actions are almost as readily recognized as those expressed by verbs denoting sensible motions. Such are *penser, admirer, considérer, juger,* etc.

It is less easy to see that real action or change is indicated by such verbs as *dormir, reposer, grandir,* and many others like them; but most difficult of all are a few verbs called *neuter verbs*, such as *sembler, apparaître*, and especially *être* in its various forms.

The neuter verbs are thought by many not to express action at all, but a state or condition of that which is named by the subject. A little reflection, however, will make it clear that they express action and at the same time denote a state or condition of the actor.

When it is said,

> Il **paraît** malade, *He appears ill*,

there are certain changes in the usual appearance of the person in question, signs that speak as plainly to the eye as the tongue can speak to the ear. In other words, certain parts of the person are *doing* something, when he seems or looks or appears in a manner that reveals some state of his mind or body. His general bearing, the color of his skin, the luster of his eyes, and many other agencies are, by a kind of action, making known that he is in a state described by *malade*, ill. In short, it appears that all verbs express action of some kind.

2. Action and State. — Not only does every verb indicate some kind and degree of activity, but it *expresses or implies a state or condition of the actor or agent.* Thus, when it is said,

> L'enfant marche, pense, dort, et grandit, *The child walks, thinks, sleeps, and grows,*

each of the verbs denotes a special kind of activity as well as an accompanying state. The boy not only performs the act of walking, but he is in a state or condition such that he may be called a walking boy. He is in a condition of walking, of thinking, of sleeping, of growing. When the boy walks or thinks, we notice the *action* but the *state* is scarcely ever considered; when he *sleeps* and *grows*, we notice the *state* rather than the *action*.

Hence, all verbs might be arranged in a series beginning with verbs that make action prominent and state slight, or unnoticeable, and ending with those in which state is the conspicuous feature and action is obscure or unnoticeable.

3. Classification of Verbs According to Form. Verbs are divided, with respect to their *form*, into three comprehensive classes: *regular*, *irregular*, and *defective*.

1. **Le verbe régulier,** the regular verb, is a verb that forms all its tenses by modifications in its endings only; as, *je parle*, *nous parlions*, *vous parlâtes*.

2. **Le verbe irrégulier,** the irregular verb, is a verb whose stem, root, or radical, as well as ending, changes in its inflection; as, *je reçois*, *nous recevons*, *reçu*.

3. **Le verbe défectif,** the defective verb, is a verb that is used in but few of its modes and tenses; as, *choir*, to fall (used in the infinitive only).

4. Classification of Verbs According to Significa-tion. — Verbs are also divided, with respect to their *significa-tion*, into two classes: *transitive* and *intransitive*.

1. **Le verbe transitif,** the transitive verb, is a verb that expresses an action which has some person or thing for its object; as,

L'enfant { a tué un oiseau,   *The child* { killed a bird.
        { chante une chanson,   { sang a song.
        { a résolu un problème,   { solved a problem.

In these examples, the action performed by the child operates upon, or affects, something besides the actor him-self—a bird, a song, a problem. These words are called the *direct objects*, or merely the *objects*, of the verbs. Verbs so used are called transitive verbs, because the action denoted by the verb seems to go over (*transire*, to go over) the verb, from the name of the actor to the name of that which receives the action.

Transitive verbs may be divided, according to their use, into two classes; namely, *simple transitive verbs*, and *trans-itive active verbs*. When so distinguished **simple transitive**

verbs are those verbs that may have a direct object, but have no such object expressed; as, *L'enfant mange*, the child eats. And **transitive active verbs** are those verbs that have their direct objects expressed; as, *L'enfant mange son dîner*, the child eats his dinner.

2. **Le verbe intransitif**, the intransitive verb, is a verb that expresses an action which has no person or thing for its object; as,

$$L'enfant \begin{cases} \textbf{marche,} \\ \textbf{pense,} \\ \textbf{court,} \end{cases} \qquad The\ child \begin{cases} walks. \\ thinks. \\ runs. \end{cases}$$

In these examples, the action denoted by the verb does *not* go over, so to speak, from an actor to a receiver. These verbs are often termed **verbes neutres**, neuter verbs.

5. **Uses of Verbs: Impersonal, Passive, Reflexive.**

1. Some verbs may be so used that the actions denoted by them cannot be attributed to any person or thing as their subject; when so used these verbs are called **verbes impersonnels**, impersonal verbs. Thus,

> Il neige, *It snows.*
> Il pleut, *It is raining.*

2. A verb may be so used as to represent that its subject, or what the nominative expresses, is acted upon; when so used it is called a **verbe passif**, passive verb. Thus,

> Le maître **est aimé** de ses élèves, *The teacher is loved by his pupils.*
> Le lièvre **a été tué** par le chasseur, *The hare has been killed by the hunter.*

3. A verb may be so used as to represent its subject as receiving the action denoted by the verb; it is then termed a **verbe réflectif**, reflexive verb. Thus,

> Je me lave, *I wash myself.*
> Elle se lave, *She washes herself.*

INFLECTION OF THE VERB

6. Conjugaison. — Verbs are inflected, or changed in form, in consequence of some change in their meaning or use. The inflection of verbs is called their **conjugation.** The word *conjugation* is derived from two Latin words meaning to join together. In the conjugation of a verb, the various inflections of the word are so arranged as to be seen or heard *together*, thus enabling the different changes to be more easily recognized and compared. The inflections of verbs are divided into four classes: (1) for *mode*, (2) for *tense*, (3) for *number*, (4) for *person*.

Conjugaison is an orderly arrangement of the various modes, tenses, numbers, and persons of a verb.

MODE—MODE

7. Function of Mode. — The sentence *je marche* takes before the mind the form of a mere statement; that is, the guise or mode of the thought is that of a statement or declaration. The thought is merely stated or indicated.

But with the help of certain other words, the thought may be expressed as conditional or dependent upon something else; it then assumes before the mind another *fashion* or *mode*.

Même **si** je me dépêchais, je serais en retard,
Even if I should hurry, I would be late.

Again, the thought may be conceived or recognized as being in the mode or dress of a command or an imperative, as in the following:

Marche, *Walk.*
Restez tranquille, *Keep quiet.*
Dépêchez-vous, *Hurry up.*

Or, the action or state may take the form of mere mention without especial reference to any person as acting or being. This is a case of action, or being, in general, as a mere abstract noun and without predication.

> **Marcher** est un excellent exercice, *To walk is an excellent exercise.*

These different attitudes that a complete thought or a mere verbal idea assume before the mind are called **modes;** and, since these differences depend largely on the form of the verb and the way in which it is used, the verb itself is said to be in this or that mode.

Mode is that form or use of a verb by which is shown the sentential construction employed to express the thought.

8. The Six Modes. — There is no definite agreement among grammatical authorities as to the number of modes in French. Most grammarians, however, assume the following six modes: (1) *le mode indicatif*, the indicative mode; (2) *le mode conditionnel*, the conditional mode; (3) *le mode impératif*, the imperative mode; (4) *le mode subjonctif*, the subjunctive mode; (5) *le mode infinitif*, the infinitive mode; (6) *le mode participe*, the participial mode.

9. Le Mode Indicatif. — The word *indicate* means to point out, to show. When a thought is expressed in the form or guise that *affirms* or *denies*, or in that of a mere *inquiry*, the predicating verb is in the indicative mode.

> La terre **est** une planète, *The earth is a planet.*
> Il ne **viendra** pas, *He will not come.*
> **Comprend**-il? *Does he understand?*

Le mode indicatif is that form or use of a verb by which a thought is predicated as a simple statement or question.

10. Le Mode Conditionnel. — When a verb expresses that an action would take place if a certain condition were fulfilled, it is in the conditional mode.

> Je **marcherais** si je pouvais, *I would walk if I could.*
> Il **irait** à Paris s'il avait de l'argent, *He would go to Paris if he had the money.*

Le mode conditionnel is that form or use of a verb which indicates that an action would take place if a certain condition were fulfilled.

11. **Le Mode Impératif.** — The word *imperative* means commanding, but in grammar its meaning is extended to include every use of the verb between commanding and mere permission.

> **Venez; partons,** *Come; let us go.*
> **Ayez** pitié des pauvres, *Have pity for the poor.*
> **Restez** tranquille, *Keep quiet.*
> **Allez** en paix, *Go in peace.*

The verb in this mode regularly omits its subject, which, however, is always understood.

Le mode impératif is that form or use of a verb by which a sentence is shown to be a command, an exhortation, an entreaty, or a mere permission.

12. **Le Mode Subjonctif.** — The subjunctive mode is so named because it is found only in subjoined, or dependent, clauses. The student must not assume, however, that the predicating verb in every subordinate clause is in this mode.

The subjunctive mode is used when *doubt* or *denial* is expressed, or to express a *wish*, a mere *supposition*, or to denote *uncertainty*, etc.

Le mode subjonctif is that form or use of a verb by which a subordinate clause expresses something as doubtful or merely supposed.

13. **Le Mode Infinitif.** — The word *infinitive* means *not limited*. The infinitive mode of the verb is so named because it takes no change of form in consequence of any change in the person and number of its subject. The infinitive *does not predicate* as do other modes, but it *names* an *act* very much as a common noun names a *thing*.

Le mode infinitif is that use of a verb by which action or state is represented, not as predicated, but as merely named.

14. Le Mode Participe. — A verb in the participial mode has the use or function of an adjective. It has its *form* from the verb, and like other forms of the verb it may have a direct object.

> **ayant** appris la grammaire, *having learned grammar*
> **louant** Dieu, *praising God*

Le mode participe is a form of a verb used as an adjective.

_____

PERSONNES–PERSONS

15. Functions of the Persons. — The action expressed by the verb may be (1) of the person speaking, as *je marche, nous mangeons;* (2) of the person addressed, as *tu marches, vous mangez;* or (3) of the person or thing of whom it is spoken, as *il marche, ils mangent.* These various forms, assumed by the verb to express to whom or to which the action expressed by it is to be attributed, are termed the **persons** of the verb. When the speaker is the actor, the verb is in the **first person;** when the person addressed is the actor, the verb is in the **second person;** and when the person or thing spoken of is the actor, the verb is in the **third person.** Verbs agree with their subjects in person, and in consequence of changes in the person of their subjects, verbs undergo certain modifications or inflections.

Personnes are the relations or modifications that distinguish the speaker, the person or thing spoken to, and the person or thing spoken of; also the forms or inflections indicating such relation.

_____

NOMBRE–NUMBER

16. Verbs have two numbers: *le singulier,* the singular, and *le pluriel,* the plural. A verb is in the **singular number** when the action it denotes is of one person or thing, or of one class of persons or things. It is in the **plural number** when that action is of more than one person or thing, or class of persons or things. Verbs agree with their subjects in number, as in person, and in consequence of changes in the number of their subjects, verbs undergo further modifications, or inflections.

TEMPS—TENSE

17. Function of Tense. — By its form sometimes, but also by the way in which it is used, a verb may reveal the time of an action or state. Thus, in *je suis, je vois, je cours*, the verbs show by their forms that the action expressed is to be understood as taking place in the *present* time; but if the forms be changed into *j'étais, je vis, je courus*, the time of the action belongs to the *past*. This peculiarity of the verb by which it reveals the time of an action or a state, is called *tense*, a word meaning time.

Temps is that form or use of a verb by which the time and the degree of completeness of the expressed action or state is indicated.

18. Divisions of Time. — There are three principal divisions of time — the *present*, the *past*, and the *future*. There are, therefore, three *principal tenses:* the *present tense*, the *past tense*, and the *future tense*.

19. Relation of the Tenses With Respect to Time. The word present in ordinary speech does not mean *now — this instant*. Strictly, now — the present — is the point where the past and future meet; it has no extent, and is always moving. But, in ordinary speech, the present is a variable portion of time extending into both the past and the future. *Je travaille* does not mean that action of the kind called *travail* is done just at the present instant; but the idea conveyed is, that as time passes, from day to day and from year to year, my habitual activity is described by the verb *travailler*. A verb so used is in the present tense.

The past and future, being composed of an infinite number of instants, admit degrees of priority and posteriority; hence, there are several varieties of past and future tenses. The present admits of only one tense, because it is indivisible. Boileau has aptly said: *"Le moment où je parle est déjà loin de moi,"* "The moment in which I am speaking is already far from me."

THE TENSES OF A FRENCH VERB

20. Mode Indicatif.—**Le présent,** the present, expresses action that is taking place at the time of speaking; as, *Je* **marche,** I am walking.

L'imparfait, the imperfect, denotes action as going on synchronously with some other action; as, *Je* **lisais** *quand il est entré,* I was reading when he came in.

Le passé défini, the past definite, expresses action as having occurred at a definite time now past; as, *Je* **voyageai** *l'année dernière,* I traveled last year.

Le passé indéfini, the past indefinite, expresses a completed past action as having occurred in past, but not yet necessarily completed time; as, *J'ai* **chanté,** I have sung.

Le passé antérieur, the past anterior, expresses action that occurred immediately before another past action; as, *Quand j'*eus **lu,** *je partis,* When I had read, I departed.

Le plus-que-parfait, the pluperfect, expresses a past action completed before the beginning of another past action; as, *J'*avais **fini** *quand il arriva,* I had finished when he arrived.

Le futur simple, the simple future, represents action as about to take place at a time not yet arrived; as, *Je* **sortirai** *demain,* I shall go out tomorrow.

Le futur antérieur, the future anterior (known in English as the future perfect), expresses action to be completed before some other future action begins; as, *J'*aurai **fini** *quand il arrivera,* I shall have finished when he comes.

21. Mode Conditionnel.—**Le conditionnel présent,** the present conditional, expresses action that would take place provided a certain condition were fulfilled; as, *Je* **chanterais** *si je pouvais,* I would sing, if I could.

Le conditionnel passé, the past conditional, represents action that would have taken place if a certain condition had been fulfilled; as, *J'aurais lu si j'avais eu un livre,*
I would have read, if I had had a book.

22. **Le Mode Impératif.** — L'imperatif, the imperative, is generally said to have but one tense, *le présent,*
because the time it represents is always present with regard
to the giving of the command, even though the action
expressed may not take place until some time in the future.
Strictly speaking, however, the time denoted by the imperative is conditional upon the sense of the clause, or sentence,
in which it is used.

But, since some time must necessarily elapse between the
giving of a command and its fulfilment, it is sometimes
contended that the time of the imperative reaches from the
immediate present into the distant future, and two imperatives are then distinguished — the *present imperative* and the
future imperative. This distinction, however, is not widely
recognized in modern languages.

Since the person or thing commanded is generally directly
addressed, the imperative ordinarily has its subject in the
second person singular or plural, or in the first person plural;
but that subject is not usually expressed. Thus, *chante,* sing
(thou); *chantons,* let us sing; *chantez,* sing (you, *pl.*).

23. **Le Mode Subjonctif.** — This mode has four tenses,
as will be explained hereafter: *le présent l'imparfait, le passé,
le plus-que-parfait.*

24. **Le Mode Infinitif.** — This mode has two tenses:
le présent, as *finir,* to finish; and *le passé,* as *avoir fini,* to
have finished.

25. **Le Mode Participe.** — The participle also has two
tenses: *le présent,* as, *finissant,* finishing; and *le passé,* as,
fini, finished.

26. **Temps Simples et Composés.** — With regard to
their form, the tenses of a verb may be divided into two
classes, *simple,* simple, and *composé,* compound. Any tense of

a verb formed solely by modifications in the ending or stem of the verb, is called a **simple tense;** any tense formed both by changing the ending or stem of the verb and at the same time linking that modified form with another verb to help in its conjugation, is called a **compound tense.** Any verb used to help in the conjugation of another verb, is called a **secondary,** or **auxiliary,** verb. Thus,

Simple Tenses	Compound Tenses
je marche	j'ai marché
je finissais	j'avais fini
je parlerai	je serais sorti

VERBES AUXILIAIRES — AUXILIARY VERBS

27. **Le verbe auxiliaire,** the auxiliary verb, is a verb used to help conjugate another verb. There are two auxiliary verbs in the French language: *avoir*, to have, and *être*, to be. The English auxiliaries, *do*, *shall*, *will*, *can*, and *may*, with their variations, have no literal equivalents in French, but are generally expressed by some peculiar inflection of the French verb. *Être* and *avoir* are auxiliaries only when used to help in the conjugation of some other verb.

In the following examples *être* and *avoir* are not auxiliaries: *J'ai un livre*, I have a book; *Je* **suis** *médecin*, I am a physician.

In these examples *être* and *avoir* are auxiliaries: *j'*ai *marché; j'*avais *fini; je* serais *sorti*.

The auxiliary **avoir** is used in the compound tenses of:

I.   Active verbs; as, *J'ai écrit trois lettres, J'ai lu un livre.*

II.   Most neuter verbs; as, *J'ai dormi, Il a marché.*

III.   Most impersonal verbs; as, *Il a plu, Il a neigé.*

The auxiliary **être** is used:

(*a*)   In all tenses of passive verbs; as, *Je suis aimé, J'ai été aimé.*

(*b*)   In the compound tenses of reflexive verbs; as, *Je me suis promené, Il ne s'est pas trompé.*

(*c*) In the compound tenses of the following neuter verbs:

aller, *to go*	partir, *to depart*
arriver, *to arrive*	rester, *to stay*
accourir, *to run*	tomber, *to fall*
descendre, *to go down*	sortir, *to go out*
entrer, *to enter*	venir,*a to come*
monter, *to go up*	résulter, *to result*
mourir, *to die*	rentrer, *to return (home)*
naître, *to be born*	retourner, *to return*

CONJUGATION OF THE AUXILIARY VERB AVOIR

INDICATIF

Présent

j'ai, *I have*
tu as, *thou hast*
il }
elle } a, *he* *she* }has
nous avons, *we have*
vous avez, *you have*
ils }
elles } ont, *they have*

Passé Indéfini

j'ai eu, *I have had*
tu as eu, *thou hast had*
il }
elle } a eu, *he* *she* }has had
nous avons eu, *we have had*
vous avez eu, *you have had*
ils }
elles } ont eu, *they have had*

Imparfait

j'avais, *I had*
tu avais, *thou hadst*
il avait, *he had*
nous avions, *we had*
vous aviez, *you had*
ils avaient, *they had*

Plus-que-Parfait

j'avais eu, *I had had*
tu avais eu, *thou hadst had*
il avait eu, *he had had*
nous avions eu, *we had had*
vous aviez eu, *you had had*
ils avaient eu, *they had had*

Passé Défini

j'eus, *I had*
tu eus, *thou hadst*
il eut, *he had*
nous eûmes, *we had*
vous eûtes, *you had*
ils eurent, *they had*

Passé Antérieur

j'eus eu, *I had had*
tu eus eu, *thou hadst had*
il eut eu, *he had had*
nous eûmes eu, *we had had*
vous eûtes eu, *you had had*
ils eurent eu, *they had had*

---

*a*Être is also used with the compounds of *venir;* as, *convenir,* to agree; *devenir,* to become; *parvenir,* to succeed; *revenir,* to come back.

NOTE.—Some of these verbs, when primarily expressing *action* rather than *state*, are conjugated with *avoir* in their compound tenses instead of with *être*.

Futur	*Futur Antérieur*
j'aurai, *I shall have*	j'aurai eu, *I shall have had*
tu auras, *thou wilt have*	tu auras eu, *thou wilt have had*
il aura, *he will have*	il aura eu, *he will have had*
nous aurons, *we shall have*	nous aurons eu, *we shall have had*
vous aurez, *you will have*	vous aurez eu, *you will have had*
ils auront, *they will have*	ils auront eu, *they will have had*

Conditionnel

Présent

j'aurais, *I should have*
tu aurais, *thou wouldst have*
il aurait, *he could have*
nous aurions, *we should have*
vous auriez, *you would have*
ils auraient, *they would have*

Passé

j'aurais eu, *I should have had*
tu aurais eu, *thou wouldst have had*
il aurait eu, *he would have had*
nous aurions eu, *we should have had*
vous auriez eu, *you would have had*
ils auraient eu, *they would have had*

Impératif

aie, *have, have thou*
ayons, *let us have*
ayez, *have, have ye*

Subjonctif

Présent

que j'aie, *that I may have*
que tu aies, *that thou mayst have*
qu'il ait, *that he may have*
que nous ayons, *that we may have*
que vous ayez, *that you may have*
qu'ils aient, *that they may have*

Passé

que j'aie eu, *that I may have had*
que tu aies eu, *that thou mayst have had*
qu'il ait eu, *that he may have had*
que nous ayons eu, *that we may have had*
que vous ayez eu, *that you may have had*
qu'ils aient eu, *that they may have had*

Imparfait

que j'eusse, *that I might have*
que tu eusses, *that thou mightst have*
qu'il eût, *that he might have*
que nous eussions, *that we might have*
que vous eussiez, *that you might have*
qu'ils eussent, *that they might have*

Plus-que-Parfait

que j'eusse eu, *that I might have had*
que tu eusses eu, *that thou mightst have had*
qu'il eût eu, *that he might have had*
que nous eussions eu, *that we might have had*
que vous eussiez eu, *that you might have had*
qu'ils eussent eu, *that they might have had*

INFINITIF

Présent	*Passé*
avoir, *have, to have*	avoir eu, *to have had*

PARTICIPE

Présent	*Passé*
ayant, *having*	eu, ayant eu, *had, having had*

28. Every tense of every verb may be conjugated in four different ways; namely, in the *affirmative, negative, interrogative-affirmative,* or *interrogative-negative.* To form the negative, *ne . . . pas* is used: the first part *ne*, being placed immediately after the subject before the verb; the second part *pas*, being put after the verb in a simple, or after the auxiliary in a compound tense. Thus,

AFFIRMATIVE	NEGATIVE
j'ai, *I have*	je n'ai **pas,** *I have not*
j'avais, *I had*	je n'avais **pas,** *I had not*
il aura, *he will have*	il n'aura **pas,** *he will not have*

The interrogatives are made by placing the pronoun subject immediately after the verb in a simple tense, and after the auxiliary in a compound tense. In interrogative forms the pronoun is joined to the verb by a hyphen. Thus,

INTERROGATIVE-AFFIRMATIVE	INTERROGATIVE-NEGATIVE
ai-je? *have I?*	n'ai-je pas? *have I not?*
avais-je? *had I?*	n'avais-je pas? *had I not?*
aurai-je? *shall I have?*	n'aurai-je pas? *shall I not have?*

29. Concerning Avoir. — The following words, though used in English with *to be*, require *avoir* in French: *chaud*, warm; *froid*, cold; *faim*, hunger; *soif*, thirst; *raison*, right; *tort*, wrong; *honte*, shame; *peur*, fear; *sommeil*, sleep. Thus,

> Avez-vous faim ou soif?—Je n'ai ni faim ni soif,
> *Are you hungry or thirsty?—I am neither hungry nor thirsty.*

> Vous avez tort de ne pas avoir peur du froid,
> *You are wrong not to be afraid of the cold.*

Age is also expressed in French with *avoir*. Thus,

> Quel âge avez-vous?—J'ai vingt ans, *How old are you? I am twenty years old.*

CONJUGATION OF THE AUXILIARY VERB ÊTRE

INDICATIF

Présent

je suis, *I am*
tu es, *thou art*
il } elle } est, *he, she* } *is*
nous sommes, *we are*
vous êtes, *you are*
ils } elles } sont, *they are*

Passé Indéfini

j'ai été, *I have been*
tu as été, *thou hast been*
il } elle } a été, *he, she* } *has been*
nous avons été, *we have been*
vous avez été, *you have been*
ils } elles } ont été, *they have been*

Imparfait

j'étais, *I was*
tu étais, *thou wast*
il était, *he was*
nous étions, *we were*
vous étiez, *you were*
ils étaient, *they were*

Plus-que-Parfait

j'avais été, *I had been*
tu avais été, *thou hadst been*
il avait été, *he had been*
nous avions été, *we had been*
vous aviez été, *you had been*
ils avaient été, *they had been*

Passé Défini

je fus, *I was*
tu fus, *thou wast*
il fut, *he was*
nous fûmes, *we were*
vous fûtes, *you were*
ils furent, *they were*

Passé Antérieur

j'eus été, *I had been*
tu eus été, *thou hadst been*
il eut été, *he had been*
nous eûmes été, *we had been*
vous eûtes été, *you had been*
ils eurent été, *they had been*

Futur

je serai, *I shall be*
tu seras, *thou wilt be*
il sera, *he will be*
nous serons, *we shall be*
vous serez, *you will be*
ils seront, *they will be*

Futur Antérieur

j'aurai été, *I shall have been*
tu auras été, *thou wilt have been*
il aura été, *he will have been*
nous aurons été, *we shall have been*
vous aurez été, *you will have been*
ils auront été, *they will have been*

Conditionnel

Présent

je serais, *I should be*
tu serais, *thou wouldst be*
il serait, *he would be*
nous serions, *we should be*
vous seriez, *you would be*
ils seraient, *they would be*

Passé

j'aurais été, *I should have been*
tu aurais été, *thou wouldst have been*
il aurait été, *he would have been*
nous aurions été, *we should have been*
vous auriez été, *you would have been*
ils auraient été, *they would have been*

Impératif

sois, *be (thou)*
soyons, *let us be*
soyez, *be (you)*

Subjonctif

Présent

que je sois, *that I may be*
que tu sois, *that thou mayst be*
qu'il soit, *that he may be*
que nous soyons, *that we may be*
que vous soyez, *that you may be*
qu'ils soient, *that they may be*

Passé

que j'aie été, *that I may have been*
que tu aies été, *that thou mayst have been*
qu'il ait été, *that he may have been*
que nous ayons été, *that we may have been*
que vous ayez été, *that you may have been*
qu'ils aïent été, *that they may have been*

Imparfait

que je fusse, *that I might be*
que tu fusses, *that thou mightst be*
qu'il fût, *that he might be*
que nous fussions, *that we might be*
que vous fussiez, *that you might be*
qu'ils fussent, *that they might be*

Plus-que-Parfait

que j'eusse été, *that ı might have been*
que tu eusses été, *that thou mightst have been*
qu'il eût été, *that he might have been*
que nous eussions été, *that we might have been*
que vous eussiez été, *that you might have been*
qu'ils eussent été, *that they might have been*

INFINITIF

Présent	*Passé*
être, *to be*	avoir été, *to have been*

PARTICIPE

Présent	*Passé*
étant, *being*	été, ayant été, *been, having been*

CONJUGATION OF FRENCH VERBS

30. **Radical et Terminaison.** — A verb is always formed of two distinct parts: (1) a part called the *radical* or *root;* and (2) a changeable part called the *termination* or *ending.* For example, in *je marche, nous marchons, vous marcherez,* the **root** is *march,* which expresses the action of walking; and the syllables **e, ons, erez,** which follow the root and mark the different inflections of the verb, are called **terminations.**

31.   **Four Regular Conjugations.** — A verb in the infinitive has one of four different endings which will mark it as belonging to one of the following conjugations:

er: as, *chanter*, *donner*, *penser*, which belong to the first conjugation.

ir: as, *finir*, *devenir*, *partir*, which belong to the second conjugation.

oir: as, *recevoir*, *devoir*, *pouvoir*, which belong to the third conjugation.

re: as, *prendre*, *rendre*, *vendre*, which belong to the fourth conjugation.

Grammarians are generally agreed upon the four conjugations as classified above. Some grammarians, however, make three conjugations only, suppressing the third (*oir*); while a few make five, dividing the verbs ending in *ir* into two classes.

NOTE. — The French language comprises about 4,000 simple verbs. Of these 3,600 end in *er;* 360 in *ir;* 10 in *oir;* and 50 in *re*. Thus it will be seen that the first is by far the most important conjugation. With but two exceptions, all its verbs are regular. Nearly all the new verbs that are being constantly added to the French language are put in the first conjugation; a few are placed in the second, but none are added to either the third or the fourth.

MODEL OF A VERB OF THE FIRST CONJUGATION

Chanter, *to sing*

INDICATIF

Présent

je chante, *I sing*
tu chantes, *thou singst*
il } chante, he } sings
elle }   she }
nous chantons, *we sing*
vous chantez, *you sing*
ils } chantent, *they sing*
elles }

Passé Indéfini

j'ai chanté, *I have sung*
tu as chanté, *thou hast sung*
il } a chanté, he } has sung
elle }   she }
nous avons chanté, *we have sung*
vous avez chanté, *you have sung*
ils } ont chanté, *they have sung*
elles }

Imparfait

je chantais, *I was singing*
tu chantais, *thou wast singing*
il chantait, *he was singing*
nous chantions, *we were singing*
vous chantiez, *you were singing*
ils chantaient, *they were singing*

Passé Défini

je chantai, *I sang*
tu chantas, *thou sangst*
il chanta, *he sang*
nous chantâmes, *we sang*
vous chantâtes, *you sang*
ils chantèrent, *they sang*

Plus-que-Parfait

j'avais chanté, *I had sung*
tu avais chanté, *thou hadst sung*
il avait chanté, *he had sung*
nous avions chanté, *we had sung*
vous aviez chanté, *you had sung*
ils avaient chanté, *they had sung*

Passé Antérieur

j'eus chanté, *I had sung*
tu eus chanté, *thou hadst sung*
il eut chanté, *he had sung*
nous eûmes chanté, *we had sung*
vous eûtes chanté, *you had sung*
ils eurent chanté, *they had sung*

Futur

je chanterai, *I shall sing*
tu chanteras, *thou wilt sing*
il chantera, *he will sing*
nous chanterons, *we shall sing*
vous chanterez, *you will sing*
ils chanteront, *they will sing*

Futur Antérieur

j'aurai chanté, *I shall have sung*
tu auras chanté, *thou wilt have sung*
il aura chanté, *he will have sung*
nous aurons chanté, *he shall have sung*
vous aurez chanté, *you will have sung*
ils auront chanté, *they will have sung*

Conditionnel

Présent

je chanterais, *I should sing*
tu chanterais, *thou wouldst sing*
il chanterait, *he would sing*
nous chanterions, *we should sing*
vous chanteriez, *you would sing*
ils chanteraient, *they would sing*

Passé

j'aurais chanté, *I should have sung*
tu aurais chanté, *thou wouldst have sung*
il aurait chanté, *he would have sung*
nous aurions chanté, *we should have sung*
vous auriez chanté, *you would have sung*
ils auraient chanté, *they would have sung*

IMPÉRATIF

chante, *sing (thou)*
chantons, *let us sing*
chantez, *sing (you)*

SUBJONCTIF

Présent

que je chante, *that I may sing*
que tu chantes, *that thou mayst sing*
qu'il chante, *that he may sing*
que nous chantions, *that we may sing*
que vous chantiez, *that you may sing*
qu'ils chantent, *that they may sing*

Passé

que j'aie chanté, *that I may have sung*
que tu aies chanté, *that thou mayst have sung*
qu'il ait chanté, *that he may have sung*
que nous ayons chanté, *that we may have sung*
que vous ayez chanté, *that you may have sung*
qu'ils aient chanté, *that they may have sung*

Imparfait

que je chantasse, *that I might sing*
que tu chantasses, *that thou mightst sing*
qu'il chantât, *that he might sing*
que nous chantassions, *that we might sing*
que vous chantassiez, *that you might sing*
qu'ils chantassent, *that they might sing*

Plus-que-Parfait

que j'eusse chanté, *that I might have sung*
que tu eusses chanté, *that thou mightst have sung*
qu'il eût chanté, *that he might have sung*
que nous eussions chanté, *that we might have sung*
que vous eussiez chanté, *that you might have sung*
qu'ils eussent chanté, *that they might have sung*

INFINITIF

Présent	*Passé*
chanter, *to sing*	avoir chanté, *to have sung*

PARTICIPE

Présent	*Passé*
chantant, *singing*	chanté, *sung*

32. The Affirmative, Negative, Interrogative-Affirmative, and Interrogative-Negative Forms. As seen in Art. **28**, every tense may be conjugated in four ways. The rules given in that article apply to all verbs.

Thus, for the verb *chanter:*

AFFIRMATIVE	NEGATIVE
je chante, *I sing*	je **ne** chante **pas,** *I do not sing*
j'ai chanté, *I have sung*	je **n'**ai **pas** chanté, *I have not sung*
je chanterais, *I should sing*	je **ne** chanterais **pas,** *I should not sing*

INTERROGATIVE-AFFIRMATIVE	INTERROGATIVE-NEGATIVE
ai-je chanté? *have I sung?*	**n'**ai-je **pas** chanté? *have I not sung?*
chanterais-je? *shall I sing?*	**ne** chanterais-je **pas?** *should I not sing?*

The juxtaposition of two vowels is avoided in French whenever possible. To prevent such juxtaposition resort is had to the following devices:

1. The *e* of *je*, *ne*, *de*, *me*, *te*, *se*, *le*, and *que*, when followed by a word beginning with a vowel or silent *h*, is dropped and replaced by an apostrophe. Thus,

> j'ai, *I have*
> je n'ai pas, *I have not*
> je n'ai pas chanté, *I have not sung*
> qu'il chante, *that he may sing*

2. The phrase *est-ce-que* is used instead of the inverted order to prevent the meeting of two mute syllables to express the interrogation of the first person present indicative of verbs of the first conjugation. *Est-ce-que* is equivalent in such constructions to the English word *do*. Thus,

> **Est-ce que** je chante? *Do I sing?*
> **Est-ce que** je parle? *Do I speak?*

3. When the interrogative form of the third person of a verb ends in a vowel, a euphonic *t* is placed between the verb and the pronoun *il* or *elle*. Thus,

a-t-il? *has he?*
chante-t-il? *does he sing?*
parle-t-elle? *does she speak?*

Note.—In verbs of the first conjugation, the *t* in these instances is not really euphonic, for it existed in the old conjugation of these verbs. Formerly, the forms of the third person were *il aimet*, *il chantet*. At that time the endings of all verbs were uniform in the third person singular; thus, *il aimet, il finit, il reçoit, il rompt*. The *t*, which has disappeared in the first conjugation, has been restored in the interrogative form of that conjugation.

33. Every simple tense has its corresponding compound tense. This may be seen at a glance by referring to the tables previously given, where it will be noticed that the compound tense corresponding to a simple tense is formed by conjugating with the past participle of the verb that tense of *avoir* or *être*, as the case may be, which represents the tense of the simple verb.

34. Peculiarities in the Inflection of Some Verbs of the First Conjugation.—All verbs ending in *er* in the infinitive (with but two exceptions: *aller*, to go, and *envoyer*, to send) are regular, and consequently are conjugated like *chanter*, as already illustrated. A few of these verbs, however, have peculiar variations.

(*a*) **Verbs ending in cer; as, commencer, annoncer, menacer.**—In French, *c* before *a*, *o*, or *u* naturally has the hard sound of *k*. If *c* is not to be sounded like *k*, it is printed with a cedilla, as in *nous commençons, je commençai*. The following verbs follow this rule:

avancer, *to advance*	lancer, *to throw*
balancer, *to balance*	menacer, *to menace*
enfoncer, *to sink*	percer, *to pierce*
ensemencer, *to sow*	pincer, *to pinch*
forcer, *to force*	prononcer, *to pronounce*
glacer, *to freeze*	renoncer, *to renounce*
influencer, *to influence*	tracer, *to trace*

(*b*) **Verbs ending in ger; as, manger, changer.** These verbs are similar to the preceding. *G* naturally has a hard sound when placed before *a*, *o*, or *u*. To preserve its soft sound in the expressions *nous mangeons*, *je mangeai*, *e* is inserted after the *g*. The following verbs follow this rule:

affliger, *to afflict*	partager, *to divide*
allonger, *to lengthen*	plonger, *to plunge*
arranger, *to arrange*	protéger, *to protect*
changer, *to change*	ranger, *to range*
charger, *to charge*	ravager, *to ravage*
corriger, *to correct*	ronger, *to gnaw*
interroger, *to interrogate*	saccager, *to sack*
juger, *to judge*	songer, *to dream*
manger, *to eat*	venger, *to revenge*
nager, *to swim*	voyager, *to travel*

NOTE. — The use of the cedilla in verbs ending in *cer*, as well as the addition of an *e* in verbs ending in *ger*, arises from a general French law of phonetics which demands that the elements in the pronunciation of a word, whether noun or verb, shall be preserved in all the forms and derivatives of that word. Since the infinitive is the general form of the verb and the foundation of its pronunciation in all its forms, and since the *c* and the *g* have soft sounds in the infinitives of verbs ending in *cer* and *ger*, the same soft sounds must be preserved throughout the entire conjugation.

(*c*) **Verbs ending in ayer, oyer, uyer; as, payer, employer, essuyer.** — These verbs change the *y* to *i* before an unaccented *e*. Thus,

je paie	j'emploie	j'essuie
je paierai	j'emploierai	j'essuierai

(*d*) **Verbs ending in eler and eter; as, appeler and jeter.** — In most languages, one syllable of a word is accented more strongly than another. That syllable is said to bear the **tonic accent**, or *to be accented*. The tonic accent usually falls upon the last syllable of a French word; but if the last syllable be mute, the tonic accent falls upon the syllable next preceding. The accented syllable of a French word must be sonorous; when it is not so by nature, the following changes are made:

When the present indicative and present subjunctive of these verbs are formed according to the general rule for the formation of those tenses, the last and the next to the last syllables are both mute in the three persons singular and the third person plural. Therefore, in order that the next to last syllable may be accented, the *l* or the *t* is doubled. Thus,

> j'appelle, tu appelles, il appelle, ils appellent;
> > que j'appelle, que tu appelles, qu'il appelle,
> > qu'ils appellent.

> je jette, tu jettes, il jette, ils jettent; que je
> > jette, que tu jettes, qu'il jette, qu'ils jettent.

Notice that the *l* and the *t* are not doubled in other persons and tenses, because the last syllable has the tonic accent. Thus,

> nous appelons, j'appelais; je jetai, j'ai jeté, etc.

To avoid having two successive mute syllables in the future and in the conditional, the *l* and *t* are doubled in those tenses. Thus,

> j'appellerai, nous appellerions; il jettera, vous
> > jetteriez, etc.

The following verbs are conjugated like *appeler* and *jeter:*

appeler, *to call*	crocheter, *to pick (a lock)*
atteler, *to hitch*	décacheter, *to unseal*
chanceler, *to stagger*	empaqueter, *to pack*
épeler, *to spell*	épousseter, *to dust*
étinceler, *to sparkle*	feuilleter, *to turn over*
ficeler, *to tie (with a string)*	jeter, *to throw*
niveler, *to level*	projeter, *to project*
rappeler, *to call back*	rejeter, *to reject*
cacheter, *to seal*	souffleter, *to slap*

EXCEPTIONS. — In the following verbs neither the *l* nor the *t* is doubled; instead, a grave accent is put over the *e* preceding the *l* or *t* where those letters would be doubled according to rule (*d*).

acheter, *to buy*	marteler, *to hammer*
geler, *to freeze*	modeler, *to model*
harceler, *to harass*	étiqueter, *to label*
peler, *to peel*	haleter, *to pant for breath*

(*e*) **Verbs having e mute before the last syllable of the infinitive; as, promener, lever.** — These verbs take a grave accent over the *e* when the following syllable is mute. Thus,

> je promène, je promènerai; je lève, je lèverai,

but we write

> nous promenons, vous promenez; nous levons,
> vous levez.

The following verbs are conjugated like *promener* and *lever:*

dépecer, *to cut in pieces*	peser, *to weigh*
enlever, *to take away*	se promener, *to take a walk*
lever, *to lift*	ramener, *to bring back*
mener, *to lead*	relever, *to raise again*

(*f*) **Verbs having an acute accent over the e before the last syllable of the infinitive; as, espérer, posséder.** — These verbs change the acute accent into a grave accent when the last syllable is mute, thus making that syllable more sonorous. Thus,

> j'espère, ils espèrent; tu possèdes, qu'ils pos-
> sèdent.

In the future tense, however, the acute accent remains, for here the syllable containing the *e* does not have the tonic accent, and an acute accent is sufficient merely to avoid the meeting of the two mute syllables. Thus,

> j'espérerai, il possédera.

The following verbs are conjugated like *espérer* and *posséder:*

accélérer, *to accelerate*	modérer, *to moderate*
céder, *to cede*	opérer, *to operate*
célébrer, *to celebrate*	persévérer, *to persevere*
décéder, *to die*	préférer, *to prefer*
digérer *to digest*	tolérer, *to tolerate*
espérer, *to hope*	alléger, *to disburden*
libérer, *to liberate*	assiéger, *to besiege*

35. Verbs of the First Conjugation. — The following is a list of the most common verbs of the first conjugation:

abriter, *to shelter*

abuser de, *to abuse*

accabler, *to overwhelm*

accepter, *to accept*

accompagner, *to accompany*

accorder, *to grant*

accrocher, *to hook*

accuser, *to accuse*

achever, *to finish*

acquitter, *to acquit*

additionner, *to add*

admirer, *to admire*

adresser, *to address*

aider, *to help*

aimer, *to like*, *to love*

allumer, *to light*

arracher, *to pull out*

arriver, *to arrive*

arroser, *to water*

attacher, *to fasten*

attraper, *to catch*

avouer, *to confess*

arrêter, *to stop*

baîller, *to gape*

boutonner, *to button*

briller, *to shine*

blesser, *to wound*

briser, *to break*

broder, *to embroider*

caresser, *to pet*

causer, *to chat*

casser, *to break*

calculer, *to calculate*

chasser, *to hunt*

chatouiller, *to tickle*

cirer, *to blacken (shoes)*

compter, *to count*

converser, *to converse*

conseiller, *to advise*

conserver, *to keep*

couper, *to cut*

coûter, *to cost*

danser, *to dance*

dater, *to date*

débarquer, *to land*

déchirer, *to tear*

décrocher, *to unhook*

délier, *to untie*

demander, *to ask*

dépenser, *to spend*

demeurer, *to dwell*

dicter, *to dictate*

digérer, *to digest*

discuter, *to discuss*

donner, *to give*

doubler, *to line*

durer, *to last*

écouter, *to listen*

éclairer, *to enlighten*

effacer, *to rub off*

empêcher, *to prevent*

empoisonner, *to poison*

emprunter, *to borrow*

enfermer, *to lock up*

enflammer, *to inflame*

enseigner, *to teach*

envelopper, *to wrap up*

escompter, *to discount*

espérer, *to hope*

estimer, *to esteem*

étonner, *to astonish*

éviter, *to avoid*

frapper, *to knock*

fumer, *to smoke*

garder, *to keep*

gâter, *to spoil*

graver, *to engrave*

gronder, *to scold*

imprimer, *to print*

indiquer, *to indicate*

jouer, *to play*

laisser, *to leave*

laver, *to wash*

louer, *to let*

manquer, *to miss*

menacer, *to menace*

mendier, *to beg*
meubler, *to furnish*
montrer, *to show*
nager, *to swim*
nier, *to deny*
nommer, *to name*
noyer *to drown*
offenser, *to offend*
oublier, *to forget*
pardonner, *to forgive*
parler, *to speak*
passer, *to pass*
pêcher, *to fish*
pécher *to sin*
penser, *to think*
pleurer, *to weep*
porter, *to carry*
pousser, *to push*
prêcher, *to preach*
présenter, *to present*
priver, *to deprive*
prononcer, *to pronounce*
questionner, *to question*
quitter, *to leave*
raconter, *to relate*
raisonner, *to argue*
ramasser, *to pick up*

ramer, *to row*
remarquer, *to remark*
regarder, *to look at*
repasser, *to iron*
respirer, *to breathe*
ressembler, *to look like*
rester, *to stay*
rêver, *to dream*
saluer, *to salute*
sauter, *to jump*
semer, *to sow*
serrer, *to squeeze*
siffler, *to whistle*
soigner, *to take care*
sonner, *to ring*
soupçonner, *to suspect*
sucrer, *to sweeten*
tacher, *to stain*
tirer, *to shoot*
tousser, *to cough*
travailler, *to work*
trouver, *to find*
user, *to wear out*
veiller, *to watch*
venger, *to avenge*
voler, *to fly*

MODEL OF A VERB OF THE SECOND CONJUGATION

Finir, *to finish*

INDICATIF

Présent

je finis, *I finish*
tu finis, *thou finishst*
il finit, *he finishes*
nous finissons, *we finish*
vous finissez, *you finish*
ils finissent, *they finish*

Passé Indéfini

j'ai fini, *I have finished*
tu as fini, *thou hast finished*
il a fini, *he has finished*
nous avons fini, *we have finished*
vous avez fini, *you have finished*
ils ont fini, *they have finished*

Imparfait

je finissais, *I was finishing*
tu finissais, *thou wast finishing*
il finissait, *he was finishing*
nous finissions, *we were finishing*
vous finissiez, *you were finishing*
ils finissaient, *they were finishing*

Plus-que-Parfait

j'avais fini, *I had finished*
tu avais fini, *thou hadst finished*
il avait fini, *he had finished*
nous avions fini, *we had finished*
vous aviez fini, *you had finished*
ils avaient fini, *they had finished*

Passé Défini

je finis, *I finished*
tu finis, *thou finishedst*
il finit, *he finished*
nous finîmes, *we finished*
vous finîtes, *you finished*
ils finirent, *they finished*

Passé Antérieur

j'eus fini, *I had finished*
tu eus fini, *thou hadst finished*
il eut fini, *he had finished*
nous eûmes fini, *we had finished*
vous eûtes fini, *you had finished*
ils eurent fini, *they had finished*

Futur

je finirai, *I shall finish*
tu finiras, *thou wilt finish*
il finira, *he will finish*
nous finirons, *we shall finish*
vous finirez, *you will finish*
ils finiront, *they will finish*

Futur Antérieur

j'aurai fini, *I shall have finished*
tu auras fini, *thou wilt have finished*
il aura fini, *he will have finished*
nous aurons fini, *we shall have finished*
vous aurez fini, *you will have finished*
ils auront fini, *they will have finished*

CONDITIONNEL

Présent

je finirais, *I should finish*
tu finirais, *thou wouldst finish*
il finirait, *he would finish*
nous finirions, *we should finish*
vous finiriez, *you would finish*
ils finiraient, *they would finish*

Passé

j'aurais fini, *I should have finished*
tu aurais fini, *thou wouldst have finished*
il aurait fini, *he would have finished*
nous aurions fini, *we should have finished*
vous auriez fini, *you would have finished*
ils auraient fini, *they would have finished*

IMPÉRATIF

finis, *finish (thou)*
finissons, *let us finish*
finissez, *finish (you)*

SUBJONCTIF

Présent

que je finisse, *that I may finish*
que tu finisses, *that thou mayst finish*
qu'il finisse, *that he may finish*
que nous finissions, *that we may finish*
que vous finissiez, *that you may finish*
qu'ils finissent, *that they may finish*

Passé

que j'aie fini, *that I may have finished*
que tu aies fini, *that thou mayst have finished*
qu'il ait fini, *that he may have finished*
que nous ayons fini, *that we may have finished*
que vous ayez fini, *that you may have finished*
qu'ils aient fini, *that they may have finished*

Imparfait

que je finisse, *that I might finish*
que tu finisses, *that thou mightst finish*
qu'il finît, *that he might finish*
que nous finissions, *that we might finish*
que vous finissiez, *that you might finish*
qu'ils finissent, *that they might finish*

Plus-que-Parfait

que j'eusse fini, *that I might have finished*
que tu eusses fini, *that thou mightst have finished*
qu'il eût fini, *that he might have finished*
que nous eussions fini, *that we might have finished*
que vous eussiez fini, *that you might have finished*
qu'ils eussent fini, *that they might have finished*

INFINITIF

Présent	Passé
finir, *to finish*	avoir fini, *to have finished*

PARTICIPE

Présent	Passé
finissant, *finishing*	fini, *finished*

36. Verbs Conjugated Like Finir. — The following is a list of the most important verbs that are conjugated like *finir:*

accomplir, *to accomplish*
adoucir, *to soften*
affaiblir, *to weaken*
affermir, *to strengthen*
affranchir, *to prepay*, *to free*
agir, *to act*
agrandir, *to enlarge*
applaudir, *to applaud*
approfondir, *to deepen*
avertir, *to warn*
arrondir, *to round*
assortir, *to match*

amincir, *to thin*
bannir, *to banish*
bâtir, *to build*
bénir, *to bless*
blanchir, *to whiten*
bondir, *to leap*
chérir, *to cherish*
choisir, *to choose*
convertir, *to convert*
divertir, *to divert*
durcir, *to harden*
établir, *to establish*

embellir, *to embellish*
éclaircir, *to clear*
élargir, *to widen*
s'évanouir, *to faint*
fleurir, *to blossom*
fournir, *to supply*
flétrir, *to fade*
gémir, *to groan*
garnir, *to trim*
grandir, *to grow tall*
guérir, *to cure*
garantir, *to guarantee*
haïr, *to hate*
jaunir, *to yellow*
jouir, *to enjoy*
jaillir, *to gush*

maigrir, *to grow thin*
mûrir, *to ripen*
moisir, *to mold*
noircir, *to blacken*
nourrir, *to feed*
pâlir, *to grow pale*
polir, *to polish*
punir, *to punish*
pourrir, *to decay*
remplir, *to fill*
réussir, *to succeed*
réfléchir, *to reflect*
rétrécir, *to narrow*
rougir, *to blush*
vernir, *to varnish*
vieillir, *to grow old*

37. The preceding verbs add *iss* to the root before the endings of all tenses except the past definite, the present infinitive, and the past participle. About thirty-five verbs do not take *iss*, and, for this reason, some grammarians have made a special conjugation of them. The verb *partir*, to depart, is given here as a model, not only because of that peculiarity, but also because it is conjugated with *être* in its compound tenses. It must not be inferred from this, however, that all verbs conjugated like *partir* take the auxiliary *être*. Only those described in Art. **27,** (*c*), require *être;* others take *avoir*.

Partir, *to depart*

INDICATIF

Présent

je pars, *I depart*
tu pars, *thou departst*
il }
elle } part, he } she } *departs*
nous partons, *we depart*
vous partez, *you depart*
ils }
elles } partent, *they depart*

Passé Indéfini

je suis parti, *I have departed*
tu es parti, *thou hast departed*
il est parti, he }
elle est partie, she } *has departed*
nous sommes partis, *we have departed*
vous êtes partis, *you have departed*
ils sont partis, }
elles sont parties, } *they have departed*

Imparfait

je partais, *I was departing*
tu partais, *thou wast departing*
il
elle } partait, *he*
she } *was departing*
nous partions, *we were departing*
vous partiez, *you were departing*
ils
elles } partaient, *they were departing*

Plus-que-Parfait

j'étais parti, *I had departed*
tu étais parti, *thou hadst departed*
il était parti, *he*
elle était partie, *she* } *had departed*
nous étions partis, *we had departed*
vous étiez partis, *you had departed*
ils étaient partis,
elles étaient parties, } *they had departed*

Passé Défini

je partis, *I departed*
tu partis, *thou departedst*
il
elle } partit, *he*
she } *departed*
nous partîmes, *we departed*
vous partîtes, *you departed*
ils
elles } partirent, *they departed*

Passé Antérieur

je fus parti, *I had departed*
tu fus parti, *thou hadst departed*
il fut parti, *he*
elle fut partie, *she* } *had departed*
nous fûmes partis, *we had departed*
vous fûtes partis, *you had departed*
ils furent partis,
elles furent parties, } *they had departed*

Futur

je partirai, *I shall depart*
tu partiras, *thou wilt depart*
il
elle } partira, he
she } *will depart*
nous partirons, *we shall depart*
vous partirez, *you will depart*
ils
elles } partiront, *they will depart*

Futur Antérieur

je serai parti, *I shall have departed*
tu seras parti, *thou wilt have departed*
il sera parti,   he
elle sera partie,   she } *will have departed*
nous serons partis, *we shall have departed*
vous serez partis, *you will have departed*
ils seront partis,
elles seront parties, } *they will have departed*

CONDITIONNEL

Présent

je partirais, *I should depart*
tu partirais, *thou wouldst depart*
il
elle } partirait, he
she } *would depart*
nous partirions, *we should depart*
vous partiriez, *you would depart*
ils partiraient,
elles partiraient, } *they would depart*

Passé

je serais parti, *I should have departed*
tu serais parti, *thou wouldst have departed*
il serait parti,   he
elle serait partie,   she } *would have departed*
nous serions partis, *we should have departed*
vous seriez partis, *you would have departed*
ils seraient partis,
elles seraient parties, } *they would have departed*

IMPÉRATIF

pars, *depart (thou)*
partons, *let us depart*
partez, *depart (you)*

SUBJONCTIF

Présent

que je parte, *that I may depart*

que tu partes, *that thou mayst depart*

qu'il   ⎫
qu'elle ⎰ parte, *that* ⎰ *he* ⎱ *may depart*
            ⎱ *she* ⎰

que nous partions, *that we may depart*

que vous partiez, *that you may depart*

qu'ils   ⎫
qu'elles ⎰ partent, *that they may depart*

Passé

que je sois parti, *that I may have departed*

que tu sois parti, *that thou mayst have departed*

qu'il soit parti,   ⎫
qu'elle soit partie, ⎰ *that* ⎰ *he* ⎱ *may have departed*
                   ⎱ *she* ⎰

que nous soyons partis, *that we may have departed*

que vous soyez partis, *that you may have departed*

qu'ils soient partis,   ⎫
qu'elles soient parties, ⎰ *that they may have departed*

Imparfait

que je partisse, *that I might depart*

que tu partisses, *that thou mightst depart*

qu'il   ⎫
qu'elle ⎰ partît, *that* ⎰ *he* ⎱ *might depart*
            ⎱ *she* ⎰

que nous partissions, *that we might depart*

que vous partissiez, *that you might depart*

qu'ils   ⎫
qu'elles ⎰ partissent, *that they might depart*

Plus-que-Parfait

que je fusse parti, *that I might have departed*

que tu fusses parti, *that thou mightst have departed*

qu'il fût parti,   ⎫
qu'elle fût partie, ⎰ *that* ⎰ *he* ⎱ *might have departed*
                 ⎱ *she* ⎰

que nous fussions partis, *that we might have departed*

que vous fussiez partis, *that you might have departed*

qu'ils fussent partis,   ⎫
qu'elles fussent parties, ⎰ *that they might have departed*

INFINITIF

Présent	*Passé*
partir, *to depart*	être parti, *to have departed*

PARTICIPE

Présent	*Passé*
partant, *departing*	parti, *departed*

38. It will be noticed that the past participle conjugated with *être* has inflections for gender and number; it is treated as an adjective. It takes the same gender and number as the subject; that is, an *e* in the feminine and an *s* in the plural. This is not the case with the past participle conjugated with *avoir*, as will be seen elsewhere.

39. Verbs Conjugated Like Partir. — The following list contains the most important verbs that are conjugated like *partir:*

bouillir, *to boil*	mentir, *to lie*
consentir, *to consent*	servir, *to serve*
dormir, *to sleep*	sentir, *to feel*
démentir, *to belie*	sortir, *to go out*

MODEL OF A VERB OF THE THIRD CONJUGATION

Recevoir, *to receive*

INDICATIF

Présent	*Passé Indéfini*
je reçois, *I receive*	j'ai reçu, *I have received*
tu reçois, *thou receivest*	tu as reçu, *thou hast received*
il reçoit, *he receives*	il a reçu, *he has received*
nous recevons, *we receive*	nous avons reçu, *we have received*
vous recevez, *you receive*	vous avez reçu, *you have received*
ils reçoivent, *they receive*	ils ont reçu, *they have received*

Imparfait	*Plus-que-Parfait*
je recevais, *I was receiving*	j'avais reçu, *I had received*
tu recevais, *thou wast receiving*	tu avais reçu, *thou hadst received*
il recevait, *he was receiving*	il avait reçu, *he had received*
nous recevions, *we were receiving*	nous avions reçu, *we had received*
vous receviez, *you were receiving*	vous aviez reçu, *you had received*
ils recevaient, *they were receiving*	ils avaient reçu, *they had received*

Passé Défini	*Passé Antérieur*
je reçus, *I received*	j'eus reçu, *I had received*
tu reçus, *thou receivedst*	tu eus reçu, *thou hadst received*
il reçut, *he received*	il eut reçu, *he had received*
nous reçûmes, *we received*	nous eûmes reçu, *we had received*
vous reçûtes, *you received*	vous eûtes reçu, *you had received*
ils reçurent, *they received*	ils eurent reçu, *they had received*

Futur

je recevrai, *I shall receive*
tu recevras, *thou wilt receive*
il recevra, *he will receive*
nous recevrons, *we shall receive*
vous recevrez, *you will receive*
ils recevront, *they will receive*

Futur Antérieur

j'aurai reçu, *I shall have received*
tu auras reçu, *thou wilt have received*
il aura reçu, *he will have received*
nous aurons reçu, *we shall have received*
vous aurez reçu, *you will have received*
ils auront reçu, *they will have received*

CONDITIONNEL

Présent

je recevrais, *I should receive*
tu recevrais, *thou wouldst receive*
il recevrait, *he would receive*
nous recevrions, *we should receive*
vous recevriez, *you would receive*
ils recevraient, *they would receive*

Passé

j'aurais reçu, *I should have received*
tu aurais reçu, *thou wouldst have received*
il aurait reçu, *he would have received*
nous aurions reçu, *we should have received*
vous auriez reçu, *you would have received*
ils auraient reçu, *they would have received*

IMPÉRATIF

reçois, *receive (thou)*
recevons, *let us receive*
recevez, *receive (you)*

SUBJONCTIF

Présent

que je reçoive, *that I may receive*
que tu reçoives, *that thou mayst receive*
qu'il reçoive, *that he may receive*
que nous recevions, *that we may receive*
que vous receviez, *that you may receive*
qu'ils reçoivent, *that they may receive*

Passé

que j'aie reçu, *that I may have received*
que tu aies reçu, *that thou mayst have received*
qu'il ait reçu, *that he may have received*
que nous ayons reçu, *that we may have received*
que vous ayez reçu, *that you may have received*
qu'ils aient reçu, *that they may have received*

Imparfait

que je reçusse, *that I might receive*
que tu reçusses, *that thou mightst receive*
qu'il reçût, *that he might receive*
que nous reçussions, *that we might receive*
que vous reçussiez, *that you might receive*
qu'ils reçussent, *that they might receive*

Plus-que-Parfait

que j'eusse reçu, *that I might have received*
que tu eusses reçu, *that thou mightst have received*
qu'il eût reçu, *that he might have received*
que nous eussions reçu, *that we might have received*
que vous eussiez reçu, *that you might have received*
qu'ils eussent reçu, *that they might have received*

INFINITIF

Présent	Passé
recevoir, *to receive*	avoir reçu, *to have received*

PARTICIPE

Présent	Passé
recevant, *receiving*	reçu, *received*

40. This conjugation has only six verbs conjugated like *recevoir;* they are:

apercevoir, *to perceive*	devoir, *to owe*
concevoir, *to conceive*	percevoir, *to perceive*
décevoir, *to deceive*	redevoir, *to owe still*

These verbs all end in *evoir* in the infinitive. On account of their small number, some French grammarians do not consider them as forming an independent conjugation, but classify them with irregular verbs.

MODEL OF A VERB OF THE FOURTH CONJUGATION

Vendre, *to sell*

INDICATIF

Présent

je vends, *I sell*
tu vends, *thou sellst*
il vend, *he sells*
nous vendons, *we sell*
vous vendez, *you sell*
ils vendent, *they sell*

Passé Indéfini

j'ai vendu, *I have sold*
tu as vendu, *thou hast sold*
il a vendu, *he has sold*
nous avons vendu, *we have sold*
vous avez vendu, *you have sold*
ils ont vendu, *they have sold*

Imparfait

je vendais, *I was selling*
tu vendais, *thou wast selling*
il vendait, *he was selling*
nous vendions, *we were selling*
vous vendiez, *you were selling*
ils vendaient, *they were selling*

Plus-que-Parfait

j'avais vendu, *I had sold*
tu avais vendu, *thou hadst sold*
il avait vendu, *he had sold*
nous avions vendu, *we had sold*
vous aviez vendu, *you had sold.*
ils avaient vendu, *they had sold*

Passé Défini

je vendis, *I sold*
tu vendis, *thou soldst*
il vendit, *he sold*
nous vendîmes, *we sold*
vous vendîtes, *you sold*
ils vendirent, *they sold*

Passé Antérieur

j'eus vendu, *I had sold*
tu eus vendu, *thou hadst sold*
il eut vendu, *he had sold*
nous eûmes vendu, *we had sold*
vous eûtes vendu, *you had sold*
ils eurent vendu, *they had sold*

Futur

je vendrai, *I shall sell*
tu vendras, *thou wilt sell*
il vendra, *he will sell*
nous vendrons, *we shall sell*
vous vendrez, *you will sell*
ils vendront, *they will sell*

Futur Antérieur

j'aurai vendu, *I shall have sold*
tu auras vendu, *thou wilt have sold*
il aura vendu, *he will have sold*
nous aurons vendu, *we shall have sold*
vous aurez vendu, *you will have sold*
ils auront vendu, *they will have sold*

CONDITIONNEL

Présent

je vendrais, *I should sell*
tu vendrais, *thou wouldst sell*
il vendrait, *he would sell*
nous vendrions, *we should sell*
vous vendriez, *you would sell*
ils vendraient, *they would sell*

Passé

j'aurais vendu, *I should have sold*
tu aurais vendu, *thou wouldst have sold*
il aurait vendu, *he would have sold*
nous aurions vendu, *we should have sold*
vous auriez vendu, *you would have sold*
ils auraient vendu, *they would have sold*

Impératif

vends, *(sell thou)*
vendons, *let us sell*
vendez, *(sell you)*

Subjonctif

Présent

que je vende, *that I may sell*
que tu vendes, *that thou mayst sell*
qu'il vende, *that he may sell*
que nous vendions, *that we may sell*
que vous vendiez, *that you may sell*
qu'ils vendent, *that they may sell*

Passé

que j'aie vendu, *that I may have sold*
que tu aies vendu, *that thou mayst have sold*
qu'il ait vendu, *that he may have sold*
que nous ayons vendu, *that we may have sold*
que vous ayez vendu, *that you may have sold*
qu'ils aient vendu, *that they may have sold*

Imparfait

que je vendisse, *that I might sell*
que tu vendisses, *that thou mightst sell*
qu'il vendît, *that he might sell*
que nous vendissions, *that we might sell*
que vous vendissiez, *that you might sell*
qu'ils vendissent, *that they might sell*

Plus-que-Parfait

que j'eusse vendu, *that I might have sold*
que tu eusses vendu, *that thou mightst have sold*
qu'il eût vendu, *that he might have sold*
que nous eussions vendu, *that we might have sold*
que vous eussiez vendu, *that you might have sold*
qu'ils eussent vendu, *that they might have sold*

INFINITIF

Présent	*Passé*
vendre, *to sell*	avoir vendu, *to have sold*

PARTICIPE

Présent	*Passé*
vendant, *selling*	vendu, *sold*

41. Verbs Conjugated Like Vendre. — The following is a list of the most important verbs that are conjugated like *vendre:*

attendre, *to wait for*	pendre, *to hang*
confondre, *to confound*	perdre, *to lose*
correspondre, *to correspond*	pondre, *to lay eggs*
défendre, *to defend*	prétendre, *to pretend*
dépendre, *to depend*	rendre, *to render*
descendre, *to go down*	répandre, *to spill*
entendre, *to hear*	répondre, *to answer*
étendre, *to extend*	suspendre, *to suspend*
fendre, *to split*	tendre, *to hold out*
fondre, *to melt*	tondre, *to shear*
mordre, *to bite*	tordre, *to twist*

FRENCH GRAMMAR
(PART 3)

LE VERBE–THE VERB–(Continued)

FORMATION OF THE TENSES

1. From the models of regular verbs already given, the following rules to govern the formation of the tenses may be deduced:

LE MODE INDICATIF

2. Présent.—In the present tense the first person singular of a verb always ends in *e*, *s*, or *x* (*s* and *x* were equivalent in old French). *J'ai* of *avoir* is the only exception. When the first person ends in *e*, the second person has the ending *es* and the third person the ending *e*. Thus,

j'aime, tu aimes, il aime.

When the first person ends in *s* or *x*, the ending of the second person is the same as the ending of the first. To form the third person, the *s* or *x* is changed to *t*, except in verbs ending in *ds* or *ts*, when the *s* is suppressed and no *t* added. Thus,

$$\text{je} \begin{cases} \text{veux} \\ \text{finis} \\ \text{prends} \\ \text{mets} \end{cases} \quad \text{tu} \begin{cases} \text{veux} \\ \text{finis} \\ \text{prends} \\ \text{mets} \end{cases} \quad \text{il} \begin{cases} \text{veut} \\ \text{finit} \\ \text{prend} \\ \text{met} \end{cases}$$

The first person plural always ends in *ons* (*nous sommes* excepted). To form the second person plural, the *ons* of the first person plural is changed to *ez* (*vous êtes, vous dites, vous faites* excepted), and to form the third person plural, *ons* is changed to *ent* (*ils ont, ils sont, ils font, ils vont* excepted). So, when the first persons singular and plural of the present indicative are given, the complete tense may be formed. In the Table of Irregular Verbs, the first persons singular and plural are given, together with exceptions for changes in their roots.

3. Imparfait. — The endings of the imperfect are identical in all verbs. They are *ais, ais, ait, ions, iez, aient*. The root of the verb in this tense is the same as in the first person plural of the present indicative. So that to form the imperfect, it is necessary only to replace the ending *ons* of the present by the endings of the imperfect. Thus,

nous $\begin{cases} \text{aim}\textbf{ons}, \text{ j'aim}\textbf{ais} \\ \text{finiss}\textbf{ons}, \text{ tu finiss}\textbf{ais} \\ \text{rend}\textbf{ons}, \text{ il rend}\textbf{ait} \end{cases}$ nous $\begin{cases} \text{part}\textbf{ons}, \text{ nous part}\textbf{ions} \\ \text{voul}\textbf{ons}, \text{ vous voul}\textbf{iez} \\ \text{ten}\textbf{ons}, \text{ ils ten}\textbf{aient} \end{cases}$

The only exception is the imperfect of the verb *être*, which is *j'étais*.

4. Passé Défini. — To obtain general rules for forming the past definite, verbs may be divided into two classes:

1. *All verbs ending in* **er** *in the infinitive* form the past definite by adding the endings *ai, as, a, âmes, âtes, èrent* to the root of the verb. Thus,

Parler

je parl**ai**	nous parl**âmes**
tu parl**as**	vous parl**âtes**
il parl**a**	ils parl**èrent**

2. *All Other Verbs, Regular and Irregular.* — With comparatively few exceptions, there is much similarity in sound between the endings of the past participle and the first person of the past definite of these verbs. It is to be noted, however, that the first person singular of the past definite

of these verbs always ends in *s*, while the past participle may
end in some other letter.   Thus,

Past Participle	Past Definite
fini, *finished*	je finis, *I finished*
pris, *taken*	je pris, *I took*
dit, *said*	je dis, *I said*
lu, *read*	je lus, *I read*
reçu, *received*	je reçus, *I received*

Exceptions.— In the following verbs and others conjugated like them, these two forms are unlike both in pronunciation and spelling:

Past Participle	Past Definite
ouvert, *opened*	j'ouvris, *I opened*
vendu, *sold*	je vendis, *I sold*
conduit, *conducted*	je conduisis, *I conducted*
craint, *feared*	je craignis, *I feared*
écrit, *written*	j'écrivis, *I wrote*
battu, *beaten*	je battis, *I beat*
vêtu, *clad*	je vêtis, *I clad*
cousu, *sewed*	je cousis, *I sewed*
vaincu, *vanquished*	je vainquis, *I vanquished*
rompu, *broken*	je rompis, *I broke*
né, *born*	je naquis, *I was born*
vu, *seen*	je vis, *I saw*
fait, *made*	je fis, *I made*
mort, *dead*	je mourus, *I died*
venu, *come*	je vins, *I came*

The first person singular of the past definite in all verbs,
regular or irregular, is formed as illustrated above.   The
full past definite of *avoir* and *être* provides the endings of the
other persons of this tense.

Past Definite	Past Definite
Avoir	*Etre*
j'eus, *I had*	je fus, *I was*
tu eus, *thou hadst*	tu fus, *thou wast*
il eut, *he had*	il fut, *he was*
nous eûmes, *we had*	nous fûmes, *we were*
vous eûtes, *you had*	vous fûtes, *you were*
ils eurent, *they had*	ils furent, *they were*

The endings of the past definite are *s, s, t, ^mes, ^tes, rent.* To form the past definite of any verb, add these endings in their proper order to the verb stem of the first person. Thus,

PAST DEFINITE

Finir	*Mourir*	*Venir*
je finis	je mourus	je vins
tu finis	tu mourus	tu vins
il finit	il mourut	il vint
nous finîmes	nous mourûmes	nous vînmes
vous finîtes	vous mourûtes	vous vîntes
ils finirent	ils moururent	ils vinrent

5. Futur. — In all conjugations, the future is formed by adding to the infinitive, in proper order, the old forms of the present of *avoir;* namely, *ai, as, a, ons, ez, ont.*

In the fourth conjugation, before adding these endings, the final *e* of the infinitive is suppressed. Thus,

Aimer	*Rendre*
j'aimerai	je rendrai
tu aimeras	tu rendras
il aimera	il rendra
nous aimerons	nous rendrons
vous aimerez	vous rendrez
ils aimeront	ils rendront

Irregularities in the future are pointed out in the Table of Irregular Verbs.

NOTE. — The French future had its origin in Classical Latin, where such expressions as *habeo cantare, J'ai à chanter,* I have to sing, are found. Later, the auxiliary *avoir* was placed after the verb; finally it was joined to the verb, thus forming only one word. Consequently, the French future is not, properly speaking, a single tense, but a compound of the infinitive and an auxiliary. The future tense of the third conjugation has been formed from Norman infinitives. The infinitives *voir, recevoir, devoir, mouvoir, pouvoir, savoir, vouloir, valoir,* were, respectively, in the dialect of Normandy, *veer, recever, dever, mouver, pouer, saver, vouler,* and *valer.* Some changes were made when the future was formed from these infinitives; *e* preceding final *r* was suppressed, as, *je recevrai,* for *je receverai; je mouvrai,* for *je mouverai.* Furthermore, when the root ended in a vowel, as in *pou er,* the *r* was doubled, *je pourrai.* The verb *envoyer,* which, too, is irregular in its future, was formed from the Norman infinitive *envé er;* future: *J'enverrai.* The Norman infinitive was used to form the future, because that form was lighter and more elegant than the heavy *-oir* form of the third conjugation.

LE MODE CONDITIONNEL

6. Conditionnel. — The conditional is formed from the infinitive by adding to it the imperfect indicative of *avoir*, suppressing, however, *av*. The endings are then: *ais, ais, ait, ions, iez, aient*. Thus,

Aimer	*Rendre*
j'aimer**ais**	je rendr**ais**
tu aimer**ais**	tu rendr**ais**
il aimer**ait**	il rendr**ait**
nous aimer**ions**	nous rendr**ions**
vous aimer**iez**	vous rendr**iez**
ils aimer**aient**	ils rendr**aient**

Since the future and conditional are formed from the infinitive, their verb roots are identical.

LE MODE IMPÉRATIF

7. Impératif. — The second person singular of the imperative of all verbs is made from the first person singular of the present indicative by suppressing the pronoun *je*.

PRESENT INDICATIVE	IMPERATIVE
je chante, *I sing*	chante, *sing* (thou)
je viens, *I come*	viens, *come* (thou)

The first and second persons plural of the imperative are formed, respectively, from the first and second persons plural of the present indicative by the suppression of the pronouns *nous* and *vous*. Thus,

PRESENT INDICATIVE	IMPERATIVE
nous parlons, *we speak*	parlons, *let us speak*
vous finissez, *you finish*	finissez, *finish* (you)

LE MODE SUBJONCTIF

8. Subjonctif Présent. — The endings of the present subjunctive are much like the endings of the present indicative of verbs of the first conjugation. They are *e, es, e, ions, iez, ent*. It will be seen that they differ only in the first and second persons plural, where *ions* and *iez* in the present subjunctive replace the *ons* and *ez* of the present indicative. This tense may be formed by substituting, in their proper order, for the ending *ons* of the first person plural of the present indicative, the endings above given. Thus,

PRESENT INDICATIVE	PRESENT SUBJUNCTIVE
nous aim**ons**	que j'aim**e**
nous finiss**ons**	que tu finiss**es**
nous rend**ons**	qu'il rend**e**
nous part**ons**	qu'elle part**e**
nous conduis**ons**	que nous conduis**ions**
nous dis**ons**	que vous dis**iez**
nous achet**ons**	qu'ils achèt**ent**

EXCEPTIONS.—1. Certain irregular verbs form the present subjunctive regularly from the root form that appears in the first person of this tense. They are,

INFINITIVE	PRESENT SUBJUNCTIVE
faire, *to make*	que je **fasse,** que tu fasses
pouvoir, *to be able*	que je **puisse,** que tu puisses
savoir, *to know*	que je **sache,** que tu saches

2. The stem of the present indicative first person plural determines the formation of the first and second persons plural of the present subjunctive; while, on account of the tonic accent, the stem of the third person plural indicative is used to form the three persons singular and the third person plural of the subjunctive. This rule applies to the following verbs and those conjugated like them:

PRESENT INDICATIVE	PRESENT SUBJUNCTIVE
nous acqu**é**r**ons**	que nous acquérions, que vous acquériez
ils acqui**è**r**ent**	{ que j'acquière, que tu acquières, qu'il acquière, qu'ils acquièrent
nous recev**ons**	que nous recevions, que vous receviez
ils reçoiv**ent**	{ que je reçoive, que tu reçoives, qu'il re**ç**oive, qu'ils reçoivent
nous buv**ons**	que nous buvions, que vous buviez

ils boi**vent**	{ que je boive, que tu boives, qu'il boive, qu'ils boivent
nous mour**ons**	que nous mourions, que vous mouriez
ils meur**ent**	{ que je meure que tu meures, qu'il meure, qu'ils meurent
nous ven**ons**	que nous venions, que vous veniez
ils vienn**ent**	{ que je vienne, que tu viennes, qu'il vienne, qu'ils viennent

3. The following verbs change *y* to *i* before a mute syllable:

PRESENT INDICATIVE	PRESENT SUBJUNCTIVE
nous voyons	que je voie, que nous voyions
nous fuyons	que je fuie, que nous fuyions
nous croyons	que je croie, que nous croyions
nous envoyons	que j'envoie, que nous envoyions

4. The present subjunctive of the impersonal verbs *pleuvoir* and *falloir* is *qu'il pleuve* and *qu'il faille*.

5. The first persons singular and plural of *aller*, *valoir*, and *vouloir* are as follows:

PRESENT SUBJUNCTIVE

aller, *to go*	{ **que j'aille,** que tu ailles, qu'il aille, qu'ils aillent **que nous allions,** que vous alliez
valoir, *to be worth*	{ **que je vaille,** que tu vailles, qu'il vaille, qu'ils vaillent **que nous valions,** que vous valiez
vouloir, *to be willing*	{ **que je veuille,** que tu veuilles, qu'il veuille, qu'ils veuillent **que nous voulions,** que vous vouliez

6. The present subjunctives of *avoir* and *être*, also irregular, are as follows:

PRESENT SUBJUNCTIVE

Avoir	*Être*
que j'aie	que je sois
que tu aies	que tu sois
qu'il ait	qu'il soit
que nous ayons	que nous soyons
que vous ayez	que vous soyez
qu'ils aient	qu'ils soient

9. Imparfait du Subjonctif. — To form the imperfect subjunctive, the following endings are added in proper order to the second person singular of the past definite: *se, ses, t, sions, siez, sent*. Thus,

tu **donnas**
que je donnasse, que nous donnassions
que tu donnasses, que vous donnassiez
qu'il donnât, qu'ils donnassent

tu **finis**
que je finisse, que nous finissions
que tu finisses, que vous finissiez
qu'il finît, qu'ils finissent

tu **vins**
que je vinsse, que nous vinssions
que tu vinsses, que vous vinssiez
qu'il vînt, qu'ils vinssent

It will be noticed that in the third person singular the *s* disappears, to be replaced by a circumflex accent.

10. Temps Composés. — All compound tenses are made by conjugating the auxiliaries *avoir* or *être*, as the case may be, with the past participle of the verb. In the Table of Irregular Verbs the past participle of all verbs is given, so that all compound tenses may be easily formed.

11. Participe Présent. — The present participle always ends in *ant*, and may be formed from the first person plural of the present by changing *ons* into *ant*. Thus,

nous
mangeons, mangeant
finissons, finissant

The present participle, the third person plural of the present indicative, the imperfect indicative, and the present subjunctive, ordinarily have the same root; consequently, when one of these forms is known, it is easy to find the others. The identity of the root in these four tenses is due to the fact that all have endings beginning with a vowel, and consequently, the original roots must be modified in the same manner before being joined to their respective endings.

ANOTHER THEORY OF THE FORMATION OF TENSES

12. Most grammarians give another theory of the formation of tenses which differs slightly from that just given. As this method is the one followed in colleges and required for entrance examination in French, we feel obliged to give it here:

The tenses of a verb are divided into *primitive* (or *principal*) and *derivative*. The **primitive tenses** are those that serve to form **derivative tenses.** Of course, this division is purely artificial, for it is not true that the primitive tenses actually served to form the others.

The primitive tenses, or principal parts, of a verb are five in number: the *infinitive*, the *present participle*, the *first person present indicative*, the *past definite*, and the *past participle*.

From the infinitive are formed two tenses: (*a*) The future by changing *r*, *oir*, or *re* into *rai*, *ras*, *ra*, *rons*, *rez*, *ront*. (*b*) The present conditional by changing *r*, *oir*, or *re* into *rais*, *rais*, *rait*, *rions*, *riez*, *raient*.

From the present participle, three tenses are formed: (*a*) The plural of the present indicative, by changing *ant* into *ons*, *ez*, *ent*. (*b*) The imperfect indicative by changing *ant* into *ais*, *ais*, *ait*, *ions*, *iez*, *aient*. (*c*) The present subjunctive by changing *ant* into *e*, *es*, *e*, *ions*, *iez*, *ent*.

From the present indicative, the imperative is formed by the suppression of the pronoun subjects, and by the suppression of *s* of the second person singular of the verbs of the first conjugation.

From the past definite, the imperfect subjunctive is formed by changing *ai* into *asse*, etc. for the first conjugation; and by the addition of *se*, etc. in the three other conjugations.

From the past participle all compound tenses are formed by the addition of the auxiliary *avoir* or *être*.

13. The principal parts of a verb are best tabulated as illustrated below:

PRINCIPAL PARTS OF A VERB

Infinitive	Present Participle	Present Indicative	Past Definite	Past Participle
donner	donnant	je donne	je donnai	donné
vivre	vivant	je vis	je vécus	vécu
devenir	devenant	je deviens	je devins	devenu
recevoir	recevant	je reçois	je reçus	reçu
retenir	retenant	je retiens	je retins	retenu
mourir	mourant	je meurs	je mourus	mort
aller	allant	je vais	j'allai	allé

LIST OF IRREGULAR VERBS

14. A simple verb may be used to form a compound verb by the addition of a *prefix*. Thus, from *courir*, for example, have been formed *accourir, concourir, discourir, parcourir*, etc. A compound verb is generally conjugated like the simple verb from which it has been formed; therefore, the conjugation of simple verbs only, printed in heavy type, has been given in the Table of Irregular Verbs which follows this list.

absoudre, *to absolve* [like résoudre, except past participle, absous (*m.*), absoute (*f.*)]

s'abstenir, *to abstain* (like venir)

abstraire, *to abstract* (like traire)

accourir, *to run to* (like courir)

accroître, *to increase* (like paraître)

accueillir, *to welcome* (like cueillir)

acquérir, *to acquire*

adjoindre, *to adjoin* (like craindre)

advenir, *to befall* (like venir)

admettre, *to admit* (like mettre)

aller, *to go*

apparaître, *to appear* (like paraître)

appartenir, *to belong* (like venir)

apprendre, *to learn* (like prendre)

assaillir, *to assail* (like cueillir except the future: j'assaillirai)

asseoir, *to sit*

astreindre, *to compel* (like craindre)

atteindre, *to reach* (like craindre)

battre, *to beat*

boire, *to drink*

bouillir, *to boil*

ceindre, *to gird* (like craindre)

circonscrire, *to circumscribe* (like écrire)

commettre, *to commit* (like mettre)

comparaître, *to appear* (like paraître)

complaire, *to please* (like plaire)

comprendre, *to understand* (like prendre)

compromettre, *to compromise* (like mettre)

conclure, *to conclude*

concourir, *to concur* (like courir)

conduire, *to lead*

confire, *to preserve*

conjoindre, *to unite* (like joindre)

connaître, *to know* (like paraître)

conquérir, *to conquer* (like acquérir)

construire, *to build* (like conduire)

contenir, *to contain* (like venir)

contraindre, *to constrain.* (like craindre)

contredire, *to contradict* (like dire, except in the present: vous *contredisez*)

contrefaire, *to counterfeit* (like faire)

convenir, *to agree* (like venir)

coudre, *to sew*

courir, *to run*

couvrir, *to cover* (like ouvrir)

craindre, *to fear*

croire, *to believe*

croître, *to grow* (like paraître)

cueillir, *to gather*

cuire, *to cook* (like conduire)

découvrir, *to discover* (like ouvrir)

décrire, *to describe* (like écrire)

décroître, *to decrease* (like paraître)

se dédire, *to retract* (like dire)

déduire, *to deduct* (like conduire)

défaillir, *to faint* (like assaillir)

défaire, *to undo* (like faire)

démentir, *to belie* (like partir)

se démettre, *to dismiss* (like mettre)

dépeindre, *to depict* (like craindre)

déplaire, *to displease* (like plaire)

desservir, *to remove* (like partir)

déteindre, *to fade* (like craindre)

détenir, *to detain* (like venir)

détruire, *to destroy* (like conduire)

devenir, *to become* (like venir)

dévêtir, *to undress* (like vêtir)

dire, *to tell*

discourir, *to discourse* (like courir)

disjoindre, *to disjoin* (like craindre)

disparaître, *to disappear* (like paraître)

dissoudre, *to dissolve* [like résoudre, except past participle, dissous (*m.*), dissoute (*f.*)]

distraire, *to divert* (like traire)

dormir, *to sleep* (like partir)

éconduire, *to dismiss* (like conduire)

écrire, *to write*

élire, *to elect* (like lire)

émettre, *to emit* (like mettre)

émouvoir, *to affect* (like mouvoir)

encourir, *to incur* (like courir)

endormir, *to put to sleep* (like partir)

enduire, *to coat* (like conduire)

enfreindre, *to infringe* (like craindre)

s'enfuir, *to flee* (like fuir)

s'enquérir, *to inquire* (like acquérir)

s'ensuivre, *to result* (like suivre)

entreprendre, *to undertake* (like prendre)

s'entretenir, *to converse* (like venir)

envoyer, *to send*

éteindre, *to extinguish* (like craindre)

extraire, *to extract* (like traire)

exclure, *to exclude* (like conclure)

faillir, *to fail*

faire, *to make*

falloir, *to be necessary*

feindre, *to feign* (like craindre)

fuir, *to flee*

inscrire, *to inscribe* (like écrire)

induire, *to induce* (like conduire)

instruire, *to instruct* (like conduire)

interdire, *to interdict* (like dire, except in the present: vous interdisez)

intervenir, *to intervene* (like venir)

introduire, *to introduce* (like conduire)

joindre, *to join* (like craindre)

lire, *to read*

luire, *to shine* (like conduire) .

maintenir, *to maintain* (like venir)

maudire, *to curse*

méconnaître, *to ignore* (like paraître)

médire, *to slander* (like dire, except in the present: vous médisez)

mentir, *to lie* (like partir)

se méprendre, *to be mistaken* (like prendre)

mettre, *to put*

moudre, *to grind*

mourir, *to die*

mouvoir, *to move*

naître, *to be born*

nuire, *to harm* (like conduire)

obtenir, *to obtain* (like venir)

offrir, *to offer* (like ouvrir)

omettre, *to omit* (like mettre)

ouvrir, *to open*

paître, *to graze* (like paraître. No past definite, subjunctive imperfect, and past participle)

paraître, *to appear*

partir, *to depart*

peindre, *to paint* (like craindre)

permettre, *to permit* (like mettre)

plaindre, *to pity* (like craindre)

se plaindre, *to complain* (like craindre)

plaire, *to please*

pleuvoir, *to rain*

poindre, *to dawn* (like craindre)

poursuivre, *to pursue* (like suivre)

pourvoir, *to provide* (like voir, except in the past definite: Je pourvus; future: Je pourvoirai)

pouvoir, *to be able*

prédire, *to predict* (like dire, except vous prédisez)

prendre, *to take*

prescrire, *to prescribe* (like écrire)

prévaloir, *to prevail* (like valoir, except in the subjunctive present: que je prévale)

prévenir, *to prevent* (like venir)

prévoir, *to foresee* (like voir, except the future: Je prévoirai)

produire, *to produce* (like conduire)

promettre, *to promise* (like mettre)

proscrire, *to proscribe* (like écrire)

provenir, *to proceed* (like venir)

reconduire, *to reconduct* (like conduire)

refaire, *to do again* (like faire)

recoudre, *to sew again* (like coudre)

recouvrir, *to recover* (like ouvrir)

recueillir, *to collect* (like cueillir)

redire, *to tell again* (like dire)

réduire, *to reduce* (like conduire)

rejoindre, *to rejoin* (like craindre)

relire, *to read again* (like lire)

reluire, *to glitter* (like conduire)

remettre, *to remit* (like mettre)

renaître, *to revive* (like naître)

reparaître, *to reappear* (like paraître)

repeindre, *to paint again* (like craindre)

se repentir, *to repent* (like partir)

reprendre, *to retake* (like prendre)

reproduire, *to reproduce* (like conduire)

résoudre, *to resolve*

restreindre, *to restrict* (like craindre)

retenir, *to detain* (like venir)
revenir, *to come back* (like venir)
revêtir, *to clothe* (like vêtir)
revivre, *to revive* (like vivre)
revoir, *to see again* (like voir)
rire, *to laugh*
satisfaire, *to satisfy* (like faire)
savoir, *to know*
secourir, *to succor* (like courir)
séduire, *to seduce* (like conduire)
sentir, *to feel* (like partir)
servir, *to serve,* (like partir)
sortir, *to go out* (like partir)
souffrir, *to suffer* (like ouvrir)
soumettre, *to submit* (like mettre)
sourire, *to smile* (like rire)
souscrire, *to subscribe* (like écrire)
soustraire, *to subtract* (like traire)
soutenir, *to sustain* (like venir)
se souvenir, *to remember* (like venir)
subvenir, *to assist* (like venir)
suffire, *to suffice* (like conduire)
suivre, *to follow*

surfaire, *to overcharge* (like **faire)**
surprendre, *to surprise* (like prendre)
survenir, *to supervene* (like venir)
survivre, *to survive* (like vivre)
taire, *to keep silent* (like plaire)
teindre, *to dye* (like craindre)
tenir, *to hold* (like venir)
traduire, *to translate* (like **con**duire)
traire, *to milk*
transcrire, *to transcribe* (like écrire)
transmettre, *to transmit* (like mettre)
tressaillir, *to start* (like assaillir)
vaincre, *to vanquish*
valoir, *to be worth*
venir, *to come*
vêtir, *to clothe*
vivre, *to live*
voir, *to see*
vouloir, *to be willing*

TABLE OF IRREGULAR VERBS

INFINITIVE Future and Conditional		PRESENT INDICATIVE Imperfect, *no Exception* Present Participle *Exception: sachant,* Present Participle of *savoir*	PRESENT SUBJUNCTIVE	PAST PARTICIPLE All Compound Tenses	PAST DEFINITE Imperfect Subjunctive
Infinitive	Irregular Future	Present Indicative	Irregular Present Subjunctive	Past Participle	Past Definite
acquérir	j'acquerrai	j'acquiers nous acquérons ils acquièrent		acquis	j'acquis
aller	j'irai	je vais tu vas il va nous allons ils vont	que j'aille	allé	j'allai
asseoir	j'assiérai	j'assieds nous asseyons		assis	j'assis
battre		je bats nous battons		battu	je battis
boire		je bois nous buvons ils boivent		bu	je bus
bouillir		je bous nous bouillons		bouilli	je bouillis
conclure		je conclus nous concluons		conclu	je conclus
conduire		je conduis nous conduisons		conduit	je conduisis
confire		je confis nous confisons		confit	je confis
coudre		je couds nous cousons		cousu	je cousis
courir	je courrai	je cours nous courons		couru	je courus
craindre		je crains nous craignons		craint	je craignis
croire		je crois nous croyons ils croient		cru	je crus
cueillir	je cuillerai	je cueille nous cueillons		cueilli	je cueillis
dire		je dis nous disons vous dites		dit	je dis
écrire		j'écris nous écrivons		écrit	j'écrivis
envoyer	j'enverrai	j'envoie nous envoyons j'enverrai		envoyé	j'envoyai

TABLE OF IRREGULAR VERBS—(*Continued*)

Infinitive — Future and Conditional		Present Indicative — Imperfect, *no Exception* — Present Participle — *Exception: sachant*, Present Participle of *savoir*	Present Subjunctive	Past Participle — All Compound Tenses	Past Definite — Imperfect Subjunctive
Infinitive	Irregular Future	Present Indicative	Irregular Present Subjunctive	Past Participle	Past Definite
faillir		je faux / nous faillons		failli	je faillis
faire	je ferai	je fais / nous faisons / vous faites / ils font	que je fasse	fait	je fis
falloir	il faudra	il faut	qu'il faille	fallu	il fallut
fuir		je fuis / nous fuyons / ils fuient		fui	je fuis
lire		je lis / nous lisons		lu	je lus
maudire		je maudis / nous maudissons		maudit	je maudis
mettre		je mets / nous mettons		mis	je mis
moudre		je mouds / nous moulons		moulu	je moulus
mourir	je mourrai	je meurs / nous mourons / ils meurent		mort	je mourus
mouvoir	je mouvrai	je meus / nous mouvons / ils meuvent		mu	je mus
naître		je nais / nous naissons		né	je naquis
ouvrir		j'ouvre / nous ouvrons		ouvert	j'ouvris
paraître		je parais / nous paraissons		paru	je parus
partir		je pars / nous partons		parti	je partis
plaire		je plais / nous plaisons		plu	je plus
pleuvoir	il pleuvra	il pleut		plu	il plut
pouvoir	je pourrai	je peux / nous pouvons / ils peuvent	que je puisse	pu	je pus
prendre		je prends / nous prenons / ils prennent		pris	je pris

INFINITIVE Future and Conditional		PRESENT INDICATIVE Imperfect, *no Exception* Present Participle *Exception: sachant,* Present Participle of *savoir*	PRESENT SUBJUNCTIVE	PAST PARTICIPLE All Compound Tenses	PAST DEFINITE Imperfect Subjunctive
Infinitive	Irregular Future	Present Indicative	Irregular Present Subjunctive	Past Participle	Past Definite
résoudre		{ je résous { nous résolvons		résolu	je résolus
rire		{ je ris { nous rions		ri	je ris
savoir	je saurai	{ je sais { nous savons	que je sache	su	je sus
suivre		{ je suis { nous suivons		suivi	je suivis
traire		{ je trais { nous trayons { ils traient		trait	no past **Def.**
vaincre		{ je vaincs { il vainc { nous vainquons		vaincu	je vainquis
valoir	je vaudrai	{ je vaux { nous valons	que je vaille	valu	je valus
venir	je viendrai	{ je viens { nous venons { ils viennent		venu	je vins
vêtir		{ je vêts { nous vêtons		vêtu	je vêtis
vivre		{ je vis { nous vivons		vécu	je vécus
voir	je verrai	{ je vois { nous voyons { ils voient		vu	je vis
vouloir	je voudrai	{ je veux { nous voulons { ils veulent	que je veuille	voulu	je voulus

VERBES PASSIFS—PASSIVE VERBS

15. **Passive verbs** are conjugated in all their tenses with the auxiliary *être*. The active forms may be changed into the passive without changing the sense of the sentence. Thus,

ACTIVE

La mère gronde l'enfant, *The mother scolds the child.*

Le jardinier plante ces arbres, *The gardener plants these trees.*

PASSIVE

L'enfant est grondé par la mère, *The child is scolded by the mother.*

Ces arbres sont plantés par le jardinier, *These trees are planted by the gardener.*

Notice that passive verbs take the preposition *par* as illustrated above, but when the passive form denotes a moral action, the preposition *de* is used. Thus,

Le maître est aimé de ses élèves, *The teacher is loved by his pupils.*

Ce monsieur est admiré de tout le monde, *This gentleman is admired by everybody.*

The passive is not so extensively used in French as in English. The active voice, giving more life to the sentence, is generally preferred. Many English expressions cannot be rendered passively in French; instead the pronoun *on* must be used with the active form of the verb. Thus,

On nous l'a dit, *We have been told.*

On l'attend, *He is expected.*

On veut que vous soyez instruit, *You are requested to be educated.*

On me prie de sortir, *I am requested to go out.*

On vous trompera, *You will be deceived,* etc.

A passive verb, being conjugated with *être*, the past participle is treated as an adjective, and consequently agrees in gender and number with its subject.

MODEL OF A PASSIVE VERB

Etre aimé, *to be loved*

INDICATIF

Présent

je suis aimé, *I am loved*
tu es aimé, *thou art loved*
il est aimé,   *he* ⎱
elle est aimée, *she* ⎰ *is loved*
nous sommes aimés, *we are loved*
vous êtes aimés, *you are loved*
ils sont aimés,   ⎱
elles sont aimées, ⎰ *they are loved*

Passé Indéfini

j'ai été aimé, *I have been loved*
tu as été aimé, *thou hast been loved*
il a été aimé,   *he* ⎱
elle a été aimée, *she* ⎰ *has been loved*
nous avons été aimés, *we have been loved*
vous avez été aimés, *you have been loved*
ils ont été aimés,   ⎱
elles ont été aimées, ⎰ *they have been loved*

Imparfait

j'étais aimé, *I was loved*
tu étais aimé, *thou wast loved*
il était aimé,   *he* ⎱
elle était aimée, *she* ⎰ *was loved*
nous étions aimés, *we were loved*
vous étiez aimés, *you were loved*
ils étaient aimés,   ⎱
elles étaient aimées, ⎰ *they were loved*

Plus-que-Parfait

j'avais été aimé, *I had been loved*
tu avais été aimé, *thou hadst been loved*
il avait été aimé,   *he* ⎱
elle avait été aimée, *she* ⎰ *had been loved*
nous avions été aimés, *we had been loved*
vous aviez été aimés, *you had been loved*
ils avaient été aimés,   ⎱
elles avaient été aimées, ⎰ *they had been loved*

Passé Défini

je fus aimé, *I was loved*
tu fus aimé, *thou wast loved*
il fut aimé, 　　*he* ⎫
elle fut aimée, *she* ⎬ *was loved*
nous fûmes aimés, *we were loved*
vous fûtes aimés, *you were loved*
ils furent aimés, 　　⎫
elles furent aimées, ⎬ *they were loved*

Passé Antérieur

j'eus été aimé, *I had been loved*
tu eus été aimé, *thou hadst been loved*
il eut été aimé, 　　*he* ⎫
elle eut été aimée, *she* ⎬ *had been loved*
nous eûmes été aimés, *we had been loved*
vous eûtes été aimés, *you had been loved*
ils eurent été aimés, 　　⎫
elles eurent été aimées, ⎬ *they had been loved*

Futur

je serai aimé, *I shall be loved*
tu seras aimé, *thou wilt be loved*
il sera aimé, 　　*he* ⎫
elle sera aimée, *she* ⎬ *will be loved*
nous serons aimés, *we shall be loved*
vous serez aimés, *you will be loved*
ils seront aimés, 　　⎫
elles seront aimées, ⎬ *they will be loved*

Futur Antérieur

j'aurai été aimé, *I shall have been loved*
tu auras été aimé, *thou wilt have been loved*
il aura été aimé, 　　*he* ⎫
elle aura été aimée, *she* ⎬ *will have been loved*
nous aurons été aimés, *we shall have been loved*
vous aurez été aimés, *you will have been loved*
ils auront été aimés, 　　⎫
elles auront été aimées, ⎬ *they will have been loved*

Conditionnel

Présent

je serais aimé, *I should be loved*
tu serais aimé, *thou wouldst be loved*
il serait aimé,   *he* ⎱
elle serait aimée, *she* ⎰ *would be loved*
nous serions aimés, *we should be loved*
vous seriez aimés, *you would be loved*
ils seraient aimés,   ⎱
elles seraient aimées, ⎰ *they would be loved*

Passé

j'aurais été aimé, *I should have been loved*
tu aurais été aimé, *thou wouldst have been loved*
il aurait été aimé,   *he* ⎱
elle aurait été aimée, *she* ⎰ *would have been loved*
nous aurions été aimés, *we should have been loved*
vous auriez été aimés, *you would have been loved*
ils auraient été aimés,   ⎱
elles auraient été aimées, ⎰ *they would have been loved*

Impératif

sois aimé, *be loved* (*thou*)
soyons aimés, *let us be loved*
soyez aimés, *be loved* (*you*)

Subjonctif

Présent

que je sois aimé, *that I may be loved*
que tu sois aimé, *that thou mayst be loved*
qu'il soit aimé,   *that* ⎰*he* ⎱ *may be loved*
qu'elle soit aimée,   ⎱*she*⎰
que nous soyons aimés, *that we may be loved*
que vous soyez aimés, *that you may be loved*
qu'ils soient aimés,   ⎱
qu'elles soient aimées, ⎰ *that they may be loved*

Passé

que j'aie été aimé, *that I may have been loved*
que tu aies été aimé, *that thou mayst have been loved*
qu'il ait été aimé,   *that* ⎰*he* ⎱ *may have been loved*
qu'elle ait été aimée,   ⎱*she*⎰
que nous ayons été aimés, *that we may have been loved*
que vous ayez été aimés, *that you may have been loved*
qu'ils aient été aimés,   ⎱
qu'elles aient été aimées, ⎰ *that they may have been loved*

Imparfait

que je fusse aimé, *that I might be loved*
que tu fusses aimé, *that thou mightst be loved*
qu'il fût aimé,
qu'elle fût aimée, *that* $\begin{Bmatrix} he \\ she \end{Bmatrix}$ *might be loved*
que nous fussions aimés, *that we might be loved*
que vous fussiez aimés, *that you might be loved*
qu'ils fussent aimés,
qu'elles fussent aimées, $\Big\}$ *that they might be loved*

Plus-que-Parfait

que j'eusse été aimé, *that I might have been loved*
que tu eusses été aimé, *that thou mightst have been loved*
qu'il eût été aimé,
qu'elle eût été aimée, *that* $\begin{Bmatrix} he \\ she \end{Bmatrix}$ *might have been loved*
que nous eussions été aimés, *that we might have been loved*
que vous eussiez été aimés, *that you might have been loved*
qu'ils eussent été aimés,
qu'elles eussent été aimées, $\Big\}$ *that they might have been loved*

INFINITIF

Présent	*Passé*
être aimé, *to be loved*	avoir été aimé, *to have been loved*

PARTICIPE

Présent	*Passé*
étant aimé, *being loved*	ayant été aimé, *having been loved*

VERBES RÉFLECTIFS—REFLEXIVE VERBS

16. **Reflexive verbs** are verbs that *throw back*, or *reflect*, the action begun by the subject upon the subject itself. The subject of these verbs is repeated, in the form of a pronoun, as the object of the verb. Thus,

Je me blesse, *I wound myself.*
Je me lave, *I wash myself.*

(*a*) Verbs reflexive in English are reflexive also in French; as, *se laver*, to wash oneself; *se blesser*, to wound oneself.

(*b*) A verb reflexive is often used in French to express an English passive form. Thus,

Ce livre se vend cinq francs, *This book is sold
for five francs* (literally, *sells itself*).

Vous vous trompez, *You are mistaken* (literally,
you mistake yourself).

(*c*) The reflexive form is also used in French to express
the mutual action of several subjects, one upon another.
For example, *Ils se frappent*, They are striking one another,
means that each of the persons "striking" is also struck.
The form may be used of two or more subjects.

(*d*) Finally, many reflexive verbs in French express a
simple verb in English. The most important of these are:

s'abonner à, *to subscribe*	se fâcher, *to get angry*
s'abstenir, *to abstain*	se fier à, *to trust*
s'adresser à, *to apply to*	se garder de, *to beware*
s'agenouiller, *to kneel*	s'habituer à, *to get accustomed*
s'approcher de, *to draw near*	s'imaginer, *to fancy*
s'asseoir, *to sit down*	se marier avec, *to get married*
s'attendre à, *to expect*	se mêler de, *to meddle with*
s'attrister, *to grieve*	se moquer de, *to make fun of*
se débarrasser de, *to get rid of*	s'occuper de, *to be busy about*
se dédire, *to retract*	se plaindre, *to complain*
se dépêcher, *to hurry*	se promener, *to take a walk*
s'écrier, *to exclaim*	se rappeler, *to recollect*
s'efforcer de, *to endeavor*	se réfugier, *to take refuge*
s'éloigner de, *to go away from*	se réjouir, *to rejoice*
s'emparer de, *to seize*	se rendre à, *to go to*
s'empresser de, *to hasten*	se repentir, *to repent*
s'en aller, *to go away*	se reposer, *to rest*
s'endormir, *to fall asleep*	se retourner, *to turn round*
s'enfuir, *to run away*	se séparer, *to part*
s'enrhumer, *to catch cold*	se souvenir, *to remember*
s'étonner, *to wonder*	se taire, *to be silent*
s'entretenir, *to converse*	se tenir debout, *to stand up*
s'évader, *to escape*	se trouver mal, *to faint*
s'éveiller, *to wake*	se vanter, *to boast*
s'excuser, *to apologize*	se venger, *to avenge*

Reflexive verbs are conjugated according to the model of
the conjugation to which they belong, except that in compound tenses they take *être* instead of *avoir*.

When the second personal pronoun is a direct object of the
verb reflected, the past participle agrees with it in gender
and number.

MODEL OF THE CONJUGATION OF A REFLEXIVE VERB

Se laver, *to wash oneself*

INDICATIF

Présent

je me lave, *I wash myself*
tu te laves, *thou washst thyself*
il se lave,   *he* } *washes* { *himself*
elle se lave, *she* }   { *herself*
nous nous lavons, *we wash ourselves*
vous vous lavez, *you wash yourselves*
ils se lavent,   } *they wash themselves*
elles se lavent, }

Passé Indéfini

je me suis lavé, *I have washed myself*
tu t'es lavé, *thou hast washed thyself*
il s'est lavé,   *he* } *has washed* { *himself*
elle s'est lavée, *she* }   { *herself*
nous nous sommes lavés, *we have washed ourselves*
vous vous êtes lavés, *you have washed yourselves*
ils se sont lavés,   } *they have washed themselves*
elles se sont lavées, }

Imparfait

je me lavais, *I was washing myself*
tu te lavais, *thou wast washing thyself*
il se lavait,   *he* } *was washing* { *himself*
elle se lavait, *she* }   { *herself*
nous nous lavions, *we were washing ourselves*
vous vous laviez, *you were washing yourselves*
ils se lavaient,   } *they were washing themselves*
elles se lavaient, }

Plus-que-Parfait

je m'étais lavé, *I had washed myself*
tu t'étais lavé, *thou hast washed thyself*
il s'était lavé,   *he* } *had washed* { *himself*
elle s'était lavée, *she* }   { *herself*
nous nous étions lavés, *we had washed ourselves*
vous vous étiez lavés, *you had washed yourselves*
ils s'étaient lavés,   } *they had washed themselves*
elles s'étaient lavées, }

Passé Défini

je me lavai, *I washed myself*
tu te lavas, *thou washedst thyself*
il ⎫
elle ⎬ se lava, *he / she* } *washed* { *himself / herself*
nous nous lavâmes, *we washed ourselves*
vous vous lavâtes, *you washed yourselves*
ils ⎫
elles ⎬ se lavèrent, *they washed themselves*

Passé Antérieur

je me fus lavé, *I had washed myself*
tu te fus lavé, *thou hadst washed thyself*
il se fut lavé, *he* ⎫
elle se fut lavée, *she* ⎬ *had washed* { *himself / herself*
nous nous fûmes lavés, *we had washed ourselves*
vous vous fûtes lavés, *you had washed yourselves*
ils se furent lavés, ⎫
elles se furent lavées, ⎬ *they had washed themselves*

Futur

je me laverai, *I shall wash myself*
tu te laveras, *thou wilt wash thyself*
il se lavera, *he* ⎫
elle se lavera, *she* ⎬ *will wash* { *himself / herself*
nous nous laverons, *we shall wash ourselves*
vous vous laverez, *you will wash yourselves*
ils se laveront, ⎫
elles se laveront, ⎬ *they will wash themselves*

Futur Antérieur

je me serai lavé, *I shall have washed myself*
tu te seras lavé, *thou wilt have washed thyself*
il se sera lavé, *he* ⎫
elle se sera lavée, *she* ⎬ *will have washed* { *himself / herself*
nous nous serons lavés, *we shall have washed ourselves*
vous vous serez lavés, *you will have washed yourselves*
ils se seront lavés, ⎫
elles se seront lavées ⎬ *they will have washed themselves*

Conditionnel

Présent

je me laverais, *I should wash myself*
tu te laverais, *thou wouldst wash thyself*
il se laverait,   *he* ⎱ *would wash* ⎰ *himself*
elle se laverait, *she* ⎰   ⎱ *herself*
nous nous laverions, *we should wash ourselves*
vous vous laveriez, *you would wash yourselves*
ils se laveraient,   ⎱ *they would wash themselves*
elles se laveraient, ⎰

Passé

je me serais lavé, *I should have washed myself*
tu te serais lavé, *thou wouldst have washed thyself*
il se serait lavé,   *he* ⎱ *would have washed* ⎰ *himself*
elle se serait lavée, *she* ⎰   ⎱ *herself*
nous nous serions lavés, *we should have washed ourselves*
vous vous seriez lavés, *you would have washed yourself*
ils se seraient lavés,   ⎱ *they would have washed themselves*
elles se seraient lavées, ⎰

Impératif

lave-toi, *wash thyself*
lavons-nous, *let us wash ourselves*
lavez-vous, *wash yourself*

Subjonctif

Présent

que je me lave, *that I may wash myself*
que tu te laves, *that thou mayst wash thyself*
qu'il se lave,   *that he* ⎱ *may wash* ⎰ *himself*
qu'elle se lave, *that she* ⎰   ⎱ *herself*
que nous nous lavions, *that we may wash ourselves*
que vous vous laviez, *that you may wash yourselves*
qu'ils se lavent,   ⎱ *that they may wash themselves*
qu'elles se lavent, ⎰

Passé

que je me sois lavé, *that I may have washed myself*
qu tu te sois lavé, *that thou mayst have washed thyself*
qu'il se soit, lavé,   *that he* ⎱ *may have washed* ⎰ *himself*
qu'elle se soit lavée, *that she* ⎰   ⎱ *herself*
que nous nous soyons lavés, *that we may have washed ourselves*
que vous vous soyez lavés, *that you may have washed yourselves*
qu'ils se soient lavés,   ⎱ *that they may have washed themselves*
qu'elles se soient lavées, ⎰

Imparfait

que je me lavasse, *that I might wash myself*
que tu te lavasses, *that thou mightst wash thyself*
qu'il se lavât, *that he* ⎱ *might wash* ⎰ *himself*
qu'elle se lavât, *that she* ⎰ ⎱ *herself*
que nous nous lavassions, *that we might wash ourselves*
que vous vous lavassiez, *that you might wash yourselves*
qu'ils se lavassent, ⎫
qu'elles se lavassent, ⎭ *that they might wash themselves*

Plus-que-Parfait

que je me fusse lavé, *that I might have washed myself*
que tu te fusses lavé, *that thou mightst have washed thyself*
qu'il se fût lavé, *that he* ⎱ *might have washed* ⎰ *himself*
qu'elle se fût lavée, *that she* ⎰ ⎱ *herself*
que nous nous fussions lavés, *that we might have washed ourselves*
que vous vous fussiez lavés, *that you might have washed yourselves*
qu'ils se fussent lavés, ⎫
qu'elles se fussent lavées, ⎭ *that they might have washed themselves*

INFINITIF

Présent	*Passé*
se laver, *to wash oneself*	s'être lavé, *to have washed oneself*

PARTICIPE

Présent	*Passé*
s'étant lavé, *having washed oneself*	été lavé, *have washed*

17. The interrogative-affirmative is formed according to the rule given for other verbs; that is, by putting the pronoun subject of the affirmative sentence after the verb in a simple tense, but after the auxiliary in a compound tense, the order of the other words remaining unchanged. Thus,

AFFIRMATIVE	INTERROGATIVE-AFFIRMATIVE
tu te laves	te laves-**tu**?
il se lèvera	se lèvera-t-**il**?
vous vous êtes promenés	vous êtes-**vous** promenés?
ils se sont trompés	se sont-**ils** trompés?

The interrogative negative is formed by putting the pronoun subject of a negative sentence after the verb in a simple tense, but after the auxiliary in a compound tense, the order of the other words remaining unchanged. Thus,

NEGATIVE	INTERROGATIVE-NEGATIVE
tu ne te laves pas	ne te laves-**tu** pas?
il ne se lèvera pas	ne se lèvera-t-**il** pas?
vous ne vous êtes pas trompés	ne vous êtes-**vous** pas trompés?
ils ne s'étaient pas trompés	ne s'étaient-**ils** pas trompés?

For euphony, *est-ce-que* is used in the interrogative form, especially in the first person singular as with other verbs. Thus,

Est-ce-que je me promène?

Est-ce-que je me lève?

This *est-ce-que* may be regarded as the equivalent of the English *do* or *did* used in questions.

18. In the imperative of reflexive verbs, the pronominal object is expressed and is placed after the verb if the imperative is affirmative; but before the verb, if the imperative is negative. Thus,

AFFIRMATIVE	NEGATIVE
lève-**toi**	ne **te** lève pas
promenons-**nous**	ne **nous** promenons pas
lavez-**vous**	ne **vous** lavez pas

VERBES IMPERSONNELS — IMPERSONAL VERBS

19. There are, in French, a certain number of verbs that express an action which cannot be attributed to any determinate person as a subject. Thus, *neiger*, to snow, *pleuvoir*, to rain, which express certain phenomena of nature. Those verbs that express an action that cannot be attributed to any person are called, for this reason, **verbes impersonnels,** impersonal verbs. They are conjugated in the third person singular only, and are preceded by the pronoun *il*. Their inflection is like that of the verbs of the conjugation to which they belong. The most important are:

geler, *to freeze*	neiger, *to snow*
dégeler, *to thaw*	pleuvoir, *to rain*
grêler, *to hail*	tonner, *to thunder*

Many other verbs may be used impersonally with *il* as their subject. Thus,

> il suffit, *it is sufficient*
> il paraît, *it appears*
> il semble, *it seems*
> il importe, *it is of consequence*
> il s'agit, *the question is*

Falloir, to be necessary, is impersonally used in French as an equivalent of the English *must*. Thus,

Il faut qu'il travaille, *He must work.*
Il faudra que vous lisiez, *You will be obliged to read*.
Il lui fallait partir, *He had to go.*

MODEL OF AN IMPERSONAL VERB

Pleuvoir, *to rain*

INDICATIF

Présent	*Passé Indéfini*
il pleut, *it rains*	il a plu, *it has rained*
Imparfait	*Plus-que-Parfait*
il pleuvait, *it was raining*	il avait plu, *it had rained*
Passé Défini	*Passé Antérieur*
il plut, *it rained*	il eut plu, *it had rained*
Futur	*Futur Antérieur*
il pleuvra, *it will rain*	il aura plu, *it will have rained*

CONDITIONNEL

Présent	*Passé*
il pleuvrait, *it would rain*	il aurait plu, *it would have rained*

IMPÉRATIF

The imperative having no third person, an impersonal verb can consequently have no imperative.

SUBJONCTIF

Présent	*Passé*
qu'il pleuve, *that it may rain*	qu'il ait plu, *that it may have rained*
Imparfait	*Plus-que-Parfait*
qu'il plût, *that it might rain*	qu'il eût plu, *that it might have rained*

INFINITIF

Présent	*Passé*
pleuvoir, *to rain*	avoir plu, *to have rained*

PARTICIPE

Présent	*Passé*
pleuvant	plu, *rained*

20.　Y Avoir. — The English expressions *there is* and *there are*, are translated in French by *avoir* with the adverb *y*, there, preceding. Thus,

> il y a, *there is*, or *are*
> il y avait, *there was*
> il y eut, *there was*
> il y aura, *there will be*
> il y aurait, *there would be*
> qu'il y ait, *that there may be*
> qu'il y eût, *that there might be*
> il y a eu, *there has been*
> il y avait eu, *there had been*
> il y eut eu, *there had been*
> il y aura eu, *there will have been*
> il y aurait eu, *there would have been*
> qu'il y ait eu, *that there may have been*
> qu'il y eût eu, *that there might have been*

NOTE. — *Il y a* has been given as the equivalent of *there is* or *there are;* and *voici, voilà* have also been translated, respectively, by *here is* or *here are* and *there is* or *there are*. These phrases are, however, used differently. The first part, *voi*, of *voici* and *voilà* comes from *voir*, to see; the second part, *ci* (abbreviation of *ici*) and *là*, mean, respectively, *here* and *there*. Their literal meanings are then, *see here* and *see there*. They refer to objects that are in sight and may be pointed out; but *il y a* is used in stating a fact. Thus,

> Il y a huit chambres dans notre maison, *There are eight rooms in our house.*
> Il y a beaucoup de monde dans cet hôtel, *There are many guests in this hotel.*
> Lisez; voici des journaux, *Read; here are newspapers.*
> Ecrivez, voilà une plume, *Write; there is a pen.*

PARTICIPE – PARTICIPLE

21.　Le Participe. — The participle, so called because it participates in the nature of a verb and an adjective, is a word derived from a verb. It shares in the nature of a verb in that it possesses the same fundamental signification and may take a direct object; and it has the nature of an adjective in that it may qualify a noun. In this double rôle, the participle sometimes resembles a verb more than it does an adjective; at other times it has more of the characteristics of the adjective. In the first instance, the participle is said to be in the *verbal form*, and is then invariable; but in most cases of the second instance, its form changes so as to agree in gender and number with the noun it modifies; it is then said to be a *verbal adjective*.

22.　Participes, Présent et Passé. — There are two kinds of participles: the *participe présent*, present participle, and the *participe passé*, past participle.

23.　Participe Présent. — The term *present participle* is defective, because the so-called present participle does not necessarily refer to present time. It may refer to past, present, or future time, according to the tense of the verb with which it is associated in the sentence. Perhaps a better term would be **participe actif.** Thus, for example, in the expression *des enfants riant*, children laughing, no more notion of the time is conveyed than of the degree, place, or manner of their laughter. Observe, in the following sentences, how the time of the action of the participle is wholly dependent upon the tense of the verb:

Je m'instruis en lisant, *I learn by reading.*

En lisant hier, je me suis instruit, *By reading yesterday, I learned.*

En lisant demain, je me distrairai, *By reading tomorrow, I shall divert myself.*

Every present participle ends in *ant*.

24. Adjectif Verbal. — When the function of the present participle becomes primarily adjectival, it loses its participial character and sometimes its participial form; it is then called a **verbal adjective.** Like the present participle, the verbal adjective ends in *ant*, except in a few verbs in which the *ant* is changed to *ent*. The verbal adjective agrees in gender and number with the noun it qualifies; the present participle never changes its form.

Any word ending in *ant* whose most prominent concept is that of an action, is a present participle; any word ending in *ant* whose most prominent feature, or function, is that of quality or qualification, is a verbal adjective. Thus,

PRESENT PARTICIPLE

Ces messieurs **arrivant** de bonne heure, eurent les meilleures places, *These gentlemen, arriving early, had the best places.*

Il voyagea longtemps, **visitant** toute l'Europe, *He traveled a long time, visiting all Europe.*

VERBAL ADJECTIVE

Ces dames sont très **obligeantes,** *These ladies are very obliging.*

Il faut prendre garde aux eaux **dormantes,** *You must beware of stagnant waters.*

The present participle is often preceded by the preposition *en*, and, in such cases, it marks the simultaneity of the two events, or actions, described by the participle and the verb of the sentence or clause in which the two stand. Thus,

Il lit en se promenant, *He reads while walking.*

25. **Differences in the Spelling of Certain Present Participles and Their Corresponding Verbal Adjectives.**—1. While the present participle ends in *ant* in the following words, the verbal adjective ends in *ent:*

PRESENT PARTICIPLE	VERBAL ADJECTIVE
adhérant, *adhering*	adhérent, *adherent*
affluant, *gathering*	affluent, *affluent*
différant, *differing*	différent, *different*
divergeant, *diverging*	divergent, *divergent*
équivalant, *being equivalent*	équivalent, *equivalent*
excellant, *excelling*	excellent, *excellent*
expédiant, *expediting*	expédient, *expedient*
négligeant, *neglecting*	négligent, *negligent*
précédant, *preceding*	précédent, *precedent*
présidant, *presiding*	président, *president*
résidant, *residing*	résident, *resident*
violant, *violating*	violent, *violent*

2. The following end in *ant*, but differ in the final consonant of the stem:

PRESENT PARTICIPLE	VERBAL ADJECTIVE
convainquant, *convincing*	convaincant, *convincing*
extravaguant, *exaggerating*	extravagant, *extravagant*
fabriquant, *manufacturing*	fabricant, *manufacturing*
fatiguant, *fatiguing*	fatigant, *fatiguing*
intriguant, *intriguing*	intrigant, *intriguing*
suffoquant, *suffocating*	suffocant, *choking*
vaquant, *vacating*	vacant, *vacant*

26. **Le Participe Passé.**—The **past participle** has been said to express past time with reference to the verb of the sentence or clause in which it stands, but the term is defective because the past participle does not necessarily express such time. It sometimes represents mere passive action and might perhaps have been better termed the **participe passif.** Unlike the present participle the past participle may be either variable or invariable in form, according to circumstances. The nice distinctions governing its agreement with nouns will be discussed under Syntax.

FRENCH GRAMMAR
(PART 4)

L'ARTICLE—THE ARTICLE

1. What the Articles Are.—The articles are peculiar adjectives and are the most common words in a language. Formerly they were classed as a separate part of speech, but grammarians are now generally agreed that they are neither more nor less than adjectives and consequently classify them as such. For purposes of reference and convenience, however, they are treated in this work as a separate part of speech. The work that the article does in the sentence, is to *limit* or *extend* the sense of the noun with which it is used.

2. The Articles.—The French language, like the English, has two articles; namely, **le**, *the*, and **un**, *a* or *an*. The article *le* was derived from the old Latin pronoun *ille, illa, illud*. The article *un* has much of the sense of the numeral *un* and probably owes its existence to the frequent use of that numeral. Both *le* and *un* are inflected so as to agree with the nouns with which they are used in number and in gender. Thus,

SINGULAR	PLURAL
masculine, le	les
feminine, la	les
masculine, un	—
feminine, une	—

Observe the following examples: *le père, le frère; la mère, la sœur; les pères, les mères; un père, un frère; une mère, une sœur.*

For euphony, the *e* of *le* and the *a* of *la* are elided and replaced by an apostrophe whenever the next word begins with a vowel or *h* mute.   Thus,

> l'honneur, *for* le honneur
> l'âme, *for* la âme

3. The Partitive Article. — The partitives *some* and *any*, which are often understood in English, must always be expressed in French.   The partitive sense is given a noun by using before it the expression *une partie de*, a part of. This combination occurs in the following four forms:

(*a*)   With the masculine article, as in
> une partie de le pain, *some*, or *any bread*.

(*b*)   With the feminine article, as in
> une partie de la viande, *some*, or *any meat*.

(*c*)   With a noun beginning with a vowel, as in
> une partie de l'eau, *some*, or *any water*.

(*d*)   With a plural noun, as in
> une partie de les légumes, *some*, or *any vegetables*.

But, in practice, the phrase *une partie* is not usually expressed, and the foregoing expressions might be written simply *de le pain, de la viande, de l'eau, de les legumes*.   But since *de* and *le* are usually contracted to *du, de le pain* becomes *du pain;* so also, since *de* and *les* are contracted to *des, de les légumes* becomes *des légumes*.

The words *du, de la, de l'*, and *des* are called the **partitive articles,** because they make the noun with which they are used refer only to a part of the whole class named by the noun.

4.   The partitive article can be used only when it immediately precedes a noun; it can never be used with an adjective.   When it is desired to give the partitive sense to a noun preceded by an adjective, the preposition *de* is used in place of the partitive article.   Thus,

> de bon pain, *some*, or *any good bread*
> de bonne viande, *some*, or *any good meat*
> de bonne eau, *some*, or *any good water*
> de bons légumes, *some*, or *any good vegetables*

5. After a negation, *de* must be used instead of the partitive article to give a noun the partitive sense. Thus,

> Je n'ai pas de pain, *I have no bread.*
> Je n'ai pas de viande, *I have no meat.*
> Je n'ai pas d'eau, *I have no water.*
> Je n'ai pas de légumes, *I have no vegetables.*

6. After adverbs of quantity, such as *assez*, *beaucoup*, *plus*, etc., *de* must always be used instead of the partitive article. Thus,

> J'ai beaucoup de pain, *I have much bread.*
> J'ai assez de viande, *I have enough meat.*
> J'ai peu d'eau, *I have little water.*
> J'ai plus de légumes, *I have more vegetables.*

7. Other Contractions of the Article. — When the article is used with the preposition *à* before it, the article is subject to the following contractions:

1. When the noun is in the masculine singular *à le* is contracted into *au.*

2. When the noun is in the feminine singular, the form *à la* is not contracted.

3. The form *à l'* is not contracted before a noun beginning with a vowel or an *h* mute.

4. When the noun is in the plural, *à les* is contracted into *aux.*

TABLE I

DIFFERENT FORMS OF THE ARTICLE

	Without a Preposition	With the Preposition *à*	With the Proposition *de*
Masculine	le	au	du
Feminine	la	à la	de la
Before a vowel or *h* mute	l'	à l'	de l'
Plural	les	aux	des

LE NOM—THE NOUN

8. The Noun.—A **noun** is any word or expression, whether long or short, that is used in speech or writing as the *name* of anything. Nouns are divided into *two principal classes: Noms communs*, common nouns, and *noms propres*, proper nouns.

NOMS COMMUNS—COMMON NOUNS

9. Class Names.—Most French nouns are **class names;** that is, nouns applied in common to things of the same class. The word *common* is derived from two words and means *bound together*. The things denoted by a common noun are united or *bound together* into one group by certain likenesses—certain common qualities. Thus, the word *garçon*, boy, is not a name given to one particular thing and to no other; it is a name of any one of a *class* composed of millions of objects that are alike in certain particulars. These class, or *generic*, names, are common nouns.

A **common noun** is a noun used to name a *class* of things.

NOMS PROPRES—PROPER NOUNS

10. It is often necessary to distinguish one thing very clearly from every other in its class. This can be done by giving it a name of its own; as Boston, Henry Clay, etc. Such names are *proper nouns;* they are so called from the Latin word *proprius*, meaning one's own. A proper noun is usually set apart for the purpose of naming a particular person or object; and if its work is to be done perfectly, the name must be used for no other purpose. A common noun distinguishes one class from every other class; a proper noun distinguishes one thing from every other thing.

A **proper noun** is a noun used as a special or an **individual** name.

NOTE.—Strictly speaking, a proper name could be applied to one individual only; but, in practice, such names are applied to many individuals at the same time. All the proper nouns known as first, or Christian, names, as *Louis*, *Pierre*, *Paul*, etc., are given to many individuals. These words are, consequently, true proper nouns only when used with a family name; and vice versa, a family name is a true proper name only when used with a Christian name. The cause of this apparent contradiction between the real nature and the use of a proper noun is to be found in the original nature of the noun itself. Originally, most proper nouns were but common nouns suggesting:

1. A quality or a defect of the mind or the body of the person to whom applied: *Legrand*, the tall one; *Lerouge*, the red one; *Sans Souci*, without care.

2. A profession: *Charpentier*, carpenter; *Meunier*, miller.

3. A place of habitation: *Dumont*, from the mountains; *Dumarais*, from the marshes.

4. A place of origin: *Breton*, from Britany; *Germain*, from Germany.

11. Classes of Common Nouns.—Common nouns have been variously subdivided, but all of them may be included under the following two great classes:

1. *Names of Things Sensible.*—This class comprises the names of substances that are material, and are, therefore, capable of being perceived by the senses; as, *arbre*, *cheval*, *odeur*, *poids*, etc.

2. *Names of Things Rational.*—This group includes the class names of all things that are merely conceived or thought of as existing, and cannot be recognized by the direct aid of any of the senses; as, *bonté*, *vérité*, *absence*, *peur*, *regret*.

3. Some of the nouns belonging in these classes have been grouped as follows:

(*a*) *Noms Collectifs.*—These are sometimes called *nouns of multitude*, because they denote many things united and thought of as in one group; as, *armée*, *jury*, *famille*, *multitude*, *troupe*.

(*b*) *Noms Composés.*—These are formed of one or several words, ordinarily joined together by a hyphen; as, *basse-cour*, *chou-fleur*.

INFLECTIONS OF THE NOUN

12. Inflection. —The word *inflection* is one that is much used in grammar. It comes from two Latin words that mean *in* and *a bending;* it denotes that something is bent or changed from one form or condition into another. Thus, we speak of the inflections of the voice, meaning its changes from certain tones to others that are higher or lower. As used in grammar, **inflection** signifies those changes in the form of a word that come from changes in its use or meaning.

13. Nouns Have Two Kinds of Inflections. —French nouns are inflected for two purposes:

1. *To Denote Number.* —That is, to show whether a noun signifies *one* of the objects it names, or *more than one* of them; as, *garçon, garçon*s; *cheval, chev*aux; *cheveu, cheveux*.

2. *To Denote Sex.* —Many nouns have one form for *males* and another for *females.* Thus, *lion, lion*ne; *comte, com*tesse; *acteur, act*rice.

Note. —*To Denote Person.* —When a noun is so used in a sentence as to name or denote the *speaker*, the *person spoken to*, or the *person spoken of*, it is sometimes said to be inflected for person. This, however, is not strictly an inflection, for an inflection implies a change of form. The noun remains unchanged, whether it denotes the speaker, the person addressed, or the person or thing spoken about in the sentence.

NUMBER IN NOUNS

14. Definition of Number. —Whether a noun means one or more than one of the objects it names, is known from one or both of two facts:

1. Its form; as, *livres, chevaux, cheveux.*
2. Its use; as, *Le fils est jeune, Les fils sont jeunes.*

The *number* of a word is that form or use of it by which it denotes one or more than one.

The *singular number* of a word is that form of use of it by which it denotes one. Thus,

un livre, le cheval

The *plural number* of a word is that form or use of it by which it denotes more than one. Thus,

les livres, trois chevaux

15. **General Rule for Forming the Plural of Nouns.**
Many nouns are arbitrary in the formation of their plurals,
and for this reason cannot be brought under the operation of
any rule. The following rule, however, includes most
French nouns: *Most nouns form their plural by adding* s *to
the singular.* Thus,

livre, livres; boîte, boîtes; église, églises.

The *s* of the plural is never sounded in French.

Note.—Historical grammar explains the origin of the use of the
letter *s* to form the plural of nouns. Of the six cases of the Latin
declension, two, the *nominative* (subject) and the *accusative* (object),
still endured in the 5th century, so that every noun then had two
forms in the singular and two in the plural. Besides, all nouns were
divided into three classes, or *declensions*, modeled after the old Latin
declension. Thus,

First Declension

Singular	Plural
Nominative, la rose	*Nominative*, les roses
Accusative, la rose	*Accusative*, les roses

Second Declension

Nominative, li murs	*Nominative*, li mur
Accusative, le mur	*Accusative*, les murs

Third Declension

Nominative, li lerre	*Nominative*, li larron
Accusative, le larron	*Accusative*, les larrons

In the 14th century, these declensions were still further simplified.
Since the accusative form of a noun was the one most used in
sentential structure, that form persisted until it finally came to play
the part of either subject or object according to its use. The old
nominative form, on the other hand, gradually disappeared.

From the above table it will be seen that nouns ended in *s* in the
accusative plural; consequently, with the preservation of the accusative
case, it was but natural that the *s* sign of its plural should come to be
regarded as the general sign of the plural number.

16. **Special Cases.**—1. *Nouns Ending in* s, x, *or* z.
When a singular noun ends in one of the letters *s*, *x*, or *z*,
that noun does not change its form in the plural. Thus,

fils, fils; croix, croix; nez, nez.

Note.—Most nouns ending in *s*, *x*, or *z* are formed from the nominative of the second declension just given. It will be noticed that
the nominative *li murs* ended in *s*; but since the accusative plural
les murs became the plural of the new French word, and since that
old accusative plural had the same form as the nominative singular,
it is clear that no changes were necessary in making the plural of the
new French word. It must not be forgotten that in old French, the
three letters *s*, *x*, or *z* were indifferently used one for the other,
and that *la voix*, the voice, for example, could have been correctly
written *voix*, *vois*, or *voiz*.

2. *Nouns Ending in al.*—Nearly all nouns ending in *al* in the singular change that *al* into *aux* in the plural. Thus,

cheval, chevaux; mal, maux; animal, animaux.

But the following words form their plurals by adding *s* to the singular: *aval*, below; *bal*, ball; *carnaval*, carnival; *chacal*, jackal; *narval*, narwhal; *nopal*, nopal; *pal*, pale; *régal*, feast.

NOTE.—The old declension of one of these words (as *mal*, for example), was as follows:

SINGULAR	PLURAL
Nominative, li mals	*Nominative*, li mal
Accusative, le mal	*Accusative*, les mals

It is seen that at first the plural of these words was regularly formed by adding *s* to the singular. It soon became customary, however, to change *l* into *u* before a consonant; thus the accusative plural became *les maus*. As has been said, *s* and *x* were equivalent letters, but in this case the *x* remained, and the plural form became *les maux*.

3. *Plural of Nouns Ending in au, eau, eu.*—These nouns form their plurals by adding *x* to the singular. Thus,

chapeau, chapeaux; tuyau, tuyaux; jeu, jeux.

The only exception is *landau*, the plural of which is *landaus*.

NOTE.—This exception is explained by the fact that the final *u* of these words was formerly an *l*. This case is thus seen to be similar to the preceding exceptions.

4. *Plural of Nouns Ending in ou.*—Nouns of this class follow the general rule; that is, they take *s* to form their plurals. Thus,

clou, clous; verrou, verrous; filou, filous.

Seven of these nouns, however, form their plurals by adding *x*. They are: *bijou*, jewel; *caillou*, pebble; *chou*, cabbage; *genou*, knee; *hibou*, owl; *joujou*, plaything; *pou*, louse.

NOTE.—As in the two preceding cases, the *u* was formerly an *l* and the plural formed by adding *s* or *x*. Usage determined upon the *s*; only the seven nouns just given have the *x*.

5. *Plural of Nouns Ending in ail.*—Most of the nouns of this class take *s* to form their plurals. Thus,

portail, portails; gouvernail, gouvernails.

The following, however, change *ail* into *aux* in the plural: *bail*, lease; *corail*, coral; *émail*, enamel; *soupirail*, air hole; *travail*, work; *vitrail*, glass window; *vantail*, folding door.

NOTE.—The reason for these irregularities is that words ending in *ail* today, formerly ended in *al*, and that some follow rule 2, while others add *s*.

17. **Nouns Having a Double Plural.**—The plural of *aïeul* is *aïeux* when the word has the general sense of ancestors; its plural is *aïeuls* when it means specifically the maternal or paternal grandfather.

The plural of *ciel* is *cieux* when it means heavens, firmament, sky; but *ciels* in the expression *ciels-de-lits*, the tester of a bed; *ciels* also when it has the meaning of the climate of a country, or that portion of a painting representing the sky.

The plural of *œil*, the eye, is *yeux*. But its plural is *œils* when the first part of a compound noun, in such expressions as *œil-de-bœuf*, round or oval window; *œil-de-chat*, cat's eye.

The plural of *bétail*, cattle, is *bestiaux*.

NOTE.—Until the 17th century, *bétail* had another form, viz., *bestail;* it is from this latter form that the plural *bestiaux* has been derived.

The plural of *travail*, work, is *travaux*. But when the word means trave, the plural is formed by adding *s* to the singular—*travails*.

In ordinary language the plural of *ail*, garlic, is *aulx*, but in botanical language, its plural is *ails*.

18. **Complement of a Noun.**—When a class name like *nid*, nest, for example is mentioned, there comes to us at once the mental picture of a vast class. The picture includes every kind of nest we can imagine; consequently, the word, or class name, expresses only an incomplete sense. We cannot tell what kind of *nest* may be in the mind of the speaker. But if the expressions *un nid de mousse, un nid de moineaux* are used, an immense number of nests are shut out from our mental picture and our class concept is much smaller and more definite. The expressions *de mousse, de* *moineaux* thus added to *nid* to restrict its meaning, are said to be *modifiers*, or *complements of the noun*, because they complete its sense. In French, these modifiers are usually joined to the first noun by one of the prepositions *de*, *à*, *en*, *pour*, or *par*. Thus,

> le chant de l'alouette, *the song of the lark*
> un verre à vin, *a wine glass*
> un voyage par eau, *a trip by water*
> la foi en Dieu, *faith in God*

19. **Pluralization of Modifiers.**—A modifier is in the *singular* number when taken in a collective sense. Thus,

> un nid de mousse, meaning *made of moss*.

A modifier is in the plural when taken in an individual sense, or when the context expresses plurality. Thus,

> un panier de pommes (containing apples)
> une paire de souliers (idea of plural)

20. **Plural of Compound Nouns.**—Nouns and adjectives only are pluralized in compound nouns; even these words are pluralized only under the following limited conditions:

1. *Two Nouns.*—When a compound noun is formed of two nouns, the second used adjectively, both nouns are pluralized. Thus,

> un chef-lieu, *a chief town;* des chefs-lieux
> un loup-cervier, *a lynx;* des loups-cerviers

2. *A Noun and an Adjective.*—Both noun and adjective take the plural mark. Thus,

> une basse-cour, *a poultry yard;* des basses-cours
> un rouge-gorge, *a robin redbreast;* des rouges-gorges

3. *Two Nouns United by a Preposition.*—In this case, the first noun only is pluralized. Thus,

> un chef-d'œuvre, *a masterpiece;* des chefs-d'œuvre
> un arc-en-ciel, *a rainbow;* des arcs-en-ciel

Note.—The plurals of *Hotel-Dieu*, hospital; *appui-main*, painter's maulstick, etc., follow the preceding rule, because, in old French, compound nouns were formed without the aid of the preposition, and these expressions are now equivalent to *Hotel-de-Dieu*, *appui de la main*, etc.

4. *A Noun and an Invariable Word.*—The noun alone takes the mark of the plural. Thus,

> un contre-ordre, *a counter-order;* des contre-ordres
> un contre-poison, *an antidote;* des contre-poisons
> une avant-garde, *a vanguard;* des avant-gardes

5. *A Verb and a Noun.*—The noun alone takes the plural mark. Thus,

> un tire-bouchon, *a corkscrew;* des tire-bouchons
> un cure-dent, *a toothpick;* des cure-dents
> un garde-fou, *a hand rail;* des garde-fous

21. Plural of Foreign Nouns.—Nouns of foreign origin, when frequently used in French, take *s* to form their plurals. Thus,

> des forums, des ladys, des pensums, des solos,
>   des villas, etc.

But if this foreign noun denotes a prayer, a church hymn, or is formed of several words, it does not change in the plural. Thus,

> des pater, des in folio, des Te Deum.

Note.—The Italian words *carbonaro, cicerone, dilettante, lazzarone, quintetto*, and the Latin words *maximum, minimum*, form their plurals as follows: *carbonari, ciceroni, dilettanti, lazzaroni, quintetti, maxima, minima*.

22. Plural of Proper Nouns.—When a proper noun is applied to a limited group of individuals, it is not pluralized. Thus,

> Les deux Corneille; Les deux Napoléon.

But proper nouns are pluralized when they denote an entire class. Thus,

> Les Racines sont rares, meaning *Men like the poet Racine are rare.*

Again, proper nouns are pluralized when they designate certain historical families. Thus,

Les Bourbons, Les Horaces.

Names of countries are pluralized. Thus,

Les deux Amériques, les trois Guyanes.

GENDER IN NOUNS

23. The French language has only two genders, the *masculine* and the *feminine*. The **masculine gender** is that form or use of a word by which it denotes the **male** sex. The **feminine gender** is that form or use of a word by which it denotes the **female** sex.

Animals alone have sex in the usual sense; and with the exception of the highest classes of these, their sex is not generally regarded as of sufficient importance to be noted in language. Strange enough, the French language has classified all nouns in either the masculine or the feminine gender, even when no sex is implied by the thing represented by the noun. As a general rule, it may be said that feminine nouns of the old Latin have remained feminine in the derived French, but masculine and neuter nouns of the old Latin have become masculine in French.

24. The gender of French nouns is always very perplexing to foreigners. Rules for the classification of genders are very intricate; consequently, we advise students, when learning a new word, to study it with its proper article before it. *Le* or *un* indicates that the noun is masculine; *la* or *une* that it is feminine. The following rules will indicate the gender of most French nouns:

1. Nouns are in the masculine gender when they are:

(*a*) The names of male animals.

(*b*) The names of seasons, days, and months.

(*c*) The names of trees and metals.

(*d*) The names of colors and cardinal points.

(*e*)   The names of the measures of the metric system.

(*f*)   Adjectives, verbs, prepositions, or adverbs used as substantives.

2.   Nouns are in the feminine gender when they are:

(*a*)   Names denoting female animals.

(*b*)   Names of fruit, science, and art, except *l'abricot*, *le citron*, *le coing*, *le raisin*, *le dessin*.

(*c*)   Names of virtues and qualities.

(*d*)   Dimensions.

25. Formation of the Feminine from the Masculine. — In general, the feminine of the names of persons or animals, is formed from the masculine:

1.   By adding *e*; as,

Allemand, Allemande	Louis, Louise
ami, amie	Justin, Justine
Chinois, Chinoise	géant, géante
marquis, marquise	Français, Française

NOTE. — In the masculine form, the last consonant of the noun is not sounded; but in the feminine form, because the new syllable is formed by the addition of *e*, that consonant is always sounded.

2.   By changing *e* into *esse;* as,

tigre, tigresse	prophète, prophétesse
maître, maîtresse	hôte, hôtesse
prêtre, prêtresse	comte, comtesse

3.   By changing *teur* into *trice;* as,

instituteur, institutrice	lecteur, lectrice
acteur, actrice	opérateur, opératrice
conducteur, conductrice	exécuteur, exécutrice
créateur, créatrice	fondateur, fondatrice

4.   Some nouns ending in *teur* change the last *r* into *se;* as,

acheteur, acheteuse	solliciteur, solliciteuse
frotteur, frotteuse	porteur, porteuse

5.   Some ending in *ien* by adding *ne;* as,

Brésilien, Bresilienne	chrétien, chrétienne
chien, chienne	Parisien, Parisienne
musicien, musicienne	plébéien, plébéienne
gardien, gardienne	paroissien, paroissienne

6. In the following cases, the feminine forms, while being closely connected with the masculine, present some peculiarities:

lion, lionne	gouverneur, gouvernante
chat, chatte	serviteur, servante
loup, louve	neveu, nièce
époux, épouse	canard, cane
fils, fille	compagnon, compagne
veuf, veuve	héros, héroïne

26. Different Words for the Masculine and the Feminine. — The following list contains nearly all the nouns that have different words for the masculine and feminine genders:

MASCULINE	FEMININE	MASCULINE	FEMININE
bélier	brebis	mari	femme
bœuf	vache	monsieur	madame
cerf	biche	neveu	nièce
coq	poule	oncle	tante
Dieu	Déesse	papa	maman
frère	sœur	parrain	marraine
garçon	fille	père	mère
gendre	bru	pigeon	colombe
homme	femme	roi	reine
jars	oie	sanglier	laie
lièvre	hase	singe	guenon
mâle	femelle	taureau	genisse

27. Other Irregularities. — The word *mâle* for the masculine, and *femelle* for the feminine is added to the names of some birds; as, *le rossignol mâle, le rossignol femelle, la fauvette mâle, la fauvette femelle.*

Nouns denoting professions usually filled by men preserve their masculine form even when applied to women; as, *une femme auteur, une femme peintre, une femme médicin.*

28. Nouns Having Two Genders. — A few nouns have two genders; as, *amour, délice, orgue* are masculine in the singular, but feminine in the plural. Thus,

un fol amour, de folles amours
un grand délice, de grandes délices
un bel orgue, de belles orgues

NOTE. — *Amour* and *orgue* were feminine in the old French. In the 16th century, they became masculine — a fact that explains the confusion in their genders.

Aigle is masculine when it means the bird *eagle* or a decoration picturing the eagle, and feminine when it has the sense of *banner*.

Hymne is feminine only when it means a *church hymn;* it is masculine in all other cases.

Gens. — Adjectives preceding the word *gens* are feminine; but adjectives following *gens* take the masculine form. Thus, *ces gens là sont heureux, voilà de bonnes gens.*

29. **Nouns Having Different Meanings According to Their Different Genders.** — The following list comprises those nouns whose meanings vary with their gender:

MASCULINE	NOUNS	FEMININE
assistant	*aide*	support
alder tree	*aune*	ell (measure)
modillion	*cartouche*	cartridge
husband and wife	*couple*	pair, two
crape	*crêpe*	pancake
echo	*écho*	a nymph
ensign	*enseigne*	sign board
keeper	*garde*	hilt
judge office	*greffe*	graft
guide	*guide*	reins for driving
book	*livre*	pound
handle	*manche*	sleeve
workman	*manœuvre*	maneuver
bill	*mémoire*	memory
mode	*mode*	fashion
mold	*moule*	mussels
ship boy	*mousse*	moss
divine service	*office*	pantry
attendant	*page*	page (book)
comparison	*parallèle*	parallel
pendulum	*pendule*	clock
stove	*poêle*	frying pan
military station	*poste*	post office
slumber	*somme*	sum
smile	*souris*	mouse
trick	*tour*	tower
veil	*voile*	sail

30. **Other Rules for Distinguishing the Gender of Nouns.** — Rules based upon the endings of nouns may be formulated for distinguishing the genders of nouns. Only those rules so formulated, which have but few exceptions, and are therefore easily mastered, are given here.

1. All nouns ending in *b, c, d, g, h, k, l, o, p, q, z* are masculine.

2. All nouns ending in *a* are masculine; except *la villa.*

3. All nouns ending in *f* are masculine; except *la soif, la nef, la clef.*

4. All nouns ending in *i* are masculine; except *la fourmi, la foi, la loi.*

5. All nouns ending in *m* are masculine; except *la faim.*

6. All nouns ending in *r* are masculine; except *la chair, la mer, la tour,* and some nouns ending in *eur.*

7. All nouns ending in *s* are masculine; except *la brebis, la fois, la souris, la vis.*

8. All nouns ending in *t* are masculine; except *la dent, la dot, la forêt, la jument, la mort, la nuit, la part.*

9. All nouns ending in *u* are masculine; except *la glu, la tribu, la vertu, l'eau, la peau.*

10. All nouns ending in *ance* or *ence,* are feminine; except *le silence.*

11. All nouns ending in *o, au, aux, aus* are masculine; except *la peau, la chaux, la faux, l'eau.*

12. All nouns ending in *ace* are feminine; except *l'espace.*

13. All nouns ending in *ade* are feminine; except *le grade.*

14. All nouns ending in *age* are masculine; except *la cage, l'image, la nage, la page* (of a book), *la plage, la rage.*

15. All nouns ending in *ége* are masculine; except *l'allége* (window sill).

16. All nouns ending in *aire* are masculine; except *l'affaire, l'aire, la chaire, la circulaire, la grammaire, la paire, la perpendiculaire.*

17. All nouns ending in *oire* are feminine; except *le déboire, l'ivoire, le purgatoire, le territoire, le répertoire, l'observatoire.*

18. All nouns ending in *ure* are feminine; except *le mercure, le parjure, le murmure.*

19. All nouns ending in *al* are masculine.

20. All nouns ending in *ain* or *ien* are masculine.

21. All nouns ending in *ion* are feminine; except *le bastion, le billion, le camion, le million, le scorpion, le septentrion.*

22. All nouns ending in *at* are masculine.

23. All nouns ending in *ant* or *ent* are masculine; except *la dent* and *la gent.*

24. All nouns ending in *té* are feminine; except *le bénédicité, le comté, le comité, le côté, l'été, le pâté, le traité.*

25. All nouns ending in *ie* are feminine; except *le foie, le génie, l'incendie, le parapluie.*

COMPARISON OF NOUNS

31. The Comparison of Nouns. — Nouns have no comparison by themselves, but the character, measure, or quantity of one object or class of objects may be compared with another object or class of objects with the aid of other words. For example, one might have *as much*, or *more*, or *less* of one object than of another. So three degrees of comparison are to be recognized:

1. *Equality.* — The expressions, as much . . . as, as many . . . as, are rendered by *autant de . . . que de.* Thus,

> J'ai mangé **autant de** pain **que de** viande,
> *I have eaten as much bread as meat.*

> Vous avez **autant de** garçons **que de** filles,
> *You have as many boys as girls.*

2. *Superiority.* — The expression, more . . . than is rendered by *plus de . . . que de.* Thus,

> Il a bu **plus de** vin **que d'**eau, *He drank more wine than water.*

> Nous avous eu **plus de** plaisir **que de** soucis,
> *We had more pleasure than care.*

3. *Inferiority.* — The expression, less or fewer . . . than, is rendered by the phrase *moins de . . . que de* before nouns. Thus,

> J'ai mis **moins de** vinaigre **que d** 'huile,
> *I put less vinegar than oil.*

> Nous récolterons **moins de** poires **que de** pêches, *We shall gather fewer pears than peaches.*

Note the differences in the comparison of nouns and adjectives. See Art. **47.**

ADJECTIF — ADJECTIVE

32. The Function of the Adjective. — The **adjective** has been defined as a word used to modify the meaning of a noun or a pronoun. When, as the name *adjective* implies, this element is joined directly to a noun, the effect in each case is to restrict or limit to a particular number, or kind, or other group, the objects named by the noun. This is to *modify* or *measure* the meaning of the noun in the extent of its application. Thus, every object answering a certain description is included by the noun *arbre*. But, when modifiers are joined to the noun, the number of denoted objects is reduced by excluding all except such as are:

(*a*) Of a certain *kind* or *quality;* as, **grands** *arbres*, *arbres* **verts.**

(*b*) Of a certain *number*, definite or indefinite; as, **six** *arbres*, **plusieurs** *arbres*.

(*c*) In a certain *condition* of change or action; as, *arbres* **morts,** *arbres* **tombés.**

(*d*) Definitely *pointed out;* as, **cet** *arbre*, **mes** *arbres*.

In these and many other ways, the adjective enables us to separate in thought the object or objects named by the noun from all others that we wish to consider.

33. Classification of Adjectives. — All adjectives modify, but most of them do so by denoting some quality in the thing indicated by the modified word, and for that reason they are called by grammarians **adjectifs qualificatifs,** qualifying adjectives. The number of this class is immense, including all that denote *qualities* perceived directly by the senses; as, *rouge, long, lourd,* etc., and qualities inferred by the mind from something perceived by the senses; as, *honnête, vrai, affectueux,* etc.

The other class, called **adjectifs déterminatifs,** determinative adjectives, are joined to the noun to *denote, determine,* or render *precise* its signification. For example, in *ma maison,* the word *ma* attaches to the word *maison* the idea of possession. *Ma* signifies that the house referred to belongs to me. The noun *maison* then represents a definite, well determined object.

34. **Division of Determinate Adjectives.** — 1. When these adjectives denote number, they are called **adjectifs numéraux,** numeral adjectives. Of these there are two classes: *cardinal,* as, *un, deux, trois,* etc.; and *ordinal,* as *premier, second, troisième,* etc.

2. Adjectives used to point out are called **adjectifs démonstratifs,** demonstrative adjectives, because, in the case of some of them, the effect is much the same as when one points with the finger; as, *cet arbre, ces messieurs.*

3. Adjectives that determine the noun by adding to it the idea of possession are called **adjectifs possessifs,** (pronominal) possessive adjectives; as, *mon chapeau, mes pommes.*

4. Finally, a certain class of adjectives determine the noun, but in a way less precise than the other determinatives, and are called for that reason **adjectifs indéfinis,** indefinite adjectives; as, *certain, tel, tout,* etc.

TABLE OF THE ADJECTIVE

Adjectives
{
QUALIFYING; as, bon, petit, blanc

DETERMINATIVE
{
Numeral; as, un, deux, troisième
Demonstratives; as, ce, cette, ces
Possessives; as, mon, notre, leur
Indefinite; as, tel, nul, autre
}

ADJECTIFS QUALIFICATIFS — QUALIFYING ADJECTIVES

35. **Inflections of the Adjective.** — By itself, the adjective has neither gender nor number; however, it changes its termination for both gender and number to better mark its relation with the noun it qualifies.

FORMATION OF THE FEMININE OF ADJECTIVES

36. **General Rule.** — To form the feminine of adjectives, an *e* is added to the masculine. Thus,

> vrai, vraie; grand, grande; petit, petite; ingrat, ingrate.

37. **Principal Exceptions to the General Rule.** 1. Adjectives ending in an unaccented *e* in the masculine do not change in the feminine. Thus,

> honnête, honnête; aimable, aimable.

2. Adjectives ending in *el*, *eil*, *ien*, *on*, *et* form their feminines by doubling the last consonant, *l*, *n*, or *t*, before the addition of *e*. Thus,

> tel, telle; pareil, pareille; ancien, ancienne; bon, bonne; muet, muette.

NOTE. — The effect of adding *e* is to render the last syllable *le*, *ne*, *te* mute, so that the syllable next to the last is accented in the feminine. To render it more sonorous, the consonant is doubled.

The words *complet*, *concret*, *discret*, *secret*, *inquiet*, *replet*, though ending in *et*, do not double the *t* before adding *e*, but take a grave accent over the *e* before the *t*, which has the same effect as the doubling of the *t* for purposes of accentuation. Thus,

> complète, concrète, discrète, secrète, inquiète, replète.

The words *gros*, *gras*, *épais* become *grosse*, *grasse*, *épaisse* in the feminine. The *s* is here doubled before adding the *e*, because otherwise *s* would fall between two vowels in the feminine and would then have the sound of *z*.

3. *Adjectives Ending in f or x in the Masculine.*—These adjectives form their feminines by changing *f* into *ve* and *x* into *se*. Thus,

neuf, neuve; heureux, heureuse.

But the adjectives *doux, faux, roux* have the feminine forms *douce, fausse, rousse.*

NOTE.—Most adjectives in *f* came from Latin words ending in *v*; this letter reappears in the feminine of the French words. *Faux* and *roux* were formerly spelled *faus, rous*, hence the feminine *rousse, fausse.*

4. *Jumeau, beau, nouveau, fou, mou, vieux* have the feminines *jumelle, belle, nouvelle, folle, molle, vieille.*

NOTE.—In the masculine, these words were formerly *jumel, bel, nouvel, fol, mol, vieil.* These forms are still used before a noun beginning with a vowel or *h* mute, and from them the present feminines were derived.

5. Note the irregularities in the following words: blanc, blanche; franc, franche; sec, sèche; frais, fraîche; public, publique; caduc, caduque; grec, grecque; turc, turque; long, longue; oblong, oblongue; bénin, benigne; malin, maligne; favori, favorite; devin, devineresse.

6. *Aigu, ambigu, contigu, exigu,* form their feminines by adding *e* with the dieresis (ë). Thus,

aiguë, ambiguë, contiguë, exiguë.

7. *Feminine of Adjectives Ending in eur.*—Adjectives ending in *eur* generally form their feminines in *euse*. Thus,

danseur, danseuse; vendeur, vendeuse; trompeur, trompeuse.

This rule governing the feminine of adjectives ending in *eur* is, however, subject to the following exceptions:

(*a*) Adjectives ending in *érieur* form their feminines by adding *e* to the masculine. Thus,

extérieur, extérieure; supérieur, supérieure.

Also *majeur, mineur, meilleur,* which have the feminines *majeur*e, *mineur*e, *meilleur*e.

(*b*)   Adjectives ending in *teur* make their feminines in *trice*. Thus,

> accusateur, accusa**trice**; protecteur, protec**trice**;
> conducteur, conduc**trice**.

(*c*)   *Vengeur, enchanteur,* and *défendeur* have the feminines *vengeresse, enchanteresse,* and *défenderesse.*

(*d*)   The following have two feminines, according to their meaning:

> bailleur, bailleuse, *yawner;* bailleresse, *lessor*
> vendeur, vendeuse, *seller;* venderesse, *vendor*
> pêcheur, pêcheuse, *fisher;* pécheresse, *sinner*
> demandeur, demandeuse, *applicant;* demanderesse, *plaintiff*

(*e*)   Masculine adjectives in *eur* that denote conditions and qualities generally applied to men, do not change in the feminine: *amateur, auteur, docteur,* etc.

8.   French adjectives end in *e* in the feminine. *Grand* follows the general rule except in the following words, which should be committed to memory: *grand'mère, grand'route, grand'messe, grand'peur, grand'peine,* and *grand'chose.*   These words are the only exceptions to the general rule.

NOTE.—In Latin, *grand* and a few other adjectives had but the one form *grandis* in both masculine and feminine. So it was in early French also; but of these adjectives *grand* is now the only one that does not always change its form. Long ago grammarians, believing *grand* to be but an abbreviation for *grande* wrongly introduced the apostrophe to compensate for the *e* which they supposed to have been elided, but which in reality never existed except in the Latin neuter.

NUMBER IN ADJECTIVES

38.   General Rule. — French adjectives, like nouns, form their plurals by the addition of *s*, either to the masculine or feminine form. Thus,

> un bon dîner, de bons dîners; une bonne per-
> sonne, de bonnes personnes.

REMARKS.—When the singular of the adjective ends in *s* or *x*, it does not change in the plural. Thus,

> un homme gros, des hommes gros; un homme
> heureux, des hommes heureux.

39. Exceptions to the General Rule. — Note the following exceptions:

1. Adjectives ending in *eau* take *x* in the plural. Thus,

    beau, beaux; nouveau, nouveaux.

2. Adjectives ending in *eu* or *ou* take *s*. Thus,

    un oiseau bleu, des oiseaux bleus; un homme fou, des hommes fous.

Hébreu has the plural *hébreux*.

3. Adjectives ending in *al* form their plurals in *aux*. Thus,

    un homme libéral, des hommes libéraux; l'honneur national, les honneurs nationaux.

But the following words form their plurals by adding *s* to the singular:

astral	glacial	naval
austral	instrumental	papal
automnal	jovial	pascal
bancal	lingual	pénal
boréal	magistral	sentimental
diamétral	matinal	virginal
fatal	mental	
final	natal	

But since all adjectives ending in *al* in the masculine singular end in *ale* in the feminine singular, all these adjectives form their plurals by adding *s*. Thus,

    une loi libérale, des lois libérales; une fête nationale, des fêtes nationales.

AGREEMENT OF ADJECTIVES

40. As has been said, the adjective by itself has neither gender nor number, but takes the gender and number of the noun it qualifies. Thus,

    le bon père, les bons pères; la bonne mère, les bonnes mères.

When an adjective qualifies two nouns, that adjective is always in the plural; three cases are then to be considered to determine its gender:

55—10

1. When the two nouns are masculine, the adjective is put in the masculine plural. Thus,

<blockquote>l'oncle et le neveu intelligents.</blockquote>

2. When the two nouns are feminine, the adjective is put in the feminine plural. Thus,

<blockquote>la tante et la nièce intelligentes.</blockquote>

3. When one noun is masculine, and the other feminine, the adjective is put in the masculine plural. Thus,

<blockquote>le neveu et la nièce intelligents.</blockquote>

41. Exceptions.—1. When an adjective qualifies several nouns in the singular, having about the same signification, it generally agrees with the last noun. Thus,

<blockquote>Cet homme a une inclination, un penchant-
démesuré pour le jeu.</blockquote>

2. When two nouns are united by the conjunction *ou*, the adjective generally agrees with the last noun. Thus,

<blockquote>un livre ou une brochure nouvelle.</blockquote>

3. An adjective may be used adverbially when it is joined to a verb or a participle; as in the expressions **court** *vêtu*, *marcher* **droit**, *parler* **fort**. In such cases, the adjective does not change in the plural. Thus,

<blockquote>Ces hommes parlent haut, These men speak
loudly.</blockquote>

<blockquote>Elles ne raisonnent pas toujours juste, They
do not always reason rightly.</blockquote>

<blockquote>Ils vendent cher, They sell dearly.</blockquote>

However, after *être, devenir, sembler, paraître*, an adjective can never be taken in an adverbial sense, and we write:

<blockquote>Ces étoffes sont chères; elles me semblent
chères; elles me paraissent chères, These
goods are, seem, appear, expensive.</blockquote>

42. Remarks Upon Some Adjectives.—The following adjectives present some peculiarities:

Some Nouns Used Adjectively to Denote Color. — When a noun is used as an adjective to denote color, that noun is invariable in form. Grammarians explain this peculiarity by assuming that the word *couleur* is understood before it. Among such nouns are: *marron*, chestnut; *ponceau*, red-poppy; *orange*, orange; *carmin*, carmine; etc. Thus,

> des chapeaux marron, *chestnut-colored hats*
> des étoffes ponceau, *red-poppy colored stuffs*
> des gants orange, *orange-colored gloves*

EXCEPTIONS. — Some words, originally nouns, have come to be considered as both nouns and adjectives, and when used as adjectives, therefore follow the general rule of agreement governing adjectives. The most important are: *violette*, voilet; *cramoisi*, crimson; *rose*, rose; *écarlate*, scarlet. Thus,

> des robes roses, *some rose-colored dresses*
> des robes violettes, *some violet-colored dresses*
> des étoffes écarlates, *some scarlet goods*

43. Adjectives Used Adverbially. — Adjectives may be used adverbially, and when so used, are invariable like other adverbs. Thus,

> Elles chantent juste, *They sing in tune.*
> Ils parlent trop haut, *They are speaking too loud.*
> Ces marchands vendent cher, *These merchants sell at high prices.*

COMPARISON OF ADJECTIVES

44. Adjectives have another kind of inflection called **comparison.** Most adjectives denoting quality are inflected to express the *degrees* of the quality denoted. Thus, we may say of one thing that it is *pretty* or *beautiful;* of another, that it is the *prettier*, or the *more beautiful* of two; of a third, that it is the *prettiest*, or the *most beautiful* of three or more.

Such adjectives as are compared, or inflected for quality, have three degrees of comparison: the *positive*, the *comparative*, and the *superlative*.

45. **The Positive Degree.** — The objects that we know and have names for we become acquainted with through their qualities or through their relations to other things. Thus, when we say *orange*, the word calls up in the mind certain ideas of *shape*, *size*, *color*, *taste*, *smell*, etc. We know it by its *sensible* qualities.

Again, *honesty* is the name of a rational quality belonging to a man's conduct when related in a certain way to other human beings. If man habitually acts so and so under particular circumstances, his conduct illustrates some quality, as honesty, and we speak of him as *an* **honest** *man*.

Now, it is by means of these qualities, sensible and rational, and by the various relations among things, that we are able to recognize objects and distinguish them from one another. By their differences and resemblances, and by their relations, and in no other way, do we become acquainted with them.

But before we can say that anything is *large*, for example, we must have a notion of average size for objects of that kind. This notion we get by experience in comparing many things of that class. When one says, *a* **large** *house*, *tree*, *animal*, the expression implies that he has seen and compared **many** *houses*, **many** *trees*, **many** *animals*, and that he has in his mind a general notion or type with respect to the size of each kind of thing mentioned. This type is not often the same with different persons, for it is derived from experience, and this is very various. The wider the experience, the more valuable the type.

This typical notion of quality is the *positive degree* of that quality. It is expressed by the simple uninflected form of the adjective; as, *grand*, *petit*, *rouge*.

The **positive degree** of an adjective is that form or use of it that implies the comparison of one thing or group of things with many others of the same class.

46. **The Comparative Degree.** — In the use of an adjective in the positive degree, the comparison is only implied or taken for granted; in the comparative degree, the comparison of one thing with another must actually be made. Only *two objects* or *two groups* of objects are considered — one having a certain quality, and the other having it in a *higher* or *lower* or an *equal* measure or degree. Thus, one thing may be *sweet* or *pretty*, or *long* or *small*, and the other *sweeter*, *prettier*, *longer*, or *smaller* than the first; or, again, one thing may be *as sweet*, *as pretty*, *as long*, *as small*, as another. An adjective used to express one of these comparisons is said to be in the *comparative degree*.

These three kinds of comparison are known as the comparatives of *inferiority*, *superiority*, and *equality*.

The **comparative degree** of an adjective is that form or use of it by which a comparison with respect to some quality is made between two things or groups of things.

47. **To Form the Comparative Degree.** — *Comparative of Equality*. — This type of the comparative of adjectives is made by placing the adjective to be compared between the adverbs *aussi* and *que*, just as its English equivalent is formed by putting the adverb *as* both before and after the adjective; thus, **aussi** *long* **que**, as long as. Mon frère est **aussi** jeune **que** le vôtre, *my brother is as young as yours*. Ma sœur est **aussi** belle **que** la sienne, *my sister is as pretty as his or hers*.

But in negative sentences *aussi* is replaced by *si;* thus,

> Elle n'est pas **si** grande **que** moi, *She is not so large as I.*

> Ce monsieur n'est pas **si** âgé **que** l'autre, *This man is not so old as the other.*

2. *Comparative of Superiority*. — To express the comparative of superiority *plus* is put before the adjective and *que* after *it*, just as in English *more . . . than* is used; thus,

> Je suis **plus** jeune **que** votre frère, *I am younger than your brother.*

> Elle est **plus** aimable **que** sa sœur, *She is more amiable than her sister.*

3. *Inferiority.*—This comparative is formed by placing *moins* before the adjective and *que* after it (less . . . than). Thus,

> Vous êtes **moins** agé que mon frère, *You are not so old as (are less old than) my brother.*

> Ces messieurs sont **moins** riches **que** votre ami, *These gentlemen are not so rich as your friend.*

48. **The Superlative Degree.**—When the superlative degree of an adjective is used, the least number of objects or groups of objects considered is *three*. One of them, as compared with the others—two or more—is seen to have the *highest* or *lowest* degree of some quality; and to denote this, a form or use of the adjective known as the **superlative degree** is required. This degree also, like the comparative, requires an actual comparison. At least, three pretty, or good, or little objects must be compared before we can say that one of them is the prettiest, the best, the least. The word *superlative* means surpassing, above, or beyond all others.

The **superlative degree** of an adjective is the form or use of it by which a comparison with respect to some quality is made among *three* or *more* things or groups of things.

49. **To Form the Superlative Degree.**—There are evidently two kinds of superlatives, one denoting *superiority* and the other *inferiority*. The first is formed by placing *le* (or *la*, or *les*) *plus* before the adjective, and the second by placing *le* (or *la*, or *les*) *moins* before it. Thus,

> La rose est **la plus** belle des fleurs, *The rose is the most beautiful of flowers.*

> L'hiver est la saison **la moins** agréable, *Winter is the least agreeable season.*

50. **Irregularities.** — Three adjectives, *bon*, *mauvais*, and *petit* form their comparatives of superiority and superlatives irregularly. They are:

POSITIVE	COMPARATIVE	SUPERLATIVE
bon, *good*	meilleur, *better*	le meilleur, *the best*
mauvais, *bad*	pire, *worse*	le pire, *the worst*
petit, *small*, or *little*	moindre, *or*, plus petit, *less*	le moindre, *or*, le plus petit, *the least*

ADJECTIFS DETERMINATIFS — DETERMINATIVE ADJECTIVES

51. There are four kinds of determinative adjectives: (1) *adjectifs démonstratifs*, demonstrative adjectives; (2) *adjectifs possessifs*, (pronominal) possessive adjectives; (3) *adjectifs numéraux*, numeral adjectives; (4) *adjectifs indéfinis*, indefinite adjectives.

ADJECTIFS DEMONSTRATIFS — DEMONSTRATIVE ADJECTIVES

52. Demonstrative adjectives are adjectives used to *point out*. This class is named *demonstrative* from the fact that the Latin word *demonstrare* means to show, point out, or indicate.

The demonstrative adjectives are:

ce before a masculine noun beginning with a consonant. Thus,

ce livre, *this*, or *that book*

cet before a masculine noun beginning with a vowel or *h* mute. Thus,

cet enfant, *this*, or *that child*
cet homme, *this*, or *that man*

cette before a feminine noun. Thus,

cette table, *this*, or *that table*

ces before a plural noun. Thus,

ces tables, *these*, or *those tables*

53. Distinction Between This and That, These and Those. — The demonstrative adjective in the simple forms given above, translates *this* and *that*, or *these* and *those*. When a closer distinction between the relations of two things must be made, the following means are used:

ci (abbreviation of *ici*, here), or **là**, there, are added to the noun and joined to it by a hyphen. *Ci* refers to this and these, and *là* to that, and those. Thus,

ce livre-ci, *this book*	ce livre-là, *that book*
cet enfant-ci, *this child*	cet enfant-là, *that child*
cette table-ci, *this table*	cette table-là, *that table*
ces enfants-ci, *these children*	ces enfants-là, *those children*

ADJECTIFS POSSESSIFS—POSSESSIVE ADJECTIVES

54. Possessive adjectives (pronominal possessive adjectives) denote the possessor of the object represented by the noun. When I say: *J'ai mon livre*, the possessive adjective *mon* denotes that the book spoken of belongs to me.

Possessive adjectives in French do not agree with the word denoting the possessor, but with the noun that follows.

TABLE II

POSSESSIVE ADJECTIVES AND THEIR ENGLISH EQUIVALENTS

	Masculine	Feminine	Plural
my	mon	ma	mes
thy	ton	ta	tes
his, her, *or* its . . .	son	sa	ses
our	notre	notre	nos
your	votre	votre	vos
their	leur	leur	leurs

55. When a feminine noun begins with a vowel or *h* mute, it is, for euphony, preceded by *mon, ton, son* instead of *ma, ta, sa.* Thus,

> mon âme (*for* ma âme), *my soul*
> ton amie (*for* ta amie), *thy friend*
> son écurie (*for* sa écurie), *his, her,* or *its stable*

56. In French, possessive adjectives are repeated before each noun they are intended to modify. Thus,

> Apportez-moi mon verre, ma fourchette, mon couteau, et ma cuillère, *Bring me my glass, fork, knife, and spoon.*

57. Possessive adjectives are not used in combination with a reflexive verb; in such cases the article is used instead. Thus,

> Je me lave la figure, *I wash my face.*
> Chauffez-vous les mains, *Warm your hands.*
> Il s'est coupé le doigt, *He cut his finger.*

ADJECTIFS NUMERAUX—NUMERAL ADJECTIVES

58. Numeral adjectives denote a certain number of persons or things. Of these, there are two kinds:

1. *Adjectifs numéraux cardinaux*, cardinal adjectives, used to denote quantity; as, *cinq, cent, mille.*

2. *Adjectifs numéraux ordinaux*, ordinal adjectives, used to denote rank or order; as, *deuxième, vingtième.*

59. Cardinal Adjectives.—The names of the numbers are:

1, un (*fem.* une)	24, vingt-quatre	79, soixante-dix-neuf
2, deux	30, trente	80, quatre-vingts
3, trois	31, trente et un	81, quatre-vingt-un
4, quatre	32, trente-deux	82, quatre-vingt-deux
5, cinq	33, trente-trois	90, quatre-vingt-dix
6, six	40, quarante	91, quatre-vingt-onze
7, sept	41, quarante et un	92, quatre-vingt-douze
8, huit	42, quarante deux	93, quatre-vingt-treize
9, neuf	50, cinquante	94, quatre-vingt-quatorze
10, dix	51, cinquante et un	100, cent
11, onze	52, cinquante-deux	101, cent un
12, douze	60, soixante	102, cent deux
13, treize	61, soixante et un	103, cent trois
14, quatorze	62, soixante-deux	200, deux cents
15, quinze	70, soixante-dix	201, deux cent un
16, seize	71, soixante et onze	206, deux cent six
17, dix-sept	72, soixante-douze	1,000, mille, mil
18, dix-huit	73, soixante-treize	1,700, dix-sept cents
19, dix-neuf	74, soixante quatorze	2,843, deux mille huit **cent**
20, vingt	75, soixante-quinze	quarante-trois
21, vingt et un	76, soixante-seize	1,000,000, un million
22, vingt-deux	77, soixante-dix-sept	
23, vingt-trois	78, soixante-dix-huit	

60.   Concerning the Numbers. — The cardinal numerals, except *un*, have no distinction for gender; the feminine of *un* is *une*.

In French, there are no separate names for *seventy*, *eighty*, *ninety* (as shown in the table). After *sixty-nine* we say *sixty-ten*, *sixty-eleven*, etc., and so *fourscore* for *eighty*, *fourscore-ten* for *ninety*, etc.

The old forms *septante*, 70; *octante*, 80; and *nonante*, 90; more rational than the present terms, are no longer used. In some provinces of France, they are still occasionally heard, but they are no longer sanctioned.

A hyphen is always inserted between *dix* and a unit immediately following, but not when *et* stands between; the hyphen is not used after *cent* or *mille*.

Un, one, is not used before *cent* or *mille*.   Thus,

cent un, 101; mille trois 1,003.

Instead of *mille cent*, 1,100, *mille deux cents*, 1,200, say *onze cents*, *douze cents* up to *dix-neuf cents;* but this form must not be used after *deux mille*.

Et, and, is used only in the numbers 21, 31, 41, 51, 61, 71; not with 81, 91, nor with any number greater than one hundred; as, *cent un*, 101.

61.   Concerning Vingt and Cent. — When *vingt* and *cent* are preceded by a multiplying adjective, they take *s* if not followed by any other number.   Thus,

quatre-vingts francs, *eighty francs*
trois cents livres, *three hundred books*

On the contrary, *vingt* and *cent*, although in the plural, do not change if they are followed by another word.   Thus,

quatre-vingt-dix francs, *ninety francs*
trois cent quinze livres, *three hundred and fifteen books*

62.   Concerning Mille. — When *mille* designates a date, it is spelled *mil* in the singular, and *mille* in the plural.   Thus,

En mil six cent quarante, *In the year one thousand six hundred and forty*

En deux mille sept cent, *In the year two thousand and seven hundred*

In all other cases, it is spelled *mille* without any variation for gender or number.

63. Pronunciation of Numerals. — For the pronunciation of numerals, see French Grammar, Part I, Art. **46**.

64. Numeral Ordinals. — Numeral ordinals, as seen from Table III, are formed by adding *ième* to the cardinal numbers:

TABLE III

ORDINAL AND CARDINAL NUMBERS

Cardinals	Ordinals
Un . .	premier unieme; used only after *vingt, trente*, etc., as *vingt-et-unième*
Deux . .	second deuxième
Trois . .	troisième
Quatre .	quatrième; the *e* is dropped before adding the *ième*
Cinq . .	cinquième; *u* is added after *q* before *ième*
Six. . .	sixième
Sept . .	septième
Huit . .	huitième
Neuf . .	neuvième; *f* is changed to *v* before adding *ième*
Dix . .	dixième

Because numeral ordinals end in *e*, they are used in both genders without variation, with the exception of *premier* and *second*, the feminines of which are, respectively, *première* and *seconde*.

There is no difference between *second* and *deuxième*. The two words are used indifferently, one for the other. However, *second* is preferable when only two objects are referred to, and *deuxième* when the second rank of a series of objects is spoken of. Thus,

> Voici le second volume, *Here is the second volume* (meaning, a work in two volumes).

> Voice le deuxième volume, *Here is. the second volume* (of a work which contains more than two volumes).

NOTE.—Formerly, the ordinals were expressed as follows: *prime*, first which has remained in *de prime abord*, at first; *prime-saut*, at the first effort; *printemps*, spring—the first time of the year; *second*, second; *tiers*, third (feminine *tierce*), which has given *tiers-état*, third estate; *tiers-ordre*, third order; *tiers-parti*, third party; *quarte*, fourth (feminine *quarte*); as in *fièvre quarte*, intermittent fever rising every 4 days; *quinte*, fifth (feminine *quinte*), in *Charles-quint*, Charles the fifth; *intervalle de quinte*, fifth interval *in music*; *sexte*, sixth; *octave*, eight; *none*, ninth; *dime*, tenth.

65. Concerning Ordinal Numbers.—In French, cardinal adjectives are used instead of ordinals, except, however, with the first day of the month and for the first sovereign of the name. In such cases the ordinal adjective is used. Thus,

> Le premier mars, *The first of March*
> Le deux, trois, quatre, etc. mars, *The second, third, fourth of March*
> Napoléon Premier, *Napoleon the first*
> Napoléon III (trois), *Napoleon the third*
> L'an mil huit cent, *The year eighteen hundred*

In case *vingt* and *cent* are used for *vingtième* and *centième*, they are not changed in form; as, *page quatre-vingt, l'an mil huit cent*.

66. Fractions.—Note the following method of expressing fractions:

$\frac{1}{2}$ une demi		$\frac{4}{5}$ quatre cinquièmes	
$\frac{1}{3}$ un tiers		$\frac{3}{8}$ trois huitèmes	
$\frac{3}{4}$ trois quarts		$\frac{15}{22}$ quinze vingt-deuxièmes	

Half is translated by *demi* (adjective), and by *la moitié* (noun). Thus,

Quelle est la moitié de quinze? *What is half of fifteen?*
Donnez-moi un demi-verre de vin, *Give me half a glass of wine.*

67. Collective Numbers.—Collective numbers are formed by adding *aine* to the cardinal numbers, suppressing the final *e* when it exists. Usage allows only these combinations:

une huitaine, *eight, about eight*   une trentaine
une dizaine, *ten, some ten*   une quarantaine
une douzaine, *a dozen*   une cinquantaine
une quinzaine, *about fifteen*   une soixantaine
une vingtaine, *about twenty*   une centaine

68. Proportional Numbers.—The following are the only proportional numbers sanctioned by usage:

simple, *simple*   sextuple, *sextuple*
double, *double*   septuple, *septuple*
triple, *triple*   octuple, *octuple*
quadruple, *quadruple*   décuple, *decuple*
quintuple, *quintuple*   centuple, *centuple*

The others are supplied by circumlocution; as,

neuf fois autant,⎱
neuf fois plus, ⎰ *nine times as many, or more.*

ADJECTIFS INDÉFINIS—INDEFINITE ADJECTIVES

69. Indefinite adjectives are so called because they modify the noun in an indefinite way. The most important indefinite adjectives are:

aucun (*m.*), aucune (*f.*),⎱
nul (*m.*), nulle (*f.*), ⎰ *no, not any*
certain (*m.*), certaine (*f.*), *certain*
quel (*m. sing.*), quels (*m. pl.*),⎱
quelle (*f. sing.*), quelles (*f. pl.*), ⎰ *which, what*
tel (*m.*), telle (*f.*), *such*
tout (*m. sing.*), tous (*m. pl.*),⎱
toute (*f. sing.*), toutes (*f. pl.*), ⎰ *all*
chaque, *each*
plusieurs, *several*
quelque, *a few*
quelconque, *whatever*
même, *same*
autre, *other*

Quel is often used in questions, when it is also known as an *interrogative adjective;* as in,

Quel chapeau avez-vous?　　*What hat have you?*
Quels livres lisez-vous?　　*What books do you read?*
Quelle robe mettez-vous?　　*What dress are you wearing?*
Quelles leçons étudiez-vous?　　*What lessons are you studying?*

FRENCH GRAMMAR

(PART ·5)

LE PRONOM—THE PRONOUN

1. The **pronoun** has been defined as a word used instead of, or as a substitute for, a name. This definition comes from the literal meaning of the word *pronoun* (*pro*, for; *noun*, a name), but it is not exactly true of all pronouns. When *Jean* says of himself *Je mange*, the meaning is somewhat different from what it would be if he should say *Jean mange*. In the former case, *je* represents the speaker, and shows by its form that it does so; in the latter example, *Jean* may denote the speaker, but nothing about the form of the word denotes that it does.

When of himself and *Henri*, to whom he speaks, *Jean* says *Nous mangeons*, the expression is not equivalent to *Jean et Henri mangent*. But if the pronoun were an exact substitute for a noun, these pairs of sentences would be exact equivalents. By its form, *je* denotes the speaker, but gives no hint of who he is—it shows only that somebody, present and known without being named, is speaking. It would serve equally well if the name of the speaker were unknown, or even if he had no name.

In like manner,

nous = *je* + *vous* (the speaker + the listener), and
nous = *je* + *vous* + *il* (the speaker + the listener + Henri)

In this last case, *il* is a real substitute for a noun, but *vous* and *je* are not. Hence, *je* denotes that some one, whose name is unknown or does not need to be known, is in the relation of speaker. *Nous* denotes that some one is speaking for himself and for others that have been referred to or are present. What their names are is generally a matter of no importance. *Vous* denotes some one in the relation of listener to some one speaking; it is used whether the listener's name is known or not. *Il, elle, ils,* etc. are real substitutes for names.

It appears, therefore, that the definition usually given for the pronoun is objectionable from the fact that it does not exactly describe the functions of all the pronouns. Doubtless, however, it is the best that can be devised. Perhaps the definition already given is somewhat less open to objection than that usually met with in grammars.

A **pronoun** is a word that denotes persons or things without naming them.

___

CLASSES OF PRONOUNS

2. Although the number of pronouns is small, they are divided into several classes, which are usually grouped under five heads: *personnel*, personal; *démonstratif*, demonstrative; *possessif*, possessive; *relatif*, relative; and *indéfini*, indefinite.

___

PRONOMS PERSONNELS–PERSONAL PRONOUNS

3. The **personal pronouns** are those that, by their form, indicate persons: (*a*) the speaker, as *je, me, moi, nous;* (*b*) the person addressed, as *tu, te, toi, vous;* (*c*) the person or thing spoken of, as *il, lui, elle, leur.*

The personal pronouns that play the part of subjects, have already been given with the conjugations of the verb. They are:

	SINGULAR	PLURAL
First person,	je	nous
Second person,	tu	vous
Third person,	il, elle	ils, elles

Tu, thou, is used only among intimate friends and persons closely related; as, parents and children, man and wife, etc.

It denotes familiarity or affection. In refined society, it is never used; *vous*, you, being employed instead.

Personal pronouns may be connected immediately with a verb, as subject or object, and are sometimes called *conjunctive personal pronouns*. When not so used, they are called *disjunctive*.

4. Conjunctive Personal Pronouns. — Besides the conjunctive personal pronouns given above, we have also the following:

SINGULAR	PLURAL
me, *me,* or *to me*	nous, *us,* or *to us*
te, *thee,* or *to thee*	vous, *you,* or *to you*
le, *him;* lui, *to him* ⎫	les, *them;* leur, *to them*
la, *her;* lui, *to her* ⎭	

To these must be added *se*, *en*, and *y*.

5. Place of Conjunctive Personal Pronouns. — The place of the pronoun in the sentence is not the same in French as in English. In French, pronouns are placed after the subject but before the verb; immediately after *ne* in a negative sentence. Thus,

Il **me** gâte, *He spoils me.*

Il **me** parle, *He speaks to me.*

Il ne **vous** parle pas, *He does not speak to you.*

Je ne **les** accompagne pas, et je ne **leur** parle pas, *I do not accompany them, and I do not speak to them.*

Lui avez-vous parlé? *Have you spoken to him* (or *to her*).

Ne **te** donne-t-il rien? *Does he give thee nothing?*

Notice also that in speaking of inanimate things, *le* or *la* is used for *it*, and *les* for *them*. Since French has no neuter gender, and every noun is either masculine or feminine, no neuter pronoun is required. Thus,

Avez-vous le livre? — Je l'ai. *Have you the book? I have it* (*him*).

Mangez-vous la viande? — Je **la** mange. *Do you eat meat? I eat it* (*her*).

55—11

6. The pronoun *se* is sometimes called a **reflexive pronoun,** because it is used in the conjugation of reflexive verbs. When used with the infinitive it means *oneself;* as, *se laver,* to wash oneself; *se tuer,* to kill oneself. It is also used with the third persons singular and plural, and then means *himself, herself,* or *themselves.* Thus,

Il se lave, *He washes himself.*
Elle ne s'habille pas, *She is not dressing herself.*
Ils se lavent, *They wash themselves.*

7. **En** is a pronoun when it means *of it, of him, of her, of them.* It is equivalent to a pronoun and the preposition *de* (*de lui, d'elle, d'eux, d'elles, de cela*). Thus,

Je vous en remercie, *I thank you for it* (*of it*).
Je parle de Charles, j'en parle, *I am speaking about* (*of*) *Charles, I am speaking of him.*

En is often used partitively, standing for a noun with the partitive preposition *de.* Thus,

Avez-vous du pain?—J'en ai, *Have you any bread?—I have some.*

Here *en* stands for *du pain.* In all but similar cases, *en* is a preposition. Thus,

Je vais en Europe, *I am going to Europe.*
Je l'ai vu en allant à la gare, *I saw him when going to the station.*

8. **Y** is the equivalent of a pronoun with the preposition *à* (*à lui, à elle, à eux, à elles, à cela*), and means *to him, to her, to them, to it.* Thus,

Pensez-vous à cela?—Oui; j'y pense, *Are you thinking of* (*to*) *that?—Yes, I am thinking of* (*to*) *it.*
Pense-t-il à Louis?—Oui; il y pense, *Is he thinking of* (*to*) *Louis?—Yes, he is thinking of him.*

In other cases, *y* is an adverb and means *there.*

9. Place of the Conjunctive Pronouns in the Imperative. — If the imperative is affirmative, pronouns are used after the verb (as in English) and joined to it with a hyphen. Instead of *me* and *te*, the pronouns *moi* and *toi* are used in this case. Thus,

> Donnez-**moi** un livre, *Give me a book.*
> Apportez-**lui** son déjeûner, *Bring him his breakfast.*
> Parlons-**leur,** *Let us speak to them.*

If the imperative is negative, however, the pronouns are placed before the verb, immediately after *ne*. Thus,

> Ne **me** donnez pas ce livre, *Do not give me that book.*
> Ne **lui** apportez pas son déjeûner, *Do not bring him his breakfast.*
> Ne **leur** parlons pas, *Let us not speak to them.*

10. Double Pronoun. — When one of the pronouns *le, la,* or *les,* is used with another pronoun, the order of words is as follows:

$$\left.\begin{matrix} \text{me} \\ \text{nous} \\ \text{vous} \end{matrix}\right\} \left.\begin{matrix} \text{le} \\ \text{la} \\ \text{les} \end{matrix}\right\} \left\{\begin{matrix} \text{lui} \\ \text{leur} \end{matrix}\right.$$

That is, the pronoun *le, la,* or *les* follows *me, nous,* or *vous,* but precedes *lui* or *leur.* Thus,

> Il **me le** donne, *He gives it to me.*
> Elle ne **nous les** donne pas, *She does not give them to us.*
> Ils **vous l'**ont promis, *They have promised it to you.*
> Il ne **la lui** passera pas, *He will not pass it to him* (or *to her*).
> Nous les leur donnerons, *We shall give them to them.*

The pronouns *en* and *y* used with other pronouns, are placed last. **Thus,**

> Il **lui en** a donné, *He has given him some.*
> Je **vous y** conduirai, *I shall take you there.*

In the imperative negative, the same order is followed. Thus,

>Ne **nous les** montrez pas, *Do not show them to us.*
>Ne **les leur** donnez pas, *Do not give them to them.*

But in the imperative affirmative, *le*, *la*, or *les* always comes immediately after the verb. Thus,

>>Apportez-le **moi**, *Bring it to me.*
>>Dites-le-leur, *Tell it to them.*
>>Montrez-les-nous, *Show them to us.*

11. Disjunctive Personal Pronouns. — Personal pronouns are called **disjunctive** when not placed close to the verb. In that case, they are always preceded by a preposition other than the preposition *à*; as, *pour*, *avec*, *de*. Disjunctive personal pronouns are always placed after the verb. These pronouns are:

	SINGULAR	PLURAL
First person,	moi, *me*	nous, *us*
Second person,	toi, *thee*	vous, *you*
Third person,	lui, *him;* elle, *her*	eux, *them* (masc.); elles, *them* (fem.)

The following are examples in which the pronoun follows the verb:

>>Comptez **sur moi**, *Rely on me.*
>>Demeurez **avec nous**, *Live with us.*
>>Ce chapeau est **pour lui**, *This hat is for him.*
>>Elle n'est pas **chez elle**, *She is not at home.*
>>Passez **devant eux**, *Go before them* (masc.).
>>Je parle **d'elles**, *I speak of them* (fem.).

12. Other Uses of Disjunctive Pronouns. — (*a*) Disjunctive pronouns are used in French, when the verb with which they should be immediately connected, is not expressed. Thus,

>>Qui a fait cela? — Moi, *Who has done that?*
>>*I* (*me*).
>>Qui vous l'a dit? — Lui, *Who told you so?*
>>*He* (*him*).

Elle est plus grande que toi, *She is taller than thou (thee)*.

Faites comme eux, *Do as (them) they do.*

(*b*) For emphasis, the disjunctive pronouns are used with *même*, self. These forms correspond to *myself, thyself,* etc. in English. They are:

moi-même, *myself*   nous-mêmes, *ourselves*
toi-même, *thyself*   vous-mêmes, *yourselves*
lui-même, *himself*   eux-mêmes, *themselves* (masc.)
elle-même, *herself*   elles-mêmes, *themselves* (fem.)

(*c*) After the expressions *c'est* and *ce sont*, the disjunctive pronouns are used. Thus,

C'est moi, *It is I.*
C'est toi, *It is thou.*
C'est lui, *It is he.*
C'est elle, *It is she.*
C'est nous, *It is we.*
C'est vous, *It is you.*
Ce sont $\begin{cases} \text{eux (masc.),} \\ \text{elles (fem.),} \end{cases}$ *It is they.*

(*d*) When more than one pronoun, or one pronoun and a noun are subjects of the same verb, the disjunctive form of the pronoun is used. Thus,

Lui et moi sommes arrivés les premiers, *He and I arrived first.*

Eux et leurs amis sont partis, *They and their friends have departed.*

(*e*) The subject pronoun, if separated from a verb by an expression other than the negative *ne*, must take the disjunctive form. Thus,

Lui, comprenant le français, n'avait pas de peine à se faire comprendre, *He, understanding French, had no trouble in making himself understood.*

Eux seuls réussirent, *They alone succeeded.*

13. Soi. — In French, the disjunctive form of the reflexive pronoun *se* is *soi;* this form is used when it relates to an indefinite subject. Thus,

> On a souvent besoin d'un plus petit que soi,
> *One often needs the help of those smaller than oneself.*

> Quand on est égoïste, on ne pense qu'à soi,
> *When one is an egotist, one thinks only of oneself.*

PRONOMS DÉMONSTRATIFS—DEMONSTRATIVE PRONOUNS

14. Ce has the value of a **demonstrative pronoun** when it is the subject of *être*, to be, in its various tenses. Thus,

> C'est moi, *It is I.*

> Que lisez-vous? — C'est un roman, *What do you read? — This is a novel.*

Ce, as the antecedent of *que* or *qui*, may be either the direct object of a preceding verb, or the subject of a following verb. Thus, Ce que vous dites est vrai, *What you say is true.*

> Faites ce que vous voudrez, *Do what you please.*

> Dites-moi ce que vous voulez, *Tell me what you wish.*

> Je fais ce qui me plaît, *I do what pleases me.*

> Ce qui vous plaira, me plaira, *What will please you, will please me.*

Sometimes *ce* also precedes *dont*, and then has the meaning of *what*, or *that of which*. Thus,

> Dites-lui ce **dont** vous avez besoin, *Tell him what you need.*

> Avez-vous ce **dont** vous avez besoin? *Have you what you need,* (that of which you are in need)?

15. Ceci and Cela. — Two adverbs, *ci*, here (abbreviation for *ici*), and *là*, there, may be joined to the pronoun *ce* to form the two expressions *ceci*, this, *literally*, this (thing) here, and *cela*, there, *literally*, that (thing) there. They are used in an indefinite way without reference to any particular object expressed. Thus,

> Prenez ceci, ne prenez pas cela, *Take this, do not take that.*
>
> Que pensez-vous de cela? *What do you think of that?*

16. **Other Demonstrative Pronouns.** — The pronoun *ce*, when joined to the disjunctive pronouns *lui*, *elle*, *eux*, *elles*, forms the following demonstrative pronouns:

> *celui*, for the masculine singular
> *celle* (for *ce elle*) for the feminine singular
> *ceux* (for *ce eux*) for the masculine plural
> *celles* (for *ce elles*) for the feminine plural

These pronouns are used as antecedents of the relative pronouns *qui*, *que*, or *dont*, to render the English expressions *he*, *she*, or *they*, followed by *who*, *whom*, or *that;* also to translate the expressions *the one*, or *the ones*. Thus,

> Celui qui étudie beaucoup apprend bien, *He who studies much learns well.*
>
> Celle qui étudie beaucoup apprend bien, *She who studies much learns well.*
>
> Ceux qui étudient beaucoup apprennent bien, *They who study much learn well.*
>
> Celles qui étudient beaucoup apprennent bien, *They who study much learn well.*
>
> Celui que vous voyez là-bas est mon frère, *He whom you see yonder is my brother.*
>
> Celle que vous voyez là-bas est ma sœur, *She whom you see yonder is my sister.*
>
> Ceux que vous voyez là-bas sont mes frères, *They whom you see yonder are my brothers.*
>
> Celles que vous voyez là-bas sont mes sœurs, *They whom you see yonder are my sisters.*

These pronouns may also be used with the preposition *de* to express an English possessive. Thus,

> C'est mon ami et celui de mon frère, *He is my friend and my brother's.*

> C'est mon amie et celle de ma sœur, *She is my friend and my sister's.*

> Ce sont mes amis et ceux de mon frère, *They are my friends and my brother's.*

> Ce sont mes amies et celles de ma sœur, *They are my friends and my sister's.*

17. Celui-ci, Celui-là; Celle-ci, Celle-là; Ceux-ci, Ceux-là; Celles-ci, Celles-là. — It is obvious that these pronouns are formed from the preceding ones, with the addition of the adverbs *ci* (for *ici*), here, and *là*, there. By their meaning, it can easily be seen that when *ci* is used after the pronoun, this pronoun will be used to denote objects near the speaker, and when used with *là*, it will denote objects far from the speaker.

As to their use, let us consider the sentence: *Voici deux livres; ce livre-ci est grand, ce livre-là est petit*, here are two books; this book is large, that book is small. In English, this may be expressed in a different way, as follows: Here are two books; this one is large, that one is small. In this case, *this one* and *that one* represent *this book* and *that book*. In French, we have the same thing, but instead of *ce livre-ci* and *ce livre-là*, the pronouns *celui-ci* and *celui-là* are used, and the whole sentence is: *Voici deux livres: celui-ci est grand, celui-là est petit.*

If the noun is feminine, *celle-ci* and *celle-là* are used. Thus,

> Voici deux tables; celle-ci est grande, celle-là est petite, *Here are two tables; this one is large, that one is small.*

Ceux-ci and *ceux-là* are used to represent the masculine, and *celles-ci* and *celles-là* to represent the feminine of plural nouns. Thus,

Voici des livres: ceux-ci sont grands, ceux-là
sont petits, *Here are books: these are large,
those are small.*

Voici des tables: celles-ci sont grandes, celles-là
sont petites, *Here are tables: these are large,
those are small.*

**18. Comparison of Demonstrative Adjectives and
Pronouns.** — The differences in the forms of the demonstrative adjectives and demonstrative pronouns may be seen
from the following comparative table:

PRONOUNS	ADJECTIVES
celui-ci, *this one*	{ **ce** livre-**ci,** *this book* { **cet** enfant-**ci,** *this child*
celui-là, *that one*	{ **ce** livre-**là,** *that book* { **cet** enfant-**là,** *that child*
celle-ci, *this one*	**cette** table-**ci,** *this table*
celle-là, *that one*	**cette** table-**là,** *that table*
ceux-ci, *these*	**ces** livres-**ci,** *these books*
ceux-là, *those*	**ces** livres-**là,** *those books*
celles-ci, *these*	**ces** tables-**ci,** *these tables*
celles-là, *those*	**ces** tables-**là,** *those tables*
ce, *this, that, it*	
ceci, *this* } indefinite **cela,** *that*	
celui (masc.), } *the one* **celle** (fem.),	
celles (fem.), } *the ones* **ceux** (masc.),	

PRONOMS POSSESSIFS–POSSESSIVE PRONOUNS

19. Let us consider the following sentences:

J'ai votre livre et mon livre, *I have your book
and my book.*

J'ai votre plume et ma plume, *I have your pen
and my pen.*

J'ai vos livres et mes livres, *I have your books
and my books.*

> J'ai vos plumes et mes plumes, *I have your pens and my pens.*

In English, as in French, these sentences could have been put in the following way:

> J'ai votre livre et **le mien,** *I have your book and mine.*
>
> J'ai votre plume et **la mienne,** *I have your pen and mine.*
>
> J'ai vos livres et **les miens,** *I have your books and mine.*
>
> J'ai vos plumes et **les miennes,** *I have your pens and mine.*

It can be seen that the word *mine* translated into French assumes one of the following four forms: *le mien* (for *mon livre*), *la mienne* (for *ma plume*), *les miens* (for *mes livres*), *les miennes* (for *mes plumes*). These expressions stand for a noun and a possessive adjective and are called **possessive pronouns.** These pronouns denote possession by absorbing the possessive adjectives, as may be seen from the illustrations just given. This does not mean that they are used in the possessive case, but that they take into their meaning the idea of possession; their function is always nominative or objective.

In French, these pronouns have different inflections for gender and number. They do not agree with the possessor, but are of the same number and gender as the noun they represent.

20. **Different Possessive Pronouns.** — The possessive pronouns are as follows:

mine
{
le mien for *mon* and a masculine singular noun
la mienne for *ma* and a feminine singular noun
les miens for *mes* and a masculine plural noun
les miennes for *mes* and a feminine plural noun
}

thine
{
le tien for *ton* and a masculine singular noun
la tienne for *ta* and a feminine singular noun
les tiens for *tes* and a masculine plural noun
les tiennes for *tes* and a feminine plural noun
}

his,
or
hers
- *le sien* for *son* and a masculine singular noun
- *la sienne* for *sa* and a feminine singular noun
- *les siens* for *ses* and a masculine plural noun
- *les siennes* for *ses* and a feminine plural noun

ours
- *le nôtre* for *notre* and a masculine singular noun
- *la nôtre* for *notre* and a feminine singular noun
- *les nôtres* for *nos* and a masculine plural noun
- *les nôtres* for *nos* and a feminine plural noun

yours
- *le vôtre* for *votre* and a masculine singular noun
- *la vôtre* for *votre* and a feminine singular noun
- *les vôtres* for *vos* and a masculine plural noun
- *les vôtres* for *vos* and a feminine plural noun

theirs
- *le leur* for *leur* and a masculine singular noun
- *la leur* for *leur* and a feminine singular noun
- *les leurs* for *leurs* and a masculine plural noun
- *les leurs* for *leurs* and a feminine plural noun

21. Concerning Possessive Pronouns. — Note that the feminines and plurals of these pronouns are regularly formed according to the rules given for the formation of the feminines and plurals of adjectives; except *leur*, which has the same form in both the masculine and feminine genders.

A circumflex accent is put over the *o* in the pronouns *le nôtre* and *le vôtre*, but there is none over the *o* in the adjectives *notre* and *votre*. The effect of the circumflex accent is to make the pronunciation of the *o* broader and longer in duration.

_____

PRONOMS RELATIFS—RELATIVE PRONOUNS

22. Function of the Relative Pronoun. — The relative pronouns have double functions in sentences: they stand for a noun or an equivalent of a noun, and they connect clauses. Thus,

Mon père est mort hier + Mon père était avocat	=	Mon père, **qui** est mort hier, était avocat. *My father, who died yesterday, was a lawyer.*
Ce chien est à vendre + **Ce chien** a gagné le premier prix	=	Ce chien, **qui** a gagné le premier prix est à vendre. *This dog, that won the first prize, is for sale.*

$$\left.\begin{array}{c} \text{Cet homme possède la maison} \\ + \\ \text{Jean a bâti la maison} \end{array}\right\} = \begin{array}{l} \text{Cet homme posséde la} \\ \text{maison que Jean a bâtie.} \\ \textit{This man possesses the house} \\ \textit{that John built.} \end{array}$$

In the first sentence, *qui* stands for *mon père*, and connects the two clauses; it is, besides, the subject of *est mort*. In the second sentence, the function of *qui* is exactly similar to that in the first sentence. *Que* in the last sentence connects the clauses and is the object of *bâtie;* this is because it takes the place of *la maison* in the second of the united clauses. The words *père*, *chien*, and *maison*, to which the pronouns relate, are called **antecedents**—meaning words that go before: *père* is the antecedent of *qui* and *maison* of *que*.

Because these pronouns relate to a noun previously expressed, they are called **relatives;** and because they join two clauses together, they are also called **conjunctives.**

23. The most common relative pronouns are *qui* and *que*. When they are not preceded by a preposition, the first stands for the subject of a verb and the second for the object. Both of them may refer to persons or things of any gender or number. Thus,

> Je vois Louis **qui** arrive, *I see Louis, who is coming.*
> C'est vous **qui** avez raison, *It is you who are right.*
> C'est lui **que** j'attends, *It is he whom I am expecting.*
> Prêtez-moi le livre **que** vous avez, *Lend me the book that you have.*

24. *Qui* may also be used as the object of a verb. In that case, it is preceded by a preposition. Thus,

> Voilà l'homme **à qui** j'ai donné cinq francs, *There is the man to whom I gave five francs.*
> Voilà les dames **chez qui** je demeure, *Here are the ladies at whose house I live.*

When used with a preposition, *qui* can represent persons only. To refer to things, *lequel* is used with the following inflections for gender and number:

SINGULAR

	Masculine	Feminine
SUBJECT, DIRECT OBJECT, }	lequel	laquelle, *which*
WITH PREPOSITION DE,	duquel	de laquelle, *of which*
WITH PREPOSITION À,	auquel	à laquelle, *to which*

PLURAL

	Masculine	Feminine
SUBJECT, DIRECT OBJECT, }	lesquels	lesquelles, *which*
WITH PREPOSITION DE,	desquels	desquelles, *of which*
WITH PREPOSITION À,	auxquels	auxquelles, *to which*

The following illustrate the uses of *lequel* and its compounds:

l'homme **auquel** (or, **à qui**) je l'ai donné, *the man to whom I have given it.*

Voilà les maisons dans **lesquelles** vous demeurez, *There are the houses in which you live.*

25. After *parmi*, among, *lequel* is always used; never *qui*. **Lequel, laquelle,** etc. are also used instead of *qui* or *que* as the subject or the object of a verb when the use of either *qui* or *que* would make the sense ambiguous; that is, when a difference of genders must be shown. Thus,

L'oncle de Mme. Loubet, lequel a fait fortune en Amérique, vient d'arriver, *Mrs. Loubet's uncle, who made a fortune in America, has just arrived.*

In this case, by using *qui* in place of *lequel*, the sentence would be ambiguous, for we could not tell whether Mrs. Loubet or the uncle had made the fortune. By using *lequel*, however, the pronoun being masculine undoubtedly refers to the uncle.

26. When *qui* or *lequel* is preceded by the preposition *de*, the relative pronoun *dont*, meaning *of whom*, *of which*, *whose*, is often used. Thus,

> J'ai vu mon ami dont le fils est ici, *I saw my friend whose son is here.*
> C'est le monsieur dont je vous ai parlé, *He is the gentleman of whom I spoke to you.*

27. *Quoi* may also be used as a relative. It is then taken in a general or indefinite sense. It does not refer to a single antecedent, but to a whole clause. Thus,

> Je ne sais **quoi** dire, *I do not know what to say.*
> Il me parla, après **quoi** il s'en alla, *He spoke to me, after which he went away.*

28. The adverb *où* may also be used as a relative pronoun, when taken in the sense of *lequel* preceded by a preposition. Thus,

> Voilà la maison où (*for*, dans laquelle) je demeure, *There is the house in which I live.*

29. As has been said in discussing demonstrative pronouns, the pronoun used as the antecedent of a relative is not the personal pronoun, as in English, but the demonstratives, *ce* and *celui*, etc.

(*a*) *Ce qui* and *ce que* are translated in English by *what* or *that which*. Thus,

> Il m'a dit **ce qu'**il pensait, *He told me what he thought.*
> Dites-moi **ce que** vous en pensez, *Tell me what you think of it.*
> Il achète **ce qui** lui plaît, *He buys what pleases him.*

(*b*) *Ce dont* means *of what*, or *that of which*. Thus,

> Avez-vous ce dont vous avez besoin, *Have you what you need.*
> C'est ce dont il se plaint, *It is that of which he is complaining.*

(*c*)   *Celui qui*, or *que* means *he who* or *the one which*. Thus,

> C'est celle que j'aime, *It is she whom I love.*
> Celui qui étudie beaucoup fait des progrès, *He who studies much makes progress.*

30.   The relative pronoun, which is often omitted in English, must always be expressed in French. Thus,

> Les livres qu'il a achetés sont très chers, *The books he bought are very dear.*
> La maison que j'ai achetée est très belle, *The house I bought is very beautiful.*

31.   **Interrogative Pronouns.** — Most relative pronouns may be used in interrogations, and when so used are called **interrogative pronouns.**   Thus,

> Qui est là?   *Who is there?*
> Que voulez-vous?   *What do you want?*
> De quoi parlez-vous?   *Of what do you speak?*
> Lequel de ses frères est marié?   *Which of his brothers is married?*

Dont is never used in interrogations.

Instead of using simply *qui* as an interrogative pronoun, the following forms are very largely employed: *qui est-ce qui?* who (*literally*, who is it who?), and *qui est-ce que?* whom (*literally*, who is it that?)   Thus,

> Qui
> Qui est-ce qui } a parlé?   *Who spoke?*

> Qui
> Qui est-ce que } vous demandez?   *Whom are you asking for?*

In the same way, instead of the simple form *que* (*qu'* before a vowel) the idiomatic expressions *qu'est-ce qui?* what, for the subject, and *qu'est-ce que?* or even *qu'est ce que c'est que?* (*literally*, what is it that, and what is this that this is that?) what, for the object, are very common expressions in conversational French. Thus,

> Que vous manque-t-il?
> Qu'est-ce qui vous manque? } *What do you need* (*lack*)?

Que désirez-vous?
Qu'est-ce que vous désirez?   } *What is it that*
Qu'est-ce que c'est que vous désirez?   *you want?*

32. How to Translate What. — (*a*) When **what** is placed before a noun, it is translated by *quel* with its different inflections.   Thus,

Quel chapeau avez-vous?   *What hat have you?*
Quelle leçon apprenez-vous?   *What lesson are you learning?*
Quels livres avez-vous lus?   *What books did you read?*
Quelles plumes préférez-vous?   *What pens do you prefer?*

Sometimes the noun is not expressed, but merely understood.   This is the case when *what* is placed before the verb *to be*.   Thus,

Quels sont ces livres?   *What (books) are these books?*

Quelles sont les principales villes de France?
   What (cities) are the principal cities of France?

(*b*)   What is translated by *que* (or, *qu'est-ce qui*, *qu'est-ce que*, see preceding article) when placed before a verb other than the verb *être*.   Thus,

Que mangez-vous?   *What do you eat?*
Que dites-vous?   *What do you say?*
Qu'est-ce qui vous manque?   *What do you need (lack)?*
Qu'est-ce que vous désirez?   *What do you want?*

(*c*)   *Que* used for *what* is changed into *quoi* if preceded by a preposition.   Thus,

A quoi pensez-vous?   *What are you thinking of (to)?*
De quoi parlez-vous?   *What are you speaking of?*

(*d*)   What, in the sense of *this*, *that*, or *that which*, etc., is translated by *ce que* or *ce qui*.   Thus,

Je sais ce qui me manque, *I know what I need.*
Donnez ce que vous avez, *Give what you have.*

PRONOMS INDÉFINIS—INDEFINITE PRONOUNS

33. Function of the Indefinite Pronoun.—As its name indicates, an **indefinite pronoun** stands for names, but denotes the things themselves with vagueness and uncertainty. Thus,

On frappe à la porte, *Some one is knocking at the door*.
Quelqu'un nous appelle, *Somebody is calling us*.
The principal indefinite pronouns are:

(*a*) Those that never change:

autrui, *others*	quiconque, *whoever*
on, *one, they, people*	plusieurs, *several*
personne, *no one*	rien, *nothing*

(*b*) Those having inflection for gender and number:

MASCULINE

	Singular	*Plural*
no one,	aucun	aucuns
other,	autre	autres
certain,	certain	certains
each,	chacun	
no one,	nul	
somebody,	quelqu'un	quelques-uns
such a one,	tel	tels
all,	tout	tous
one another, or *the one and the other,*	l'un l'autre	les uns les autres
both,	l'un et l'autre	les uns et les autres
either, or *one or the other,*	l'un ou l'autre,	les uns ou les autres
neither,	ni l'un ni l'autre	ni les uns ni les autres

FEMININE

	Singular	*Plural*
no one,	aucune	aucunes
other,	autre	autres
certain,	certaine	certaines
each,	chacune	
no one,	nulle	
somebody,	quelqu'une	quelques-unes
such a one,	telle	telles
all,	toute	toutes

one another, or *the one and the other*,	l'une l'autre	les unes les autres
both,	l'une et l'autre	les unes et les autres
either, or *one or the other*,	l'une ou l'autre	les unes ou les autres
neither,	ni l'une ni l'autre	ni les unes ni les autres

L'ADVERBE—THE ADVERB

34. Functions of the Adverb.—In treating of the adjective, it was stated that its function is to narrow the extension and enlarge the comprehension of the noun's meaning. The same is true of the *adverb* in its relation primarily to a verb; and secondarily, to an adjective or another adverb. The **adverb** generally limits the meaning of the word with which it is used in time, place, manner, or degree. Thus,

Je parle **peu,** *I speak little.*

Il est **très** bon, *He is very kind.*

Vous parlez **très bien,** *You speak very well.*

It will be observed that the adverb briefly expresses what would otherwise require several words—often a preposition followed by a noun; thus, *here*, in this place; *now*, at this time; *very*, in a high degree. So in the sentence, *il parle poliment*, he speaks politely, the adverb *poliment* is equivalent to the prepositional phrase, with politeness.

Since the adjective, the adverb, and the verb, the words with which the adverb is associated, have by themselves neither gender nor number, the adverb has no inflection.

35. Classification of Adverbs.—Adverbs may be divided, with regard to their meaning, into four general classes; namely, adverbs of time, of place, of manner, and of degree.

1. *Adverbes de temps*, adverbs of time, answer the questions, when? how long? how soon? etc.; as, *j'irai* **demain.**

2. *Adverbes de lieu*, adverbs of place, answer the questions, where? whither? whence? etc.; as, *j'irai* **ici.**

3. *Adverbes de manière*, adverbs of manner, answer the questions, how? in what way? etc.; as, *j'irai* **gaiement.**

4. *Adverbes de quantité*, adverbs of degree, answer the questions, how much? how little? etc.; as, *j'irai* **peu.**

Adverbs may also be divided, according to their use, into four general classes: namely, adverbs expressing interrogation, affirmation, doubt, or denial.

1. *Adverbes interrogatifs*, adverbs of interrogation, are used in asking questions relative to the time, place, manner, or cause of an action or state; as **quand** *ira-t-il?*

2. *Adverbes d'affirmatifs*, adverbs of affirmation, are used to express consent, or to modify the general meaning of a sentence or clause; as, **oui,** *j'irai;* **volontiers,** *j'irai.*

3. *Adverbes de doute*, adverbs of doubt, are used to express uncertainty or indecision; as, *j'irai* **probablement.**

4. *Adverbes de négation*, adverbs of denial, are used to express negation or unbelief; as, **non;** *je* n'*irai* **pas.**

36. **Adverbs of Place.** — The principal **adverbs of place** are:

ici, *here*	ailleurs, *elsewhere*	dessous, *under*
là, *there*	deçà, *on this side*	dedans, *inside*
y, *there*	delà, *on that side*	dehors, *outside*
où, *where*	partout, *everywhere*	devant, *in front of*
en, *from there*	çà, *here*	derrière, *behind*
loin, *far*	dessus, *on*	

37. **Concerning là, en, and y.** — The adverb *là*, always written with the grave accent, should be carefully distinguished from *la*, the article and pronoun, never written with the accent. Thus,

Il la trouva là pendant la nuit, *He found it there during the night.*

En and *y* serve as either adverbs or pronouns according to their use. When used as adverbs they have the sense of *from there* and *there* respectively. Thus,

Connaissez-vous Paris? — J'en arrive et j'y retourne, *Do you know Paris? — I came from there and I am going there again.*

But when used as pronouns, *en* means *from* or *of him, her, it*, or *them*, while *y* means *to him, her, it,* or *them*. Thus,

> Pensez-vous à votre ami?—Oui; j'y pense, *Are you thinking of your friend?—Yes; I am thinking of him.*
>
> Parlez-vous de votre ami?—Oui; j'en parle, *Are you speaking of your friend?—Yes, I am speaking of him.*

38. Adverbs of Time.—The most important **adverbs of time** are:

quand, *when*	maintenant, *now*	jadis, *formerly*
puis, *then*	jamais, *never*	lors, *then*
depuis, *since*	aujourd'hui, *today*	alors, *then*
souvent, *often*	demain, *tomorrow*	longtemps, *long time*
toujours, *always*	hier, *yesterday*	enfin, *at last*
ensuite, *afterwards*	aussitôt, *as soon as*	encore, *yet, again*

39. Adverbs of Manner.—The most common **adverbs of manner** are:

bien, *well*	à la hâte, *hastily*	ainsi, *thus*
mal, *badly*	à la mode, *fashionably*	à tort, *wrongfully*
volontiers, *willingly*	exprès, *purposely*	à raison, *rightfully*

To these adverbs of manner belong a long list of adverbs ending in *ment;* indeed there are but few adjectives in French from which such adverbs have not been formed. The adverbial ending *ment* is derived from the Latin substantive *mens*, manner, and corresponds closely with the English adverbial ending *ly*. Hence *tendrement*, tenderly, means in a tender manner, etc. Adverbs in this ending are formed in various ways:

(*a*) By adding the termination *ment* to the feminine form of the adjective. Thus,

ADJECTIVES		ADVERBS
Masculine	*Feminine*	
active, actif	active	activement
low, bas	basse	bassement
beautiful, beau	belle	bellement

discreet, discret	discrète	discrètement
sweet, doux	douce	doucement
fresh, frais	fraîche	fraîchement
long, long	longue	longuement
glorious, glorieux	glorieuse	glorieusement
malicious, malin	maligne	malignement
neat, net	nette	nettement
late, tardif	tardive	tardivement

(*b*) If, however, the adjective ends with a vowel in the masculine, *ment* is added to the masculine form. Thus,

ADJECTIVE	ADVERB
hardi	*hardiment*
poli	*poliment*
vrai	*vraiment*

It will be seen that this addition of *ment* to the masculine form of certain adjectives is equivalent to adding it to their feminine forms with the feminine ending *e* suppressed. Consequently, one might expect that the final vowel of such masculine adjectives would acquire a circumflex accent in the adverb to compensate for the suppression of the *e*. The French Academy, however, has warranted the use of the circumflex accent for this cause only in the adverbs *assidûment, crûment, dûment,* and *indûment;* except that the Academy authorizes also either the retention of the *e* or the use of the circumflex in a few adverbs; as in *atermoiement,* or *atermoîment; gaiement,* or *gaîment.*

(*c*) In adjectives ending in *ant* or *ent* in the masculine, the final *nt* is changed into *m* before adding *ment*. Thus,

ADJECTIVES	ADVERBS
fluent, courant	couramment
frequent, fréquent	fréquemment
prudent, prudent	prudemment
learned, savant	savamment
violent, violent	violemment

Lent, slow, has, however, for its corresponding adverb *lentement*, slowly.

(*d*) The following adjectives form adverbs irregularly:

ADJECTIVES	ADVERBS
blind, aveugle	aveuglément
brief, brief	brièvement
common, commun	communément
according, conforme	conformément
confuse, confus	confusément
enormous, énorme	énormément
immense, immense	immensément
precise, précis	précisément
treacherous, trîatre	traîtreusement

40. Adverbs of Quantity. — The principal adverbs of quantity are:

assez, *enough*
autant, *as much, as many*
beaucoup, *much, many*
bien, fort, très, *very*
davantage, *more*
combien, *how much, how many*

guère (ne), *but little, but few*
peu, *little, few*
presque, *almost*
tant, *so much, so many*
trop, *too much, too many*
trop peu, *too little.*

Adverbs of quantity may be used with nouns. They are then followed, or supplemented by the preposition *de* before the noun. Thus,

Avez-vous assez de pain, *Have you enough bread?*

The pronoun *en* is sometimes used in place of the preposition *de* and its objective noun. Thus,

Oui, j'en ai assez, *Yes; I have enough* (*of it*).

41. Adverbs of Interrogation. — Interrogative adverbs are always placed before the verb. They are as follows:

combien, *how much, how many*
comment, *how*
où, *where*

d'où, *whence*
pourquoi, *why*
quand, *when*

42. Adverbs of Affirmation. — The principal adverbs of affirmation are:

certes, *certainly*
oui, si, *yes*
sans doute, *undoubtedly*

soit, *be it so*
volontiers, *willingly*
d'accord, *agreed*

43. Adverbs of Negation. — The most important **adverbs of negation** are *non*, no, and *ne*, not. *Ne* is used alone in but few cases; when it occurs with a verb, it generally appears in one of the following combinations:

ne . . . pas, *not*	ne . . . aucunement, *by no means*
ne . . . point, *not* (emphatic)	ne . . . nullement, *by no means*
ne . . . plus, *no longer*	ne . . . que, *but, only*
ne . . . jamais, *never*	ne . . . guère, *little, but little*

44. Adverbs of Doubt. — The most common **adverbs of doubt** are *peut-être*, perhaps, and *probablement*, probably.

45. Adjectives Used as Adverbs. — Certain adjectives are sometimes used as adverbs to express manner. When so used they are subject to all the conditions governing the correct use of adverbs proper. Therefore they cannot then have inflections for either number or gender. Those most frequently so employed are:

cher, *dear*	bas, *in a low voice*
faux, *out of tune*	juste, *correctly*
haut, *loud*	fort, *very*

46. Compound Adverbs. — The **compound adverbs** in most common use are the following:

à jamais, *forever*	en avant, *forwards*
à la fois, *at the same time*	jusque là, *so far*
à part, *aside*	là-dessus, *thereupon*
après-demain, *day after tomorrow*	ni plus ni moins, *neither more nor less*
à présent, *at present*	
au moins, *at least*	non plus, *not either*
avant-hier, *day before yesterday*	par hasard, *by chance*
ci-contre, *on the other side*	quelque part, *somewhere*
ci-inclus, *enclosed*	sans doute, *undoubtedly*
d'abord, *at first*	tour à tour, *in turn*
d'ailleurs, *moreover*	tôt ou tard, *sooner or later*
de plus, *besides*	tout à l'heure, *just now*
de suite, *in succession*	tout de suite, *immediately*
d'ici, *from here*	tout à coup, *suddenly*
d'ordinaire, *usually*	tout d'un coup, *in a stroke*

47. Comparison of Adverbs. — Like adjectives, certain adverbs may have varying degrees of comparison. Such are (1) adverbs of manner ending in *ment*, (2) adverbs of degree, (3) adjectives used as adverbs, and (4) *bien, mal, peu, fort, loin, près, tôt, tard, vite, volontiers.*

Adverbs are compared in the same way as adjectives. Thus,

POSITIVE	COMPARATIVE	SUPERLATIVE
souvent, *often*	plus souvent, *oftener*	le plus souvent, *oftenest*
tard, *late*	plus tard, *later*	le plus tard, *latest*

Three adverbs, *bien, mal, peu,* form their comparatives irregularly, as follows:

POSITIVE	COMPARATIVE	SUPERLATIVE
bien, *well*	mieux, *better*	le mieux, *best*
mal, *badly*	pis, *worse*	le pis, *worst*
peu, *few*	moins, *fewer*	le moins, *least*

Note the similarity between the compared forms of these adverbs and the corresponding forms of their correlated adjectives.

POSITIVE	COMPARATIVE	SUPERLATIVE
bon, *good*	meilleur, *better*	le meilleur, *best*
mauvais, *bad*	pire, *worse*	le pire, *the worst*
petit, *small*	moindre, *smaller*	le moindre, *the smallest*

The expressions *plus mauvais, plus petit,* and *plus mal* may also be used, but never *plus bien, plus bon,* nor *plus peu.*

48. Concerning Some Adverbs. — *Beaucoup,* much, cannot be used with another adverb to be modified in meaning. Thus, *très beaucoup, trop beaucoup, si beaucoup* cannot be correctly said.

Bien, when used before an adverb, means *very* or *quite;* but after an adverb it has the meaning of *well.* Thus,

bien tard, *very late*   assez bien, *pretty well*
bien assez, *quite enough*   très bien, *very well*

Plus and *davantage* are synonymous in meaning, but are not interchangeable in use. *Davantage* cannot modify an adjective or be followed by *de* or *que.* It is to be preferred to *plus* at the end of a sentence or a sentential phrase or clause. *Plus tôt* means *sooner;* it is the comparative of *tôt,* soon. *Plutôt* has the meaning of *rather.*

LA PRÉPOSITION—THE PREPOSITION

49. Definition of the Preposition.—The **preposition** is almost the only part of speech that has been defined substantially in the same terms by nearly all grammarians. It is used to connect words and show the relation between them. It should be noted, however, that this word relation may be taken in different meanings in grammar. For example, in the sentence, *Paul est ennuyé*, Paul is weary, the word *est* placed between *Paul* and *ennuyé* establishes between them the relation of subject and attribute, and denotes that relation. But, when it is said that the preposition expresses a relation between two words, it is meant that the general sense of one is modified by the presence of the other. The expression *le livre*, the book, denotes any kind of book, a book in general. On the contrary, in *le livre de Pierre*, the signification which the word *livre* possessed before that addition is changed considerably; for, instead of being applied to all books in existence, it applies only to that book of which Peter has the property. There is then relation between *livre* and *Pierre*.

Between two words, relations of very different natures may be established. For example, between *je suis* and *eau* there may be a great many relations. We may have: *Je suis* **dans** *l'eau; je suis* **sur** *l'eau; je suis* **sous** *l'eau; je suis* **devant** *l'eau; je suis* **derrière** *l'eau; je suis* **contre** *l'eau;* etc. The kind of each of these relations is indicated by a different preposition.

The preposition is so called because it is always placed before (*pre*, before; position) the second term of the relation established. The prepositions are invariable, because the general idea of a relation between two objects does not seem to approach one more than the other, and there is no more reason for making the preposition agree with the preceding term than with the second; nor the second, than the preceding.

50. Origin of Prepositions. — The French language has taken most of its simple prepositions from the Latin. But in Latin, with its complicated system of declensions, prepositions were not of so much importance as in French after the suppression of declensions. More prepositions had then to be created. They have been derived from nouns, adjectives, verbs, and adverbs.

(*a*) *From Nouns.* — From the Latin word *casa*, house, has come *chez*, at, or to the house of; *parmi* comes from *per medium*, literally, *par le milieu*, by the middle; *malgré* from *mal* and *gré* (*volonté*) in spite of; etc.

(*b*) *From Adjectives.* — The preposition *sauf*, save, comes from the adjective *salvus;* etc.

(*c*) *From Imperative Verbs.* — Two prepositions, *voici* and *voilà*, are derived from old French imperatives. These words are composed of the adverbs *ci* and *là*, here and there, and of *voi*, which is the old imperative form of *voir*, to see. Originally, the imperative *vois* had no *s*. *Voici le livre*, therefore, signifies *Voyez ici le livre*, See the book here.

(*d*) From *past participles* have been derived the prepositions: *passé, vu, excepté, attendu*, to which may be added *hormis*, equivalent to *mis hors*, put out.

(*e*) From *present participles* of the verbs *durer, pendre, suivre, concerner, toucher* have come the prepositions *durant, pendant, suivant, concernant, touchant*.

(*f*) Most compound prepositions have been derived from adverbs coupled with the preposition *de;* as, *loin de, autour de, au devant de;* etc.

51. List of Prepositions. — The following is a list of the most commonly used prepositions:

à, *to,* or *at*	chez, *at,* or *to the house of*	de, *of,* or *from*
après, *after*		depuis, *since*
avant, *before*	contre, *against*	derrière, *behind*
avec, *with*	dans, *in*	dès, *as soon as*

devant, *before*
en, *in*
entre, *between*
envers, *toward*
hormis, *excepted*
hors, *out*
malgré, *in spite of*

nonobstant, *notwith-*
   standing
outre, *besides*
par, *by*
parmi, *among*
pendant, *during*
pour, *for*
près de, *near*

sans, *without*
selon, *according to*
sous, *under*
sur, *on*
vers, *toward*
voici, *here is, here are*
voilà, *there is, there are*

52. Compound Prepositions—The principal **compound prepositions** are:

à cause de, *on account of*
à côté de, *by the side of*
à l'exception de, *with the exception of*
à force de, *by dint of*
à propos de, *to the purpose of*
au dedans de, *inside of*
au devant de, *in the front of*
au dessus de, *above*

au dessous de, *below*
autour de, *around of*
en dépit de, *in spite of*
jusqu'à, *as far as*
loin de, *far from*
près de, *near to*
quant à, *as to*
vis à vis de, *opposite*

53. Classes of Prepositions. — Prepositions, being but the signs of relations between other words, have by themselves only an incomplete meaning. That word which completes their signification is generally called the **complement** of the preposition. Thus, in *aller à Paris, travailler pour lui*, the words *Paris* and *lui* are considered as the complements of the prepositions *à* and *pour*. In French the preposition, with its complement, is considered to be the *indirect object* of the verb. Thus, *à Paris, pour lui* are indirect objects of *aller* and *travailler*. These indirect objects have an adverbial value since they modify the meaning of the verb.

With reference to their adverbial value, prepositions have been divided into several groups. They denote:

(*a*) *place;* as, auprès, autour, sous, devant, derrière
(*b*) *time;* as, en, dans, depuis
(*c*) *end;* as, envers, pour, concernant
(*d*) *cause;* as, par, moyennant, attendu, vu
(*e*) *order;* as, avant, après, dès
(*f*) *union;* as, avec, pendant, selon, durant
(*g*) *separation;* as, sans, excepté, hors, hormis
(*h*) *opposition;* as, contre, malgré, nonobstant

54. **Concerning Some Prepositions.** — *A* with a grave accent is a preposition; but *a* without such accent is the third person singular of *avoir*. Thus,

> Cette dame **a** des amis **à** Paris, *This lady has friends in Paris.*

Des, as a preposition, takes the grave accent over its *e;* but *des*, the partitive article, has no accent. Thus,

> Je suis parti **dès** le matin pour **des** affaires sérieuses, *I started early in the morning* (literally, *as soon as morning*) *to look after* (literally, *for*) *important business.*

Sur and *sous* are prepositions and thus require an object, while *dessus* and *dessous* are adverbs and can have no object. Thus,

> Mon livre est **sous** la table; mettez le **dessus**, *My book is under the table,* put *it upon the table* (literally, *over*).
>
> Mon livre est **sur** la table; mettez-le **dessous**, *My book is on the table; put it under.*

Hors and *dans* are prepositions; their corresponding adverbs are *dehors*, and *dedans*. Thus,

> Il est **hors** la loi, *He is an outlaw.*
>
> Elle est **dans** sa chambre, *She is in her room.*
>
> Il fait froid **dehors**; venez **dedans**, *It is cold outside; come inside.*

Autour and *avant* are prepositions; their corresponding adverbs are *alentour* and *auparavant*. Thus,

> Si vous partez **avant** moi, écrivez-moi **auparavant**, *If you go before me, write to me beforehand.*
>
> Ils s'assirent **autour** du feu, pendant que les autres dansaient **alentour**, *They sat around the fire, while others were dancing about.*

LA CONJONCTION—THE CONJUNCTION

55. Functions of the Preposition and the Conjunction Compared.—As the word implies, a **conjunction** is, like the preposition, a word used for joining or connecting other sentential elements. There are, however, some differences that are easily seen between these two classes of words. Some of them are as follows:

1. Conjunctions sometimes connect sentences; prepositions never. Thus,

> Marie est allée à la ville, **mais** Catherine est
> restée à la maison, *Mary went to the city,*
> *but Kate remained at home.*

Here, the two sentences are joined by the conjunction *mais;* the preposition *à* connects *est allée* and *ville,* and *est restée* and *maison.*

2. Conjunctions connect words belonging to the same part of speech, or words used in the same way; prepositions may connect different parts of speech.

3. Conjunctions do not, and prepositions always do, take after them a noun or pronoun to form phrases that modify other words.

CLASSES OF CONJUNCTONS

56. Conjunctions are divided into two principal classes, *conjonctions de coordination*, coordinating conjunctions, and *conjonctions de subordination*, subordinating conjunctions.

57. Coordinating Conjunctions.—The word *coordinating* means making of equal rank or importance. The conjunctions of this class are so called because they unite two elements without at the same time reducing one of them to the inferior rank of a mere modifier of the meaning of the other element. Hence, these conjunctions serve mainly to connect. The conjunctions belonging to this class are: *et, ou, ni, mais,* or, *car, donc.* Of these, the conjunction *et,* and, is perhaps oftener used than all other conjunctions taken together. It may be regarded as the plus sign of the language; for, when placed between two words, phrases, or sentences, it denotes that they are to be thought of as united—their sum of meaning is to be taken.

58. **Subordinating Conjunctions.**—We have seen that coordinating conjunctions may connect words, phrases, or clauses. This, however, is not the case with the subordinating conjunction; for it is almost invariably used to unite clauses. It does this in such a manner as to make one of the clauses a mere modifier; and in consequence of this inferior or subordinate relation of the modifying clause, the conjunction that introduces it is called a **subordinating conjunction.** Thus,

Vous tomberez **si** vous ne faites pas attention,
You will fall if you are not careful.

On le renvoya **parce qu'**il n'était pas capable,
He was dismissed because he was incompetent.

In these sentences, the subordinate clauses have the value of adverbs, and they generally modify the meaning of the entire independent or principal clause.

59. **Subdivisions of Subordinating Conjunctions.** Subordinating conjunctions, in consequence of differences in adverbial meaning or value, are subdivided into the following classes:

1. *Time,* quand, pendant que, comme, jusqu'à.
2. *Cause and condition,* parce que, si, à moins que, néanmoins, quoique.
3. *Purpose,* que, pour que.

60. **Concerning Conjunctions.**—*Que* may be either a relative pronoun, an adverb, or a conjunction. In the first case it represents a noun; in the second, it has the sense of *how*, *how much;* in the third, it serves to unite two propositions. Thus,

PRONOUN: L'homme **que** je vois est âgé, *The man I see is old.*

ADVERB: **Que** vous êtes riche!   *How rich you are!*

CONJUNCTION: Il est aussi grand **que** mon frère, *He is as tall as my brother.*

Ou, or, when a conjunction has no accent; the adverb *où*, where, has a grave accent over the *u*. Thus,

ADVERB: **Où** allez-vous?   *Where are you going?*

CONJUNCTION: Je vais à Paris **ou** à Londres, *I am going to Paris or London.*

L'INTERJECTION–THE INTERJECTION

61. The Use of the Interjection.—As the word indicates, **interjections** (*inter*, among, and *jectus*, thrown) are thrown among the words of a sentence to indicate feeling, not thought. Strong feeling of every kind—hatred, joy, fear, anger—is expressed by the interjection.

The principal interjections are:

ah! *hah!*	ha! *ah!*	oh! *oh!*
aïe! *ay!*	hélas! *alas!*	ouais! *dear me!*
bah! *pooh!*	hem! *humph!*	ouf! *oh!*
bast! *pooh!*	hein! *what!*	oui-dà! *indeed!*
chut! *hush!*	hé! *hey!*	or ça! *now!*
crac! *crack!*	hé bien! *well!*	paf! *bang!*
eh! *eh!*	hé quoi! *what!*	parbleu! *zounds!*
eh bien! *well!*	ho! *ho, ahoy!*	pouah! *faugh!*
fi! *fie!*	holà! *hallo!*	pouf! *bang!*
fi donc! *for shame!*	O! *O!*	zest! *pshaw!*

Besides these interjections, many other words, such as nouns, adjectives, verbs, and compound expressions, may be employed as interjections. Thus,

adieu! *good by!*	tiens! *well!*
courage! *courage!*	ma foi! *upon my faith!*
paix! *hush!*	grand Dieu! *heavens!*
silence! *hush!*	juste ciel! *dear me!*
allons! *go ahead!*	miséricorde! *dear me!*
bon! *good!*	gare! *look out!*

FORMATION OF WORDS

62. Origin of Words. — In all languages, words have their history; none have been formed spontaneously. When one studies them attentively, either in their forms or articulations, he is soon impressed with the analogy that exists between their structure and the ideas it is their purpose to convey to the mind. One is soon convinced that words do not owe their creation to hazard, but that many of them have been formed by **onomatopœia,** which means that the sound of a word is like the echo of the object represented. When, for example, it is said that the wind *souffle*, blows; that the door *grince*, creaks, that the sheep *bêle*, bleats, that the cat *miaule*, mews, etc., the analogy between these diverse articulations and the ideas they express strikes the mind immediately.

Not only are words used to paint phenomena that are perceived by the sense of hearing, but the human voice can also imitate, to a certain extent, the form, the action, and the manner of objects perceived by other senses. This is done by articulations that may be strong or feeble, grave or sharp, rude or soft, slow or rapid; in short, by sounds suggesting the phenomena it is desired to present to the mind. Even phenomena of a moral order, that is to say, those of which the idea is not directly perceived by the senses, present very close relations between the word and the idea. Between physical and moral ideas, analogies are in fact so easy to establish that a moral fact, according to the relation it has with a physical fact, and according to the painful or agreeable impression it produces upon the mind, has necessarily been characterized by the same signs and manifested in the language by the same articulations as its analogical signs of the physical order.

63. Derivation.—With onomatopœia, two other principles presided over the formation of words, *derivation* and
agglutination. A language composed of roots or stems
formed by onomatopœia would be very poor if, to express
all sensations, all ideas, it possessed nothing but those
simple and primitive words furnished by imitation. Once
the primitive words invented, they acquired certain modifications to correspond to those of the general thought they
express. An example will more clearly illustrate this
principle: the onomatopœia in *coquerico*, cock-a-doodle-do,
awakens in the mind the idea of an animal, *Le coq*, the cock.
If to the stem *coq* we add *et*, which is a diminutive, we
obtain *coquet* or *cochet*, a small cock, or, figuratively, a man
who has the gait, conduct, or carriage of a cock. The
addition of *er* indicates the action of the *coquet*, and gives
coqueter. The feathers of the *coq*, serving as a sign of rally-
ing, will be called *cocarde*. A flower, the color of which
resembles the cock's comb, is called *le coquelicot*, wild
poppy, etc. In the same way, the stem *cri* has formed
crier, *crieur*, *criard*, etc. These terminations thus added to
the stem are called *suffixes*.

64. Agglutination or Composition.—Agglutination may be made in two different manners:
1. By uniting in one word two or more simple words—
noun, adjective, or verb—sometimes joined by a hyphen,
sometimes not; as, *garde-fou*, hand-rail; *portefeuille*, pocket-
book, etc.
2. By placing before the stem one or more particles
called *prefixes*, which modify the sense of that stem by joining to it their own signification. Thus, from *faire*, to do,
the following are formed by adding prefixes: *défaire*, to
undo; *refaire*, to do again; *contrefaire*, to counterfeit; *par-
faire*, to perfect; *surfaire*, to overcharge.

TABLE I

LATIN PREFIXES

Prefix	Modified Forms	Meaning	Examples
a	ab, abs, av	from, away	aversion, abjurer, abuser, abject, abstraction, abstenir, amovible
ad	ap, af, ac, ag, at, as, an, al, ar, a	to, at, toward	apporter, admission, acclimater, affaiblir, agglomérer, attention, assister, annihiler, allier, arriver, avis
anti	ante, anté	before, against	antichambre, antiphrase, antédiluvien, antechrist, antisocial
bis	bi	twice	bicolore, biscuit, bimane, bipède
circum	circom, circon	about, around	circonscrire, circonférence, circumnavigation
con	com, col, cor, co	together, with	concitoyen, compère, collision, corrompre, cohabiter
contra	contro, contre	counter, against	contraste, contredire, contrevent, controverser
dé	des	remove	décourager, déshonorer, déranger
dis	di, dif	away, apart	discontinuer, disjoindre, disparaître, diffamer, divulguer
éx	é, es, ef	out	éborgner, échauder, exhumer, expatrier, effeuiller, effacer
extra		beyond, out of	extravagant, extraordinaire
in	im, en, em, il, ir	in, into, not, upon	inanimé, imberbe, illégal, irréparable, emporter, enterrer
inter	entre	between	intéresser, interdire, intermédiaire
intro		in, within	entresol, introduire
mé	mes, mal	ill, badly	médire, mécontent, mésaventure, maléfice
ob	oc, of, op	against, before	obstacle, occasion, offrir, opposer, oppresser
per	par	through, by, very	perfection, parcourir
post		after	postérieur, postérité
pré		before	prévision, précéder, précoce
pro	por, pour	for, forth, forwards	projeter, pronom, pourvoir, poursuivre, portrait
re	red, ré, r	again, back	rebâtir, reconnaître, réformer, rhabiller, ravoir
rétro		back, backwards	retrograde, rétrocession, rétroactif
sé		apart, aside	sécurité, sédition, séparer
siné	sin, sim	without	sinécure, sincère, simple

TABLE I – (Continued)

Prefix	Modified Forms	Meaning	Examples
sub	sup, suf, suc, sug, su, sou, sous, se, subter	under, up	subir, subjonctif, supporter, suffire, suffoquer, succomber, suggérer, sujet, soutenir, souscrire, secourir, subterfuge
super	sur, sus	above, over	superflu, surcroît, suspendre, supérieur, superlatif
trans	tra, très, tré	beyond, over	transplanter, transatlantique, trépasser, travestir

TABLE II
GREEK PREFIXES

Prefix	Modified Forms	Meaning	Examples
a	an	privation, without	acéphale, anarchie, athée, atone
amphi		two, double	amphibie, amphithéatre
ana		aside, change	anachorète, anagramme
anti	ant	against	antithèse, antonyme
auto		self	autographe, automobile
apo	aph	from, away	apologie, aphorisme
archi		high degree	archipel, architecte
dia		through	diadème, diaphane, diagonale, diamètre, dialogue
epi	eph	upon	épitaphe, épidémie, épilogue
hemi		half	hémicycle, hémisphère
hypo		under	hypoténuse, hypothèse, hypocrisie
méta		beyond, over	métaphysique, métaphore, métamorphose
mono		one, alone	monogramme, monomanie
para	par	against, beside	paradoxe, parabole, paragraphe, parodie, parasite, parallèle
peri		around	pericarpe, périhélie, périmètre
pan	panto	all	panacée, panoplie, panorama, pantographe, pantomime
poly		several	polysyllabe, polyglotte, polygone
syn	sym, syl, sy	together	syntaxe, sympathie, syllabe

PREFIXES

65. List of Prefixes. — **Prefixes,** though chiefly prepositions, are sometimes adverbs, and are taken from the Latin, Greek, or French language itself. The Latin and Greek prefixes are inseparable; that is, they are always joined to the stem to form a new word, while most French prefixes are separated from the stem by a hyphen.

66. French Prefixes. — Besides prefixes taken from the Latin or Greek languages, the French has also formed new words by using its own prefixes taken from the following prepositions:

après, *after*	entre, *between*
avant, *before*	sans, *without*
arrière, *behind*	sous, *under*
contre, *against*	sur, *upon*

Compounds have also been formed from the adverb *non,* no.

These prefixes are not joined directly to the noun, but are separated from it by a hyphen, — except *sur,* which is joined directly to the radical. Thus,

après-demain, *the day after tomorrow*	non-valeur, *waste*
après-midi, *afternoon*	sans-façon, *off-hand manner*
arrière-cour, *backyard*	sans-culotte, *soldier of the French Revolution*
arrière-garde, *rear guard*	sous-lieutenant, *second lieutenant*
contre-ordre, *counter order*	
contre-poison, *antidote*	sous-louer, *to sublet*
entre-deux, *middle space*	surnaturel, *supernatural*
entre-temps, *meantime*	surnommer, *to surname*
non-sens, *nonsense*	

SUFFIXES

67. As the word indicates (*literally,* fixed at the end), **suffixes** are the syllables that end words; they express secondary ideas added to the principal idea. Suffixes have not so much power in modifying the fundamental meaning of a word as prefixes. For this reason, their influence is often too subtle to be recorded, and it would be impossible to prepare a system of general rules that would indicate the different shades of meaning given words to which suffixes are added. The most important of these suffixes will be studied from the point of view of their resemblance to English suffixes.

Many words of Latin origin have passed from French into English, either without alteration, or with such slight changes as English spelling has required.

COMPARISON OF FRENCH AND ENGLISH SUFFIXES

68. able. — This suffix, which is the same in French and English, is added to a verb to form an adjective. It implies the ability to do the action expressed by the verb. Thus,

aimable, *amiable*	acceptable, *acceptable*
admirable, *admirable*	remarquable, *remarkable*
charitable, *charitable*	passable, *passable*

69. ace. — Many nouns ending in *ace* are the same in French and English. Thus,

grâce, *grace*	menace, *menace*
place, *place*	race, *race*
surface, *surface*	trace, *trace*

These words are all feminine, with the exception of *espace*, space.

70. ade. — Most nouns having this suffix are the same in both languages. They are all feminine, with the exception of *le grade*, the grade. Thus,

brigade, *brigade*	grade, *grade*
camarade, *comrade*	limonade, *lemonade*
parade, *parade*	ambuscade, *ambuscade*

71. age. — This suffix, common to both languages, forms many nouns and a few adjectives. Thus,

âge, *age*	village, *village*
page, *page*	rage, *rage*
image, *image*	courage, *courage*

These nouns are generally masculine, with few exceptions (see Part 4, Art. **30,** 14).

72. ain. — The suffix *ain* becomes *an* in English, and is used to form nouns and adjectives, most of which denote nationality. Thus,

Africain, *African*	républicain, *republican*
Américain, *American*	puritain, *puritan*
Romain, *Roman*	humain, *human*

These nouns are masculine.

73. aire. — With this suffix, both adjectives and nouns are formed. The English suffix, however, is *ary* for nouns, and *ary* or *ar* for adjectives. Thus,

vocabulaire, *vocabulary*	nécessaire, *necessary*
dictionnaire, *dictionary*	vulgaire, *vulgar*
notaire, *notary*	populaire, *popular*

Nouns ending in *aire* are generally masculine. (See exceptions, Part 4, Art. **30,** 16).

74. al. — Nouns and adjectives formed with the suffix *al* are the same in French and English. Thus,

général, *general*	moral, *moral*
canal, *canal*	final, *final*
animal, *animal*	légal, *legal*

Nouns ending in *al* are masculine.

75. ance. — Nouns ending in *ance* are generally common to both languages, and are all feminine. Thus,

chance, *chance*	assurance, *assurance*
tempérance, *temperance*	balance, *balance*
alliance, *alliance*	assistance, *assistance*

76. ant.—Many nouns common to both languages are formed with the suffix *ant*. The present participle, in French, also ends in *ant*, and is equivalent to *ing* in English. It may be used as an adjective. Thus,

pédant, *pedant*   finissant, *finishing*
ascendant, *ascendant*   rendant, *rendering*
vigilant, *vigilant*   charmant, *charming*

Nouns ending in *ant* are masculine

77. at.—A few French nouns ending in *at* end in *ate* in English. These nouns are all masculine. Thus,

candidat, *candidate*   consulat, *consulate*
sénat, *senate*   certificat, *certificate*
prélat, *prelate*   magistrat, *magistrate*

78. ége.—A small number of nouns ending in *ége* are common to both languages. Thus,

collége, *college*   siége, *siege*
privilége, *privilege*   sacrilége, *sacrilege*

These nouns are masculine with the exception of *l'allége*, the window sill.

79. el.—This suffix serves to form adjectives and corresponds to *al* in English. Thus,

annuel, *annual*   sensuel, *sensual*
paternel, *paternal*   maternel, *maternal*
personnel, *personal*   fraternel, *fraternal*

80. ence.—Almost all nouns ending in *ence* are the same in both languages. A few, however, in English end in *cy*. They are all feminine, except *le silence*, silence. Thus,

prudence, *prudence*   clemence, *clemency*
indolence, *indolence*   urgence, *urgency*
violence, *violence*   patience, *patience*

81. ent.—Many nouns and adjectives having this suffix are the same in both languages. Thus,

instrument, *instrument*   accident, *accident*
absent, *absent*   content, *content*
moment, *moment*   diligent, *diligent*

Nouns ending in *ent* are masculine, with the exception of *la dent*, the tooth, and *la gent*, the race.

82. eur. — Many nouns and a few adjectives have the suffix *eur*, which becomes *or* in English. Thus,

directeur, *director*   docteur, *doctor*
ambassadeur, *ambassador*   supérieur, *superior*
professeur, *professor*   antérieur, *anterior*

83. eux. — A certain number of adjectives ending in *eux* correspond to English adjectives terminating in *ous*. Thus,

ambitieux, *ambitious*   studieux, *studious*
courageux, *courageous*   laborieux, *laborious*
envieux, *envious*   dangereux, *dangerous*

84. ible. — Many adjectives are formed by joining this suffix to a verb, and are common to both languages. Thus,

terrible, *terrible*   horrible, *horrible*
sensible, *sensible*   invisible, *invisible*
possible, *possible*   insensible, *insensible*

85. ice. — Many French and English nouns are formed with the suffix *ice*. Thus,

avarice, *avarice*   notice, *notice*
justice, *justice*   service, *service*
vice, *vice*   sacrifice, *sacrifice*

86. atie, ie. — These suffixes form a certain number of nouns, but the suffix *atie* becomes *acy* in English, and *ie* becomes *y*. Thus,

anarchie, *anarchy*   aristocratie, *aristocracy*
folie, *folly*   démocratie, *democracy*
furie, *fury*   diplomatie, *diplomacy*

87. ien. — This suffix, which is changed into *ian* in English, is used to form nouns and adjectives. Thus,

musicien, *musician*   Egyptien, *Egyptian*
Italien, *Italian*   logicien, *logician*
Parisien, *Parisian*   comédien, *comedian*

Nouns ending in *ien* denote nationality or profession, and are masculine.

88. **if.**—Many adjectives are formed with this suffix, which becomes *ive* in English. Thus,

attentif, *attentive*   instructif, *instructive*
actif, *active*   pensif, *pensive*
passif, *passive*   décisif, *decisive*

89. **il, ile.**—Many adjectives and nouns common to both languages are formed from these suffixes. Thus,

civil, *civil*   stérile, *sterile*
volatil, *volatile*   fragile, *fragile*
fossile, *fossil*   fertile, *fertile*

90. **in.**—This suffix, *ine* in English, is added to many words. Thus,

féminin, *feminine*   sanguin, *sanguine*
masculin, *masculine*   aquilin, *aquiline*
marin, *marine*   cristallin, *crystalline*

91. **ique.**—This suffix corresponds to the *ic* of English nouns and the *ic* or *ical* of English adjectives. Thus,

musique, *music*   pacifique, *pacific*
république, *republic*   logique, *logical*
logique, *logic*   historique, *historical*

92. **ion.**—Many nouns with this suffix are common to both languages. Thus,

nation, *nation*   notion, *notion*
position, *position*   portion, *portion*
passion, *passion*   profession, *profession*

They are generally feminine.

93. **oire.**—This suffix, *ory* in English, has been added to many French words. Thus,

obligatoire, *obligatory*   histoire, *history*
gloire, *glory*   directoire, *directory*
victoire, *victory*   conservatoire, *conservatory*

94. **ède, ide, rbe, rde, rme, sme, ste, xte, xe.** — The words common to both languages formed with these suffixes, drop the final *e* in English. Thus,

bipède, *biped*   spasme, *spasm*
acide, *acid*   artiste, *artist*
verbe, *verb*   prétexte, *pretext*
corde, *cord*   préfixe, *prefix*
terme, *term*   suffixe, *suffix*

95. **té.** — This suffix is changed into *ty* in English. Thus,

charité, *charity*   liberté, *liberty*
beauté, *beauty*   qualité, *quality*
député, *deputy*   société, *society*

96. **tre, bre.** — Many nouns ending in *tre* or *bre* in French end in *ter* or *ber* in English. Thus,

neutre, *neuter*   décembre, *December*
octobre, *October*   nombre, *number*

97. **ure.** — This suffix is the same in both languages and appears in many nouns. Thus,

agriculture, *agriculture*   littérature, *literature*
culture, *culture*   censure, *censure*
nature, *nature*   aventure, *adventure*

DIMINUTIVE SUFFIXES

98. These suffixes are added to a word to indicate that its meaning is restricted or depreciated. The following are the most important:

aille,
{ ferraille, *old iron;* from fer, *iron*
{ pierraille, *broken stones;* from pierre, *stone*

as, asse (fem.),
{ paperasse, *old paper;* from papier, *paper*
{ coutelas, *cutlas;* from couteau, *knife*

âtre,
{ blanchâtre, *whitish;* from blanc, *white*
{ noirâtre, *blackish;* from noir, *black*

cule,
{ animalcule, *animalcule;* from animal, *animal*
{ monticule, *hillock;* from mont, *hill*

eau, el, elle, { cordeau, *line;* from corde, *cord*
                { ruelle, *lane;* from rue, *street*

et, ette,   { fillette, *small girl;* from fille, *girl*
                { jardinet, *small garden*; from jardin, *garden*

ille,   { faucille, *sickle;* from faux, *scythe*
                { flottille, *flotilla;* from flotte, *fleet*

on,   { cordon, *twist;* from corde, *cord*
                { carafon, *small flagon;* from carafe, *decanter*

WORDS USED AS NOUNS

99. Other parts of speech may be used as nouns; as, for example:

1. The infinitive. Thus,

le manger, *the eating*   le rire, *the laugh*
le boire, *the drinking*   le dormir, *the sleep*

2. The present participle. Thus,

le vivant, *the person alive*   le tranchant, *the edge*

3. The past participle. Thus,

un fait, *a fact*   un reçu, *a receipt*
une entrée, *an entrance*

4. The adjective. Thus,

le beau, *the beautiful*   le riche, *the rich man*
le pauvre, *the poor man*

5. Adverbs, prepositions, and conjunctions. Thus,

le pourquoi, *the wherefore*
le pour et le contre, *the pro and con*
les si et les mais, *the ifs and buts*

FRENCH GRAMMAR

(PART 6)

THE STUDY OF SENTENCES

ANALYSE—ANALYSIS

1. Analyse.—The word *analysis* means a taking apart; it is the opposite of *synthesis*, a putting together. In its general sense, **analysis** is the decomposition of the whole into its constitutive parts, into its primordial elements. This word has many significations. It is used in speaking of physical things, as the analysis of a liquid, of a substance; also in speaking of moral things, as the analysis of the faculties of the soul; finally in speaking of the works of intelligence, as the analysis of a book.

In grammar, **analysis** is the decomposition of a phrase into its different elements.

2. Different Kinds of Analysis in Grammar.—We may consider words to be the elements of a sentence, or we may consider the sentence to be formed of clauses or propositions. In the first case, the decomposition of a sentence into words constitutes *analyse grammaticale*, grammatical analysis. In the second case, the decomposition of the sentence is called *analyse logique*, logical or sentential analysis.

ANALYSE GRAMMATICALE—GRAMMATICAL ANALYSIS

3. Grammatical analysis decomposes the sentence into words. When a being or object is presented to the mind, we necessarily examine it from a triple point of view. We first examine its nature, to ascertain whether it is a plant

§ 21

or an animal; what kind of plant, what kind of animal. When its nature has been determined, we examine its form. If it is a dog, we notice in what respects it differs from other dogs. The study of its form will tell us whether the dog is male or female, young or old, handsome or ugly, fat or thin, large or small. Having learned both its nature and form, we need only to know its function to complete our idea. Does it watch the house? or is it used for hunting? etc.

In the same way grammar teaches us to study words under three aspects: their *nature*—to ascertain whether they are adjectives or verbs, articles or nouns; their *form*—to find out whether they are masculine or feminine in gender, singular or plural in number; and finally to examine their *function* in the sentence—to learn whether they are subjects, or objects. When a word has thus been studied, our idea about that word is complete.

The preceding parts of this grammar have given us the means of finding the nature and the form of a word. It remains now to study the function of words in sentences.

FUNCTION OF WORDS

LE SUJET—THE SUBJECT

4. Le Sujet.—In any sentence, a word or phrase may make the action denoted by the verb or be in the state or condition expressed by the verb. This word or phrase is then said to be **le sujet,** the subject, of the verb. Thus, in the sentence, *L'enfant étudie sa leçon*, The child is studying his lesson, *l'enfant* is doing the action expressed by the verb *étudier* and is called the subject of the verb.

The same word may be at the same time the subject of several verbs, for the same individual may, at the same time, perform several actions. Thus,

Charles va à l'école, travaille beaucoup et fait des progrès, *Charles goes to school, works much, and makes progress.*

In this sentence Charles is the subject of *va*, *travaille*, and *fait*.

Several words may also be the subject of a single verb, for several beings may perform together the same action. Thus,

Jean et sa sœur vont à l'école, *John and his sister go to school*.

5. Of the ten classes of words, the verb is the only word that expresses an action, and consequently is the only word that can have a subject. The subject of the imperative form of the verb is generally understood. Thus,

(Vous) venez, (*you*) *come;* (vous) allez, (*you*) *go*.

6. **Words That May Be the Subject.** — The subject of a verb may be represented by:

1. A noun. Thus,

Le **printemps** est le peintre de la nature, *Spring is the painter of nature*.

Le **malheur** nous rend très bons ou très mauvais, *Misfortune makes us very good or very bad*.

2. A pronoun. Thus,

Celui qui n'a pas ce qu'il aime, doit aimer ce qu'il a, *He who has not what he likes, must like what he has*.

On est bien près d'être ingrat quand **on** discute la valeur d'un service rendu, *One comes very near to being ungrateful in discussing the value of a rendered service*.

3. Any word taken as a noun. Thus,

Trois et **quatre** font sept, *Three and four are seven*.

Le **mieux** est l'ennemi du bien, *The best is the enemy of the good*.

4. By an infinitive. Thus,

Mourir pour sa patrie est le sort le plus beau, *To die for one's country is the most happy fate*.

Aimer ne dépend pas de la volonté, *To love does not depend upon the will*.

5. By a proposition. Thus,

Il vous faut est fort bon, mon moulin est à moi tout aussi bien, au moins, que la Prusse est au roi, *You must have is very good, my mill belongs to me just as well, at least, as Prussia belongs to the king.*

COMPLÉMENTS — COMPLEMENTS

7. Compléments, complements, in grammar, are any words or phrases that serve to complete an idea expressed by another word or phrase. Words that may have a complement are the *verb*, the *noun*, the *adjective*, the *participle*, the *preposition*, and the *adverb*. Thus,

Il chante une chanson, *He is singing a song.*

Elle a un cœur de mère, *She has a mother's heart.*

Il est plein d'ambition, *He is full of ambition.*

Cet enfant est chéri de ses parents, *This child is cherished by his parents.*

Il est venu avec moi, *He came with me.*

Il a beaucoup de courage, *He has much courage.*

COMPLEMENTS OF THE VERB

8. The verb may have three kinds of complements: *complément direct*, direct object; *complément indirect*, indirect object; *complément circonstanciel*, circumstantial complement.

9. Complément Direct. — The **direct object** is the word that receives *directly*, that is to say *without* the aid of a preposition, the action expressed by the verb. Thus,

Elevez bien votre **fils,** et il consolera votre **vieillesse,** *Bring up your son well, and he will comfort you in your old age.*

Fils is the direct object of *élevez*, and *vieillesse* of *consolera.*

The direct object of a verb may be:

1. A noun. Thus,

Le chagrin compte les **secondes;** le bonheur oublie les **heures,** *Chagrin counts the seconds; happiness forgets the hours.*

2. A pronoun. Thus,

Celui qui **vous** flatte est votre ennemi, *He who flatters you is your enemy.*

Elle s'est brûlée, *She has burned herself.*

3. An infinitive. Thus,

Celui qui ne sait pas **obéir** ne sait pas **commander,** *He who does not know how to obey, does not know how to command.*

4. A clause or proposition. Thus,

Dieu dit: "Que la lumière soit," et la lumière fut, *God said: "Let there be light," and there was light.*

Transitive verbs only can have a direct object.

10. **Complément Indirect.** — The **indirect object** is the word that receives indirectly; that is to say, *with* the aid of a preposition, the action expressed by the verb. Thus,

L'exilé songe **à sa patrie,** *The exile thinks of his country.*

Rome fut prise **par les Gaulois,** *Rome was taken by the Gauls.*

Je **lui** parle, *I am speaking to him.*

11. **Complément Circonstanciel.** — Circumstantial complements are complements that complete the sense of the verb by adding to it a definite idea of place, time, manner, cause, etc. They are, in fact, mere adverbial phrases. Thus,

PLACE: On va **de France, en Italie, par la Suisse,** *One goes from France to Italy through Switzerland.*

TIME: La plupart des oiseaux partent **avant l'hiver,** et reviennent **au printemps,** *Most birds depart before winter and return in the spring.*

MANNER: Il régna **avec sagesse,** *He reigned with wisdom.*

CAUSE: On étudie **pour s'instruire,** *One studies to be learned.*

There is a close resemblance between the form of the indirect object and that of the circumstantial complement. The first, however, answers the questions in what, to whom, with what, etc., while the second answers the questions where, when, how, why, etc.

COMPLEMENTS OF THE NOUN

12. Every word that completes the sense of a noun, with or without a preposition, is said to be a **complement of the noun**. Thus,

Les yeux sont le miroir **de l'âme**, *The eyes are the mirror of the soul.*

J'ai rencontré votre professeur **de musique**, *I met your music teacher.*

COMPLEMENTS OF THE ADJECTIVE

13. The sense of the adjective, like that of the noun, may be completed by a preposition followed by a noun. Thus,

L'avare est digne **de pitié**, *The miser is deserving of pity.*

A **quelque chose** malheur est bon, *Misfortune is good for something.*

COMPLEMENTS OF THE PARTICIPLE

14. Any word that completes the sense of the participle without the aid of a preposition is called the **complement of the participle**. Thus,

Votre mère est une personne obligeant **tout le monde**, *Your mother is an obliging person to everybody.*

COMPLEMENTS OF THE PREPOSITION

15. Prepositions are the signs of relation, and have, by themselves, an incomplete sense. The words which complete that sense are called the **complements of the preposition**. Thus,

Je parle de **mes amis**, *I am speaking of my friends.*

In this sentence *mes amis* is the complement of the preposition *de*.

Many grammarians, and with good reason, contend that the preposition has no complement. In the sentence above, *de mes amis* is considered as the indirect object of *parle*, and *de* is analyzed as a preposition showing the relation between *parle* and *mes amis*. In Latin, prepositions had an effect on the form of the following word. So in that language the preposition may be said to have really had a *régime*. The preposition has no such influence in French. Because in all cases the old word *regime* was translated by *complément*, French grammarians have said that the preposition has a complement, while its most important function is to indicate relation.

COMPLEMENTS OF THE ADVERB

16. The adverb, having a complete sense in itself, generally has no complement. The following adverbs, however, must be excepted:

1. *Adverbs of Quantity.*—The adverbs *assez, autant, beaucoup, bien, combien, guère, infiniment, moins, beu, plus, que, tant, telle, trop* take a complement introduced by the preposition *de*. Thus,

assez de paroles, *enough words*
beaucoup de monde, *many people*
combien d'hommes, *how many men*
moins de bruit, *less noise*

2. *Adverbs of Manner.*—Some adverbs of manner derived from adjectives also take a complement; as, *conformément, contrairement, relativement*, etc.

APPOSITION—APPOSITION

17. A noun or pronoun is said to be in **apposition** with another noun or pronoun when the two are placed together in the same case and denote the same person or thing. Thus,

Je suis Charles, votre ami, *I am Charles, your friend.*
La ville de Paris, *The city of Paris.*

Ami and *Paris* are, respectively, in apposition with *Charles* and *ville*.

PLEONASME—PLEONASM

18. Pleonasme.—The word **pleonasm** is derived from a Greek word meaning more. Pleonasm is the introduction or use of superfluous words in a sentence. The pleonastic construction is used to add emphasis to the statement made.

When rightly employed, pleonasm adds much to the impressiveness and elegance of a sentence; but when abused, it is one of the worst faults of poor composition. The French language is peculiarly rich in pleonastic construction; indeed it is one of the most striking beauties of this language. Observe its effect in these examples:

Le roi, il est mort, *The king, he is dead.*

Ecouter, c'est s'instruire, *To listen, that is to instruct oneself.*

L'Etat, c'est moi, *I am the state.*

MODEL OF GRAMMATICAL ANALYSIS

19.   Deux renards entrèrent la nuit par surprise dans un poulailler; ils étranglèrent le coq, les poules et les poulets; après ce carnage, ils apaisèrent leur faim, *Two foxes stole into a chicken yard by surprise during the night; they strangled the cock, the hens, and the chickens; after this carnage, they appeased their hunger.*—FÉNELON, *The Two Foxes.*

deux	Numeral cardinal adjective; determines *renards*
renards	Common noun, masculine plural; subject of *entrèrent*
entrèrent	Past definite indicative of the neuter verb *entrer*, third person plural, first conjugation
la	Definite article, feminine singular; indicates that *nuit* is taken in a determinate sense
nuit	Common noun, feminine singular, circumstantial complement of time of *entrèrent;* joined to the verb by the preposition *pendant* understood
par	Preposition; shows the relation between *entrèrent* and *surprise*
surprise	Common noun, feminine singular; circumstantial complement of manner of *entrèrent;* joined to the verb by the preposition *par*
dans	Preposition; shows a relation of place between *entrèrent* and *poulailler*
un	Indefinite article, masculine singular; determines *poulailler*
poulailler	Common noun, masculine singular, circumstantial complement of place of *entrèrent*
ils	Personal pronoun, third person masculine plural, in place of *renards;* subject of *étranglèrent*

étranglèrent	Past definite indicative of the active verb *étrangler*, third person plural, first conjugation
le	Definite article; indicates that *coq* is taken in a determinate sense
coq	Common noun, masculine singular; direct object of *étranglèrent*
les	Definite article, feminine plural; indicates that *poules* is taken in a determinate sense
poules	Common noun, feminine plural, direct object of *étranglèrent*
et	Conjunction; unites *poules* and *poulets*
les	Definite article, masculine plural; indicates that *poulets* is taken in a determined sense
poulets	Common noun, masculine plural; direct object of *étranglèrent*
après	Preposition; shows the relation between *carnage* and *apaisèrent*
ce	Demonstrative adjective, masculine singular; determines *carnage*
carnage	Common noun, masculine singular, circumstantial complement of manner of *apaisèrent*
ils	Personal pronoun, third person masculine plural, in place of *renards;* subject of *apaisèrent*
apaisèrent	Past definite indicative of the active verb *apaiser*, third person plural, first conjugation
leur	Possessive adjective, feminine singular; determines *faim*
faim	Common noun, feminine singular; direct object of *apaisèrent*

ANALYSE LOGIQUE—LOGICAL ANALYSIS

20. Unit of Thought in Grammar.—Every subject
has some central point of interest—some object or matter of
consideration that is of greater importance than any other
and to which everything else is secondary. Thus, in orthography, the word is the central idea; so, in grammar, there
must be some leading idea or *unit* that is of the greatest
interest and importance.

In orthography and etymology, it is the word that fixes
the attention; but these are divisions of grammar that are
only preparatory to the study of a very much more important
branch of the subject—syntax, the science of the sentence.
Grammar deals primarily with thought and the forms in

which thought is expressed by speech and writing. It is true that words are necessary to the expression of thought; but there is nothing fixed or constant about words. All the words that we use have been divided into classes, but there are thousands of them that cannot be classified until it is ascertained what duty or function they perform in a sentence. It is in the sentence, therefore, that words perform the functions for which they were devised; it is in the sentence that they have their usefulness, their interest, and their full significance. They are the materials of which men construct the wonderful edifice of expressed thought. Therefore, the **unit of thought** in grammar is the sentence.

21. Syntax. — The word **syntax** is derived from *syntaxis*, a Greek military term meaning to draw up into line a body of soldiers. In a similar manner, words are arranged, each in its proper place, to form a sentence that will express, in the best possible manner, a given thought. The syntax of a language treats of the combination of words into sentences, the various forms of sentences, the relation and government of their constituent parts.

Clearness is the distinctive quality of the French language: as this language has no declension, clearness depends essentially on the arrangement of words, and the construction of the sentence is therefore subject to exact laws.

THE SENTENCE

GENERAL CONSIDERATIONS

22. Arrangement of Words. — There are two ways in which words may be arranged: (1) independently, or out of relation to one another; (2) dependently, or in relation to one another. Thus, we may utter or write a number of words so that they will convey no thought. Thus,

est qui Dieu se l'souvient Cieux homme un tombé des.

Here, whatever meaning the words may have separately, they are all used independently, just as much so as a column of words in a spelling book. They are entirely out of relation; that is, the meaning of no word has any influence upon that of any other. They do not help one another to express a thought. Let us now place them in relation; that is, so that each one will do its share in expressing a thought — in making known some truth. Thus,

L'homme est un Dieu tombé qui se souvient des Cieux, *Man is a fallen God who remembers Heaven.*

The words used here are the same as in the preceding example, but the result is different. The words are now in relation, and they have a meaning, not only individually, but collectively. They are joined in such way as to express a thought, and the thought is complete. We see then that words are arranged in relation when by their union they help one another to express some meaning different from any of the meanings expressed by the words when taken separately.

23. Sentence Defined. — A word is usually defined as the sign of an idea. Thus, the word *homme*, man, calls up in the mind a mental image or representation of a particular kind of object, and the word *marche*, walks, a mental picture of an action performed by something that acts. These mind

pictures considered separately are *ideas*. But when we bring
two or more ideas into proper relation, we have a *thought*,
provided certain essential elements are present; and when,
either in speech or in writing, we properly join the words
that call up these ideas, the result is a sentence. Hence,
it appears that a sentence does for a thought just what a
word does for an idea; that is to say, if a spoken or a written
word is the sign of an idea, a spoken or written sentence is
the sign of a thought.

A **sentence** is a collection of uttered or written words
arranged in such order or relation as to express a complete
thought.

24. **Words Implied or Understood.** — Sentences sometimes seem to consist of but one word; as, *regardez*, look;
venez, come. The student will observe that these words
express action. Now, it is clear that every such word
requires us to think of an actor, although the word denoting
the actor is not expressed. Words that are thus necessary
to the completeness of a thought, but are not expressed,
are said to be *sous-entendus*, understood. . If, in the one-word
sentences just given, every necessary word were expressed,
the sentences would be (*vous*) *regardez;* (*vous*) *venez*.

In order, therefore, that a sentence may express a complete thought, it must consist of words arranged in proper
relation; and in order that this shall be possible, at least
two words are required. Of these two words, one may be
understood, but it must be clearly implied.

25. **Different Uses or Functions of Sentences.** — In
the communication of thought among men, there are only
three different uses or purposes that are served by sentences:

1. *To Make a Statement or Declaration.* — If a person has
some knowledge or information that he wishes to convey to
others, that is, if he wishes to *tell* something, he makes use
of a form of sentence called a **statement** or **declaration.**
Thus,

Celui qui vous flatte est votre ennemi, *He who flatters you
is your enemy.*

La reconnaissance est la mémoire du cœur, *Gratitude is memory of the heart.*

Celui qui a dix amis n'en a pas un, *He who has ten friends has not one.*

2. *To Ask a Question.* — A person may desire some information that he believes another person can furnish. In order to obtain it, he employs a form of sentence called a **question.** Thus,

Combien y a-t-il de Londres à Paris? *How far is it from London to Paris?*

Qu'entendez-vous par là? *What do you mean by that?*

Irez-vous à Paris l'année prochaine? *Will you go to Paris next year?*

3. *To Express a Command or an Earnest Wish or Entreaty.* A person may wish to impose his will upon others, or to have it known that he has a strong desire that something shall or shall not be or be done. To accomplish this object, he expresses his thought so as to indicate that it is a command or a wish. Thus,

Etudiez vos leçons, *Study your lessons.*

Ne m'abandonnez pas, *Do not abandon me.*

Quittez cette ville immédiatement, *Leave this city at once.*

Sentences, therefore, may be used to declare or tell, to inquire or question, and to command or entreat.

26. **Exclamatory Sentences.** — The thought expressed in sentences may be so mingled with strong feeling and emotions of every kind as to give the sentences an appearance of serving an entirely different use from those described above. Thus, a person may make a statement, ask a question, or express a command under the influence of such earnestness, anger, sorrow, or other emotion that the sentence becomes an *exclamation.* But utterance accompanied by feeling does not change a statement, a question, or a command into something else, for the emotion affects the sentence only in the manner of utterance. The use made of the sentence is still the same.

27. It must not be understood that every sentence has one of these three forms, for such is not the fact. Any two, or all three of these fundamental forms may be combined in a single sentence. Indeed, the variety of sentential structure is endless. Thus,

DECLARATIVE: Je vais à la gare;
INTERROGATIVE: Ne venez-vous pas avec moi?

I am going to the station; are you not coming with me?

SENTENTIAL ELEMENTS

28. Principal Parts of the Sentence. — We may say of nearly everything that can be pictured by the mind that it is capable of being or doing something; or we may deny that it has any such capacity of being or doing. Thus, of the things denoted by the word *le garçon*, the boy, many things may be affirmed or denied.

Le garçon {n'est pas studieux / n'est pas sage / n'est pas docile}   The boy {*is not studious* / *is not good* / *is not docile*}

These are *declarative* sentences. They are more frequently used than any other form of sentence. As the student has already learned, their office, or use, is to state or declare — to affirm or deny. By some slight and easy changes, they may be made *interrogative*.

Le garçon {n'est-il pas studieux? / n'est-il pas sage? / n'est-il pas docile?}   *Is not the boy* {*studious?* / *good?* / *docile?*}

In the imperative sentence, words are used in such way as to denote that some person or thing is ordered or entreated to do or be, or not to do or be, something or other.

(Vous) {soyez tranquille / ne partez pas}   (*You*) {*be quiet* / *do not go*}

In each of these sentences there are two parts; the work, or function, of each part is entirely different. The first part represents something that is capable of being or doing something or other; the second part represents this possible being or action. As long as these parts stand alone, they represent only ideas, but when they are properly joined by the verb, they express thoughts—they are sentences. Thus, we find three parts used in the sentences: *le sujet*, the subject; *le verbe*, the verb; *l'attribut*, the predicate; these three parts are called the **principal parts** of a sentence.

29.   The Verb. — French grammarians, up to the present day, have divided French verbs into two extremely unequal classes. On the one side, is placed the verb *être*, to be, which is the only verb acknowledged by them, and which is known to them as the *substantive verb*. On the other side all other verbs are placed and recognized as *attributive verbs*. Under this classification attributive verbs are thought to be formed of the verb *être*, and the present participle of the expressed attributive verb. Thus, *je marche* is equivalent to *je suis marchant; je mange*, to *je suis mangeant;* etc. This division is arbitrary, and has no foundation in the recent discoveries of grammar.

30.   Subject and Predicate Modified and Unmodified. — The subject and predicate of a sentence may each consist of one word or of many words; but, no matter how many words there are in each, there is nearly always one word that cannot be stricken from either without destroying the meaning of the entire sentence. These two parts that cannot be dispensed with sometimes consist of two words each, or even of more than two, so closely associated that they must be taken together. Thus, in the sentence, *Tous les matins, un bel oiseau au plumage brillant chante mélodieusement sous ma fenêtre*, Every morning, a beautiful bird with brilliant plumage sings melodiously under my window, the principal parts in full are: Subject, *un bel oiseau au plumage brillant;* verb, *est;* attribute, *chantant mélodieusement tous les matins sous ma fenêtre.*

When these parts are reduced to the simplest possible forms—when all modifiers of each are omitted—the sentence will be, *oiseau est chantant*. Here we have the naked or unmodified subject joined by the verb to the naked or unmodified predicate.

CLAUSE ELEMENTS

31. Definition of the Clause.—Two or more sentences may be made into one by means of conjunctions. After the union of these elements, they are no longer sentences, but *propositions*, clauses, of a sentence. Thus, the two sentences, *La terre est ronde*, The earth is round, and *Les hommes peuvent naviguer autour de la terre*, Men can sail around the earth, may be united into one sentence by using a conjunction, as any one of the following: *et, si, ainsi, alors, parce que, puisque, vu que*. Thus,

La terre est ronde **puisque** les hommes peuvent naviguer autour d'elle, *The earth is round, for men can sail around it.*

Here we have a new sentence consisting of two propositions, each having a subject, a verb, and a predicate. But sometimes, when separate sentences are united, slight changes are necessary. This happens in such cases as the following:

1. When the subjects in two or more of the sentences denote the same person or thing. Thus,

Le soleil se lève à l'est, *The sun rises in the east.*
Le soleil se couche à l'ouest, *The sun sets in the west.*
Le soleil se lève à l'est **et** se couche à l'ouest.
Les filles sont restées chez elles, *The girls stayed at home.*
Les filles ont fait l'ouvrage de la maison, *The girls did the housework.*
Les garçons sont allés se promener, *The boys went for a walk.*
Les filles sont restées chez elles, **et** ont fait l'ouvrage de la maison, **mais** les garçons sont allés se promener.

Here the statements are nearly complete, for the omitted subjects are clearly implied.

2. When two or more predicates are alike. Thus,

Le jour est triste, *The day is dreary.*
Le monde est triste, *The world is dreary.*
Ma vie est triste, *My life is dreary.*
Le jour et le monde et ma vie sont tristes.

A comparison of these sentences with those above will show that the clause elements are more nearly complete when all the predicates are retained than when only one appears. In other words, the predicate is by far the most important part of a sentence. Hence, a sentence has as many clauses as it has different predicates; for, if it be rightly constructed, the subjects that are not expressed are plainly implied. Moreover, the imperative regularly omits the subject, but the predicate can rarely be omitted.

FUNCTIONS OF CLAUSES

32. Clauses do a work in sentences as follows:

1. *A Clause May Have the Function of a Noun.*—In this relation, a clause may be:

(*a*) The subject of a sentence. Thus,

Que le prisonnier soit coupable paraît très douteux, *That the prisoner is guilty appears very doubtful.*

Ce que devint son ami n'a jamais été connu, *What became of his friend has never been known.*

(*b*) The predicate noun. Thus,

Le moment critique fut **quand il franchit le Rubicon,** *The critical moment was when he crossed the Rubicon.*

La question est, **qui fut l'inventeur de la machine à vapeur?** *The question is, who was the inventor of the steam engine?*

(*c*) The object of a verb. Thus,

Savez-vous **quand le train part pour Boston?** *Do you know when the train leaves for Boston?*

Il fit **ce qu'on lui avait dit,** *He did what he was told.*

(*d*) In apposition with a noun or pronoun. Thus,

Jeanne d'Arc, l'héroïne **qui sauva la France,** fut brûlée vive à Rouen, *Joan of Arc, the heroine who saved France, was burned at the stake at Rouen.*

2. *A Clause May Have the Function of an Adjective.* — Thus,

Le pays **que l'on découvrit** était habité par des sauvages, *The land that was discovered was inhabited by savages.*

3. *A Clause May Have the Function of an Adverb.* — Thus,

On l'enterra **où il tomba,** *They buried him where he fell.*

The clause *où il tomba* modifies the meaning of the verb *enterra.*

THE RANK OF CLAUSES

33. With respect to rank, there are two relations in which clauses may stand to one another.

1. *Clauses May Be of Equal Rank.* — When two or more sentences are united into one, the relation of the clauses in the resulting sentence is entirely dependent upon the kind of conjunction or other connective word used. If such words as *et, ou, mais, aussi,* and others of the class called **coordinating conjunctions** are used, the resulting sentence will consist of clauses equal in rank — each clause being of just as much importance as any other. Clauses connected by conjunctions of this class are *propositions coordonnées,* coordinate clauses. Thus,

Il finit son travail **et** reçut son salaire, *He finished his work, and received his salary.*

Je lirai **ou** j'écrirai, *I shall read or write.*

2. *Clauses May be of Unequal Rank.* — Clauses may be so joined in a sentence as to have unequal importance as sentential elements. For example, a clause may be nothing more than a noun in the function it fills, or it may be a mere modifier, doing the work of an adjective, or of an adverb.

Noun Clause: Il m'a montré **comment je dois lire,** *He showed me how I should read.*

Adjective Clause: Le château **que nous possédons maintenant** fut construit au XIV siècle, *The castle that we now own was built in the 14th century.*

Adverbial Clause: L'homme courageux travaille **pendant que le paresseux dort,** *The courageous man works while the idle sleeps.*

In the first sentence, the clause *comment je dois lire* is the object of the verb *a montré,* just as *sa maison* would be in the sentence *Il m'a montré sa maison.*   In the next sentence, the first clause *que nous possédons* modifies the word *château;* it is therefore an adjective clause.   In the last sentence the verb *travaille* is modified by the clause *pendant que le paresseux dort.* Clauses so used may generally be omitted without destroying the main sense of the sentence, for they serve only to add some circumstance or explanation to the meaning of a more important clause.   Such are called *propositions subordonnées,* subordinate or dependent clauses, because of their inferior importance as essential elements. The clause that expresses the main thought and has attached to it one or more helping or subordinate clause elements is called *proposition principale,* or *indépendante,* principal, or independent clause.

SUBORDINATING CONNECTIVES

34. The words used to unite principal and subordinate clauses are of three kinds: (1) Subordinating conjunctions; as, *si, à moins que, pourvu que, parce que.*   (2) Conjunctive adverbs; as, *quand, pendant que, où, après que, avant que.* (3) Relative pronouns; as, *qui, que, dont, lequel.*

FORMS OF SENTENCES

THE SIMPLE SENTENCE

35. **Twofold Classification of Sentences.** — We have seen that sentences considered with regard to the use that is made of them are divided into three classes.   If used to make a statement, they are *declarative;* if they express a question, they are *interrogative;* if used in commanding, entreating, or wishing, they are *imperative.* We have seen, too, that any one of these three classes may become *exclamatory.* But sentences have another and very important classification—one that has no regard to the use that sentences serve, but is based upon their form or structure.

36. The Simplest Sentential Structure.—The simplest sentential structure that a sentence can have is the form composed of two words, one the subject, the other the predicate (*verbe et attribut*). Thus,

Il chante. Qui frappe? Les oiseaux volent.

In the imperative sentence, the subject is generally omitted, but if it were not clearly implied there could be no thought expressed, and, therefore, no sentence. Thus,

(vous) $\begin{cases} \textbf{venez} \\ \textbf{allez} \end{cases}$ (you) $\begin{cases} come \\ go \end{cases}$

A **simple sentence** is a sentence composed of one subject, expressed or clearly implied, and one predicate.

37. Other Elements in a Simple Sentence.—The naked form of the simple sentence is not often met with in actual use; some other elements are usually added to the subject, or to the predicate, or to both. These elements may be words, but not clauses; when clauses enter, the sentence is no longer simple. Thus,

Subject	Modifiers	Predicate	Modifiers
enfants	$\begin{cases} \text{deux} \\ \text{petits} \\ \text{les mains rougies de} \\ \text{froid} \end{cases}$	passaient	$\begin{cases} \text{en ce moment} \\ \text{dans notre rue} \end{cases}$

Deux petits enfants, les mains rougies de froid, passaient en ce moment dans notre rue, *Two little children, their hands red with cold, were passing at that time in our street.*

38. Compound Members.—Two or more simple sentences may often be contracted into one sentence, which is itself simple. This is done by joining their like members by means of conjunctions.

Subjects Compounded

Jean va à l'école Sa sœur va à l'école	Jean et sa sœur vont à l'école, *John and his sister are going to school.*

La terre est-elle ronde comme une boule? La lune est-elle ronde comme une boule? Toutes les autres planètes sont-elles rondes comme une boule?	La terre, la lune, et toutes les autres planètes sont-elles rondes comme une boule? *Are the earth, the moon, and all other planets round like a ball?*

These are simple sentences with compound subjects.

Objects Compounded

Nous avons mangé du pain Nous avons mangé de la viande Nous avons mangé des légumes Nous avons mangé des fruits	Nous avons mangé du pain, de la viande, des légumes, et des fruits, *We eat bread, meat, vegetables, and fruit.*

Here we have a simple sentence with compound objects.

Predicate Nouns or Adjectives Compounded

M. Blaine était un orateur M. Blaine était un homme d'état M. Blaine était un patriote	M. Blaine était un orateur, un homme d'état et un patriote, *Mr. Blaine was an orator, a statesman, and a patriot.*

L'enfant a été sage L'enfant a été appliqué L'enfant a été heureux	L'enfant a été sage, appliqué et heureux, *The child has been good, laborious, and happy.*

Simple sentences are often very long. There is one condition necessary in order that a sentence may be simple — it must contain but one predicating verb.

THE COMPLEX SENTENCE

39. Definition of the Complex Sentence. — A sentence may be composed of two clauses of unequal rank. Thus,

Venez quand vous aurez le temps, *Come when you have time.*

Qui croit que la terre est plate? *Who believes that the earth is flat?*

"Qui êtes-vous?" **demanda-t-il,** *"Who are you?" he inquired.*

Dites-nous quelle heure il est, *Tell us what time it is.*

In these sentences, which are called *complex sentences*, the principal clauses are in black-faced type.

A sentence may contain several subordinate clauses, but so long as there is only one principal clause, it is still a complex sentence.

Il ne veut pas travailler
He does not want to work
{
bien qu'il soit jeune.
although he is young.
et qu'il soit bien portant.
and although he is in good health.
}

Quand on est riche
When one is rich
et qu'on est généreux
and when one is generous
}
on compte beaucoup d'amis,
one has many friends.

A **complex sentence** is a sentence consisting of one principal clause and one or more subordinate clauses.

THE COMPOUND SENTENCE

40. Definition of the Compound Sentence. — If, by the use of subordinating connectives, clauses be joined in such relation that one of them is more important than any of the others, the sentence is, as we have learned, complex. But, if coordinating connectives be used, the clauses joined will be of equal rank. If these coordinate clauses do not stand in an inferior or dependent relation to some more important clause, the sentence is called a *compound sentence*.

The simplest possible form of the compound sentence consists of two imperative clauses of which the subjects are
understood. Thus,

Allez et **voyez,** *Go and see.*

Lisez ou **écrivez,** *Read or write.*

Dormez et **reposez-vous,** *Sleep and rest.*

Other and longer compound sentences having two clauses
of equal rank — independent clauses and no dependent
clauses — are as follows:

Restez tranquille et **étudiez** votre leçon, *Sit still and
study your lesson.*

Nous **avons rencontré** et **repoussé** l'ennemi, *We met
and repulsed the enemy.*

Compound sentences may be lengthened by the addition
of subordinate clauses. Thus,

Quand nous partîmes, **il pleuvait,** mais **le ciel
était clair** avant que nous eussions atteint notre destination, *When we started the rain was falling, but the sky was
clear before we reached our destination.*

Ne vous fiez pas à celui qui fait beaucoup de pro-
messes, mais **fiez-vous plutôt à celui** qui en fait peu, *Do
not trust him that makes many promises, but trust rather him
that makes few.*

A **compound sentence** is a sentence composed of two
or more independent clauses, with or without subordinate
clauses.

***

SENTENTIAL ANALYSIS

ANALYSIS OF SIMPLE SENTENCES

41. To analyze simple sentences (containing one proposition only), it is necessary to find the three essential
parts — subject, verb, predicate — and to point out the modifiers, if any, of the subject and of the predicate. Let us,
for example, analyze the following sentence: *L'homme
avare est un être malheureux,* The avaricious man is an

unfortunate being. The subject is *l'homme*, modified by *le* and *avare;* the verb is *est;* the attribute is *être*, modified by *un* and *malheureux*.

42. **Analysis by Diagrams.** — In English, sentential analysis is usually done by means of diagrams, and, of these, many systems have been devised by different authors. The most serious objection that has been urged against analysis by diagrams, is that nearly all methods so separate sentential elements that the student is unable to put them together again. This objection is obviated in the scheme that is here explained.

43. **Conventional Signs.** — The principal parts of the sentence are pointed out as follows: The subject is enclosed in marks of parenthesis ( ), the verb is enclosed in brackets [ ], the predicate is indicated by two parallel lines below it =, a modifier is connected by an arrow with the element it modifies, and connectives are indicated by the sign +. When the subject or any other element is to be represented as understood, the fact is indicated by means of a cross ×.

44. **Models of Analysis by Diagrams of the Simple Sentence.** —

1.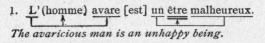
L'(homme) avare [est] un être malheureux.

The avaricious man is an unhappy being.

2. (×)   Venez   avec moi.
[Soyez] venant

(You) Come with me.

3.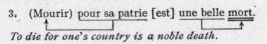
(Mourir) pour sa patrie [est] une belle mort.

To die for one's country is a noble death.

4.
La (mort)   frappe   les rois et les bergers.
[est] frappant

Death strikes kings and shepherds.

5.   L' (homme) faible

peut augmenter sa force par un régime hygiénique bien entendu.

[est] pouvant.

The feeble man can increase his strength by a well-understood hygienic diet.

6.   Ni l' (or) ni la (grandeur) ne nous   rendent   heureux.

[sont] rendant

Neither gold nor greatness make us happy.

7.   La (mémoire) des grands hommes [est] respectée par le temps.

Memory of great men is respected by time.

ANALYSIS OF COMPLEX AND COMPOUND SENTENCES

45.   In the analysis of complex and compound sentences, besides the analysis of clauses, as has been explained, it is necessary to show the relation of these clauses to one another; so that, accompanying the minute analysis of each clause, there should be a diagram showing the plan of the clauses. This diagram should be constructed as follows:

1. An independent clause should have a sign of equality at the beginning and end of a heavy horizontal line indicating the clause. Thus,

$$= \underline{\hspace{3cm}} \overset{+}{=} \underline{\hspace{2cm}} =$$

Le soleil se couche et la lune se lève.
The sun sets and the moon rises.

2. A subordinate clause should be represented by a light horizontal line, and should be separated from independent clauses and from other subordinate clauses by the sign of inequality. The opening of this sign should be turned toward the clause of which the dependent clause is an element.

$$= \underline{\hspace{3cm}} = + > \underline{\hspace{4cm}}$$

La lune s'est levée avant que le soleil soit couché.
The moon rose before the sun set.

$$+ \underline{\hspace{2cm}} < = \underline{\hspace{1cm}} =$$

S'il fait beau, nous irons.
If it is fine, we shall go.

$$+ \underline{\hspace{3cm}} < = \underline{\hspace{2cm}} = + > \underline{\hspace{1cm}}$$

Avant que je parte **je vous verrai,** si vous n'êtes

$$\underline{\hspace{2cm}} + > \underline{\hspace{3cm}}$$

pas occupé et si vous désirez ma visite.
*Before I leave, I shall see you if you are not
busy, and if you desire my visit.*

3.   If an independent clause is broken by one or more
contained subordinate clauses, the fact should be shown as
follows:

$$= \underline{\hspace{1.5cm}} + > \underline{\hspace{1cm}} < \underline{\hspace{2cm}} =$$

Le malheur qui lui est arrivé **est irréparable.**
The misfortune which happened to him is irreparable.

Here the connective *qui* is represented by the plus sign.

$$= \underline{\hspace{1.5cm}} + > \underline{\hspace{2cm}} < + > \text{-}$$

Les enfants qui étudient beaucoup et qui

$$\underline{\hspace{4cm}} < \underline{\hspace{3cm}} =$$

écoutent bien leur maître **font des progrès.**
*The children that study very much and listen
well to their teacher make progress.*

MODELS OF ANALYSIS

46. 1. $= \underline{\hspace{1cm}} = + = \underline{\hspace{1cm}} =$

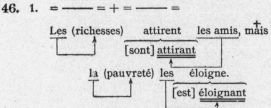

Riches attracts friends, but poverty chases them away.

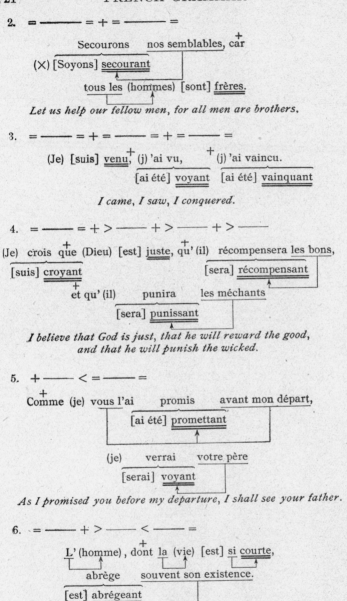

2. = ——— = + = ——— =

Secourons   nos semblables, car⁺

(✕) [Soyons] secourant

tous les (hommes) [sont] frères.

Let us help our fellow men, for all men are brothers.

3. = ——— = + = ——— = + = ——— =

(Je) [suis] venu,⁺ (j) 'ai vu, ⁺ (j) 'ai vaincu.

[ai été] voyant   [ai été] vainquant

I came, I saw, I conquered.

4. = ——— = + > ——— + > ——— + > ———

(Je) crois que⁺ (Dieu) [est] juste, qu' (il) récompensera les bons,

[suis] croyant   [sera] récompensant

et qu'⁺ (il)   punira   les méchants

[sera] punissant

*I believe that God is just, that he will reward the good,
and that he will punish the wicked.*

5. + ——— < = ——— =

Comme⁺ (je) vous l'ai   promis   avant mon départ,

[ai été] promettant

(je)   verrai   votre père

[serai] voyant

As I promised you before my departure, I shall see your father.

6. = ——— + > ——— < ——— =

L' (homme), dont⁺ la (vie) [est] si courte,

abrège   souvent son existence.

[est] abrégeant

Man, whose life is so short, often shortens his existence.

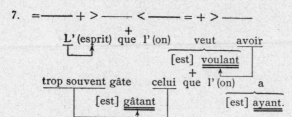

The wit, which one wishes to have, too often spoils that that one has.

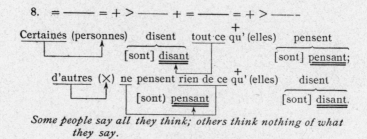

Some people say all they think; others think nothing of what they say.

47. French Model of Sentential Analysis. —

Lorsque l'enfant paraît, le cercle de famille
Applaudit à grands cris; son doux regard qui brille
Fait briller tous les yeux,
Et les plus tristes fronts, les plus souillés peut-être
Se dérident soudain à voir l'enfant paraître
Innocent et joyeux. — V. Hugo.

When the child appears, the family circle applauds with joyous cries; his sweet bright appearance makes all eyes glisten, and the saddest foreheads, the most sullied perhaps, clear at seeing the child look so innocent and joyous.

This sentence contains five propositions:

1. *Le cercle de famille applaudit (est applaudissant) à grands cris.* This is a principal proposition: Subject, *cercle,* with modifiers *le, de famille;* verb, *est;* attribute, *applaudissant,* modified by *à grands cris.*

2. *Lorsque l'enfant paraît (est paraissant).* This is a subordinate proposition, joined to the principal one by the

conjunctive of subordination *lorsque*. The subject is *enfant* with *le* as modifier; the verb is *est;* the attribute is *paraissant.*

3. *Son doux regard . . . fait (est faisant) briller tous les yeux.* This is a principal proposition, coordinate with the first. The subject is *regard* with *son* and *doux* as modifiers; the verb is *est;* the attribute is *faisant,* modified by the adverbial phrase *briller tous les yeux.*

4. *Qui brille (est brillant).* This is a subordinate proposition playing the role of a modifier of *regard.* The subject is *qui* (for, *regard*); the verb is *est;* and the attribute, *brillant.*

5. *Et les plus tristes fronts, les plus souillés peut être, se dérident soudain à voir l'enfant paraître innocent et joyeux.* This is a principal coordinate proposition. The subjects are *fronts* expressed and *fronts* understood. The first is modified by *les plus tristes* and the second by *les plus souillés peut être;* the verb is *sont;* the attribute, *déridant,* which is modified by *se, soudain, à voir l'enfant paraître innocent et joyeux.*

48. Analysis by the English Method. — Following the English method, the mapping and analysis of the above will be as follows:

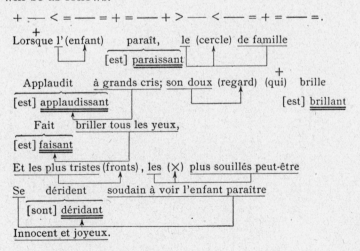

LA PONCTUATION – PUNCTUATION

GENERAL CONSIDERATIONS

49. Ponctuation. — Punctuation (Latin, *punctum*, a point) is the division of written or printed matter by significant marks or points to indicate the connection and dependence of its parts. The chief purpose of punctuation is to render clearer and more definite the meaning to be conveyed. The system of punctuation in use at the present time was entirely unknown to the ancients. It is a creation of the 16th century.

DIVISIONS OF PUNCTUATION

50. Considered with respect to use or purpose, punctuation may be *logical, rhetorical, grammatical,* or *etymological;* or for *emphasis* and *reference.*

51. Logical Punctuation. — In a printed or written document of any kind, those elements that serve to connect its sentences and paragraphs into one whole — to give unity — are logical in character. This unity, or continuity, is secured by the use of a great variety of expressions that point backwards to something that has been said before. Thus, consider the sentence, *Vous pouvez être sûr, par conséquent, que la terre est ronde,* You may be sure, therefore, that the earth is round. The words *par conséquent* are grammatically unnecessary; their effect is to establish a logical connection between this sentence and some arguments or illustrations that precede. Their function is logical, rather than grammatical. Examples of these kinds of superfluous words are the following: *en verité, de plus, conséquemment, de là, d'abord, finalement,* and innumerable other words, phrases, and clauses. Many others are used to prepare the mind for something that is to follow—they are anticipative; such are, *savoir*, *comme suit*, *ainsi*. As has been said, these transitional, or logical, elements form no necessary part of the sentences in which they occur; they are, in a sense, independent, and their independence or separateness should generally be indicated by punctuation.

52. Rhetorical Punctuation.—Closely allied in function to these logical elements are others, called *rhetorical*. They are used not to establish unity among the sentences composing a paragraph or a discourse, but to denote some peculiarity in the way the meaning expressed by a sentence is to be taken. Their general effect is to render the style lively, earnest, amusing, familiar, affectionate, etc.; some of the many expressions for this purpose are *maintenant*, *vous voyez*, *eh bien*, *vraiment*, *vous savez*, *ainsi*. Nearly all of these elements are parenthetical; and being, therefore, more or less independent, generally require to be separated by punctuation from the rest of the sentence. That a sentence is a question, an exclamation, a quotation, or a mere parenthesis, is also a rhetorical fact, and the punctuation necessary is for that reason rhetorical.

53. Grammatical Punctuation.—The flow of thought in language is not uniform and unbroken; if it were so, punctuation within the body of a sentence would be unnecessary. Logical and rhetorical elements are constantly introduced into sentences in such manner as to break their continuity, and these stand related to other elements in different degrees of remoteness. Among grammatical elements also, there are interruptions of continuity. Words, phrases, and clauses do not unite their meanings in regular, uniform sequence; but breaks of unequal length occur after long and short intervals. The only method of indicating such breaks is to punctuate; and, on account of the great variety of these interruptions, punctuation is a matter requiring the nicest judgment.

54. Etymological Punctuation.—Besides the punctuation of sentences for logical, rhetorical, and grammatical reasons, words and letters, considered as such, often require to be marked or punctuated. Thus, the fact that a word is compound, abbreviated, or contracted, is shown by marks of punctuation.

55. Punctuation for Emphasis and Reference.—A great variety of marks are used for miscellaneous purposes. Most of them are used for emphasis or to refer the reader to something else in the composition; as, the *paragraph* (¶), the *asterisk* (*), the *section* (§), etc. As they do not belong properly to the domain of grammar, they may be omitted from this treatise.

56. Signs Used in Punctuation.—The following signs are used in punctuation: *La virgule*, the comma (,); *le point-virgule*, the semicolon (;); *les deux points*, the colon (:); *le point*, the period (.); *le point d'interrogation*, the interrogation (?); *le point d'exclamation*, the exclamation (!); *les points de suspension*, the elliptic dots (. . .); *la parenthèse*, the parenthesis ( ); *les guillemets*, the quotation marks (" "); *le tiret*, the dash (—). Also the following etymological marks, which have been studied in Part 1, under the title Orthographic Marks: *Le trait d'union*, hyphen (-); *l'apostrophe*, apostrophe ('); *le trema*, dieresis (¨).

57. Taste and Judgment in Punctuation.—It must not be assumed that punctuation has been reduced to an exact science. No two writers or printers could be found that would punctuate a long paragraph, much less a magazine article or a book, in exactly the same way. The varieties possible in sentence structure and in style are practically endless, and each person will interpret expressed thought a little differently from every other person. What to one person seems important or emphatic, will usually strike another person differently. These differences in interpretation inevitably lead to differences in what is conceived to be the appropriate or necessary punctuation. Hence, taste and judgment will determine in a large measure the excellence

and consistency of each person's practice of this art. It is
clear, therefore, that no system of rules alone, however
elaborate and precise, can be applied with uniformity or
produce equally good results.

GRAMMATICAL PUNCTUATION

58. Elements of the Phrase.—Sentences are primarily made up of single words. When, however, these
separate elements are carefully considered with respect to
the work they do, it is at once seen that they do not always
enter the sentence as individual words, each representing a
separate idea; on the contrary, they often occur in groups of
closely related words that must be taken together as signs
of compound ideas. Each group has a function—does a
work—exactly similar to that done by single words. These
group elements are of two kinds, *phrases* and *clauses*.

59. Phrases and Clauses.—A **phrase** is a group of
words having a single function, but not expressing a complete thought. Thus,

au printemps, *in the spring*
près de la rivière, *by the river*
sans hésitation, *without hesitation*

The use of phrases in sentences is commonly either
adjectival or adverbial. Their functions are to modify,
narrow, or restrict, the meanings of other parts of speech;
to show their functional unity and to separate them from
neighboring elements, the meaning of which they might
otherwise improperly modify; it is often necessary to set
them off by punctuation.

A **clause** is one of two or more sentential elements,
expressing not a mere compound idea, but a complete
thought; it must therefore contain a finite verb, and when
separated from the rest of the sentence in which it is used,
it must say something completely.

60. Three Important Principles.—Whether or not
a word, a phrase, or a clause should be separated by

punctuation from other elements, depends largely on three circumstances:

1. *Its Length.* — The longer a sentential element, the more likely is it to require separation by punctuation.

2. *Its Connection.* — The need for punctuating an element increases with the remoteness of its connection with other elements.

3. *Its Position.* — When a word or a longer expression is removed from the place in which the natural and orderly flow of the thought requires it to be, it should usually be set off by some kind of punctuation.

This transposition is usually for the purpose of emphasis, or it is the result of interruption or afterthought. Thus,

Fréquemment, mais pas toujours, les méchants sont punis dans cette vie, *Frequently, but not always, are the wicked punished in this life.*

This sentence, regularly arranged, would require no punctuation. Thus,

Les méchants sont fréquemment mais pas toujours punis dans cette vie, *The wicked are frequently but not always punished in this life.*

RULES FOR PUNCTUATION

61. Insufficiency of Rules. — No code of rules for punctuation can be devised that will provide for every possible sentence form, for the number of these is practically infinite; much must be left to the judgment, taste, and intention of the writer. It may be taken as a general principle that the objects of punctuation are to aid in bringing out the exact meaning of the writer, and to prevent ambiguity.

The following rules will be found to cover all the cases that have been determined by the general practice of the best authorities.

LA VIRGULE—THE COMMA

62. General Principles.—The comma is used more frequently than any other mark of punctuation; but, almost without exception, these various uses may be included under one of the three following heads:

1. *The Interpolation of Elements.*—The flow of thought in language is not uniform and unbroken like the current of a deep river; it is more like that of a stream filled with obstructions. These obstructions to the flow of the sentence are indicated by punctuation. When an element, not really necessary to the thought, is introduced in such way as to break the continuity, it is commonly set off by commas.

2. *The Ellipsis of Elements.*—In the expression of thought, elements are often so clearly implied that they need not be repeated. This is particularly the case with the verb, though the ellipsis of other parts of speech, as, for example, the conjunction, is very common. These ellipses are usually marked by commas.

3. *The Transposition of Elements.*—Usage has established certain positions for the various sentential elements, which are often put in other places, generally for emphasis or euphony; and since in their unusual positions they obstruct in some measure the flow of thought, the fact must often be marked by punctuation.

63. Parenthetical Grammatical Elements.—Grammatical elements loosely connected are usually set off by commas, especially if they are long modifying phrases or clauses not directly joined to the expression they modify. Thus,

Ce fait, quoique embarrassant, est inévitable, *This fact, although embarrassing, is unavoidable.*

Supposez, par exemple, que la terre soit plate, *Suppose, for example, that the earth were flat.*

La lune semble, à moi du moins, plus belle que le soleil, *The moon seems, to me at least, more beautiful than the sun.*

64. **Transposed Expressions.**—Elements that for emphasis or any other reason are placed out of their natural or usual order, are usually set off by commas. Thus,

Respectueusement, nous insistâmes sur nos droits, *Respectfully, we insisted upon our rights.*

A un cœur blessé, il faut le silence et l'ombre, *To a wounded heart, silence and darkness are necessary.*

65. **Dependent Clauses.**—Dependent clauses, unless the connection is close, should be set off by commas. Thus,

Quoique la planète Vénus ressemble beaucoup à la terre, elle peut être inhabitée, *Although the planet Venus closely resembles the earth, it may be without inhabitants.*

Si vous voulez réussir dans ce que vous entreprenez, vous devez y donner toute votre attention, *If you would succeed in the thing that you undertake, you must give it close attention.*

66. **Relative Clauses.**—When not restrictive, relative clauses should be set off by commas. Thus,

Homère, qui a composé l'Illiade, était aveugle, *Homer, who composed the Iliad, was blind.*

Les roses, qu'on cultive à Provins, sont admirables, *The roses, which are raised at Provins, are admirable.*

The function of a restrictive clause is merely to modify; they are not ordinarily set off by commas. Thus,

L'oiseau qui chante là-bas est un rossignol, *The bird that sings yonder is a nightingale.*

Le monsieur que vous avez rencontré ce matin est mon père, *The gentleman whom you met this morning is my father.*

67. **Omitted Connectives.**—Similar elements not connected by conjunctions, are separated from one another by commas. Thus,

La candeur, la docilité, la simplicité, sont les vertus de l'enfance, *Candor, docility, and simplicity are the virtues of childhood.*

Le chien est doux, carressant, fidèle, *The dog is gentle, caressing, faithful.*

L'attelage suait, soufflait, était rendu, *The team was sweating, breathing, was exhausted.*

The comma is not used between two similar parts of a proposition when they are joined by one of the conjunctions *et, ou, ni.* Thus,

J'écrirai ou je lirai, *I shall write or read.*

Je n'ai pas reçu sa lettre ni la vôtre, *I have not received his letter nor yours.*

J'ai vu Paris, Londres et Berlin, *I have seen Paris, London, and Berlin.*

When the conjunctions *et, ni, ou* are repeated several times for emphasis, the comma is used. Thus,

> On égorge à la fois,
> Et la sœur et le frère,
> Et la fille et la mère. — RACINE.

They slaughter at the same time, and the sister and the brother, and the daughter and the mother.

68. Similar Propositions. — The comma is used to separate short propositions of the same nature. Thus,

Je suis venu, j'ai vu, j'ai vaincu, *I came, I saw, I conquered.*

69. Ellipsis of the Verb. — In continued sentences where a common verb is expressed in only one of the clauses and understood in others, the omitted verb is usually indicated by a comma. Thus,

Homère fut le plus grand génie; Virgile, le plus grand artiste, *Homer was the greater genius; Virgil, the better artist.*

Semiramis construisit Babylone; Didon, Carthage; Romulus, Rome, *Semiramis built Babylon; Dido, Carthage; Romulus, Rome.*

70. Similar Subordinate Propositions. — When several subordinate propositions of a certain length are used in a sentence, they should be separated by commas. Thus,

Lorsque les Espagnols eurent exploré l'Amérique, lorsqu'ils eurent exterminé la plus grande partie des naturels, lorsqu'ils se virent en possession des trésors qu'avait convoités leur cruelle avidité, ils se firent les uns aux autres une guerre furieuse et implacable. *When the Spaniards had explored America, when they had exterminated most of the natives, when they saw themselves in possession of treasures that their cruel avarice had coveted, they carried on a furious and implacable war amongst themselves.*

LE POINT-VIRGULE—THE SEMICOLON

71. Coordinate Clauses.—United clauses of equal rank, when of a certain length, should be separated by semicolons. Thus,

Aristide avait été juste avant que Socrate eût dit ce que c'était que la justice; Léonidas était mort pour son pays avant que Socrate eût fait un devoir d'aimer sa patrie; Sparte était sobre avant que Socrate eût loué la sobriété. J. J. ROUSSEAU. *Aristide had been just before Socrates had said what justice was; Leonidas had died for his country before Socrates had made it a duty to love one's country; Sparta was sober before Socrates had praised sobriety.*

72. Subdivided Clauses.—United clauses that contain elements set off by commas should generally be separated by semicolons. Thus,

Les lions ne font pas la guerre aux lions, ni les tigres aux tigres; l'homme seul, malgré sa raison, fait ce que les animaux sans raison ne firent jamais. *Lions do not make war with lions, nor tigers with tigers; man alone, in spite of his reason, does what animals without reason never did.*

Le tigre déchire sa proie, et dort; l'homme devient homicide, et veille. *The tiger tears his prey, and sleeps; man becomes homicide, and is sleepless.*

LES DEUX POINTS—THE COLON

73. There is no analogy between the semicolon and the colon. The first has a separative character—it divides, it distinguishes; the second, on the contrary, has rather a conjunctive character—it marks a relation, and could be replaced in many cases by a connective.

74. Formal Quotations.—A direct quotation or any similar matter should be preceded by a colon when formally introduced. Thus,

> Le lion tint conseil, et dit: "Mes chers amis,
> Je crois que le Ciel a permis
> Pour nos péchés cette infortune."

The lion held a council, and said: "My dear friends, I believe that heaven has permitted this misfortune on account of our sins."

75. After a general proposition followed with details, the colon is used. Also before a proposition which develops what precedes. Thus,

Tout plaît dans ce livre: la finesse des remarques, la justesse des pensées, le choix des exemples, *Everything in this book pleases: the finesse of remarks, the justness of thoughts, the choice of examples.*

Il faut autant qu'on peut obliger tout le monde: On a souvent besoin d'un plus petit que soi. *We must, as much as we can, oblige everybody: We often need help from smaller than ourselves.*

76. Enumerations.—The colon is used before an enumeration. Thus,

Il y a cinq parties du monde: L'Europe, l'Asie, l'Afrique, l'Amérique et l'Océanie, *There are five parts in the world: Europe, Asia, Africa, America, and Oceanica.*

LE POINT—THE PERIOD

77. Complete Sentences.—A complete statement or command, unless strongly exclamatory should be followed by a period. Thus,

Le paradis est le lieu où les parents sont toujours jeunes et les enfants toujours petits.—V. Hugo. *Paradise is the place where parents are always young and children always small.*

Loin des yeux, loin du cœur. *Far from the eyes, far from the heart.*

78. Direct Questions. — Every *direct question* should be followed by a mark of interrogation, but an *indirect question* by a period. Thus,

DIRECT: Les rois ne sont-ils pas sujets à la mort comme les autres hommes? *Are not kings subject to death as other men?*

INDIRECT: Il me demanda si j'avais l'intention d'aller à New-York. *He asked me if I had the intention of going to New York.*

When the interrogation is multiple, the interrogation point is used between each partial interrogation, if these are considered as forming a complete sense. Thus,

Où suis-je? Qu'ai-je fait? Que dois-je faire encore? *Where am I?   What have I done?   What have I to do yet?*

The interrogation point is used only at the end, if each part is considered as a member of the sentence. Thus,

Voulez vous, ou ne voulez-vous pas? *Will you, or will you not?*

———

LE POINT D'EXCLAMATION—THE EXCLAMATION POINT

79. Exclamatory Sentences. — An exclamation point should be placed at the end of a sentence expressing very strong emotion or implying loud outcry. Thus,

Combien je vous plains! *How I pity you!*
S'il est des jours amers, il en est de si doux! *If there are bitter days, there are also sweet ones!*

80. Exclamatory Expressions. — An exclamation point should ordinarily follow interjections. Thus,

Hélas! Hélas! qu'ai-je dit? Ecoutez! *Alas! alas! what have I spoken? Listen!*

———

LES POINTS DE SUSPENSION—THE ELLIPTIC DOTS

81. The elliptic dots are used when an emotion, a sudden thought, comes to the mind and prevents it from finishing a sentence just begun. Thus,

Quant à eux . . . mais j'ai promis de me taire, *As for them . . . but I promised to be silent.*

Et ce même Sénèque, et ce même Burrhus
Qui depuis . . . Rome alors estimait leurs vertus.

And the same Seneque, and the same Burrhus who since . . . then Rome esteemed their virtues. — RACINE.

LA PARENTHÈSE–THE PARENTHESIS

82. Words inserted in the body of a sentence or paragraph, and nearly or quite independent, so that they may be omitted without changing the sense or construction, should be enclosed in marks of parenthesis. Thus,

La peste (puisqu'il faut l'appeler par son nom) faisait aux animaux la guerre. *The plague (since we must call it by its name) was making war upon animals.*

Je croyais, moi (jugez de ma simplicité)
Que l'on devait rougir de la duplicité.

I believed, I (judge of my simplicity) that one had to blush for duplicity.

GUILLEMETS–QUOTATION MARKS

83. Direct Quotations. — Expressions that are cited or borrowed should, when written or printed, be enclosed between marks of quotation. Thus,

Sénèque a fait cette remarque: "Si vous voulez garder un secret, gardez-le vous-même," *Seneca made this remark: "If you wish your secret kept, keep it yourself."*

LE TIRET—THE DASH

84. The object of the dash is to separate the language of two persons in conversation. Thus,

Qu'est cela? lui dit-il. — Rien. — Quoi, rien? — Peu de chose. — Mais encore? — Le collier dont je suis attaché
De ce que vous voyez est peut-être la cause. — LA FONTAINE. *What is that? said he to him. — Nothing. — What, nothing? — Little thing. — But, still? — The collar with which I am tied is perhaps the cause of what you see.*

USE OF CAPITALS

LETTRES MAJUSCULES—CAPITAL LETTERS

85.   In order to give distinction to certain words, larger letters called **lettres majuscules,** capital letters, may be employed as initials.   These capitals are used as follows:

1.   At the beginning of a sentence or after a period.

2.   At the beginning of each verse in poetry.

3.   To begin the words, *Dieu,* God, and all synonymous words; as, *Providence*, *Créateur*, *Seigneur* (Lord), *Tout-Puissant*.

4.   In nouns naming a literary work, a fable, an object of art; as, *le Contrat Social*, *le Renard et le Corbeau*, *la Descente de la Croix de Rubens*, etc.

5.   In proper nouns.

Unlike English, French treats the days of the week and the months of the year as common nouns, and, consequently, they take no capital letter.   In French, proper adjectives are also written with small letters.

FRENCH GRAMMAR

(PART 7)

THE STUDY OF SENTENCES—(Continued)

SYNTAX

GENERAL CONSIDERATIONS

1. Synthetic and Analytic Languages.—A **synthetic language** expresses the relation of words by their forms—their inflections. For example, Latin is essentially a synthetic tongue. A word used as the subject of a finite verb is put in the nominative case, while a word used as the object of a verb is put in the accusative case. Such changes in the function of words are marked by changes in their endings. The order of words in a Latin sentence has no material effect on the meaning; thus, the sentence *Lupus occidit agnum*, The wolf killed the lamb, might also be written *Occidit agnum lupus*, or *Agnum occidit lupus*.

This is not true, however, of **analytic** or uninflected languages like the French. In such languages, words cannot be arranged at pleasure, for their order, nearly as much as their individual signification, determines their collective meaning. The French equivalent of the Latin sentence given above can be arranged in no other order than *Le loup a tué l'agneau*. That the wolf is the agent and the lamb the victim is indicated by the position of each word with respect to the other words of the sentence; for by merely reversing the position of the subject and object of the verb, it is the lamb that kills the wolf, *L'agneau a tué le loup*. In a language so analytic as the French, the chief characteristic of which is clearness, it is obvious that the free construction of the Latin would in time be abandoned, and that the construction of the sentence would be reduced to very exact laws.

SYNTAX OF THE SENTENCE

2. Regular Construction. — The construction of the French sentence differs but little from that of the English. The regular construction for any language is entirely arbitrary, and consists of a certain established order of the principal sentential elements. The French order of these elements is as follows:

SUBJECT	VERB	DIRECT OBJECT	INDIRECT OBJECT
Votre ami	étudie	le français	avec un professeur.
Your friend	*studies*	*French*	*with a professor.*
Charles	a reçu	un cadeau	de son oncle.
Charles	*has received*	*a present*	*from his uncle.*

There are, however, many cases in which the usual order of the parts of the sentence varies from the foregoing illustration.

INVERSION OF THE SUBJECT

3. Place of the Subject in Interrogative Sentences. Any change from the order of words indicated above is called **inversion** or **displacement**. The most frequent inversions of the subject are in the interrogative construction. The rules governing this construction are:

1. If the subject of an interrogative proposition is a personal pronoun, or one of the pronouns *ce* or *on*, it is placed after a verb of single tense form, but after the auxiliary in a compound tense. Thus,

Parle-t-il déjà bien? *Does he already speak well?*
Avons-nous bien étudié? *Have we studied well?*
Est-ce vous? *Is it you?*

A-t-on été content de moi? *Have they been satisfied with me?*

2. When the subject of a verb in a question is a noun, it is generally put first in the sentence; but in the form of one of the personal pronouns *il, ils, elle, elles*, it is repeated after the verb. In other words, the subject is first stated, and the question is then asked of it by means of a pronoun. Thus,

M. Bernard demeure-t-il ici? *Does Mr. Bernard live here?*
Cette dame a-t-elle commandé une voiture? *Has that lady ordered a carriage?*
Vos malles ne sont-elles pas arrivées? *Have not your trunks arrived?*

But the regular construction is used when the question is introduced by the expression *est-ce que*, do, did, etc. Thus,

Est-ce que M. Bernard demeure ici? *Does Mr. Bernard live here?*
Est-ce qu'on a été content de moi? *Have they been satisfied with me?*

This *est-ce que* is used to avoid a disagreeable meeting of two mute syllables; as, *est-ce que je cherche?* for *cherche-je?* It is also used to mark surprise.

3. When the interrogative pronoun *qui* represents the subject, inversion does not occur. Thus,

Qui me parle? *Who is speaking to me?*
Qui est venu vous voir? *Who came to see you?*

4. When the interrogative pronoun *que* begins a question, the subject is always inverted. Thus,

Que dites-vous? *What are you saying?*
Que fait ce monsieur? *What is this gentleman doing?*

In this case, however, a noun subject may precede *que* and the pronoun *il* or *elle* is then repeated after the verb. Thus,

Ce monsieur, que fait-il? *What is this gentleman doing?*
Cette dame, que prendra-t-elle? *What will this lady take?*

5. When the interrogative *qui* or one of the words *où, d'où, comment, quand* is used, either of the following constructions is admissible: (*a*) to place the noun after the verb; (*b*) to

place the noun before the verb, and one of the pronouns *il, elle, ils, elles* after the verb. Thus,

De qui parle votre frère?
De qui votre frère parle-t-il? } *Of whom is your brother speaking?*
Votre frère, de qui parle-t-il?

Où demeure votre ami?
Où votre ami demeure-t-il? } *Where does your friend live?*
Votre ami, où demeure-t-il?

Comment se porte monsieur votre père?
Comment monsieur votre père se porte-t-il? } *How is your father?*
Monsieur votre père, comment se porte-t-il?

Quand part le train?
Quand le train part-il? } *When does the train start?*
Le train, quand part-il?

If the verb has a direct object, however, and if the sentence also contains the interrogative *pourquoi*, the noun precedes the verb and the pronoun follows it. Thus,

A qui votre ami a-t-il donné son livre? } *To whom did your friend give his book?*
Votre ami, à qui a-t-il donné son livre?

Où votre ami prend-il ses leçons? } *Where does your friend take his lessons?*
Votre ami, où prend-il ses leçons?

Pourquoi ce monsieur s'arrête-t-il? } *Why does this gentleman stop?*
Ce monsieur, pourquoi s'arrête-t-il?

It would be incorrect to say:

A qui a donné votre ami son livre?
Où prend votre ami ses leçons?
Pourquoi s'arrête ce monsieur?

6. When the interrogative adjective *quel*, or the interrogative *combien* is joined to the subject of a verb, the regular construction is used. Thus,

Quel élève a été puni? *What pupil has been punished?*
Combien de personnes sont arrivées aujourd'hui? *How many people have come today?*

7. When *quel* or *combien* is joined to an object, inversion occurs. Thus,

Combien de livres avez-vous? *How many books have you?*
Quel cheval a-t-il acheté? *What horse has he bought?*
Combien de voyages Colomb fit-il?⎱ *How many voyages did*
Combien de voyages fit Colomb? ⎰ *Columbus make?*
Dans quelle chambre demeure votre ami?⎱ *In what room*
Dans quelle chambre votre ami demeure-⎬ *does your*
 t-il? ⎭ *friend live?*

4. Place of the Subject in Exclamatory Sentences. — The regular order of exclamatory sentences is as follows:

Que vous êtes bon! *How kind you are!*
Que cette ville est belle! *How beautiful this city is!*

But when the exclamation begins with an interrogative, inversion may take place. Thus,

O, Liberté! que de crimes ne commet-on pas en ton nom! *O, Liberty, how many crimes are committed in thy name!*
O religion, que de vertus te doivent les humains! *O religion, how many virtues do men owe thee!*

5. Place of the Principal Subject With Broken Quotations. — In French as in English, the verb is followed by the subject that denotes the author of the broken quotation. Thus,

"Il viendra," me dit-il, "j'en suis sûr," *"He will come,"* *said he to me, "I am sure of it."*
"Prenez cette chaise," me dit mon ami "et asseyez-vous," *"Take this chair," said my friend to me, "and sit down."*

6. Inversion in Optative Sentences. — In optative sentences the subject is placed after the verb when *que* or *si* is not used. Thus,

Puissiez-vous réussir, *May you (be able to) succeed.*

This construction however is frequent only with *sois*, be; *puisse*, may; *veuille*, please; *vive*, long live; *plaise* or *plût*, please; *dût*, should. In other cases, *que* is used with the subjunctive and the construction is regular.

7. Inversion to Give a Conditional Sense. — When a subjunctive is used to express a condition, inversion of the subject sometimes occurs. If the proposition were complete, it would begin with *si*, if, though. Thus,

Dût-il m'en coûter la vie, *Should it (though it should) cost me my life.*

Fussiez-vous homme ou démon, *Should you be man or demon.*

8. Inversion With Être. — When the attribute with *être* is a noun or an adjective, it may be placed first and followed by *être* and the subject. Thus,

Ses deux principaux ennemis furent les nobles et les évêques, *His two principal enemies were the nobles and the bishops.*

Telle est l'origine de ce mot, *Such is the origin of that word.*

9. Inversion After Certain Adverbs. — After certain adverbs or adverbial phrases the subject when a pronoun is placed after the verb. These adverbs are such as the following: *aussi*, accordingly; *à peine*, hardly; *encore*, besides; *peut-être*, perhaps; *en vain*, in vain; *toujours*, ever; *tout au plus*, at the utmost; *au moins* or *du moins*, at least. Thus,

Aussi est-il très riche aujourd'hui, *Accordingly, he is very rich today.*

A peine avait-il douze ans quand il quitta l'école, *He was hardly twelve when he left school.*

Peut-être paiera-t-il, *Perhaps he will pay.*

If the subject is a noun instead of a pronoun, the noun is expressed after the adverb and the corresponding pronoun repeated after the verb, as in questions. Thus,

Aussi, mon frère vous écrira-t-il, *Accordingly, my brother will write to you.*

A peine mon frère était-il arrivé, *My brother had hardly arrived,*

Peut-être votre ami viendra-t-il, *Perhaps your friend will come.*

10. Inversion When an Indirect Object Begins a Sentence.—When the sentence begins with an indirect object or with an adverb of place, or with *ainsi*, an adverb of manner, the noun subject is ordinarily placed after the verb, providing the verb has no direct object. Thus,

Ainsi périt Charles XII, *Thus died Charles XII.*

Ici fleurit jadis une ville opulente, *Here once flourished an opulent city.*

A cette première disposition fut ajoutée la suivante, *To this first disposition, was added the following.*

INVERSION OF DIRECT OBJECT

11. A Pronoun as the Direct Object.—When the direct object is a pronoun, it precedes the verb. Thus,

Je le vois, *I see him.*

Il ne nous invite pas, *He does not invite us.*

12. Place of Objects According to Their Length. When a verb has two objects of equal length, one direct, the other indirect, the regular order is preserved. Thus,

Je donne le livre à mon ami, *I give the book to my friend.*

Les Anglais vainquirent les Français à Azincourt, *The English vanquished the French at Agincourt.*

When the two objects are of different length, the shorter is placed first. Thus,

Chacun doit préférer à la fortune le témoignage d'une bonne conscience, *Everybody should prefer the testimony of a good conscience to fortune.*

13. Place of Indirect Object.—Certain verbs are preceded by the indirect object when it is emphatic or is indispensable to the sense. Thus,

A toutes mes demandes il opposa un refus formel, *To all my demands he opposed a formal refusal.*

Aux pauvres d'esprit appartient le royaume des Cieux, *To the poor in spirit the kingdom of heaven belongs.*

14. Inversion for Emphasis. — Sometimes a part of the sentence is put at the beginning for emphasis. The following are some of the varieties:

(*a*) *To Emphasize the Direct Object.* — To emphasize the direct object, it is placed at the beginning of the sentence, but is repeated by means of one of the personal pronouns, *le*, *la*, or *les*, before the verb. Thus,

Alors, Napoléon donna à Moscou l'ordre de la retraite, *Then, Napoleon gave at Moscow the order of retreat.*

To emphasize the direct object *l'ordre de la retraite*, the sentence would read: *L'ordre de la retraite, Napoléon* le *donna alors à Moscou.*

(*b*) *To Emphasize Other Elements of the Sentence.* — To emphasize other elements of the sentence, the expressions *c'est*, *ce sont*, *ce fut*, etc. may be put immediately before the part to be emphasized, and *qui* or *que* after it. Thus, the sentence, *Alors Napoléon donna à Moscou l'ordre de la retraite*, may be constructed as follows, according to the part that is to be emphasized:

Ce fut **Napoléon** qui donna alors à Moscou l'ordre de la retraite.

Ce fut **l'ordre de la retraite** que Napoléon donna alors à Moscou.

Ce fut à **Moscou** que Napoléon donna alors l'ordre de la retraite.

Ce fut **alors** que Napoléon donna à Moscou l'ordre de la retraite.

___

SYNTAX OF THE VERB

15. Relations Between the Verb and Its Subject. Every finite verb must have a subject. Thus, in the following sentence there are two finite verbs, *met* and *sait*, the subjects of which are respectively *qui* and *celui*.

Celui qui met un frein à la fureur des flots
Sait aussi des méchants arrêter les complots.

He who puts a check to the fury of the waves knows also how to stop the plots of the wicked.

In the imperative, however, the subject is generally understood. This is also true of many exclamatory sentences, as may be seen by the following examples:

Quels temoins éclatants devant moi rassemblés! *What glorious witnesses assembled before me!*

Nul bien sans mal, nul plaisir sans mélange! *No good without pain, no unalloyed pleasure!*

The verb is not expressed in the foregoing sentences, but it is understood; when completed, they would read:

Quels témoins éclatants **sont** devant moi rassemblés!

Nul bien **n'existe** sans mal, nul plaisir **n'existe** sans mélange?

The inflections of the verb for person and number depend on the person and number of the subject.

AGREEMENT OF THE VERB IN NUMBER

16. Compound Subject. — When the subject of a verb is composed of two or more words, with or without conjunctions, the verb is generally in the plural. Thus,

L'amour et la haine sont de puissants leviers, *Love and hatred are powerful levers.*

Le jeûne, la prière, la méditation exaltèrent l'imagination de Pierre l'Ermite, *Fasting, prayer, meditation exalted the imagination of Peter the Hermit.*

17. Synonymous Subjects. — When the subject of a verb is composed of two or more synonymous words, the verb agrees with the last word. Thus,

Son courage, son intrépidité étonne les plus braves, *His courage, his intrepidity, astonishes the bravest.*

The reason for this rule is that although there are several nouns, there is only one idea. Since there is unity in sense, there should be unity of words. Moreover, the conjunction *et*, being a sign of addition, must never be used between two closely synonymous words.

18. Subjects Forming a Climax.—When the words composing the subject form a climax, the verb agrees with the last word, because this is the most important word in the series. Thus,

Votre intérêt, votre honneur, Dieu même vous **commande** ce sacrifice, *Your interest, your honour, God himself orders you to make this sacrifice.*

19. Compound Subjects Summarized in One Word. One of the words *tout, rien, chacun, personne,* etc., frequently summarizes the elements of a compound subject. In such case, the verb agrees with that word. Thus,

Femmes, moines, vieillards, tout était descendu, *Women, monks, old men, all had alighted.*—LA FONTAINE.

> Vous n'êtes point à vous: le temps, les biens, la vie,
> Rien ne vous appartient, tout est à la patrie.

You do not belong to yourself; time, property, life, nothing belongs to you; everything is the country's.—GRESSET.

Grands, riches, pauvres, petits, personne ne peut se soustraire à la mort, *High, rich, poor, small, no one can escape death.*

20. Subjects United by ou.—When two subjects are connected by the conjunction *ou,* the verb agrees with the second only when the idea expressed by the verb cannot be applied to the first subject. Thus,

> Le bien ou le mal se **moissonne**
> Selon qu'on sème le mal ou le bien.

Good or bad is harvested according as evil or good is sown.

—LAMOTHE.

La paix ou la guerre sortira de cette conférence, *Peace or war will result from this meeting.*

But when the conjunction *ou* connects alternatives, that is, when the action expressed by the verb has reference to both of the subjects, the verb is in the plural. Thus,

Le temps ou la mort sont nos remèdes, *Time or death are our remedies.*—ROUSSEAU.

21. Subjects United by comme, de même que, ainsi que. — When subjects are united by *comme, de même que, ainsi que*, etc., the verb agrees with the first subject, the second being the subject of a verb understood. Thus,

L'enfant, ainsi que certaines plantes, a besoin de soutien, *The child, like certain plants, has need of support.*

This sentence is equivalent to *L'enfant a besoin de soutien, et certaines plantes ont besoin de soutien.*

A comparison is made here between *l'enfant* and *certaines plantes.* When the comparison does not exist and the subjects express a union or an enumeration, the verb is in the plural. Thus,

Bacchus ainsi qu'Hercule **étaient** reconnus pour demi-dieux, *Bacchus, as well as Hercules, was recognized as a demigod.*

22. Subjects Connected by ni. — When two subjects are united by *ni*, the verb is in the plural, except when the action can be affirmed of only one of the subjects. Thus,

Ni l'or ni la grandeur ne nous rendent heureux, *Neither gold nor grandeur renders us happy.* — LA FONTAINE.

Ni ton frère ni ton ami n'obtiendra cette place, *Neither your brother nor your friend will obtain this place.*

23. C'est and Ce Sont. — (*a*) The verb *être* preceded by *ce* is in the plural only when followed by a pronoun in the third person plural or by a plural noun. Thus,

C'est nous qui avons fait cela, *We did that.*
C'est vous qui sortirez, *You will go out.*
Ce sont eux qui viennent, ⎱
Ce sont elles qui viennent, ⎰ *They are coming.*
Ce sont deux Français, *They are two Frenchmen.*

(*b*) The verb *être* preceded by *ce* is in the singular if followed by several nouns in the singular.

C'est la vérité et la justice, *It is truth and justice.*

(*c*) If *être* is followed by several nouns, the verb is singular if the first noun is singular; otherwise, the verb is plural. Thus,

C'est le jeu et les spectacles qui le captivent.

Ce sont les spectacles et le jeu qui le captivent, *It is theater and play that captivate him.*

(*d*) When *ce* preceding *être* relates to a plural antecedent, the verb must be plural. Thus,

Quels sont les quatre **points** cardinaux?—**Ce sont** l'est, l'ouest, le nord et le sud, *What are the four cardinal points? They are the east, the west, the north, and the south.*

(*e*) *Être* followed by a plural noun is in the singular in the following cases:

1. In interrogative or exclamative sentences, when the verb *être* with *ce* forms a disagreeable sound. This rule avoids such combinations as *furent-ce, seront-ce, a-ce,* and *ont-ce.* Thus, instead of *furent-ce les Romains qui vainquirent?* the following phraseology is used:

Fut-ce les Romains qui vainquirent? *or,* Sont-ce les Romains qui vainquirent? *Was it the Romans who were victorious?*

2. With the expression *si ce n'est,* when it means *if not.* Thus,

Qui devons-nous aimer, si ce n'est nos parents? *Whom should we love, if not our parents?*

3. When the noun following *être* must be construed with another verb either as object or as an element of an adverbial modifier. Thus,

C'est des contraires que résulte l'harmonie, *It is from contraries that harmony results.*

24. Collective Noun as Subject. — A collective noun denotes many things regarded as forming a single group. When a collective noun is used as the subject of a verb, the verb is generally in the plural. Thus,

Peu de gens négligent leurs intérêts, *Few people neglect their interests.*

Une foule de nymphes étaient assises autour d'elle, *A crowd of nymphs were seated around her.*

However, if the collective unit is to be strongly emphasized in thought, the verb is in the singular. Thus,

La généralité des enfants aime mieux jouer qu'étudier, *Most children like to play better than to study.*

25. Adverbs of Quantity. — Adverbs of quantity and the collective *la plupart*, the most part, are always followed by a verb in the plural, when the determinative is plural; otherwise the verb is singular. Thus,

La plupart de ses amis l'abandonnèrent, *The majority of his friends abandoned him.*

La plupart du monde ignore ses véritables intérêts, *The majority of people ignore their true interests.*

Beaucoup de gens parlent mal, *Many people speak badly.*

Peu de gens savent se taire à propos, *Few people know how to be silent at the right time.*

26. Qui Used as the Subject. — When the subject is *qui*, the verb agrees with the antecedent of the relative. Thus,

Ces messieurs qui vous ont parlé sont nos amis, *These gentlemen who spoke to you are our friends.*

Cette dame qui est arrivée ce matin parle français, *This lady who arrived this morning speaks French.*

AGREEMENT OF THE VERB IN PERSON

27. The verb agrees in person with its subject. Thus,

Je parle, *I speak.*　　　　　Vous appelez, *You call.*

Tu demeures, *You live.*　　　Ils reçoivent, *They receive.*

Il achète, *He buys.*　　　　Elles vont à Paris, *They are going to Paris.*

Elle vend, *She sells.*

Paul donne, *Paul gives.*　　Ces messieurs parlent bien,

Nous commençons, *We begin.*　　*These gentlemen speak well.*

28. Subjects United by et. — When the subject consists of words of different persons, connected by *et* or by a conjunction equivalent to *et*, the verb is put in the plural and in the person having the priority. The first person has priority over the second, and the second over the third. Thus,

Toi et moi sommes contents, *You and I are glad.*

Vous et lui étiez présents, *You and he were present.*

Mon ami et moi avons beaucoup voyagé, *My friend and I have traveled much.*

Often, a pronoun subject summarizing the different subjects is repeated before the verb. Thus,

Mon ami et moi, nous avons beaucoup voyagé.

It will be noticed that when a compound subject is formed of two pronouns, or of a noun and a pronoun, the disjunctive form of the personal pronouns is used.

29. Subjects United by ou, or ni. — When the subjects are of different persons and are united by the conjunctions *ou* or *ni*, the verb is always in the plural. Thus,

Elle ou moi irons vous rendre visite, *She or I will return your visit.*

Mon frère ou moi partirons pour Paris la semaine prochaine, *My brother or I will start for Paris next week.*

Ni lui ni moi n'irons à Rome, *Neither he nor I will go to Rome.*

30. Qui Used as a Subject. — When the subject is *qui*, the verb agrees in person with the antecedent of the relative. Thus,

Moi qui suis, *I who am*
Toi qui es, *Thou who art*
Lui or elle qui est, *He or she who is*
Nous qui sommes, *We who are*
Vous qui êtes, *You who are*
Eux or elles qui sont, *They who are*

In certain phrases, where *qui* is preceded by a substantive, the verb may agree with that noun or with the pronoun subject of the principal proposition. Thus,

Je suis un orphelin qui ne connus ni père ni mère, | *I am an orphan who knew neither father nor mother.*
Je suis un orphelin qui ne connut ni père ni mère, |

Vous êtes le seul qui ayez réussi, | *You are the only one who has succeeded.*
Vous êtes le seul qui ait réussi, |

SYNTAX OF THE OBJECT

31. **One Direct Object.** — Although the direct object of a verb may be compound, formed of several nouns or pronouns, a verb can have only one direct object. The following from Racine has been justly criticized:

Ne vous informez pas ce que je deviendrai, *Do not investigate what will become of me.*

In this sentence the verb has the two direct objects *ce* and *vous*, which is incorrect. It should be, *Ne vous informez pas de ce que je deviendrai.*

32. **Indirect Object.** — A verb can have only one indirect object to express the same relation. It would be incorrect to say:

C'est à vous à qui je parle.
C'est de vous dont il s'agit.
C'est la ville où je vais.

The correct forms are

C'est à vous que je parle, *It is to you that I speak.*
C'est de vous qu'il s'agit, *It is of you that it is questioned.*
C'est à la ville que je vais, *It is to the city that I am going.*

33. **Proper Object.** — A verb must have the kind of object its nature requires. Thus, a direct object must not accompany a verb that requires an indirect object, nor an indirect object be given to a verb that requires a direct object. Thus, the verb *se rappeler*, to remember, coming from the active verb *rappeler* requires a direct object. We must say *Je me rappelle cette histoire*, I remember that story; *Je me la* *rappelle*, I remember it. It would be incorrect to use an indirect object and say *Je m'en rappelle*. In this case, the verb *se souvenir*, which means also *to remember* and which requires an indirect object, may be used, *Je m'en souviens*.

34. Direct Object Common to Two Verbs. — A direct object may be common to two verbs, providing each verb may have a direct object. Thus,

Le général attaqua et prit la ville, *The general attacked and took the city.*

Cet enfant aime et respecte ses parents, *This child loves and respects his parents.*

These sentences are correct, because the same kind of object is appropriate to each verb. But if the verbs cannot take the same kind of object, that is, if one requires a direct and the other an indirect object, different objects must be expressed. It would be incorrect to say *Le général attaqua et s'empara de la ville*, or *Cet enfant aime et obéit à ses parents.*

In the first sentence, *attaqua* requires a direct and *s'empara* an indirect object, whereas *de la ville*, an indirect object, is given to both. In the second sentence, *aime* requires a direct and *obéit* an indirect object. So that *à ses parents*, an indirect object, cannot be applied to both. The correct forms are *Le général attaqua la ville et* **s'en** *empara*, and *Cet enfant aime ses parents et* **leur** *obéit.*

35. Objects Must Be of Like Classes. — Similar objects of a verb must be of the same nature. If the first one is a noun, the others must be nouns; if the first is a verb form, the others must be verb forms. Thus, it would be incorrect to say *Il aime l'étude et à se promener*, He loves study and walking.

Of the two objects, *l'étude* is a noun and *se promener* a verb, which is an impossible grammatical construction, for grammar requires that the construction first introduced shall be preserved. The correct forms are, with nouns, *Il aime l'étude et la promenade;* or with verbs, *Il aime à étudier et à se promener.*

SYNTAX OF AUXILIARIES

36. Only two auxiliaries are used in the conjugation of French verbs, *avoir* and *être*. As a general principle, it may be said that *avoir* is used to express action, and *être* to mark state. From this, it is evident that all active verbs should be conjugated with *avoir*.

USE OF THE AUXILIARIES

37. Verbs Conjugated With Avoir and Être. — All verbs are conjugated with *avoir*, except in the following cases, when *être* is used:

1. All passive verbs take *être* in all their tenses, because in these verbs *state* rather than *action* is of primary importance and consequently determines the choice of the auxiliary.

2. All reflexive verbs take *être* in their compound tenses. This use of *être* in conjugating reflexive verbs is explained by the passive nature of reflexive verbs where the pronoun is the direct object, and consequently, in the compound tenses, the result of the action is considered rather than the action itself. For example, in the sentence, *Je me suis blessé*, I have wounded myself, for *when I have wounded myself*, the result to be considered is, *I am wounded*.

3. The following neuter verbs are conjugated with *être* in their compound tenses:

aller, *to go*	partir, *to depart*
arriver, *to arrive*	rentrer, *to go home*
accourir, *to run to*	rester, *to stay*
descendre, *to go down*	résulter, *to result*
entrer, *to go in*	retourner, *to return*
monter, *to go up*	sortir, *to go out*
mourir, *to die*	tomber, *to fall*
naître, *to be born*	venir, *to come*

In these verbs, the result of the action, that is, the state, and not the action itself, is considered. In *mourir*, for example, when the action of *mourir* is over, the resulting state is *death*, and this is the point to be emphasized.

38. Verbs Taking Avoir to Express Action and Être to Express State. — A great many neuter verbs may take either *avoir* or *être* according to the meaning they express. If they express an action, they are conjugated in their compound tenses with *avoir*. If, on the contrary, the state is dominant, they take *être*. The following is a list of the most important of such verbs:

ACTION SHOWN BY THE USE OF AVOIR	CONDITION SHOWN BY THE USE OF ÊTRE
Accourir. — Pourquoi n'avez-vous pas accouru aussitôt que j'ai sonné? *Why did you not run to the door as soon as I rang?*	Il y a plus d'une heure que je suis accouru à son secours, *I ran to his help more than an hour ago.*
Cesser. — Sa fièvre a cessé hier, *His fever ceased yesterday.*	La fièvre est cessée depuis hier, *Fever ceased since yesterday. (There has been no fever since yesterday).*
Changer. — J'ai changé de vêtements en rentrant, *I changed my clothes on coming home.*	Cet homme est bien changé; je ne le reconnais plus, *That man has changed a great deal; I no longer recognize him.*
Croître. — En deux heures la rivière a crû d'un pied, *In two hours the river rose a foot.*	Depuis deux jours la rivière est crue, *Since two days the river is swollen (The river has been swollen for the last two days).*
Déchoir. — Depuis ce moment, il a déchu de jour en jour, *Since that time, he has declined from day to day.*	Il est fort déchu de sa réputation, *He is greatly fallen in reputation.*
Dégénérer. — Cette race, autrefois puissante, a dégénéré pendant ces dernières années, *This race, formerly so powerful, has degenerated during these last years.*	Cette race est complètement dégénérée aujourd'hui, *This race is completely degenerated today.*
Descendre. — Le thermomètre a descendu de cinq degrés depuis midi, *The thermometer has dropped five degrees since noon.*	Il y a plus d'une heure que je suis descendu, *I have been down for more than one hour.*
Disparaître. — Elle a disparu subitement, *She disappeared suddenly.*	Elle est disparue depuis huit jours, *She has been missing for a week.*

Embellir. — Elle a embelli sa maison, *She has embellished her house.*

Comme elle est embellie! *How beautiful she has grown!*

Entrer. — J'ai entré cet article au grand livre, *I entered that item in the ledger.*

Il est entré sans mot dire, *He entered without saying a word.*

Monter. — Il a monté la montagne, *He climbed the hill.*

Il est monté à sa chambre, *He went up to his room.*

Passer. — Cet homme a passé devant chez nous ce matin, *That man passed our house this morning.*

Le mauvais temps est passé, *The bad weather is over.*

Sonner. — Une heure a sonné tout à l'heure, *One o'clock struck a little while ago.*

Midi est sonné depuis longtemps, *Noon struck a long while ago.*

Sortir. — Avez-vous sorti le cheval? *Did you take the horse out?*

Je suis sorti ce matin, *I was out this morning.*

Tomber. — Ce grand courage a tombé tout à coup, *That great courage of his suddenly collapsed.*

Le sort est tombé sur lui, *The lot fell on him.*

Monter. — Il a monté l'escalier, *He climbed the stairs.*

Il est monté à sa chambre, *He went up to his room.*

39. Verbs Whose Meaning Depends on the Auxiliary With Which They Are Conjugated. — The meaning of certain neuter verbs varies with the auxiliary with which they are conjugated; among these are the following:

Convenir. — When conjugated with *avoir* this verb means to suit; with *être*, it means to agree. Thus,

Cette maison m'*aurait* bien *convenu, This house would have suited me very well.*

Je *suis convenu* du prix, *I agreed to the price.*

Demeurer. — When conjugated with *avoir* this verb means to reside, to inhabit, to stay at, to tarry; with *être*, it means to stay, to remain behind. Thus,

Nous *avons demeuré* une année à Paris, *We lived one year in Paris.*

Il *est demeuré* en chemin, *He remained behind on the road.*

Echapper. — This verb follows the general rule, taking *avoir* to express *action* and *être* to denote the *result* of the action. It also takes *avoir* in the sense of *not being perceived*

or *discovered*, and *être* when it means *to have a thing done by negligence* or *imprudence*. Thus,

Il a dit une sottise qui n'a pas **échappé** à ses auditeurs, *He said a foolish thing which did not escape the hearers.*

Ce mot m'**est échappé**, *This word escaped me (unintentionally).*

Expirer. — This verb takes *avoir* in the sense of *to perish*, and *être* when meaning *to expire, to run out.* Thus,

Son ami **a expiré** de misère, *His friend perished of misery.* Mon bail **est expiré**, *My lease has run out.*

Rester. — The auxiliary *avoir* is used when this verb means *to dwell, to live, to stay*, and *être* in other meanings. Thus,

Il **a resté** deux jours à Lyon, *He stayed two days at Lyons.* Je l'attendais à Paris et il **était resté** à Lyon, *I was waiting for him in Paris, and he had remained at Lyons.*

REMARKS ON THE VERB ÊTRE

40. Preposition à With Être. — An infinitive preceded by the preposition *à* may be used in a passive sense as an attribute of the verb *être*. Thus,

C'est à prendre ou à laisser, *It is either to be taken or left.* Cet appartement est à louer, *This apartment is to be let.* Ma maison n'est pas à vendre, *My house is not for sale.*

41. Preposition de With Être. — When the verb *être* is followed by an adjective or a past participle, the adjective or participle is succeeded by the preposition *de*. Thus,

Je suis heureux **de** vous voir, *I am delighted to see you.* Je ne suis pas satisfait **de** votre conduite, *I am not satisfied with your conduct.* Il a été obligé **de** partir, *He has been obliged to go.* Je suis enchanté **de** faire votre connaissance, *I am delighted to make your acquaintance.*

42. Ce and Il With Être. — *Il* is generally used with *être* in statements of time; also when *être* is placed before an adjective followed by a logical subject, as in the sentences above. Thus,

Il est quatre heures, *It is four o'clock*.
Il est tard, *It is late*.

Ce is much more used than *il*, especially with the third person of *être* in the sense of *it is*, *it was*. Also when something already described is referred to, in which case *ce* might be translated by *that*. Thus,

Vous avez tort, c'est évident, *You are wrong, that is evident*.
Faites cela, c'est très facile, *Do that, it is very easy*.

43. **Etre fâché.** — This expression followed by the preposition *de* means *to be sorry for;* but when followed by *contre*, it means *to be angry with*. Thus,

Je suis bien fâché de vous déranger, *I am very sorry to disturb you*.
J'en (*of it*) suis bien fâché, *I am very sorry for it*.
Pourquoi est-il fâché contre moi, *Why is he angry with me?*

44. **Tard and en Retard, and Their Contraries.**
En retard and *tard*, although both are translated by *late* in English, cannot be used interchangeably.

Tard denotes that an action occurs later than it might have been expected. Thus,

Il est rentré très tard hier soir, *He came home very late last night*.
Pourquoi venez-vous si tard? *Why do you come so late?*

It is also used to express the end of the day. Thus,

Il se fait tard, *It is getting late*.
J'irai vous voir sur le tard, *I shall go to see you toward evening*.

En retard denotes that an action has been performed too late, or after a specified time. Thus,

Vous êtes en retard ce matin, *You are late this morning*.
Je ne pensais pas être en retard, *I did not expect to be late*.

To be late, referring to persons, is rendered by *être en retard;* referring to time, the expression is *être tard.* Thus,

Il est en retard, *He is late.*
Il est tard, *It is late.*

The opposite meanings of *tard* and *en retard* are, respectively, *de bonne heure,* early (*literally,* at a good hour), and *en avance,* early (*literally,* in advance, before time). They are used in the same way that their antonyms are used as explained above. Thus,

Ne partez pas, il est encore de bonne heure, *Do not go, it is still early.*

Il n'est que dix heures; je suis en avance, *It is only ten o'clock; I am early.*

45. Etre mieux. — *Etre mieux* is often translated *to feel better.* Thus,

Etes-vous mieux? *Do you feel better?*
Oui; je suis beaucoup mieux, *Yes; I feel much better.*

IDIOMS WITH ÊTRE

46. N'est-ce pas. — In English, the auxiliaries do, did, will, would, etc. are often repeated after an affirmative sentence in order to emphasize a question. In such cases, the repetition is expressed by the phrase *n'est-ce pas.* Thus,

Vous êtes pauvre, n'est-ce pas? *You are poor, are you not?*

Vous avez été à Paris, n'est-ce pas? *You have been in Paris, have you not?*

Vous partirez avec lui, n'est-ce pas? *You will start with him, will you not?*

Vous achèteriez cette maison si vous aviez de l'argent, n'est-ce pas? *You would buy this house if you had money, would you not?*

N'est-ce pas is used in French in a similar way even after a negative clause. Thus,

Vous n'avez rien à faire, n'est-ce pas? *You have nothing to do, have you?*

Vous n'irez pas à Paris, n'est-ce pas? *You will not go to Paris, will you?*

47. Gallicisms With Être. — *Gallicisms* are expressions peculiar to the French language. They may be illustrated by the following uses of *être:*

1. In the phrases *être que de*, or *être de* . . . , meaning *to be in the place of.* — Thus,

Si, j'étais que de vous, *or* si j'étais de vous, *If I were in your place.*

The first of these forms, however, though often used by French writers of the 17th century, is not common today.

2. *Être* used impersonally. — In this case, the verb is followed by the real or logical subject. Thus,

Il est un Dieu, *There is one God.*
Il était une fois un roi et une reine, *There was once a king and a queen.*

3. In the expressions *c'est* . . . *que* and *c'est* . . . *qui*, used to emphasize some special part of the sentence. — The first of these phrases is used to emphasize the direct or indirect object, and the second the subject. Thus,

C'est vous que j'attends, *I am waiting for you.*
C'est de moi que vous parlez, *You are speaking about me.*
C'est Louis qui a parlé, *It is Louis who spoke.*

4. The expressions *c'est à moi de* and *c'est à vous à* both mean *it belongs to me*, or, *to you to* . . . . Thus,

C'est à moi de parler, *It is my turn to speak.*
C'est à vous à jouer, *It is your turn to play.*

The expressions *si ce n'était, si ce n'eût été*, if it were not, are often contracted in French to *n'était*, or *n'eût été*. Thus,

N'était le respect que je vous dois, je vous dirais votre fait, *If it were not for the respect I owe you, I would tell you what I think.*

6. *Être* is often used in the past tense, instead of *aller*, to state that the speaker has gone somewhere and has returned. Thus,

J'ai été à Paris, *I went to Paris.*

48. Other Idioms With Être. — Besides the foregoing, the verb *être* is used in many other idioms, the most important of which are:

J'y suis, *I have the idea* (literally, *I am at it*).

Vous y êtes, *You have the idea.*

Je suis des vôtres, *I am one of you.*

Je n'en suis plus! *I have enough (am done)!*

Il n'en est rien, *Such is not the case. (There is nothing in it).*

être bien (mal) avec quelqu'un, *to be on good (bad) terms with somebody.*

être de moitié, *to go halves with*

Il en est ainsi, *So it is.*

Soit, *Well, let it be so.*

Ainsi soit-il, *So be it.*

Qu'est-ce que c'est? *What is it?*

Ce livre est à moi, *This book is mine.*

Je suis à vous dans un moment, *I shall be at your service in a moment.*

En êtes-vous encore là? *Do you still believe that?*

Voilà où nous en sommes, *Such is our present situation.*

Je n'y suis pour personne, *I am at home to no one.*

Madame n'y est pas, *My mistress is not at home.*

être de mauvaise humeur, *to be cross*

être en villégiature, *to be in the country*

être en vacances, *to enter in the holidays*

être en train de, *to be in the mood for*

être sur le point de, *to be on the point of*

être à jeun, *to fast, to be fasting*

Je ne suis pas à ce que vous dites, *I am not attentive to what you are saying.*

Je suis de toutes les fêtes, *I take part in every fête.*

Il est à son travail, *He is doing his work.*

C'est bien, *That is right.*

REMARKS ON THE VERB AVOIR

49. Preposition de With Avoir. — When *avoir* is followed by a noun taken in a general sense, the preposition *de* is required before the following infinitive. Thus,

J'ai le temps d'aller au théâtre ce soir, *I have time to go to the theater tonight.*

J'ai l'honneur de vous souhaiter le bonjour, *I have the honor to wish you good day.*

50. Preposition à With Avoir. — When *avoir* is followed by a noun taken in a partitive sense, or is not separated by a noun from the following verb, it takes the preposition *à*. Thus,

Qu'avez-vous à faire? *What have you to do?*

Je n'ai rien à faire, *I have nothing to do.*

Combien d'exercices avez-vous à faire? *How many exercises have you to write?*

J'ai du travail à faire, *I have work to do.*

J'ai quelque chose à vous dire, *I have something to tell you.*

51. Avoir Used for Être. — The following words, used in English with to be, take *avoir* in French:

chaud, *warm*	raison, *right*
froid, *cold*	tort, *wrong*
faim, *hunger*	sommeil, *sleep*
soif, *thirst*	peur, *fear*
honte, *shame*	

The reason for this difference in the use of the auxiliary in the two languages is, that in English an adjective is used with to be, while in French a noun is used with *avoir*. Thus,

N'avez-vous pas peur d'avoir froid? *Are you not afraid of being cold?*

Je n'ai ni faim ni soif, *I am neither hungry nor thirsty.*

Je n'ai pas encore sommeil, *I am not sleepy yet.*

In speaking of things, *right* and *wrong* cannot be translated by the expressions *raison* and *tort*. The following idioms are generally used to translate these words: Thus,

Ce que vous faites n'est pas bien, *What you are doing is not right.*

Ce que vous faites n'est pas convenable, *What you are doing is not becoming*.

Cette expression n'est pas juste, *or* exacte, *or* bonne, *This expression is not right*.

C'est l'homme qu'il me faut, *He is the right man for me*.

Je suis dans le bon (le mauvais) chemin, *I am in the right (wrong) way*.

L'endroit (l'envers) de cette étoffe, *The right (the wrong) side of that cloth*.

52. Age. — The verb *avoir* is used in French to express a person's age. Thus,

Quel âge avez-vous? *How old are you?*

J'ai trente-deux ans, *I am thirty-two*.

The words *vieux* (masc.), *vieille* (fem.), old, are not used in French in speaking of old age, for they are not considered respectful. *Agé*, old, is used instead. Thus,

Etes-vous plus âgé que votre frère? *Are you older than your brother?*

Il est plus âgé que moi; il a trois ans de plus que moi; il aura trente ans le mois prochain, *He is older than I; he is three years older than I; he will be thirty next month*.

53. Avoir mal. — The English expression, *to have* or *feel a pain*, is translated in French by *avoir mal*, followed by the preposition à. Thus,

Où avez-vous mal? *Where have you a pain?*

J'ai mal au doigt, *I have a pain in my finger*.

J'ai mal à la tête, *I have a headache*.

J'ai mal à l'oreille, *I have a pain in my ear*.

J'ai mal aux yeux, *I have sore eyes*.

54. Avoir lieu. — The expression *avoir lieu* means *to take place*. When followed by the preposition *de*, it means *to have reason for*. Thus,

Cette réunion aura lieu demain, *This meeting will take place tomorrow*.

Je n'ai pas lieu de me plaindre, *I have no reason for complaining*.

IDIOMS WITH AVOIR

55. The verb *avoir* appears in a great many idioms, among the most usual of which are the following:

Qu'avez-vous?   } *What ails you?*
Qu'est-ce que vous avez? } *What is the matter with you?*
J'ai à vous parler, *I must speak to you.*
En a-t-il!   *What a lot he has!*
Il y a plus, *Nay, more!*
Il y a de quoi vous amuser, *You will find amusement enough.*
Il n'y a pas de quoi, *Don't mention it.*
Il a de quoi, *He has the means.*
Je n'en ai pas les moyens, *I cannot afford it.*
Il a bon (mauvais) caractère, *He is good (bad) tempered.*
A qui en a-t-il?   *Against whom has he anything?*
avoir en horreur, *to hold in horror*
avoir l'air, *to have the appearance*
faire avoir, *to procure for*

56. Avoir beau. — When the expression *avoir beau* precedes a verb, it means that the action expressed by the verb is futile. Thus,

Vous avez beau faire, *You act in vain.*
Il a beau parler, *He speaks in vain.*

57. Y Avoir. — The expressions *there is*, *there are*, etc. are translated by the verb *avoir* used impersonally with the adverb *y*, there. Thus,

N'y a-t-il plus de vin?   *Is there no more wine?*
Y avait-il quelqu'un au salon?   *Was there any one in the parlor?*
Il y aurait du danger à sortir si tard, *There would be danger in going out so late.*

1. *Il y a* is used to translate *ago*. Thus,

Il est mort il y a trois mois, *He died three months ago.*
Je l'ai vu il y a deux ans, *I saw him two years ago.*

2. *Il y a longtemps* is translated by *it is long since*. Thus,

Y a-t-il longtemps qu'il est arrivé?   *Is it long since he arrived?*

55—18

Il n'y a pas longtemps qu'il est arrivé, *It is not long since he arrived.*

3. *Il y a loin* is the equivalent of *it is far.* Thus,

Y a-t-il loin de Calais à Douvres? *Is it far from Calais to Dover?*

Il n'y a pas loin, *It is not far.*

4. *Combien de temps y a-t-il?* is equivalent to *how long is it?* Thus,

Combien de temps y a-t-il que vous êtes ici? *How long have you been here?*

5. *Quelle distance y a-t-il?* means *how far is it?* Thus,

Quelle distance y a-t-il d'ici chez lui? *How far is it from here to his house?*

Il y a à peu près trois kilomètres, *It is about three kilometers.*

SPECIAL AND IDIOMATIC USES OF VERBS

58. Abandonner.—This verb means, to give up, to abandon. When conjugated reflexively, it requires the preposition *à* and means, *to give way to, abandons himself to.* Thus,

On a abandonné les travaux de ce bâtiment, *They have given up working at that building.*

Il s'abandonne au jeu, *He abandons himself to gambling.*

59. Aller.—This verb appears in a great many idiomatic expressions, the most important of which are:

aller en voiture, *to take a drive*
aller à cheval, *to ride* (*on horse back*)
aller à pied, *to go on foot, to walk.*
aller en chemin de fer, (en tramway, en bicyclette, etc.), *to ride on the train,* (*on the street car, on a bicycle, etc.*).

These expressions are also used with the reflexive verb *se promener.* There is, however, a difference between *aller en voiture* and *se promener en voiture.* With the former, a definite destination is in mind; with the latter, the drive is at random and merely for pleasure.

aller bien, *to fit* or *to suit*
aller, *to be* (speaking of health)
aller au devant de, *to go and meet*
aller chercher, *to go for* (literally, *to go to fetch*)
aller de pair, *to be equal in rank*
aller aux voix, *to collect the votes*
aller au fait, *to come to the point*
aller au trot, au galop, *to trot, to gallop*
aller son train, *to go one's own way*
aller en course, *to go on an errand*
aller à reculons, *to go backwards*
aller tout droit, *to go straight on*
faire aller, *to set going*
Allons donc!   *Come, then!* (*Nonsense!*)
aller aux informations, *to make inquiries*
Tous les chemins vont à Rome, *All roads lead to Rome.*
Les affaires vont bien (mal) *Our affairs are in good* (*bad*) *shape.*
Il y va de bonne foi, *He acts sincerely.*
Comme vous y allez!   *You go on at a fine rate!*
Allez toujours, *Go on.*
Il y allait de la vie, *Life was at stake.*
Il ira son chemin, *He will make his way.*
Cela va tout seul, *There is no difficulty in the thing.*
Cela n'ira pas loin, *That will not last long.*

60.   Apporter. — *To bring* is translated ty either *apporter* or *amener*. There is, however, a difference in their uses. *Apporter* is a compound of *porter*, to carry. It denotes that something is to be brought by carrying. Thus,

Apportez-moi mon déjeûner, *Bring me my breakfast.*
Apportez une chaise, *Bring a chair.*

Amener is a compound of *mener* and is used when something is to be brought otherwise than by carrying. Thus,

Amenez votre dame avec vous, *Bring your wife with you.*
Vous amènerez la voiture, *You will bring the carriage.*

To take away is also translated by two expressions, *emporter* and *emmener;* the difference between them is similar to that between *apporter* and *amener*.   Thus,

Emportez ce livre, *Take this book away.*
Emportez mon chapeau, *Take my hat away.*
Emmenez votre cheval, *Take your horse away.*
Emmenez cette voiture, *Take this carriage away.*

61.   Approuver. — This verb has the sense of the English *to approve of*. Being active in French, it does not require any preposition. Thus,

Tout le monde approuve votre conduite, *Every one approves of your conduct.*

Approuvez-vous tout ce qu'il dit?   *Do you approve of all he said?*

62.   Assister. — This verb has two meanings. Without a preposition, it means *to assist*. When followed by the preposition *à* it means *to be present at*. Thus,

Avez-vous assisté à ma leçon?   *Were you present at my lesson?*

Ma mère aime à assister les pauvres, *My mother likes to give assistance to the poor.*

Dieu vous assiste!   *God help you!*

63.   Attendre. — This verb, which means *to wait for*, is a transitive verb, and consequently requires no complementary preposition. Thus,

J'attends mon ami ce matin, *I am waiting for my friend this morning.*

Je vous ai attendu pendant une heure, *I have been expecting you for an hour.*

The reflexive form, followed by the preposition *à*, is used in the sense of *to expect*. Thus,

Je m'attends à partir demain, *I expect to leave tomorrow.*

Vous attendiez-vous à recevoir cette bonne nouvelle? *Did you expect to receive this good news?*

The more common idiomatic expressions in which *attendre* is used are:

C'est où je l'attends, *I shall have him there.*
Voilà ce qui vous attend, *This is what is reserved for you.*
Attendez! *Stay! Hold!*
Tout vient à point à qui sait attendre, *Patience brings all things about.*
Je n'attends plus qu'après cela, *I am only waiting for that.*
Il ne faut pas s'attendre à cela, *We must not rely upon that.*
Je m'y attends, *I expect it.*
Je ne m'attendais pas à cela, *I did not expect that.*
Attendez-vous y! *I wish you may get it!*
se faire attendre, *to keep people waiting*

64. Casser, Briser. — These two verbs are synonymous and mean *to break.* The former is used in speaking of fragile things, as glass or china; also with reference to a will or judgment. The other, in a moral sense. Thus,

Que vous êtes maladroit! Vous avez cassé ce verre, *How awkward you are! You have broken that glass.*
Mon cœur **est** brisé de douleur, *My heart is broken with grief.*

Among the idiomatic uses of these verbs are:

Qui casse les verres les paie, *He who breaks glasses must pay for them.*
Il est tout cassé de vieillesse, *He is worn out by old age.*
Brisons-là, *Let us say no more about it.*
casser un jugement, *to reverse a judgment*
se casser le cou, *to break one's neck*
se casser la tête, *to puzzle one's brains*

65. Compter. — This verb means either *to count* or *to intend.* Followed by the preposition *sur* it means *to rely upon.* Thus,

Savez-vous compter en français? *Do you know how to count in French?*
Vous pouvez compter sur moi, *You can rely upon me.*

Je compte travailler et gagner de l'argent, *I intend to work and earn some money.*

The most common idiomatic expressions in which *compter* is used are:

Il marche à pas comptés, *He walks with measured steps.*

Tout bien compté, j'ai perdu de l'argent dans cette affaire, *Everything reckoned, I have lost money in this business.*

Comptez là-dessus, *Rely upon that.*

Cela ne compte pas, *That is not taken into account.*

66. Convenir. — *Convenir* in the sense of *to agree* takes the preposition *de* and is conjugated with *être.* When it means *to suit* it is conjugated with *avoir.* Thus,

Nous sommes convenus de travailler ensemble, *We have agreed to work together.*

Il ne m'a pas convenu de lui répondre, *It did not suit me to answer him.*

67. Couper. — This verb is found in the following idiomatic expressions:

Je coupe mon vin avec de l'eau, *I dilute my wine with water.*

couper par tranches, *to slice, to cut into slices.*

Les sanglots lui coupent la voix, *Her sobs stifle her voice.*

pour couper court, *to be brief, in short.*

Pardonnez-moi si je vous coupe parole, *Excuse me for interrupting you.*

A qui à couper? *Whose cut is it?* (with reference to a game of cards.)

couper par le plus court, *to take the shortest way.*

68. Courir. — This verb is used in a number of idioms, the most important of which are:

courir à toutes jambes, *to run as fast as possible*
courir la chance, *to run the chance*
l'année qui court, *the present year*
par le temps qui court, *as times go*
la monnaie qui court, *the current money*
la mode qui court, *the prevailing fashion*

Le bruit court qu'elle est morte, *There is a report that she is dead.*

Il court bien des maladies, *There is much illness about.*

Il court à sa perte, *He hastens to his ruin.*

faire courir des bruits, *to spread reports*

courir les rues, *to run about the streets*

69.　Défendre. — This verb may be used actively in the sense of *to defend.* Thus,

Je défends mon honneur, *I defend my honor.*

When followed by the preposition *de*, it means *to forbid.* In this sense the verb cannot be used passively; the pronoun *on* with the active verb being used instead. Thus,

On me défend de sortir, *I am forbidden to go out.*

Vous a-t-on défendu de fumer? *Have you been forbidden to smoke?*

70.　Demander. — When this verb means *to ask for*, it is active, and the complementary preposition *for* is not required. Thus,

Que demandez-vous? *What are you asking for?*

Je demande mon livre, *I ask for my book.*

When meaning *to ask from*, or *of*, this verb takes the preposition *à; demander à* (*literally*, to ask to). If *demander* is followed by another verb, the preposition *de* is required before that verb. Thus,

J'ai demandé à Charles de venir me voir, *I asked Charles to come to see me.*

Il faut que je lui demande ce que je lui dois, *I must ask him what I owe him.*

Demander is used in the following idiomatic expressions:

demander l'aumône, *to ask alms, to beg*

On vous demande, *You are wanted.*

On demande un bon cuisinier français, *Wanted, a good French cook.*

On demande un commis sachant bien le français et l'anglais, *Wanted, a clerk well acquainted with French and English.*

Cela demande une explication, *That requires an explanation.*
Je ne demande pas mieux, *I am quite willing.*

71. Demeurer, Rester. — *Demeurer* and *rester* are closely
related. The former denotes habitual residence or a long
sojourn in one place. It means *to live* or *reside;* the second
is used for a *short stay, a stop. Demeurer* is ordinarily conjugated with *avoir*, and *rester* with *être.* Thus,

Où demeurez-vous? *Where do you live?*
Je demeure dans cette maison brune, *I live in this
brown house.*
Avez-vous demeuré à New-York? *Did you live in New
York?*
Non, je n'y suis resté qu'une semaine, *No, I remained
there only one week.*

The most common idioms used with *demeurer* and *rester*
are:

Où en êtes-vous demeuré? *Where did you leave off?*
Nous demeurons porte à porte, *We are next-door neighbors.*
Demeurons-en là, *Let us leave off there.*
Il est demeuré interdit, *He stood confused.*
ma demeure, *my residence*
C'est tout ce qu'il me reste, *It is all I have left.*
Il me reste à vous dire . . . , *I still have to tell you . . .*
Restez tranquille, *Keep quiet.*
Rester never means *to rest*, which is translated by *se reposer.*

72. Devoir. — This verb, when it means *to owe*, is
active. Thus,

Je vous dois beaucoup de reconnaissance, *I am deeply
indebted to you.*
Je lui dois cent francs, *I owe him a hundred francs.*

When expressing a *necessity*, it is translated by *must* in
English. Thus,

Je dois travailler, *I must work.*
Vous devez vous tromper, *You must be mistaken.*

Sometimes *devoir* means *ought*, or *should*, and is used to express a duty. It is then used in the conditional mode or in the imperfect of the indicative. Thus,

Il devrait partir tout de suite, *He ought to go at once.*
Vous devriez voyager, *You should travel.*

73. Donner. — Among the most important idioms formed with this verb are the following:

Je lui donne tort, *I blame him.*
Donnez-lui le bonjour, *Wish him a good day.*
donner rendez-vous, *to appoint a meeting place*
donner la chasse, *to pursue*
Cette fenêtre donne sur la rue, *This window opens on the street.*
Je donne beaucoup au hasard, *I attribute much to chance.*
C'est à vous à donner, *It is your turn to deal.*
Il a donné dans ce piège, *He fell into that trap.*
Cet arbre donne du fruit, *That tree yields fruit.*
Je donne à dîner demain, *I am to have company at dinner tomorrow.*
Ils se donnent le bras, *They go arm in arm.*
se donner la peine de, *to take the trouble to*
Cela m'a donné à penser, *That made me think.*
Le soleil donne dans ma chambre, *The sun shines into my room.*

74. Écouter. — This verb is active and means *to listen to.* It requires no complementary preposition. Thus,

Pourquoi n'écoutez-vous pas le maître? *Why do you not listen to the teacher?*
Je l'écoute toujours bien, *I always listen well to him.*

Among the idiomatic expressions in which *écouter* is used are:

Ecoutez! *Listen! Look here!*
Il n'écoute personne, *He minds nobody.*
Ne l'écoutez pas! *Never mind him!*
se faire écouter, *to obtain a hearing*

75. Entendre.—This verb is used in the following idiomatic expressions:

à vous entendre, *according to you*
Il entend un peu l'anglais, *He understands English a little.*
Entendons-nous, *Let us come to a right understanding.*
Il n'entend pas raillerie, *He cannot take a joke.*
Cet homme n'entend rien aux affaires, *This man knows nothing about business.*
Qu'entendez-vous par là? *What do you mean by that?*
Je m'entends bien, *I know very well what I mean.*
cela s'entend, *of course, to be sure*

76. Espérer.—*Espérer*, to hope for, is active and does not require a preposition. Thus,

Qu'espérez-vous? *What do you hope for?*
J'espère une faveur, *I hope for a favor.*

77. Essayer.—When used without a preposition, this verb means *to try on;* when followed by the preposition *de*, it means *to endeavor, to attempt.* Thus,

J'ai essayé mon chapeau, *I tried on my hat.*
J'ai essayé de lui faire entendre raison, *I endeavored to reason with him.*
Essayez de marcher, *Try to walk.*

78. Faire.—*Faire* has many special idiomatic uses.
1. It is used in describing the condition of the weather. Thus,

Il fait froid, *It is cold.*
Il fera chaud, *It will be warm.*

2. It is much used in the sense of *to cause to* with a following infinitive. Thus,

Faites entrer, *Show him in;* literally, *Make (him) to enter.*
Je fais faire un chapeau, *I am having a hat made.*

3. It is sometimes used to avoid the repetition of a preceding verb. Thus,

Je lui ai écrit comme je devais le faire, *I wrote to him, as I ought to do.*

* Among the idiomatic uses of *faire* are:

bonne à tout faire, *servant of all work*
faire une chambre, *to tidy a room*
faire la cuisine, *to cook*
faire cuire, *to cook (something)*
faire voir, *to show*
faire savoir, *to let one know*
faire penser, *to remind*
faire des progrès, *to improve*
faire le malade, *to sham illness*
faire semblant de, *to feign, to pretend*
faire la barbe, *to shave*
faire faillite, *to fail (in business)*
faire des emplettes, *to shop, to make purchases*
faire les malles, *to pack the trunks*
faire une question, *to ask a question*
faire son droit, *to study law*
Je n'ai que faire de lui, *I do not want him.*
Cela ne fait rien, *That does not make any difference.*
Je n'en ai que faire, *I have no need of it.*
Qu'y faire? *How can it be helped?*
Vous avez beau faire, *You act in vain.*
C'est bien fait pour lui, *It serves him right.*
Comment se fait-il? *How is it?*
Il s'est fait avocat, *He became a lawyer.*
Faites comme chez vous, *Make yourself at home.*

79. Falloir. — This verb means *to be necessary.* It is used in a great many idioms, some of which are:

Je ne sais ce qu'il lui faut, *I do not know what he wants.*
Faites cela comme il faut, *Do that properly.*
Ce sont des gens comme il faut, *They are well-bred people.*
C'est ce qu'il faudra voir! *We shall see!*
Il faut longtemps, *It takes a long time.*
peu s'en faut, *very nearly*
il s'en faut de beaucoup, *very far from it*

80. Jouer. — *Jouer*, to play, takes the preposition *de* when referring to an instrument, and the preposition *à* when referring to a game. Thus,

Ce jeune homme joue très bien du piano, *This young man plays on the piano very well.*

Savez-vous jouer aux cartes? *Do you know how to play cards?*

To play an instrument is translated in several ways:

jouer, *or* toucher du piano, *to play on the piano*
pincer de la guitare, de la harpe, *to play on the guitar, on the harp*
sonner du cor, *to play on the bugle*
battre du tambour, *to play on the drum*

Jouer is used in the following idiomatic expressions:

Nous ne jouons que l'honneur, *We play for honor.*
jouer un rôle, *to play a part*
Il s'est joué de moi, *He deceived me.*
La fortune se joue des hommes, *Fortune makes sport of mankind.*
Il joue de son reste, *He stakes his all.*
Nous jouons de malheur, *We are unfortunate.*

81. Manquer. — Without a preposition, this verb means *to lack*, *to be short of*, but with the preposition *de*, it means *to fail*, *to come near.* Thus,

Il me manque dix francs, *I am ten francs short.*

Il a manqué de mourir il y a quinze jours, *He nearly died two weeks ago.*

Ne manquez pas de venir ce soir, *Do not fail to come this evening.*

Among the idiomatic expressions using *manquer* are:

Le cœur lui manque, *He, or she faints.*
Le pied lui a manqué, *His foot slipped.*
Rien ne vous manquera, *You shall want for nothing.*
Il a manqué à sa parole, *He has broken his word.*
Il manque de tout, *He is destitute of all the necessaries of life.*

J'ai manqué une belle occasion, *I have lost a good opportunity*.

Il ne manque pas d'esprit, *He is not deficient in wit*.

Il a manqué à l'appel, *He missed the roll call*.

Vous me manquez, *I miss you*.

Je vous manque, *You miss me*.

Nous l'avons manqué belle, *We had a narrow escape*.

82. Mettre. — *Mettre*, to put on, being an active verb does not require a preposition. Thus,

Mettez votre pardessus, *Put on your overcoat*.

Avez-vous mis vos gants? *Did you put on your gloves?*

Its antonym, *ôter*, to take off, is also active. Thus,

Õtez votre pardessus, *Take off your overcoat*.

J'ôte mes gants parce qu'il fait trop chaud, *I take off my gloves because it is too warm*.

The most common idiomatic expressions in which *mettre* is used are:

mettre de côté, *to lay by*

mettre à jour, *to bring up to date*

mettre au jour, *to give birth to*

mettre le couvert, *to lay the cloth*

mettre une chose en tête à quelqu'un, *to persuade any one to do a thing*

Je l'ai mis dehors, *I turned him out of doors*.

Il met son nez partout, *He thrusts his nose everywhere*.

mettre en mer, *to set out to sea*

se mettre à table, *to sit down at table*

se mettre dans le commerce, *to take to trade*

Il se met à tout, *He turns his hand to everything*.

Il se met à écrire, *He starts writing*.

83. Obéir. — This verb, which means *to obey*, not being active, requires the preposition à. Thus,

Obéissez à vos maîtres, *Obey your teachers*.

Si vous n'obéissez pas à vos parents, vous serez punis, *If you do not obey your parents, you will be punished*.

84. Ouvrir. — The principal idioms formed with *ouvrir*, to open, are as follows:

Cela ouvre l'appétit, *That sharpens the appetite.*
Il m'a ouvert son cœur, *He unbosomed himself.*
Je peux traduire à livre ouvert, *I can translate at sight.*
ouvrir une enquête, *to institute an inquiry*
recevoir à bras ouverts, *to welcome heartily*
un compte ouvert, *a running account*
Il s'en est ouvert à moi, *He opened his mind to me about it.*

85. Parler. — The principal idioms with *parler*, to speak, are:

parler haut, bas, *to speak loud, in a low tone*
parler à l'oreille, *to whisper*
Il parle mal de vous, *He speaks ill of you.*
Il a fait parler de lui, *He is much talked of.*
Cela ne vaut pas la peine d'en parler, *It is not worth mentioning.*
Il en parle bien à son aise, *It is easy for him to say so.*
Je lui apprendrai à parler, *I will teach him to govern his tongue.*
Il trouvera à qui parler, *He will meet with his match.*
Nous avons parlé de la pluie et du beau temps, *We talked of indifferent matters.*
Il m'a parlé en maître, *He spoke to me peremptorily.*

86. Passer. — The principal idioms with *passer*, to pass, are:

Cette fleur est passée, *This flower is faded.*
Il a passé par Paris, *He passed through (by) Paris.*
Passez par ici, *Come this way.*
Il passera un jour par mes mains, *Some day or other, he will fall into my hands.*
Il faut en passer par là, *We must submit.*
Passez chez moi ce soir, *Call on me tonight.*
Cela m'a passé de l'esprit, *That has slipped my memory.*
Il a été passé par les armes, *He was shot.*
Passez votre chemin, *Go your way.*

Passez cela sous silence, *Take no notice of that.*
Voulez-vous me passer cela? *Will you hand me that?*
Ceci est passé de mode, *This is out of fashion.*

87. Penser.—Unlike its English equivalent, *penser*, to think, requires the preposition *à*, before the object. Thus,

A quoi pensez-vous? *What are you thinking of (to)?*
Je pense à mon frère, *I am thinking of (to) my brother.*

However, if this verb signifies *to have an opinion* about somebody or something, it takes the preposition *de*. Thus,

Que pensez-vous de cela? *What do you think of that?*
Vous pouvez penser de moi ce que vous voudrez, *You can think what you like of me.*

Penser requires no preposition before another verb. Thus,
Je pense partir bientôt, *I am thinking of going soon.*

The following are the most common idiomatic expressions that contain *penser:*
Je l'ai fait sans y penser, *I did it unintentionally.*
Vous pensez juste, *You think rightly.*
à ce que je pense, *in my mind*
A quoi pensez-vous de faire cela? *What do you mean by doing that?*
Il a pensé mourir, *He nearly lost his life.*

88. Pouvoir.—This verb, which means *to be able*, may be translated by can, may, or could. It is not an auxiliary, as in English, but is a primary verb. It is used in the following expressions:
Je n'y puis rien, *I cannot help it.*
Vous pouvez tout sur lui, *You have great power over him.*
Cela se peut, *That may be.*
Je n'en peux plus, *I am exhausted.*
Il se peut qu'il neige, *It may snow.*

89. Prendre.—*To take care of* is rendered by *prendre soin de.* Thus,

Prenez bien soin de vous, *Take care of yourself.*

Il a pris bien soin de ses enfants, *He took good care of his children.*

To beware is translated by *prendre garde à.* Thus,

Prenez garde à cette voiture, *Look out for this carriage.*

Among the most common idiomatic expressions using *prendre* are:

Il a pris congé de moi, *He took leave of me.*
Vous prenez mal mes paroles, *You misconstrue my words.*
Il prend les choses de travers, *He takes things amiss.*
à tout prendre, *upon the whole*
Je sais comment le prendre, *I know how to deal with him.*
Il en a pris sa bonne part, *He has had his share of it.*
Je vous y prends, *I have caught you.*
Il prend beaucoup sur lui, *He assumes much.*
Cela prend forme, *That is beginning to take shape.*
Il s'en prend à moi, *He lays the fault upon me.*

90. Regarder. — This verb, being active, requires no preposition. It means *to look at.* Thus,

Regardez cela, comme c'est beau! *Look at that, how beautiful it is!*
Cela ne me regarde pas, *That does not concern me.*

91. Répondre. — In the sense of *to answer,* this verb takes the preposition *à,* but when it means *to answer for,* the preposition *de.* Thus,

Pourquoi n'avez-vous pas répondu à ma lettre? *Why did you not answer my letter?*
Je réponds à votre lettre du dix courant, *I am answering your letter of the tenth instant.*
Je réponds de lui, *I answer for him.*

92. Ressembler. — This verb means *to resemble* and, not being active, requires the preposition *à.* Thus,

Cet enfant ressemble à sa mère, *This child resembles his mother.*

Cette photographie ne lui ressemble pas, *This photograph does not look like him.*

93. Rire. — *Rire* means *to laugh at* and requires the preposition *de.* Thus,

Je ne ris pas de vous, *I am not laughing at you.*
De qui riez-vous? *At whom are you laughing?*

Rire is used in the following common idiomatic expressions:

Il a le mot pour rire, *He is facetious.*
Il n'y a pas là de quoi rire, *There is nothing to laugh at in that.*
Rira bien qui rira le dernier, *He laughs best who laughs last.*
Vous voulez rire, *You are jesting.*
Je le disais pour rire, *I said it in jest.*
On se rit de lui, *He is laughed at.*

94. Savoir — Connaître. — These two French verbs are translated by *to know.* But they are not quite identical in meaning. *Savoir* is exclusively used with reference to things, while *connaître* is largely, though not exclusively, used with reference to persons. In a more general sense, *savoir* means *to know how,* while *connaître* has the sense of *to be acquainted with.* Thus,

Savez-vous votre leçon? *Do you know your lesson?*
Connaissez-vous ce monsieur? *Do you know that gentleman?*

95. Tarder. — This verb has two meanings. Without a preposition or with the preposition *à,* it means *to tarry, to delay.* Thus,

Ne tardez pas un moment, *Do not tarry one moment.*
Il tarde bien à venir, *He delays his coming a good deal.*

Tarder, in the sense of *to long, to be anxious for,* takes the preposition *de* and is an impersonal verb; that is, it is used in the third person singular only. Thus,

Il me tarde de voir mes parents, *I long to see my parents.*
Il lui tarde d'être riche, *He is anxious to become rich.*

96. **Tenir.**—This verb may be used without a preposition in the sense of *to keep*. Thus,

Il tient toujours sa parole, *He always keeps his word.*
Elle tient maison pour moi, *She keeps house for me.*

When followed by the preposition *à*, this verb means *to value*. Thus,

A quoi tenez-vous le plus? *What do you value most?*
C'est à ceci que je tiens le plus, *I hold this most dear.*

It may also be followed by the preposition *de*, in which case it means *to take after*. Thus,

Il tient de son père, *He takes after his father.*

Tenir lieu de means *to be instead of*. Thus,

Il m'a tenu lieu de père, *He has been a father to me.*
Elle m'a tenu lieu de mère, *She has been a mother to me.*

Tenir may be used idiomatically. Thus,

Tenez, voilà ce que je vous dois, *Here, there is what I owe you.*
Vous tenez trop de place, *You take up too much room.*
Cela m'a tenu plus que je ne pensais, *That detained me longer than I thought.*
Je le tiens pour honnête homme, *I look upon him as an honest man.*
Voilà la conduite qu'il tient, *Such is the way in which he behaves.*
Cessez de tenir ce langage, *Cease to speak in such a manner.*
Il tient table ouverte, *He keeps open house.*
Je tiendrai compte de cela, *I shall take that into consideration.*
Il tient à le faire, *He is anxious to do it.*
Il ne tient pas à moi qu'elle ne vienne pas, *It is not my fault that she does not come.*
Qu'à cela ne tienne, *Never mind!*
S'il ne tient qu'à cela, *If that is all.*
Je n'y tiens plus, *I cannot stand it any longer.*
Je m'en tiens à votre avis, *I am sticking to your advice.*

Il se tient mal à cheval, *He does not sit well on horseback.*
Tenez-vous là, *Stand there.*

97. Valoir. — *Valoir* has many meanings. The most important are:

valoir autant, moins, plus, mieux, que, *to be worth as much, less, more, better, than*
Il vaut mieux ne pas y aller, *It is better not to go there.*
Cela ne vaut rien, *That is good for nothing.*
Cet habit ne vaut plus rien, *This coat is quite worn out.*
valoir la peine, *to be worth while*
Cela ne vaut pas la peine d'y penser, *That is not worth thinking of.*
Il ne vaut pas la peine qu'on lui réponde, *He is not worth answering.*

Faire valoir has various meanings some of which are:

faire valoir une terre, *to improve an estate, to farm*
faire valoir son argent, *to turn one's money to account*
Il fait bien valoir ce qu'il sait, *He makes the best of his knowledge.*
faire valoir son droit, *to prosecute one's right*

98. Venir. — When this verb is followed by *chercher*, it means *to come for.* Thus,

Que venez-vous chercher ici? *What do you come here for?*
Je viens chercher le livre que j'ai oublié, *I come for the book I forgot.*

When followed by the preposition *de*, *venir* is translated by *to have just*, and denotes that an action has just taken place. Thus,

Elle vient d'arriver, *She has just come.*
Je viens de recevoir une lettre de lui, *I have just received a letter from him.*

Venir occurs in many idiomatic expressions. Thus,

Faites venir le médecin, *Send for the doctor.*
Je ne ferai qu'aller et venir, *I will not stay, I shall be back directly.*

Il en vint jusqu'à le menacer, *He went so far as to threaten him.*

Si ma lettre venait à se perdre, *If my letter should happen to be lost.*

D 'où vient-il que . . . ? *How is it that . . . ?*

D' où vient cela? *What is the cause of that?*

Cet arbre vient bien, *That tree thrives well.*

Où voulez-vous en venir? *What are you driving at?*

Il faut le voir venir, *We must first see what his intentions are.*

99. Vouloir. — The principal idioms formed with *vouloir* are as follows:

Je le veux ainsi, *I will have it so.*

Dieu le veuille! *God grant it!*

Ce que femme veut, Dieu le veut, *A woman must have her way.*

Je vous veux du bien, *I am your well-wisher.*

en vouloir à quelqu'un, *to bear any one ill will*

Il en voulait à l'argent, *He had an inkling for the money.*

A qui en veut-il? *Of whom has he to complain?*

Quand vous voudrez, *When you choose.*

Il veut trois mille francs de sa maison, *He asks three thousand francs for his house.*

Que veut dire cet homme? *What does that man mean?*

Que veut dire ce mot? *What is the meaning of that word?*

Je veux bien, *I am quite willing.*

Il veut ce qu'il veut, *He has a strong will.*

sans le vouloir, *unintentionally*

FRENCH GRAMMAR

(PART 8)

USES OF THE TENSES

INDICATIVE MODE

1. Uses of the Indicative Mode. — The word *indicate* means to point out, to show. When a thought is expressed in the form or guise that affirms or denies, or in that of an inquiry, the predicating verb is in the **indicative mode.** Thus,

La terre est une planète, *The earth is a planet.*
Il viendra sûrement, *He will surely come.*
Elle n'est pas arrivée, *She has not arrived.*
Comprenait-il? *Did he understand?*

PRESENT

2. Uses of the Present. — The word *present* in ordinary speech does not mean now — this instant. Strictly, now, the present, is the point where the past and future meet; it has no extent, and is always moving. But in ordinary speech, the present is a variable portion of time extending into both the past and future. So that we use the word present somewhat vaguely. When I say *Je chante*, the fact is that the performance of the act consumes time on both sides of the point called now.

The principal uses of the present tense are:

1. *To Express Present Action.* — Thus,

Je travaille maintenant, *I am working now.*
Vous marchez trop vite, *You are walking too fast.*

The progressive form in English, which represents action as going on and, therefore, as incomplete, is expressed in French by the simple present. Thus,

Je chante, *I am singing*.
Je travaille, *I am working*.

This same present also translates the emphatic English form. Thus,

Je chante, *I do sing*.
J'étudie, *I do study*.

Consequently, the same form *Je chante* renders *I sing*, *I am singing*, and *I do sing*. Similarly, *Vous chantez* translates *you sing*, *you are singing*, and *you do sing*.

2. *Universal Present.*—It has been said that the word present does not strictly mean now, but that it extends into the past and the future. This extension finds its extreme in what is called the **universal present.** This variety of the present tense is used with reference to those activities or states that are always going on—always true. Thus,

Deux et deux font quatre, *Two and two are four*.
La terre tourne autour du soleil, *The earth revolves around the sun*.

3. *In Place of a Future.*—The present is also used in French to express an immediate future. Thus,

Je suis de retour dans un moment, *I shall be back presently*.
Son procès se juge demain, *His case will be judged tomorrow*.

However, to express a remote future, the future tense should be used. It would be incorrect to say, *Je quitte la France dans quelques années*. The correct expression is, *Je quitterai la France dans quelques années*, I shall leave France in a few years.

4. *In Place of a Past Tense.*—Sometimes, when the author's intention is to give vivacity to the discourse, the present is used for a past. In such case, all verbs of the same sentence expressing past time must be in the present tense.

Turenne meurt, tout se confond, la victoire se lasse, la

paix s'éloigne, les bonnes intentions des alliés se ralentis-
sent; tout le camp demeure immobile.

*Turenne dies, all is in confusion, victory languishes, peace
vanishes, the good intentions of the allies relax; all the camp
remains motionless.* — FLÉCHIER.

However, when the discourse is long, this change of tense
is not a blemish. But the present may be correctly used
only when the action described becomes more decisive, more
lively. When these changes in the tenses are well introduced,
they give both variety and charm to the style. The following is an example of this kind, taken from Mme. de Sévigné's
description of the death of Vatel, an unfortunate cook who
committed suicide because the fish did not come in time for
the dinner he was preparing:

Les pourvoyeurs ne vinrent point. Sa tête s'échauffait, il
crut qu'il n'y aurait point d'autre marée. Il trouva Gourville; il lui dit: "Monsieur, je ne survivrai point à cet
affront-ci. Gourville se moqua de lui. Vatel monte à sa
chambre, met son épée contre la porte, et se la passe au
travers du cœur; mais ce ne fut qu'au troisième coup (car il
s'en donna deux qui n'étaient pas mortels) qu'il tomba mort.
Cependant la marée arrive de tous côtés; on cherche Vatel
pour la distribuer; on va à sa chambre, on heurte, on
enfonce la porte, on le trouve noyé dans son sang.

*The purveyors did not come. His head became hot; he
thought there would be no fish. He met Gourville, and said
to him: "Sir, I will not survive this outrage." Gourville
laughed at him. Vatel goes up to his room, puts his sword
against the door, and presses it through his heart. But it was
only at the third stroke (for he gave himself two which were not
fatal) that he fell down dead. However, fish come from all sides;
the people look for Vatel to distribute them; they go to his
room; they knock; they force the door open; they find him
drowned in his own blood.*

Notice how all these circumstances of fact, all the principal
features, are rendered by the present tense: *monte, met, passe,*
etc. Although these presents have each the value of a past,
rendering in present time a past action, they give great

vividness to the discourse. All minor details are, on the contrary, put in the past tense: *vinrent, s'échauffait, crut, trouva,* etc. And these different tenses are mixed without provoking any confusion. Literary art of this kind is one of the secrets of great writers.

5. *After Si, Meaning If.* — A conditional verb after *si* is put in the present tense when the verb of the principal proposition is in the future. Thus,

J'irai à Paris si j'ai assez d'argent, *I shall go to Paris if I have enough money.*

Je partirai demain si vous le permettez, *I shall go tomorrow if you permit me to do so.*

The future is never used in French, as it may be in English, after *si*, if. It may, however, occur after *si* used in the sense of *whether*. Thus,

Je ne sais pas encore si j'irai ou non, *I do not know yet whether I shall go there or not.*

Dites-moi s'il viendra, *Tell me whether he will come.*

6. *Past Action Continued Into the Present.* — The present is also used in French to express past action continued into the present. In such case, the phrase denoting its continuance is preceded by *depuis*, since, or *il y a*, ago. Thus,

Il est ici depuis vendredi, *He has been here since Friday.*

Combien de temps y a-t-il que vous êtes malade? *How long have you been sick?*

7. *After a Past Tense.* — The present is used after a past tense to denote an action not completed at the time of speaking. Thus,

J'ai appris que vous êtes malade, *I have learned that you are ill.*

In this example, the present tense is properly used when the person is ill at the time of speaking. But, if the person is not ill at the time of speaking, the past tense is employed. Thus,

J'ai appris que vous étiez malade la semaine dernière, *I heard that you were ill last week.*

IMPERFECT

3. Uses of the Imperfect. — The **imperfect** includes the four uses of the imperfect in English. Thus,

Je parlais, *I spoke, I did speak, I was speaking, I used to speak.*

Vous parliez, *You spoke, you did speak, you were speaking, you used to speak.*

The principal uses of the imperfect are:

1. To denote that an action was in progress at the same past time in which another action occurred. Thus,

J'écrivais quand vous êtes arrivé, *I was writing when you came.*

Il parlait à M. A quand je l'ai vu, *He was speaking to Mr. A when I saw him.*

Je m'habillais quand il est venu, *I was dressing when he came.*

This use is equivalent to the English progressive form *I was* followed by the present participle of the verb. As has already been said, the French verb has no progressive form, and the present and past English progressives are translated by the simple present or imperfect tenses of the French verb. Thus,

Je parle, *I am speaking.*

Je parlais, *I was speaking.*

If the two actions are in progress at the same time, both verbs should be in the imperfect. Thus,

J'écrivais pendant que vous lisiez, *I was writing while you were reading.*

J'étudiais pendant que vous déjeûniez, *I was studying while you were breakfasting.*

2. The imperfect is used to denote habitual past action. It may then be translated by *used to* with the English infinitive. Thus,

Je demeurais à Paris, *I used to live in Paris.*

Autrefois j'aimais beaucoup les promenades en voiture, *Formerly I greatly enjoyed driving.*

Quand j'étais jeune, j'avais une bonne santé, *When I was young, I used to have good health.*

3. If the verb of the principal proposition is in the conditional, the verb of the condition after *si* should be in the imperfect. Thus,

J'irais à Paris si j'avais assez d'argent, *I would go to Paris if I had enough money.*

Elle vous accompagnerait si vous le lui demandiez, *She would accompany you if you asked her.*

Il viendrait s'il pouvait, *He would come if he could.*

The conditional is never used after *si*, if, but may occur after *si*, whether. Thus,

Il ne m'a pas dit s'il viendrait, *He did not tell me whether he would come.*

Je ne savais pas s'il le ferait, *I did not know whether he would do it.*

4. This tense is sometimes called **descriptive,** because it is much used in descriptive narration. Thus,

Nous étions en hiver; il faisait très froid; la neige tombait à gros flocons et couvrait la terre comme un grand manteau blanc, etc., *We were having winter; it was very cold; large flakes of snow were falling and covered the ground like a great white cloak, etc.*

5. The imperfect is also used to express a past action continued up to a certain specified time; this expression of time is preceded by *il y avait* or *depuis* and so thrown into a subordinate clause. Thus,

Il y avait une heure que j'étais couché quand j'entendis un grand bruit, *I had been an hour in bed when I heard a great noise.*

Il était à Paris depuis trois jours quand il reçut la nouvelle de la mort de son père, *He had been in Paris three days when he received news of the death of his father.*

6. The imperfect is sometimes used in verbs of speaking, when the words of the speaker are quoted. Thus,

"Avouez," continuait son ami, *"Confess," continued his friend*.

"Jamais, jamais," repétait l'autre, *"Never, never," repeated the other*.

PAST DEFINITE OR PRETERIT

4. Uses of the Past Definite. — The **past definite** translates *I spoke, I finished, I sang, I did see*, etc. It is used to denote that an action occurred during a period completely elapsed, as in the expressions: I saw him last year, last month, last week, yesterday. Notice that the precise time is specified. It could not be used in the expressions I saw him this morning, this week, this month, this year, because the day, week, month, or year has not yet completely elapsed. Thus,

Ils quittèrent la ville la semaine dernière, *They left the city last week.*

Nous voyageâmes en France le mois dernier, *We traveled in France last month.*

Since the events related in history are facts completed in a time wholly elapsed, the preterit definite is chiefly used in historical narrative, and consequently has sometimes been called the **historic past.**

5. Imperfect and Past Definite Compared. — The past definite should not be confounded with the imperfect, which represents an action as going on at the time of another past action, or as being habitual. The past definite denotes past action without any relation to other action; that is, absolutely. In the sentence, *Je parlais quand il entra*, the first verb is in the imperfect, because the action is going on at the time of another past action, while the second verb is in the past definite, since it expresses absolute past action.

In English, when *I was* is or may be used with the present participle, the verb is in the imperfect tense. The same is true when *used to* precedes or may properly precede the verb. In other cases, the past definite or the past indefinite is used.

The following extract from Fénelon's Télémaque will make clearer the distinction between the past definite and the imperfect:

Calypso ne pouvait se consoler du départ d'Ulysse. Dans sa douleur, elle se trouvait malheureuse d'être immortelle. La grotte ne résonnait plus de son chant; les nymphes qui la servaient n'osaient lui parler. Elle se promenait souvent seule sur les gazons fleuris dont un printemps éternel bordait son île; mais ces beaux lieux, loin de modérer sa douleur, ne faisaient que lui rappeler le triste souvenir d'Ulysse, qu'elle y avait, vu tant de fois auprès d'elle. Souvent, elle demeurait immobile sur le rivage de la mer qu'elle arrosait de ses larmes; et elle était sans cesse tournée vers le côté où le vaisseau d'Ulysse, fendant les ondes, avait disparu à ses yeux. Tout à coup, elle aperçut les débris d'un navire qui venait de faire naufrage.

Calypso could not be comforted for the departure of Ulysses. In her grief she found herself unhappy in being immortal. Her grotto no longer echoed with her songs; the nymphs who were attending her did not dare to speak to her. She often walked alone on the green lawns with which an eternal spring covered her island; but these beautiful places, far from moderating her grief, served only to recall the sad memory of Ulysses whom she had so often seen near her there. Often, she remained motionless on the shore which she watered with her tears; and she was constantly turning toward the point where Ulysses' ship, plowing the waves, had disappeared from her eyes. Suddenly she saw the remains of a vessel that had just been wrecked.

This tense, as may be seen in the extract above, marks habitual past state, or the habitual actions of an individual.

It is not so with the past definite. Action expressed by that tense is sudden, abrupt, and momentary. It marks an event that puts an end to habitual state or action. This is well illustrated by the use of the past definite *aperçut* at the end of the above quotation. The imperfect tense makes the grief of the goddess seem to be infinite and everlasting, until something happens—something unusual, something out of the ordinary, and the past definite is used: *elle aperçut les débris d'un navire.* This ship brings Telemachus, and with him new love and the end of her sufferings.

PAST INDEFINITE

6. Uses of the Past Indefinite. — The **past indefinite** is the most widely used past tense; it denotes action as occurring in past time that may or may not be entirely elapsed, or that may not be definitely specified. Thus,

J'ai reçu une lettre de mon ami, *I received a letter from my friend.*

J'ai reçu ce matin une lettre de mon ami, *This morning I received a letter from my friend.*

J'ai reçu hier une lettre de mon ami, *Yesterday I received a letter from my friend.*

This past indefinite is sometimes used in place of a near future. Thus,

Attendez, j'ai fini dans un instant, *Wait, I (shall) have finished in a moment.*

In this case *j'ai fini* stands for *j'aurai fini.*

7. Past Definite and Past Indefinite Compared. When the past definite is used, the past time is always specified; but with the past indefinite, it may or may not be mentioned. The former tense is also used to indicate a time entirely elapsed, while the latter expresses action in a time not necessarily entirely completed. Thus,

J'ai reçu votre lettre ce matin, *I received your letter this morning.*

Je vous ai écrit cette année, *I wrote to you this year.*

It would be incorrect to say *Je reçus* and *J'écrivis,* because the morning and the year are not yet past.

In cases where the past time is entirely elapsed, it would be correct to use either of the two tenses. Thus,

Je parlai à votre père hier, ⎱
J'ai parlé à votre père hier, ⎰ *I spoke to your father yesterday.*

Nous voyageâmes en France l'année dernière,

Nous avons voyagé en France l'année dernière,

> *We traveled in France last year.*

Ils quittèrent la ville la semaine dernière,

Ils ont quitté la ville la semaine dernière,

> *They left the city last week.*

In conversation, however, the past indefinite is always used, although the past definite would be equally correct, for the latter tense sounds affected and formal. But in narrative style, either in speaking or writing, the distinction between past definite and past indefinite must be carefully observed.

NOTE.—When several pasts are used in the same sentence, and when it would be equally correct to use either the past definite or the past indefinite, the same tense should be used in each instance. It would be incorrect to say: *Je reçus hier une lettre à laquelle j'ai répondu.* The correct form is: *Je reçus hier une lettre à laquelle je répondis*, or *J'ai reçu hier une lettre à laquelle j'ai répondu.*

PLUPERFECT

8. Uses of the Pluperfect.—When two actions are expressed as having taken place in past time, the primary verb is put in the **pluperfect** when it should denote that its action had already been completed when the second past action occurred. Thus,

J'avais fini mon livre quand vous êtes arrivés, *I had finished my book when you came.*

The first verb *avais fini* is in the pluperfect, because the action of finishing the book was completed before the other past action *quand vous êtes arrivés* happened. Observe also the following examples:

Il était arrivé quand je suis parti, *He had arrived when I left.*

J'étais levé quand vous avez frappé à ma porte, *I was up when you knocked at my door.*

Il avait vendu sa maison avant de partir pour la France, *He had sold his house before starting for France.*

The verb expressing a condition after *si* is in the pluperfect, if the verb of the principal proposition is in the past conditional. Thus,

Il serait venu plus tôt s'il avait su que vous étiez là, *He would have come sooner, if he had known that you were there.*

J'aurais pris le premier train si j'avais reçu votre lettre à temps, *I would have taken the first train, if I had received your letter in time.*

The pluperfect tense should not be used as a substitute for the past indefinite, when a past action bears no relation to the past time expressed by the verb of the principal proposition. Thus,

Elle m'a dit qu'elle a vendu sa maison de campagne, *She told me that she sold her country house.*

It would be incorrect to say *qu'elle avait vendu*, because no relation is here shown between *a vendu* and some other verb that might express past action posterior to the selling of the country house. However, if such a verb is added, the pluperfect should be used. Thus,

Elle m'a dit qu'elle avait vendu sa maison de campagne quand vous m'en avez parlé, *She told me that she had sold her country house, when you spoke to me about it.*

PAST ANTERIOR

9. Uses of the Past Anterior. — The **past anterior** corresponds to the English pluperfect, but is not so frequently used. It is always preceded by an adverb of time, as *aussitôt que, quand, lorsque, à peine.* It expresses action as having taken place immediately before another action, which is usually denoted by the past definite. Thus,

Quand nous eûmes reçu notre argent, nous partîmes pour Paris, *When we had received our money, we started for Paris.*

A peine furent-ils arrivés que mon frère nous quitta, *Hardly had they come, when my brother left us.*

Il partit aussitôt qu'il eut fini son dîner, *He started as soon as he had his dinner.*

10. **Pluperfect and Past Anterior Compared.** — Both the pluperfect and the past anterior denote an action anterior to another past action. There is, however, the same distinction between these two tenses that exists between the imperfect and the past definite. The past anterior marks a precise moment, as does the past definite. This may be seen in the example, *Quand j'eus reconnu mon erreur, je fus honteux*, When I had recognized my error, I was ashamed. Here it is evident that *j'eus reconnu mon erreur* marks a precise moment. The pluperfect, however, does not independently denote a specific time; its time is purely relative to the time of some other verb either expressed or implied. So, in the sentence, *J'avais déjeûné quand il entra*, I had breakfasted when he came, the pluperfect *avais déjeûné* specifies no exact time. The action of breakfasting is merely mentioned, without any special reference to time.

FUTURE

11. **Uses of the Future.** — As in English, the **future** denotes future action. In addition, the future tense is used in the following cases:

1. In place of the imperative. Thus,

Tu ne tueras point, *Thou shalt not kill* (*Kill not*).

Vous saurez que je suis riche, *Know that I am rich.*

Un seul Dieu tu adoreras et aimeras parfaitement, *Only one God shalt thou perfectly love and adore.*

2. In a subordinate proposition, when the action represented by the verb of the principal proposition is future. Thus,

Vous direz ce qu'il vous plaira, *Tell what you please.*

Garde-toi tant que tu vivras, de juger les gens sur la mine, *Take care, as long as you live, not to judge people by their appearance.*

Venez me trouver quand il partira, *Come to see me when he goes away.*

But the verb after *si*, meaning *if*, as has already been explained, is never put in the future.

ANTERIOR FUTURE

12. Uses of Anterior Future. — The **anterior future** denotes future action to be finished before another action begins. Thus,

J'aurai fini quand vous arriverez, *I shall have finished when you arrive.*

C'est là que, lorsqu'il sera mort, elle vivra obscure et paisible, *It is there that, when he is dead, she will live alone and in quiet.*

This anterior future is sometimes used to denote that an action has probably taken place. Thus,

Il lui aura tout dit, *He must have told him everything.*

Il aura perdu son chemin, sinon il serait ici, *He has probably lost his way; if not, he should be here.*

CONDITIONAL MODE

PRESENT

13. Uses of the Present Conditional. — The **present conditional,** being a simple tense, has no equivalents for the English auxiliaries *should* and *would*.

1. This tense is used, as in English, to denote action subject to some condition. Thus,

J'irais à Paris si j'avais de l'argent, *I would go to Paris if I had the money.*

Je vous rendrais ce service avec plaisir si je pouvais, *I would render you this service with pleasure if I could.*

2. When the conditional mode is used, the verb of the condition after *si* must always be in the imperfect. But when the verb is in the indicative future, the verb of the condition after *si* is in the present. Thus,

J'irais à Paris si j'avais de l'argent, *I would go to Paris if I had the money.*

55—20

J'irai à Paris si j'ai de l'argent, *I shall go to Paris if I have the money*.

Je vous rendrais ce service si je pouvais, *I would render you this service if I could*.

Je vous rendrai ce service si je peux, *I shall render you this service if I can*.

3. The conditional mode is never used after *si* when it means *if*, but it can be used after *si*, meaning *whether*. Thus,

Je ne savais pas si vous viendriez ou non, *I did not know whether or not you would come*.

Elle ne savait pas si elle étudierait le français, *She did not know whether or not she would study French*.

4. The present conditional is also used after the past tense of verbs expressing an opinion, like *dire, savoir, penser, croire*. It is also used to represent, in a subordinate proposition, a fact as being doubtful. Thus,

On nous a dit qu'il viendrait, *We were told that he would come*.

Je ne savais pas que vous viendriez, *I did not know that you would come*.

Je pensais qu'il ne pourrait pas venir, *I thought he could not come*.

Je n'ai jamais cru qu'il réussirait, *I never thought he would succeed*.

5. But if the fact is to be represented as certain, the future should be used instead of the conditional. Thus,

On m'a assuré qu'il viendra, *I have been assured that he will come*.

J'ai toujours pensé qu'il réussira, *I have always thought that he will succeed*.

On nous a dit qu'il sera ici à dix heures, *We have been told that he will be here at ten o'clock*.

6. As in English, the conditional mode is often used in place of the indicative to soften a request, to appear less decisive, or to leave a certain doubt in the mind as to the result of the action expressed by the verb. Thus,

Je voudrais vous voir, *I should like to see you*.

Auriez-vous la bonté de venir? *Would you have the kind-ness to come?*

Je ne saurais faire ce que vous me dites, *I could not do what you tell me.*

7. When a subordinate clause is connected with the principal proposition by means of one of the conjunctive adverbs *tant que*, *partout*, etc., the verbs of the two clauses are in the same tense. Thus,

Il vous accompagnerait partout où vous iriez, *He would accompany you wherever you go.*

Il vous accompagnera partout où vous irez, *He will accompany you wherever you go.*

Il vous accompagne partout où vous allez, *He accompanies you wherever you go.*

Il vous accompagnait partout où vous alliez, *He accompanied you wherever you went.*

14. Remarks on the Conditional of Certain Verbs.

1. The conditional of *savoir*, accompanied by the negative *ne*, is sometimes used for the present indicative of the verb *pouvoir*. Thus,

Je ne saurais vous dire ce que j'éprouve, *I cannot tell you what I feel.*

Je ne saurais vous le dire, *I cannot tell you.*

2. *Could* and *might*, when a possibility is implied, are rendered by the conditional of *pouvoir*. Thus,

Pourriez-vous me dire son nom? *Could you tell me his name?*
Il pourrait le mettre, *He might put it on.*

3. *Ought to* and *should* expressing moral obligation are translated by the conditional of *devoir*. Thus,

Vous devriez me dire son nom, *You ought to tell me his name.*
Il devrait le mettre, *He should put it on.*

4. The conditional is sometimes used after *quand*, *quand même*, to state an assumed condition. Thus,

Quand même je serais pauvre, je ferais l'aumône, *Even though I were poor, I would give alms.*

5. *I should rather* is rendered by the conditional of *aimer mieux*. Thus,

J'aimerais mieux mourir que de faire cela, *I should rather die than do that.*

___

PAST CONDITIONAL

15. Uses of the Past Conditional. — With the **present conditional,** the action takes place at the present time if the condition is fulfilled; but, with the past conditional, the action would have already taken place if the condition had been fulfilled. The verb of the condition with *si*, with a past conditional, is in the pluperfect indicative. Thus,

Je serais venu ce matin si j'avais été sûr de vous trouver, *I would have come this morning if I had been sure of finding you.*

Il vous aurait écrit s'il avait su que vous étiez ici, *He would have written to you if he had known that you were here.*

___

MODE IMPERATIVE

16. Uses of the Imperative. — The **imperative** is used in French, as in English, to exhort, to command, to entreat, to permit. The tense of the imperative most used in French, is the simple present; as, *parle, parlons*, etc.

The imperative, like any other tense, may be used in all the persons. The most important persons in which it is used, however, are the first person plural, and the second persons singular and plural. Thus,

Viens, mon enfant, *Come (thou), my child.*
Venez, mes amis, *Come (you), my friends.*
Partons, il est temps, *Let us go, it is time.*

In these persons, the real subject is ordinarily understood. The third persons singular and plural are supplied from the present subjunctive, which they really are, for a governing proposition is really always understood. Thus,

Qu'il vienne, *Let him come.*
Qu'ils s'en aillent, *Let them go.*

These two sentences may be completed as follows:

Je désire qu'il vienne, *I wish him to come.*
Je désire qu'ils s'en aillent, *I wish them to go.*

The first person singular or plural may be indifferently used when a person is speaking to himself. Thus,

Rentre en toi-même, Octave, et cesse de te plaindre, *Enter into thyself, Octavius, and cease to complain.*
Vivons ·caché dans une profonde retraite, *Let me live hidden in some profound retreat.*

The imperative ordinarily marks a near future. It is for this reason that it is often replaced by a future. Thus,

Entre le pauvre et vous, vous prendrez Dieu pour juge, *Between the poor and you, you will take God as a judge.*

The same sentence may be expressed in the imperative:

Entre le pauvre et vous, prenez Dieu pour juge.

The compound tense of the imperative, rarely used in French, also expresses a future, but the future so expressed is anterior to a more remote future. Thus,

Ayez fini quand je reviendrai, *Have finished when I come back.*

SUBJUNCTIVE MODE

GENERAL CONSIDERATIONS

17. Indicative and Subjunctive. — The subjunctive is the mode of doubt, indecision, or simple possibility. When the subjunctive is used, the truth may differ greatly from the idea expressed. When the speaker wishes to indicate that he is in doubt, he should use the subjunctive mode; but to indicate that he is certain he should use the indicative mode. The following examples will illustrate:

INDICATIVE

Je cherche quelqu'un qui m'a rendu service, *I am looking for some one who rendered me a service.*

Je ferai de manière que mes parents seront contents de moi, *I shall act in such way that my parents will be satisfied with me.*

J'irai dans une retraite où je serai tranquille, *I shall go into a retreat where I shall be undisturbed.*

SUBJUNCTIVE

Je cherche quelqu'un qui puisse me rendre service, *I am looking for some one who may render me a service.*

Je ferai de manière que mes parents soient contents de moi, *I shall act in such way that my parents may be satisfied with me.*

J'irai dans une retraite où je sois tranquille, *I shall go into a retreat where I may be undisturbed.*

In the same sentence, the two modes may even be employed alternately, as in this extract from Mme. de Sévigné:

Les soldats criaient qu'on les menât au combat; qu'ils voulaient venger la mort de leur père, de leur général; qu'on les laissât faire; qu'ils étaient furieux.

The soldiers cried aloud that they be led on to fight; that they wanted to avenge the death of their father, their general; that they be left free to act; that they were mad.

Qu'on les menât and *qu'on les laissât faire* were results uncertain for the soldiers, while *qu'ils voulaient venger* and *qu'ils étaient furieux* were already known facts.

The fact that it is the peculiar function of the subjunctive to express doubt is the basis of the general and most important principle regulating its use. Upon this principle are based the following particular constructions:

18. Subjunctive in a Principal Proposition. — The word *subjunctive* means subjoined, under the dependence of. It is so called because it is almost always used in subordinate clauses. Indeed, it is rarely employed in independent clauses.

1. *Je ne sache pas*, meaning I am not aware of, and *que je sache.* Thus,

Je ne sache pas qu'une autre langue offre une semblable

ressource grammaticale, *I am not aware that any other language offers such a grammatical resource.*

Qui est entré pendant mon absence?—Personne que je sache, *Who came during my absence?—No one that I know of.*

Qui vive? Who goes there? the cry of sentinels, is also an example of the same construction.

2. The French subjunctive, like the Latin, is sometimes used to express a wish. But this use is not so extensively made in French as in Latin, and we may even suppose these propositions to be subordinate to a principal proposition understood. Thus,

Ainsi soit-il, *So be it* (*for* Je désire qu'il en soit ainsi).
Dieu vous soit en aide, *God help you.*
Puissé-je, de mes yeux y voir tomber la foudre, *May I see it struck by lightning with my own eyes.*

3. When the order of verb and subject is inverted, the subjunctive is sometimes, though rarely, used in a concessive or conditional sense. Thus,

Vienne qui voudra, je resterai ici, *Come who will, I shall stay here.*
Eût-il été bien plus fort et bien plus habile, eût-il été Richelieu ou Sully, il fût tombé de même, *Had he been much stronger and much more clever, had he been Richelieu or Sully, he would have fallen just the same.*

4. In place of a past conditional, in a hypothetic clause, the pluperfect subjunctive is sometimes used in a principal proposition. Usually the verb of the subordinate clause, if expressed, is also in the subjunctive. Thus,

Une main si habile eût sauvé l'Etat, si l'Etat eût pu être sauvé, *Such a clever hand would have saved the state, if the state could have been saved.*
En me coupant les oreilles, monsieur le marquis eût-il amélioré sa situation? *Would you, Marquis, have bettered your situation by cutting my ears?*

SUBJUNCTIVE IN SUBORDINATE CLAUSES

19. Subjunctive After Certain Verbs. — In French, the subordinate clause is usually joined to the principal clause by the conjunction *que*. Hence, in conjugating a verb, the subjunctive is denoted by this conjunction.

Whether or not the subjunctive can be used in a subordinate clause depends upon the sense of the verb of the principal proposition. If the verb of the principal clause expresses command, determination, desire, doubt, or fear, the verb of the subordinate clause is ordinarily in the subjunctive. Thus,

J'ordonne que vous parliez, *I order you to speak.*

Il veut que j'aille le voir, *He wishes me to go to see him.*

Je désire que vous soyez heureux, *I wish that you may be happy.*

Je doute que vous arriviez à temps, *I doubt whether you will arrive in time.*

Je crains qu'il n'arrive pas, *I fear that he may not arrive.*

After these verbs, it is evident that the result is uncertain; the order, wish, desire, doubt, or fear, may not be realized.

The subjunctive is generally used after the following verbs:

vouloir, *to will*

entendre, *to mean*

aimer, *to like*

aimer mieux, préférer, } *to prefer*

désirer, souhaiter, } *to wish*

attendre, *to expect*

prier, *to beg*

supplier, *to supplicate*

demander, exiger, } *to exact*

prétendre, *to pretend*

ordonner, commander, } *to command*

admettre, *to admit*

souffrir, *to suffer*

consentir, *to consent*

approuver, *to approve*

mériter, *to deserve*

permettre, *to permit*

défendre, *to forbid*

trouver bon, *to approve*

trouver mauvais, *to dislike*

Il entend, désire, veut, exige, ordonne, permet, trouve bon, etc. que vous fassiez cela, *He demands, desires, wishes, exacts, orders, permits, approves that you do that.*

REMARKS. — 1. *Dire* and *écrire* are sometimes used in the sense of *to order*, and require the subjunctive: *Je lui dis (écris) qu'il vienne*, I tell (write, order) him to come.

2. *Entendre* in the sense of *to hear* does not require the subjunctive.

3. After verbs expressing a resolution, as *arrêter, décider, résoudre, decréter, déterminer*, the subjunctive is not used.

4. After certain verbs expressing command, the future or conditional is used, if obedience to the command is thought to be certain.

5. When both the first and the second verbs have the same subject, the second verb is put in the infinitive mode instead of the subjunctive. Thus,

Je veux sortir, *I want to go out, not* Je veux que je sorte.

Il veut s'en aller, *He wishes to go, not* Il veut qu'il s'en aille.

But if the subjects are different, the second verb is put in the subjunctive according to the general rule. Thus, *Il veut s'en aller*, He wishes to go, means that *he* himself wants to go, while *Il veut qu'il s'en aille*, means that he wishes some one to go.

20. Subjunctive After Interrogation. — When verbs expressing certainty are used interrogatively, if the principal proposition is a question that leaves uncertain the action expressed in a subordinate proposition, the subjunctive is used provided the two clauses are joined by *que*. Thus,

Croyez-vous que nous soyons à Paris à dix heures? *Do you think we may be in Paris by ten o'clock?*

By using this form, the speaker not only shows that he wishes to know the opinion of the person to whom he is speaking, but that he is uncertain whether he will be in Paris at that time or not.

But if he were to say, *Croyez-vous que nous serons à Paris à dix heures*, using the future, no uncertainty would be indicated, and he would merely want to know the opinion of the listener. But the subjunctive is more used in a mere emphatic question. Thus,

. . . Madame, oubliez-vous
Que Thésée est mon père, et qu'il est votre époux?
Madam, do you forget that Theseus is my father and that he is your husband? — RACINE.

21. Subjunctive After Negation. — The subjunctive is used in a subordinate clause rendered doubtful by a negative in the principal proposition. Thus,

Je ne crois pas que vous le connaissiez, *I do not believe that you know him.*

Here the negation denotes uncertainty as to whether the person addressed knows him or not. But if the negation in the principal clause does not render doubtful the idea or action expressed by the verb of the subordinate proposition, the indicative is used. Thus,

Personne ne sait qu'il est revenu, *No one knows that he has returned.*

Here there is no uncertainty, for the meaning is, *Il est revenu, mais personne ne le sait.*

22. Subjunctive After Impersonal Verbs. — The subjunctive is generally used after an impersonal verb, with or without *que* following. Thus,

Il faut que je parte, *I must go.*
Il est nécessaire que vous arriviez de bonne heure, *It is necessary that you should arrive early.*

The indicative is used after impersonal verbs expressing certainty (*Il est certain*, etc.), probability (*il est probable*, etc.), or a positive fact (*il arrive, il s'ensuit*, etc.). Thus,

Il est certain que je l'ai vu, *I am positive that I saw him.*
Il est probable qu'il viendra ce matin, *He will probably come this morning.*
Il s'ensuit qu'il a raison, *It follows that he is right.*

If, however, these verbs are accompanied by a negative or are used in a question, the subjunctive is used. Thus,

Il ne me semble pas qu'il ait raison, *It does not seem to me that he is right.*

S'ensuit-il qu'il ait raison? *Does it follow that he is right?*

23. Subjunctive After a Relative. — The subjunctive is used after a relative pronoun and *où*, the adverb of place, when the following verb expresses something doubtful or uncertain. Thus,

Je sollicite une place que je puisse remplir, *I am looking for a place that I can fill.*

The meaning is that I am doubtful of my ability. But if I were positive that I could fill the position, I should use the indicative, and the sentence would read: *Je sollicite une place que je peux remplir.*

These distinctions are the same in the following examples, in which the verb of the subordinate proposition may be in the subjunctive or in the indicative, according as the action of the verb in the subordinate proposition expresses a possibility, an uncertainty, or a fact:

J'irai dans une retraite où je sois tranquille, *I shall go to a retreat where I may be undisturbed.*

Je cherche quelqu'un qui me rende ce service, *I am looking for some one who may render me this service.*

The subjunctive is used here, because it is possible that I may not be undisturbed in the retreat to which I intend to go, and also because the person for whom I am looking may not render me the service desired. But if the retreat and the person for whom I am looking are familiar to me, and if I am positive that I shall be undisturbed in that retreat, and that I shall obtain the desired service, these two sentences would read: *J'irai dans une retraite où je serai tranquille,* and *Je cherche quelqu'un qui me rendra ce service.*

24. Subjunctive After a Relative Preceded by a Negative Proposition. — The subjunctive is used after a relative preceded by a negative or conditional proposition, and also after a relative preceded by an interrogative proposition having a negative sense. Thus,

Il n'y a point de siècle que nous connaissions aussi bien que celui de Louis XIV, *We know no century so well as that of Louis XIV.*

Y a-t-il un homme qui ne se plaigne de ses semblables? *Is there a man who does not complain of his fellow men?*

25. **Subjunctive After a Relative Preceded by a Superlative.**—When the relative pronoun or the adverb *où* is preceded by a superlative or by analogous words (as *le seul, le premier, le dernier*), the following verb is generally put in the subjunctive. Thus,

Le chien est le seul animal dont la fidélité soit à l'épreuve, *The dog is the only animal whose fidelity has been tested.*

C'est la seule place où vous puissiez aspirer, *This is the only place to which you may aspire.*

Il y a peu d'hommes qui sachent supporter le malheur, *There are few men who know how to bear misfortune.*

In these cases, instead of the subjunctive, the indicative is used when the verb of the subordinate proposition expresses a fact. Thus,

De ces deux hommes, c'est le plus jeune que je connais, *I know the younger of these two men.*

Vouloir ce que Dieu veut est la seule science qui nous met en repos, *To wish what God wishes, is the only science that gives us peace.*

26. **Subjunctive After Conjunctions.**—1. The subjunctive is always used after conjunctions, simple or compound, that express condition, concession, or restriction. The following are the most important:

quoique,		soit que, *whether*	
bien que,	} *although*	en cas que,	} *in case that*
encore que,		au cas que,	
pourvu que, *providing that*		à moins que, *unless that*	
supposé que, *supposing that*		pour peu que, *howsoever little*	

Thus,

Il est venu quoique vous le lui ayez défendu, *He came, although you had forbidden him*.

Je vous accompagnerai, pourvu que vous preniez une voiture, *I shall accompany you, provided you take a carriage*.

Supposé qu'il vienne, que feriez-vous? *Supposing he should come, what would you do?*

Prenez ce parapluie au cas qu'il pleuve, *Take that umbrella lest it rain*.

Je partirai seul, à moins qu'il ne m'écrive, *I shall go alone unless he writes me*.

2. In the enumeration of several conditions the conjunction *que* alone may stand for one of the above compound conjunctions or for the conjunction *si;* in either of these cases the subjunctive is used. Thus,

Si le roi de France n'a qu'un million d'écus dans son trésor, et qu'il en **ait** besoin de deux, il n'a qu'à persuader à ses sujets qu'un écu en vaut deux, et ils le croient, *If the king of France has but one million crowns in his treasury and needs two, he has only to persuade his subjects that a crown is worth two, and they believe him.*

Venez me voir afin que nous parlions de cette affaire et que nous décidions quelle marche suivre, *Come to see me that we may talk about this matter and decide how to proceed.*

3. The subjunctive is also used after the following conjunctions, which nullify a fact:

non que,		sans que, *without*	
non pas que,	*not that*	loin que,	*far from*
ce n'est pas que,		bien loin que,	

Thus,

Le combat avait duré douze heures sans que la victoire **parût** se décider, *The fight had lasted twelve hours without the victory appearing to be decided.*

Loin qu'il soit pauvre, il devient toujours plus riche, *Far from being poor, he is constantly becoming richer.*

4. The subjunctive is used also after the following conjunctions denoting time:

Avant que, *before;* jusqu'à ce que, *until;* en attendant que, *till, until.*

Jouons en attendant qu'il vienne, *Let us play until he comes.*

Je vous écrirai avant que vous partiez, *I shall write to you before you go.*

5. The prepositions *afin que, pour que,* in order that, also require the subjunctive. Thus,

Pour qu'on vous obéisse, obéissez aux lois, *In order to be obeyed yourself, obey the laws.*

Dites-lui de venir me trouver, afin que je le punisse, *Tell him to come to see me, that I may punish him.*

6. The prepositions *de manière que, de façon que,* so that, govern the subjunctive if the verb of the subordinate proposition expresses an action that may not take place; but take the indicative, when it expresses a fact. Thus,

Il se conduit de manière qu'on n'a aucun reproche à lui faire, *He behaves so that no one has any reproach to make to him.*

Conduisez-vous de manière qu'on n'ait aucun reproche à vous faire, *Behave in such manner that there may be nothing for which to reproach you.*

USES OF THE SUBJUNCTIVE TENSES

27. General Considerations. — The chief function of the subjunctive mode, as has been said, is to express doubt. It replaces the indicative and conditional modes whenever doubt instead of affirmation is to be expressed. It contains only four tenses: the present and its compound the past; as, *que je reçoive* and *que j'aie reçu, que je tienne* and *que j'aie tenu;* the imperfect and its compound the pluperfect; as, *que je reçusse* and *que j'eusse reçu; que je tinsse,* and *que j'eusse tenu.* Thus it will be seen that these four subjunctive tenses take the place of the many forms of the indicative and conditional modes.

The tense of the subjunctive mode to be used in any given case, is determined by the time of the action to be expressed.

The imperfect subjunctive is of very little use in conversation, for it is considered too formal.

28. Concord of the Tenses of the Subjunctive, Indicative, and Conditional. — The present subjunctive replaces:

1. The present indicative. Thus,

Il est possible qu'il **soit** votre ami, *It is possible that he may be your friend.* But the present indicative would be used if the idea were regarded as a fact. Thus, *Il* est *votre ami, c'est possible,* He is your friend, it is possible.

2. The future indicative. Thus,

Je désire que vous **écriviez** demain, *I wish that you would write tomorrow.*

But the future indicative would express a simple affirmation. Thus,

Vous **écrirez** demain si vous faites ce que je désire, *You will write tomorrow if you do what I wish.*

The imperfect subjunctive replaces:

1. The imperfect indicative. Thus,

Il fallait que je **partisse,** *It was necessary that I should depart.*

If the dependent clause were affirmative, the expression would be,

Je **partais,** parce qu'il le fallait, *I was going, because it was necessary.*

2. The present conditional. Thus,

Il faudrait que vous **lussiez,** *It might be necessary that you should read.*

This is nearly equivalent to,

Vous **liriez** s'il le fallait, *You would read if it were necessary.*

The past subjunctive replaces: 1. The past definite or indefinite. Thus,

Je doute que vous **ayez écrit** hier, *I doubt whether you wrote yesterday.*

In the indicative mode, this would be,

Vous avez écrit (*or*, vous écrivîtes) hier, c'est ce dont je doute, *You wrote yesterday; I doubt it.*

2. The compound future. Thus,

J'ai voulu que vous **soyez admis,** *I have wished that you may be admitted.*

Vous **serez admis,** c'est ce que j'ai voulu, *You will be admitted; I wished it.*

The pluperfect subjunctive replaces: 1. The pluperfect indicative. Thus,

J'avais désiré qu'on **vous eût écouté,** *I was wishing that you had been listened to.*

The same meaning can be expressed by independent clauses. Thus,

On vous **avait écouté;** c'est ce que j'avais désiré, *They had listened to you; it is what I desired.*

3. The past conditional. Thus,

J'aurais désiré que vous **eussiez écrit** hier, *I could have wished that you might have written yesterday.*

Vous **auriez écrit** hier si vous aviez fait ce que je désirais, *You would have written yesterday, if you had done what I desired.*

29. **Table of the Concord of Tenses.** — The following table shows in a concise form the concord of the various tenses of the subjunctive, indicative, and conditional modes:

Present subjunctive replaces	present indicative future indicative
Imperfect subjunctive replaces	imperfect indicative present conditional
Past subjunctive replaces	past definite indicative past indefinite indicative anterior future
Pluperfect subjunctive replaces	pluperfect indicative past conditional

30. Other Examples. — An easy way of determining the tense of the indicative or conditional to be used, is to transform the subordinate proposition into a principal proposition. Observe the following examples:

1. Present subjunctive.

Je ne crois pas qu'il **soit** malade, *I do not believe he is ill.*

Transformed this sentence may assume any one of the following forms: Il **est** malade; c'est ce que je ne crois pas, *He is ill; this I do not believe;* Il est possible qu'il **soit** malade, *It is possible that he may be ill;* transformed; Il **est** malade; c'est possible; *He is ill; this is possible.*

Je lui ai écrit qu'elle **vienne** demain, *I wrote her to come tomorrow.*

Transformed: Elle **viendra** demain parce que je lui ai écrit, *She will come tomorrow, because I wrote to her.*

Je ne pense pas qu'il vous **écrive** bientôt, *I do not think he will write you soon.*

Transformed: Il vous **écrira** bientôt; c'est ce que je ne pense pas, *He will write you soon; that is what I do not believe.*

2. Imperfect subjunctive.

La Fontaine voulait que les actions des animaux **servissent** de leçons aux hommes, *La Fontaine wished that the actions of animals should serve as lessons to men.*

Transformed this would be: Les actions des animaux **servaient** de leçons aux hommes; c'est ce que La Fontaine voulait, *The actions of animals serve as lessons to men; that is what La Fontaine wished.*

Je ne pensais pas qu'il **étudiât** hier quand je l'ai appelé, *I did not think he studied yesterday when I called him.*

Transformed: Il **étudiait** hier quand je l'ai appelé; c'est ce que je ne pensais pas, *He was studying yesterday when I called him; that is what I did not think.*

Il voudrait que nous **sortissions** demain, *He wished that we might go out tomorrow.*

Transformed: Nous **sortirions** demain si nous faisions ce qu'il voulait, *We would go out tomorrow if we were doing what he wished.*

Bien des pères aimeraient mieux que leur fils **mourût** plutôt que de le voir fuir devant l'ennemi, *Many a father would prefer that his son might die rather than see him flee before the enemy.*

Transformed: Le fils **mourrait** plutôt que de fuir devant l'ennemi, c'est ce que bien des pères aimeraient, *The son would die rather than flee before the enemy; that is what many a father would like.*

3. Past subjunctive.

Je doute qu'il **ait travaillé** hier, *I doubt whether he worked yesterday.*

Transformed this sentence would be: Il **a travaillé** hier; c'est ce dont je doute, *He worked yesterday; I doubt it.*

Je crains que tu n'**aies payé** cela trop cher, *I fear that thou hast paid too much for that.*

Transformed: Tu **as payé** cela trop cher, je le crains, *You paid too much for that; I fear it.*

Si vous attendez qu'un enfant **ait contracté** l'habitude du mensonge, vous ne pourrez plus l'en carriger, *If you wait until a child has contracted the habit of lying, you will not be able to reform him.*

Transformed: Quand un enfant **aura contracté** l'habitude du mensonge, vous ne pourrez plus l'en corriger, *When a child has (will have) contracted the habit of lying, you cannot (will not be able to) correct him.*

J'aurai soin que vous **ayez fini** quand il arrivera, *I shall take care that you have finished when he comes.*

Transformed: Vous aurez fini quand il arrivera; c'est ce dont j'aurai soin, *You shall have finished when he comes; I shall take care of that.*

4. Pluperfect subjunctive.

Je ne savais pas que tu **eusses visité** l'Afrique du Sud, *I did not know that you had visited South Africa.*

Transformed this sentence would be: **Tu avais visité** l'Afrique du Sud; je ne le savais pas, *Thou hast visited South Africa; I did not know it.*

J'ignorais qu'il **eût écrit** hier, *I did not know that he had written yesterday.*

Transformed: Il **avait écrit** hier; c'est ce que j'ignorais, *He had written yesterday; I was ignorant of it.*

Je doute qu'il **eût réussi** sans mon assistance, *I doubt whether he would have succeeded without my help.*

Transformed: Il **aurait réussi** sans mon assistance; c'est ce dont je doute, *He would have succeeded without my assistance; I doubt it.*

Je doute qu'il **eût** mieux **réussi** que vous, *I doubt whether he might have succeeded better than you.*

Transformed: **Aurait**-il mieux **réussi** que vous? j'en doute, *Would he have succeeded better than you? I doubt it.*

FRENCH GRAMMAR

(PART 9)

SYNTAX OF THE INFINITIVE

1. The Infinitive Mode. — The word *infinitive* means *not limited*. This mode of the verb is so named because it takes no change of form in consequence of any change in the person and number of its subject. It may be regarded as the name of the verb, and as such may perform all the functions of a noun. In English a great many infinitives may be used as nouns. In French, however, only the following may be so employed:

le manger, *the eating*	le rire, *the laughter*
le boire, *the drinking*	le sourire, *the smile*
le parler, *the speaking*	le dire, *the saying*
le savoir, *the knowledge*	le savoir-faire, *the ready tact*
le dormir, *the sleep*	le savoir-vivre, *the good breeding*

Besides these listed infinitives there are a few that have been *entirely* transformed into nouns; as, *le souvenir*, the remembrance; *le devoir*, the duty; *l'être*, the being, etc.

2. Functions of the Infinitive. — The infinitive may be used as:

1. The subject of the sentence. Thus,

Parler n'est rien, agir est tout, *To speak is nothing, to act is everything.*

Mourir pour la patrie est un sort digne d'envie, *To die for one's country is a fate to be envied.*

2. The logical subject after an impersonal verb. Thus,

Il vaut mieux souffrir que mourir, *It is better to suffer than to die.*

Il fait bon servir la république, *It is a good thing to serve the republic.*

3. The attribute of a verb. Thus,

Il semble parler, *He appears to be speaking.*
Il est à plaindre, *He is to be pitied.*

4. The object of a verb. In this construction the infinitive is often used in place of a subordinate clause. Thus,

Je vous promets de venir vous voir, *I promise to come and see you.*

This sentence may also be constructed: *Je vous promets que je viendrai vous voir.* When the use of the infinitive as the object of the verb does not interfere with the clearness of the sentence, it is better to use the infinitive than an equivalent subordinate proposition, for a proposition tends to make the style diffuse and heavy. In the following examples, the second form is to be preferred:

Il est certain qu'il réussira, ⎫
Il est certain de réussir, ⎬ *He is certain to succeed.*

3. Remarks on the Infinitive. — When an infinitive is used as the subject of a verb its sense is usually repeated by a following *ce.* Thus,

Le voir, c'est l'aimer, *To see him is to love him.*

N'être bon qu'à soi, c'est n'être bon à rien, *To be good to no one but oneself, is to be good for nothing.*

To give emphasis to a sentence the predicate may be put first, in which case the sentence is introduced by *c'est*, and the infinitive is preceded by *que de.* Thus,

C'est l'aimer que de le voir, *It is to love him to see him.*

C'est n'être bon à rien que de n'être bon qu'à soi, *It is to be good for nothing to be good to no one but oneself.*

4. Time Expressed by an Infinitive. — The infinitive represents action in a vague way, and the time expressed by it is always dependent on the time expressed by the governing verb. Thus,

PRESENT: J'entends
PAST: J'ai entendu } parler,   *I hear*
FUTURE: J'entendrai   *I heard* } *speaking.*
   I shall hear

To express time anterior to the time expressed by the principal verb, the past infinitive is used. Thus,

Je suis content d'**être venu,** *I am glad to have come.*

Il se réjouit d'**avoir accepté,** *He is glad to have accepted.*

After the preposition *après*, the past infinitive is always used. Thus,

Après avoir reçu votre lettre, je suis parti, *After having received your letter, I went.*

Il s'est senti malade après s'être levé, *He felt ill after having got up.*

5. Independent Infinitives.—The infinitive may be used independently in certain interrogative or exclamatory sentences. Thus,

Comment faire?   *What to do?*

Que devenir?   *What will become of me?*

Te mesurer à moi! Qui t'a rendu si vain? *To measure swords with me! Who made you so vain?*—CORNEILLE.

PREPOSITIONS BEFORE AN INFINITIVE

6. The preposition *to*, which precedes an infinitive in English, is expressed in French by *à, de, pour;* but these prepositions cannot be interchangeably used. Sometimes no preposition is needed. It is important to observe that when a preposition is required before an infinitive, the foregoing verb, noun, or adjective determines which preposition is to be used, according as that verb, noun, or adjective governs one or another preposition. This government must therefore be ascertained. This is one of the chief difficulties in mastering the French language. Government of prepositions by nouns and adjectives will be treated elsewhere.

7. Verbs Requiring No Preposition Before a Following Infinitive. — The following verbs require no preposition before a dependent infinitive: (1) verbs that express motion from one place to another; (2) verbs that translate the English auxiliaries *can, may, will, must, let, dare*, etc.; (3) verbs expressing action of the senses; and (4) a few other verbs.

aimer mieux, *to like better*
aller, *to go*
compter, *to intend*
courir, *to run*
croire, *to think*
daigner, *to deign*
devoir, *to owe, must*
écouter, *to listen*
entendre, *to hear*
envoyer, *to send*
espérer, *to hope*
faire, *to make, to cause*
falloir, *to be necessary*
s'imaginer, *to fancy*
laisser, *to leave, to let*
mener, *to lead*

oser, *to dare*
paraître, *to appear*
penser, *to think*
pouvoir, *to be able*
préférer, *to prefer*
prétendre, *to pretend*
reconnaître, *to acknowledge*
regarder, *to look at*
savoir, *to know*
sembler, *to seem*
sentir, *to feel, to smell*
soutenir, *to maintain*
valoir mieux, *to be better*
venir, *to come*
voir, *to see*
vouloir, *to be willing*

Examples:

J'aime mieux étudier le français, *I prefer to study French.*

Je vais chercher un médecin, *I am going for a doctor.*

Nous comptons partir demain, *We expect to leave tomorrow.*

Ils doivent arriver par le train de deux heures, *They must arrive by the two o'clock train.*

J'en ai entendu parler, *I heard of it.*

Nous espérons faire beaucoup de progrès, *We hope to make much progress.*

Il s'imagine être un grand homme, *He imagines that he is a great man.*

Elle peut venir quand elle voudra, *She may come when she pleases.*

Nous ne voulons pas vous déranger, *We do not wish to disturb you.*

8. Remarks. — By a comparative study of the examples given in Art. **7,** it will be seen that when two verbs occur

together, the second is always in the infinitive. The verb
venir in the sense of *just to be, just to have*, requires *de* before
a following infinitive; when meaning *to happen* it requires
à; but, when having the sense of *to come*, it requires no
preposition. Thus,

Nous venons d'arriver, *We have just arrived.*

S'il vient à pleuvoir, mon chapeau sera endommagé, *If it
happens to rain, my hat will be spoiled.*

Il est venu vous voir hier soir, *He came to see you last night.*

**9. Verbs That Require à Before a Following
Infinitive.** — The following verbs, which generally express
a continued or progressive action, or a tendency toward
something, require *à* before a following infinitive:

s'abaisser à, *to stoop to*
aboutir à, *to end in*
s'accorder à, *to agree in*
accoutumer à, *to accustom to*
aider à, *to help to*
aimer à, *to like to*
s'amuser à, *to amuse oneself with*
animer à, *to excite to*
s'appliquer à, *to apply to*
apprendre à, *to learn to*
s'apprêter à, *to get ready to*
aspirer à, *to aspire to*
s'attendre à, *to expect to*
autoriser à, *to authorize to*
avoir à, *to have to*
chercher à, *to seek to*
commencer à, *to begin to*
condamner à, *to condemn to*
consentir à, *to consent to*
consister à, *to consist in*
contribuer à, *to contribute to*
coûter à, *to cost*
décider à, *to induce*
destiner à, *to destine to*
se déterminer à, *to resolve upon*
disposer à, *to dispose to*
donner à, *to give to*
encourager à, *to encourage to*

engager à, *to induce to*
enseigner à, *to teach to*
s'entendre à, *to be skilful in*
s'étudier à, *to study to*
exceller à, *to excel in*
exciter à, *to excite to*
exercer à, *to exercise in*
exhorter à, *to exhort to*
s'exposer à, *to expose to*
se fatiguer à, *to get tired with*
gagner à, *to gain by*
habituer à, *to accustom to*
se hasarder à, *to venture to*
hésiter à, *to hesitate to*
inviter à, *to invite to*
se mettre à, *to set about*
montrer à, *to show to*
s'obstiner à, *to persist in*
s'offrir à, *to offer to*
parvenir à, *to succeed in*
passer à, *to spend in*
penser à, *to think of*
perdre à, *to lose in*
persévérer à, *to persevere in*
persister à, *to persist in*
se plaire à, *to delight in*
prendre plaisir à, *to take pleasure*
préparer à, *to prepare to*

provoquer à, *to incite to*
recommencer à, *to begin again to*
renoncer à, *to renounce to*
se résoudre à, ⎫
réussir à,   ⎬ *to resolve to*
servir à, *to serve to* ⎭

songer à, *to think of*
tarder à, *to delay*
tendre à, *to tend to*
tenir à, *to be anxious*
travailler à, *to work*
viser à, *to aim at*

Examples:

Aidez-moi à porter ce bureau, *Help me to carry this desk.*

Il aime à se lever de bonne heure, *He likes to get up early.*

N'avez-vous pas appris à nager? *Did you not learn how to swim?*

Je m'attends à recevoir sa visite, *I expect to receive his call.*

Je vous autorise à sortir, *I authorize you to go out.*

Il n'a rien à faire, *He has nothing to do.*

Pourquoi ne cherchez-vous pas à savoir? *Why do you not seek to know?*

Je commence à croire qu'il ne viendra pas, *I begin to believe he will not come.*

Il a consenti à vous écouter, *He consented to listen to you.*

L'avez-vous décidé à nous accompagner? *Did you induce him to accompany us?*

Il est disposé à vous recevoir, *He is disposed to receive you.*

Il m'a engagé à venir vous voir, *He induced me to come to see you.*

Je ne puis m'habituer à marcher, *I cannot accustom myself to walking.*

Il hésite à vous demander de l'argent, *He hesitates to ask you for money.*

Il n'est pas parvenu à me faire croire cela, *He did not succeed in making me believe that.*

Il persiste à croire que vous avez tort, *He persists in believing that you are wrong.*

Il a réussi à vous tromper, *He succeeded in deceiving you.*

10. Remarks on the Preceding Verbs.—The verbs *coûter*, *suffire*, and *tarder*, which are given above as requiring the preposition *à*, require *de* when used as impersonal verbs. Thus,

Combien cela coûte-t-il à produire? *What does it cost to produce this?*

Il lui en coûte beaucoup de dire cela, *It is very painful for him to say that.*

Cela suffira à le satisfaire, *That will be sufficient to satisfy him.*

Il ne suffit pas de le vouloir, *To wish it is not sufficient.*

Votre ami tarde bien à venir, *Your friend delays his coming much.*

Il me tarde de voir ma mère, *I long to see my mother.*

11. Verbs Requiring de Before the Infinitive. — The verbs in the following list, most of which express a result or consequence, a turning away from, or a cessation of action, require *de* before a succeeding infinitive:

s'abstenir de, *to abstain from*
accuser de, *to accuse of*
achever de, *to finish to*
affecter de, *to pretend to*
s'affliger de, *to be grieved at*
s'agir de, *to be the question*
avertir de, *to warn of*
s'aviser de, *to bethink of*
blamer de, *to blame for*
brûler de, *to be anxious to*
cesser de, *to cease to*
se charger de, *to take charge of*
commander de, *to command to*
conjurer de, *to conjure to*
conseiller de, *to advise to*
se contenter de, *to be content with*
convenir de, *to agree*
craindre de, *to fear to*
dédaigner de, *to disdain to*
défendre de, *to forbid to*
défier de, *to defy to*
se dépêcher de, *to hasten to*
désespérer de, *to despair of*
différer de, *to delay to*
dire de, *to tell to*
discontinuer de, *to discontinue to*
disconvenir de, *to disown to*
dispenser de, *to dispense with*

dissuader de, *to dissuade from*
douter de, *to doubt*
écrire de, *to write to*
s'efforcer de, *to endeavor*
empêcher de, *to prevent to*
enrager de, *to be enraged to*
entreprendre de, *to undertake to*
essayer de, *to try to*
s'étonner de, *to be astonished at*
éviter de, *to avoid*
excuser de, *to excuse for*
exempter de, *to exempt from*
feindre de, *to feign to*
féliciter de, *to congratulate upon*
finir de, *to finish*
se flatter de, *to flatter oneself with*
frémir de, *to shudder to*
se garder de, *to take care not to*
se glorifier de, *to glory in*
se hâter de, *to hasten to*
jurer de, *to swear to*
manquer de, *to fail to*
se mêler de, *to meddle by*
menacer de, *to threaten to*
mériter de, *to deserve to*
négliger de, *to neglect to*
offrir de, *to offer to*
ordonner de, *to order to*

oublier de, *to forget to*
pardonner de, *to forgive for*
permettre de, *to permit to*
persuader de, *to persuade to*
se piquer de, *to pretend to*
plaindre de, *to pity for*
prendre soin de, *to take care of*
presser de, *to urge to*
prier de, *to request to*
promettre de, *to promise to*
proposer de, *to propose to*
être ravi de, *to be overjoyed with*
recommander de, *to recommend*
refuser de, *to refuse to*
regretter de, *to regret to*
se réjouir de, *to rejoice over*
remercier de, *to thank for*
rendre grâce de, *to thank*
se repentir de, *to repent of*

reprocher de, *to reproach for*
résoudre de, *to resolve to*
rire de, *to laugh at*
rougir de, *to blush for*
sommer de, *to summon to*
souffrir de, *to suffer to*
soupçonner de, *to suspect of*
se souvenir de, *to remember to*
suggérer de, *to suggest to*
supplier de, *to entreat to*
tâcher de, *to endeavor to*
tarder de, *to long to*
tenter de, *to attempt to*
trembler de, *to tremble at*
se trouver bien de, *to derive benefit from*
se trouver mal de, *to fare ill in*
se vanter de, *to boast of*

Examples:

Il m'a accusé de vouloir prendre sa place, *He accused me of wishing to take his situation from him.*

Il brûle de vous dire ce qu'il en pense, *He is anxious to tell you what he thinks of it.*

Je me charge de lui parler, *I assume the task of speaking to him.*

Je vous commande de vous arrêter, *I order you to stop.*

Dépêchez-vous de finir votre travail, *Make haste to finish your work.*

Je lui ai écrit de venir, *I wrote him to come.*

Il a essayé de se lever ce matin, *He tried to get up this morning.*

Pourquoi évite-t-il de me répondre? *Why does he avoid answering me?*

Il a oublié de me payer, *He forgot to pay me.*

Il vous a permis de sortir, *He allowed you to go out.*

Pourquoi avez-vous refusé de le suivre? *Why did you refuse to follow him?*

Je regrette de vous dire que vous vous conduisez mal, *I regret to tell you that you behave badly.*

Il se pique d'être un bon chasseur, *He pretends to be a good huntsman.*

12. Remarks on Verbs Taking de. — The verb *oublier*, to forget how, takes the preposition *à*. Thus,

On oublie à danser, *One forgets how to dance.*
Avez-vous oublié à jouer du piano? *Did you forget how to play on the piano?*

To the preceding list may be added the verb *avoir* when followed by a noun, and *être* when followed by an adjective. Thus,

Il a la satisfaction d'avoir rempli son devoir, *He has the satisfaction of having fulfilled his duty.*
Avez-vous regret d'avoir fait cela? *Do you regret having done that?*
Je suis heureux de vous revoir, *I am delighted to see you again.*
Elle est fâchée de vous avoir fait attendre, *She is sorry to have kept you waiting.*

13. Infinitive Preceded by Prepositions Other Than à or de. — All French prepositions except *en*, which requires the present participle, govern the infinitive. Thus,

sans mentir, *without lying*	en mentant, *in lying*
pour partir, *in order to go*	en partant, *in going*
après avoir reçu, *after having received*	il a commencé par me dire, *he began by telling me*
en ayant reçu, *in having received*	en me disant, *in telling me*

Conformably to its meaning, *après* always requires the past infinitive. Thus,

Après m'avoir salué, il sortit, *After having saluted me, he went out.*
Après s'être promené un peu, il se sentit fatigué, *After having walked a little, he felt tired.*

Before an infinitive *to* is expressed by *pour* when purpose is either expressed or understood. Thus,

Je suis venu pour vous complimenter, *I came in order to
congratulate you*.

Je vais chez moi pour changer de vêtements, *I am going
home to change my clothes*.

The present participle in English preceded by *for* explain-
ing the motive of an action, is rendered in French by *pour*
followed by the infinitive. Thus,

Il a été chassé pour avoir menti, *He was expelled for
lying*.

Il a été condamné pour avoir volé, *He was sentenced for
theft*.

SYNTAX OF THE PARTICIPLE

PRESENT PARTICIPLE

14. Present Participle and Verbal Adjective.
Both the present participle and the verbal adjective end
(except a few verbal adjectives) in *ant*. But while the
present participle is not inflected, the verbal adjective agrees
in gender and number with the noun it qualifies.

The present participle expresses *action*, while the verbal
adjective denotes *state*. **Action** is denoted when an accidental, instantaneous, short, or limited time is introduced;
state, when the sentence expresses quality or the result of
a prolonged or frequently repeated action. Thus,

Les éclairs **sillonnant** la nue, étaient continuels, *Flashes
of lightning, cutting the clouds, were continuous*.

Et nous vîmes ces soldats, **combattant** avec acharnement,
And we saw those soldiers fighting desperately.

In these sentences *sillonnant* and *combattant* express action.
Sillonnant marks an instantaneous act; *combattant* expresses
an act of long or but brief duration.

But in the sentence, *Vous avez des enfants bien* **caressants,** You have very sweet children, the verbal adjective is used, because *caressants* expresses a state, a quality, and is a true adjective.

15.   Characteristics of the Present Participle. — A word ending in *ant* is a present participle when it expresses an action.   A word ending in *ant* is a present participle:

1.   When it may be replaced by some other form of the verb.   Thus,

J'ai vu ces enfants **courant** vers la rivière, *I saw these children running toward the river.*

In this case *courant* may be replaced by *qui couraient*, who were running.

2.   When it has a direct object.   Thus,

C'est un excellent homme, **obligeant** tout le monde, *He is an excellent man, obliging everybody.*

Les hommes, **prévoyant** le danger, se tinrent sur leurs gardes, *The men, foreseeing danger, kept on their guard.*

3.   When accompanied by a negation.   Thus,

Ce sont des écoliers ne **travaillant** pas, et **n'aimant** pas l'étude, *They are scholars not working, and not fond of study.*

4.   When accompanied by the preposition *en*.   Thus,

L'appétit vient en **mangeant,** *Appetite comes while we eat.*
La fortune ne vient pas en **dormant,** *Fortune does not come during our sleep.*

PAST PARTICIPLE

16.   Cases to Be Considered. — The past participle may be used without an auxiliary, or with the auxiliary *être* or *avoir*.   Consequently, three cases must be considered:

PAST PARTICIPLE WITHOUT AN AUXILIARY

17. **Past Participle Considered as an Adjective.**
When the past participle is used without an auxiliary it is
considered to be an adjective, and thus agrees in gender and
number with the word with which it is associated.   Thus,

Vous avez mis une robe **déchirée,** *You put on a torn dress.*
Ma sœur, **frappée** de ces nouvelles, tomba évanouie, *My
sister, struck by this news, fell in a swoon.*

Enchantés de cette réception, mes frères restèrent longtemps, *Delighted by that reception, my brothers remained a
long time.*

18. **Exceptions.** — A few past participles become real
prepositions when placed before nouns, and, like prepositions, do not then agree with their dependent nouns.   They
are: *attendu*, considering; *excepté*, except; *supposé*, supposing;
ouï, heard; *passé*, past; *vu*, seeing; *y compris*, including; *non
compris*, not including; and the two participles *approuvé*,
approved, and *certifié*, certified, when used at the beginning
of a sentence in certain administrative and judicial forms.
Thus,

attendu les évènements, *considering the events*
approuvé l'écriture ci-dessus, *approved the above writing*
certifié la présente copie conforme à l'original, *certified
that the present copy conforms to the original*
non compris les dépenses, *not including the expenses*

But when these participles are placed after the noun, they
agree with it in number and gender, as do adjectives.   Thus,

les évènements attendus, *the expected events*
l'écriture ci-dessus approuvée, *the above writing approved*
la présente copie certifiée conforme à l'original, *the
present copy certified as agreeing with the original.*

PAST PARTICIPLE WITH ÊTRE

19. The past participle conjugated with *être* is held to
be an adjective and agrees in gender and number with the
subject of the verb, which may precede or follow it.   Thus,

Mon ami est **arrivé** (*masc.*), *My friend has arrived.*
Mon amie est **arrivée** (*fem.*), *My friend has arrived.*
Mes amis sont **arrivés** (*masc. pl.*), *My friends have arrived.*
Mes amies sont **arrivées** (*fem. pl.*), *My friends have arrived.*

PAST PARTICIPLE WITH AVOIR

20. **General Rule.** — A past participle conjugated with the auxiliary *avoir* agrees with the direct object when that direct object is placed before the participle. The past participle does not change its form when the direct object is placed after it, or when there is no direct object. Thus,

1. *The direct object preceding the past participle*

Voilà la ville que j'ai **visitée**, *There is the city I visited.*
Voilà les villes que j'ai **visitées**, *There are the cities I visited.*
Les arbres qu'ils ont **plantés** portent des fruits, *The trees they planted bear fruit.*
Les livres que vous m'avez **prêtés** étaient intéressants, *The books you lent me were interesting.*
Les souliers qu'il a **achetés** sont trop étroits, *The shoes he bought are too narrow.*
La maison que vous avez **vue** appartient à mon frère, *The house you saw belongs to my brother.*

2. *The direct object following the past participle*

Ils ont **planté** des arbres ce matin, *They planted trees this morning.*
J'ai **visité** toutes ces villes, *I visited all these cities.*
Il m'a **prêté** des livres intéressants, *He lent me interesting books.*
Vous avez **acheté** des souliers trop étroits, *You bought shoes too narrow.*
J'ai **vu** la maison qui appartient à votre frère, *I have seen the house that belongs to your brother.*

3. *No direct object*

Mes arbres ont **péri**, *My trees have died.*
Votre fils a bien **travaillé**, *Your son has worked well.*

Vous avez trop joué, et vous n'avez pas assez **étudié**, *You played too much, and you did not study enough.*

J'ai **dormi** toute la nuit, *I slept all night.*

Notice that the past participle with *avoir* does not agree with the subject. All variable past participles are subject to the rules given above. It is, however, often difficult to determine the direct object.

21. Past Participle of Neuter Verbs. — Neuter verbs having no direct object, they are invariable when conjugated with *avoir*. Thus,

La pluie n'a cessé de tomber pendant les deux heures que nous avons **couru**, *Rain did not cease falling during the two hours we ran.*

Les quelques heures qu'il a **dormi**, l'ont reposé, *The few hours he slept have refreshed him.*

Certain verbs may be used transitively or intransitively. When their participles are used transitively, these verbs are inflected if the direct object is placed before them; but they are invariable when used intransitively. *Courir* is intransitive when it means *to run*, and transitive in the sense of *to pursue, to be exposed to.* Thus,

Quels dangers avez-vous **courus?** *To what dangers have you been exposed?*

Les kilomètres que nous avons **couru**, *The kilometers we ran.*

Pousser in the sense of *to push* is transitive, and neuter when meaning *to grow.* Thus,

Nous les avons **poussés**, devant nous, *We pushed them before us.*

Ces champignons ont **poussé** dans une nuit, *These mushrooms grew in one night.*

Peser may be either transitive or intransitive. Thus,

La viande que j'ai **pesée**, a été vendue, *The meat I weighed has been sold.*

Les cinq kilogrammes que ce gigot a **pesé**, *The five kilograms that this leg of mutton weighed.*

Valoir is transitive in the sense of *to procure*, and neuter when it means *to be worth*. Thus,

Ce sont là les honneurs que son courage lui a **valus**, *These are the honors that his courage procured him.*

Cette propriété ne vaut plus les vingt mille francs qu'elle a **valu**, *This property is no longer worth the twenty thousand francs it once was.*

According to the Academy, the verb *coûter* is always neuter, and consequently can never be inflected when used with *avoir*. Thus,

Les vingt mille francs que cette maison m'a **coûté**, *The twenty thousand francs that this house cost me.*

Les efforts, la peine que ce travail m'a **coûté**, *The efforts, the trouble that this work has cost me.* . . . .

All grammarians and many French authors, however, consider *coûter* to be an active verb when it has the sense of *to cause, to exact*. Thus,

Après tous les ennuis que ce jour m'a **coûtés**, *After all the annoyances which this day has caused me.* — RACINE.

Vous n'avez pas oublié les soins que vous m'avez **coûtés** depuis votre enfance, *You have not forgotten the troubles that you have caused me since your childhood.* — FÉNELON.

22. Past Participle of Reflexive Verbs. — *Être* is used instead of *avoir* to form the compound tenses of reflexive verbs; but because *être* merely stands for *avoir* in such constructions, it follows the general rule given for the agreement of past participles used with *avoir*. Thus,

Elle s'est **habillée**, *She dressed herself.*
Ils se sont **battus**, *They fought.*

Some active verbs, called **essentially reflexive verbs** because they cannot be conjugated otherwise than in the reflexive form, always agree with the second pronoun. The only exception is *s'arroger*, to arrogate to oneself, which, although always used in the reflexive form, follows the general rule. Thus,

Nous nous sommes **abstenus** de toute reflexion, *We abstained from all reflection.*

Les soldats se sont **emparés** de la ville, *The soldiers took the city.*

23. Past Participle of an Impersonal Verb.—The past participle of an impersonal verb is invariable. Thus,

Il est **arrivé** des provisions, *Provisions have arrived.*

Les chaleurs qu'il a **fait** cet été ont été insupportables, *The hot weather of this summer has been intolerable.*

24. Past Participle Preceded by en.—A past participle conjugated with *avoir* and having *en* as a complement is invariable. Thus,

Avez-vous reçu des lettres?—Oui; j'en ai **reçu,** *Have you received letters?—Yes; I have received some.*

En is here used for *des lettres* in a partitive sense. It might seem that *en* should be construed as the direct object of *reçu* and that the past participle should agree with it. Recalling what was said of the partitive noun, it is obvious that *des lettres* means a part of all letters. *Des lettres* is, therefore, a complement, the direct object of the past participle being understood. This pronoun *en*, in fact, represents things considered to have neither gender nor number and is equivalent to *de cela*. *J'en ai reçu* is equivalent to *J'ai reçu de cela*. But if *en* is preceded by one of the adverbs *autant, combien, plus, moins,* suggesting the idea of plurality, the past participle is variable. Thus,

Combien n'en a-t-on pas **vus** qui étaient plus pauvres que lui! *How many of them did we not see poorer than he!*

Autant de parties il a **jouées,** autant il en a **perdues,** *As many games as he played, so many he lost (He lost every game he played).*

In a few special cases *en* has no effect upon the variation of the past participle. One of these cases is when the sentence contains a direct object of the usual type. Thus,

Mon père est à Paris; voici les nouvelles que j'en ai reçues, *My father is in Paris; here is the news I received from him.*

Here *en* has nothing to do with the agreement of the past participle, for *que*, representing *nouvelles*, is the direct object and the past participle agrees with it.

25. **Past Participle Followed by an Infinitive.** Sometimes the past participle with *avoir* is followed by an infinitive or by a preposition and an infinitive. In such cases, the direct object belongs either to the past participle or to the infinitive. If it belongs to the past participle, the past participle agrees with the direct object when the direct object precedes it. If it belongs to the infinitive, the past participle is invariable, its object being the following infinitive. It is sometimes difficult to determine the true relations of the object with the past participle and the infinitive. Thus,

Les messieurs que j'ai vus jouer étaient musiciens, *The gentlemen whom I saw playing were musicians.*

Les pièces que j'ai vu jouer étaient belles, *The plays that I have seen played were beautiful.*

In the first case, *vus* agrees with *que* as the direct object of the past participle, for it is evident that *que* (representing *messieurs*) cannot be the object of the infinitive *jouer*. But in the second case, *vu* does not change its form, for *que* (representing *les pièces*) is the object of *jouer*, and not of *vu*. The distinction may, perhaps, be more easily seen by comparing the French and English constructions. When the infinitive is translated by a present active participle the past participle agrees with the direct object; but when the infinitive is rendered in English by a passive participle the participle does not change. Thus, in the first case, the infinitive *jouer* is translated by the active participle *playing*, while in the second case it is rendered by the passive participle *played*. These rules are more fully illustrated in the following examples:

Les messieurs dont vous parlez, je les ai **vus** passer devant chez nous, *I saw the gentlemen of whom you speak passing before our house.*

Les musiciens que j'ai **entendus** jouer avaient un grand talent, *The musicians, whom I heard playing, had great talent.*

Cette dame parle bien; je l'ai **entendue** parler, *This lady speaks well; I heard her speak.*

Les propriétés que nous avons **vu** vendre étaient très belles, *The things that we saw sold were very beautiful.*

Les asperges que j'ai **vu** récolter étaient très grosses, *The asparagus that I saw picked was very large.*

Les chevaux que j'ai **vu** vendre ce matin étaient jeunes, *The horses that I saw sold this morning were young.*

Il nous a **priés** de lui écrire, *He begged us to write to him.*

Il nous a **recommandé** de lui écrire, *He recommended that we write to him.*

26. Infinitive Understood. — Certain participles, as *dû*, *permis*, *pu*, *voulu*, are invariable when they have for their object an infinitive understood. Thus,

Il a acheté tous les livres qu'il a **pu** (acheter *understood*), *He bought all the books he could.*

Elle a lu tous les romans qu'elle a **voulu** (lire *understood*), *She read all the novels she wished.*

But these past participles follow the general rule if no infinitive is understood. Thus,

Les sommes que nous lui avons **dues** sont payées, *The sums we owed her are paid.*

27. Le Representing a Proposition as Object. When *le* representing a proposition, is the direct object, the past participle is invariable. Thus,

L'affaire fut moins sérieuse que je ne l'avais **pensé,** *The affair was less serious than I thought.*

Les affaires n'ont pas tourné comme nous l'aurions **souhaité,** *The affairs did not take the turn we would have wished.*

In these examples, the first *le* stands for *qu'elle serait sérieuse,* and the second for *qu'elle ait tourné.* This pronoun *le* is a real neuter pronoun equivalent to *à cela;* consequently, the past participle must remain invariable.

28. Participle Preceded by le peu. — *Le peu* has two meanings in French: sometimes it denotes *a small quantity,* in which case the past participle agrees with the logical object of *le peu;* at other times it means *the lack of,* in which case the past participle agrees with *le peu,* (always masculine singular). Thus,

Le peu de chimie que cet industriel a **apprise,** lui a été fort utile, *The little chemistry that manufacturer learned has been very useful to him.*

Le peu de résultats que vous avez **obtenu** vous a découragé, *The lack of results you obtained discouraged you.*

SYNTAX OF THE ARTICLE

DEFINITE ARTICLE

USES OF THE ARTICLE

29. General Principle. — The article is used before nouns taken in a determinate sense; otherwise it is omitted. A noun taken in a determinate sense represents the totality of beings or objects it names; or it represents a species, or a part of the totality of the class of beings or objects that have among themselves points of resemblance; or finally, it designates one particular object or being.   Thus,

Les hommes sont mortels, *Men are mortal.*
Les oiseaux volent, *Birds fly.*
L'argent est un métal, *Silver is a metal.*
Les enfants studieux font des progrès, *Studious children make progress.*
L'homme faible se laisse gouverner par ses passions, *The weak allow themselves to be governed by their passions.*
L'homme dont vous parlez ne mérite pas votre pitié, *The man of whom you are speaking does not deserve your pity.*
Le fils de votre ami parle français, *Your friend's son speaks French.*

A noun is indeterminate when it does not denote totality, a species, or individual beings or objects, but is taken in a vague, general sense.   Such a noun is not preceded by the article, and may generally be replaced by an adjective or an adverb without destroying the sense of the sentence. Thus,

Il a été reçu avec honneur (honorablement), *He was received with honor.*

Sa vie a été pleine de sagesse (sage), *His life has been full of wisdom.*

Note.—A noun may be rendered determinate not only by an article, but also by a possessive adjective, a demonstrative adjective, an interrogative adjective, an indefinite adjective, or by a numeral.

30. Partitive Article.—Before nouns taken in a partitive sense, the article is used in connection with the preposition *de* to form the combinations *du, de la, de l', des.* These are not really articles, as they do not render the noun determinate. Take *des* for example. It has two distinct meanings. It may be a plural article contracted for *de les.* Thus,

Les pensées **des** hommes sont changeantes, *The thoughts of men are changing.*

But taken in a partitive sense, it is equivalent to *quelque*, and does not affect the extension of the noun. Thus,

La vie a **des** plaisirs, *Life has pleasures.*

The sense is that of an indefinite article. It seems to be the plural of the indefinite article *un.* Thus,

Avez-vous **un** livre? *Have you a book?*
J'ai **des** livres, *I have some books.*

Applying this to the exceptions given in the use of the partitive article, we will say that it is only the partitive article *des* that disappears before an adjective, but that *des*, the contracted article, is retained before an adjective. Thus,

Notre mérite attire l'estime **des** honnêtes gens, *Our merit attracts the esteem of honest people.*

Ceux qui s'appliquent trop aux petites choses deviennent ordinairement incapables **des** grandes, *Those who apply themselves to small things, ordinarily become incapable of great ones.*

31. Article After Aimer.—The sense of the noun may be determinate in French when the English construction would not indicate it. The article is also used after *aimer* and *aimer mieux*. Thus,

En Europe, le pain, la viande, le lait, les œufs, les légumes, le fruit sont les aliments ordinaires de l'homme; le vin, la bière, le cidre, sa boisson, *In Europe, bread, meat, milk, eggs, vegetables, fruit are the ordinary food of man; wine, beer, cider, his drink.*

J'aime mieux le café que le thé, *I like coffee better than tea.*
Aimez-vous le café? *Do you like coffee?*

32. Article in Gallicisms.—In the following Gallicisms, the article is used in French while it is avoided in English:

J'ai le temps, *I have time.*
donner, trouver, prendre le temps, *to give, to find, to take time*
vers les trois heures, vers le soir, *toward three o'clock, toward evening*
Il est parti le premier (le dernier), *He started first (last).*
Il est venu la semaine dernière (le mois passé), *He came last week (last month).*
Je le verrai l'hiver prochain, *I shall see him next winter.*
apprendre, étudier, comprendre, etc. le français, *to learn, study, understand, etc. French*
garder le silence, *to keep silence*
Soyez le bienvenu, la bienvenue, *Welcome!*
Je vous souhaite le bonjour, le bonsoir, *I wish you good day, good evening.*
Il n'a pas le sou, *He has not a farthing.*

33. Article With Names of Parts of the Body.—The article is used in French before the names of the parts of the body and the qualities of the mind, when the sense clearly indicates the relation between them and their possessor, while English usage demands the possessive adjective. Thus,

J'ai mal à la tête, *My head aches.*
Elle a le bras cassé, *Her arm is broken.*
Vous vous fatiguez l'esprit pour rien, *You weary your mind for nothing.*

34. Article Before Units of Weight and Measure.
The article is used in French before a unit of weight or measure, as the indefinite article is used in English.   Thus,

Le mouton se vend quinze sous la livre, *Mutton is sold at fifteen cents a pound.*

Ce drap coûte sept francs le mètre, *This cloth costs seven francs a meter.*

ARTICLE BEFORE PROPER NOUNS

35.   Article Before Names of Countries. — The article is used in French before the name of a country:

1.   When subject or direct object of a verb.   Thus,

La France est très peuplée, *France is very populous.*
Je connais la France, mais je ne connais pas l'Angleterre, *I am acquainted with France, but I do not know England.*

2.   After all prepositions except *en*, which always requires the suppression of the article; also in a few cases with *de.* Thus,

La Turquie a fait la paix avec la Russie, *Turkey made peace with Russia.*
Il est parti pour l'Amérique, *He started for America.*
L'année dernière j'étais en France, *Last year I was in France.*

The article is not used after *de* if the name of the country is used to qualify a preceding noun, nor when *de* has the meaning of *from.*   Thus,

l'empereur d'Allemagne, *the emperor of Germany*
J'ai acheté une histoire de France, *I bought a French history.*
J'arrive d'Italie, *I am just coming from Italy.*

36. **Article Before Proper Names of Persons and Names of Cities.** — The article is generally omitted before names of persons and cities. Thus,

Louis a couru, *Louis ran.*

Paris est la capitale de la France, *Paris is the capital of France.*

But the article is used in the following cases:

1. When the names of persons or cities are preceded by an adjective or a title. Thus,

Le docteur Charcot, *Dr. Charcot*
L'empereur Napoléon, *The Emperor Napoleon*
le bon Henri, *the good Henry*
La Nouvelle Orléans, *New Orleans*

2. For emphasis, before the names of illustrious persons; also before the names of persons used as common nouns. Thus,

Les Montesquieu, les Rousseau, les Voltaire nous ont éclairés par leurs œuvres, *Montesquieu, Rousseau, Voltaire enlightened us by their works.*

Les Racine, les Corneille, sont rares, *Poets like Racine, Corneille are rare.*

3. Before a few names of cities derived from common nouns. Thus,

Le Hâvre,	La Haye,
Le Mans,	Le Caire,
La Rochelle,	La Mecque

37. **Article Before Plus, Mieux, Moins.** — Before the adverbs *plus*, *mieux*, *moins*, the article is used to express a comparison. It is then inflected for both gender and number. Thus,

De tout le monde, ces messieurs sont les plus affligés, *These gentlemen are the most afflicted of all.*

Dans une fête, elle est toujours la plus belle, *On a holiday, she is always the most beautiful.*

EXCEPTIONS. — *Le* used before *plus*, *mieux*, *moins* to denote a quality expressed in the highest degree, but without comparison is uninflected. Thus,

C'est le matin que les fleurs paraissent le plus belles, *It is in the morning that flowers appear the most beautiful.*

Le without inflection is also used before these adverbs when they modify a verb or an adverb, because in such constructions they are adverbial. Thus,

Votre mère est celle qui donne le plus, *Your mother is giving the most.*

Racine et Boileau sont les deux poêtes qui écrivent le mieux, *Racine and Boileau are the two poets who write best.*

REPETITION OF THE ARTICLE

38. General Rule. — The article must be repeated before each noun with which it can properly be used. Thus,

Les femmes, les enfants, les vieillards furent mis en sûreté, *Women, children, old people were placed in safety.*

Paris est la ville la plus grande et la plus peuplée de la France, *Paris is the largest and most populous city of France.*

The article is not repeated, however, before nouns forming an indivisible phrase nor before nouns occurring in certain administrative and legal expressions, nor before nouns in certain idiomatic forms established by long usage. The most important of these expressions are:

les père et mère, *the father and mother*
les frères et sœurs, *the brothers and sisters*
les officiers, sous-officiers et soldats, *the officers, non-commissioned officers, and soldiers*
journal paraissant les mardi, jeudi et samedi de chaque semaine, *newspaper appearing on Tuesday, Thursday, and Saturday of each week*
les Arts et métiers, *the arts and trades*
les Ponts et Chaussées, *the bridges and roads (administration)*
les dits jour mois et an, *the said day, month, and year*
les us et coutumes, *the usages and customs*

39. **Article Before an Adjective.** — When adjectives not grouped in series qualify a succession of nouns, expressed or understood, the article is repeated before each adjective. Thus,

Le jeune soldat et le vieux, *The young and the old soldier*.

It is evident that *jeune* and *vieux* cannot qualify the same man, and that *soldat* is understood after the second adjective. It would be incorrect to say: *le jeune et vieux soldat*. But, on the contrary, when the adjectives qualify the same noun, the article is not repeated. Thus,

Le simple et bon La Fontaine est une de nos gloires littéraires, *The simple and good La Fontaine is one of our literary glories*.

OMISSION OF THE ARTICLE

40. **Article Omitted Before an Indeterminate Noun.** — The article is not used before a common noun having no specialized sense. Thus,

une table de bois, *a wooden table*
un homme sans talent, *a man without talent*

In these examples, there is nothing to indicate that it is a question of a special kind of wood or talent. These words are taken in an entirely vague, generic sense.

41. **Article Omitted in Proverbial Sentences.** Even when a noun has a specialized sense, the article is often omitted in proverbial sentences. Thus,

Patience et longueur de temps
Font plus que force ni que rage.

Patience and lapse of time accomplish more than strength or rage. — LA FONTAINE.
Pauvreté n'est pas vice, *Poverty is not vice*.

42. **Article Omitted in Enumerations.** — In enumerations, the article is often suppressed to give more liveliness, energy, and grace to the sentence. Thus,

Citoyens, étrangers, ennemis, peuples, rois, empereurs, le plaignent et le révèrent, *Citizens, foreigners, enemies, peoples, kings, emperors, pity and venerate him.*

Femmes, moines, vieillards, tout était descendu, *Women, monks, old men, all had alighted.*

43. **Article Omitted Before Nouns Joined to Certain Verbs.** — After certain verbs, like *avoir, faire, donner, mettre, parler, prendre,* etc., the article is omitted before an object complement that forms with the verb an idiomatic expression. Thus,

ajouter foi, *to give credit*

avoir besoin, *to be in need of*

avoir carte blanche, *to have full power*

avoir chaud, *to be warm*

avoir froid, *to be cold*

avoir compassion, *to commiserate*

avoir dessein, *to intend*

avoir envie, *to wish*

avoir faim, *to be hungry*

avoir soif, *to be thirsty*

avoir honte, *to be ashamed*

avoir patience, *to have patience*

avoir peur, *to be afraid*

avoir pitié, *to pity*

avoir raison, *to be right*

avoir tort, *to be wrong*

avoir soin, *to take care*

donner carte blanche, *to give full power*

faire attention, *to mind*

faire peur, *to frighten*

faire plaisir, *to do a favor*

faire semblant, *to feign*

faire tort, *to wrong*

faire voile, *to set sail*

mettre fin, *to put an end*

parler français, *to speak French*

porter bonheur, *to bring good luck*

porter malheur, *to bring bad luck*

porter envie, *to bear envy*

prendre courage, *to cheer up*

prendre garde, *to take care*

prendre patience, *to wait patiently*

prendre plaisir, *to delight*

prendre racine, *to take root*

rendre visite, *to return a visit*

tenir tête, *to cope with one*

44. **Article Suppressed Before Words in Apposition.** — The article is generally omitted before words in apposition. Thus,

Cieux écoutez ma voix; terre, prête l'oreille, *Heavens, listen to my voice; earth, give ear.*

Dieppe, ville de Normandie, est très frequentée en été, *Dieppe, city of Normandy, is a very popular resort in summer.*

45. Article Omitted After ni. — The article is not used before nouns preceded by *ni . . . ni*, meaning *neither . . . nor.* Thus,

Il n'a ni parents ni amis, *He has neither parents nor friends.*
Je n'ai ni peur ni honte, *I am neither afraid nor ashamed.*

46. Article in Negative Propositions. — The article is omitted in negative propositions before a noun used partitively as the direct object of a verb or of a preposition. Thus,

Il ne m'a pas fait de reproches, *He did not reproach me with anything.*
Il ne mange pas de viande, *He does not eat any meat.*

But if the noun is followed by a qualifying adjective, or by a determinative, the article is used. Thus,

Je ne vous ferai pas des reproches frivoles, *I will not reproach you frivolously.*
Je ne fais pas des vers quand je veux, *I do not write verses when I wish.*

47. Article in Interrogative Sentences. — In interrogative-negative sentences, the article is not used before a noun, except when a positive answer is implied. Thus,

N'avez-vous pas d'amis? *Have you no friends?*

The meaning is, I do not know whether you have friends. But we say, *N'avez-vous pas des amis?* when we wish to convey the idea that the person has friends upon whom he may rely.

___

INDEFINITE ARTICLE

48. Indefinite Article With Tel or Si. — This article corresponds to the English article *a* or *an*. It is written *un* in the masculine and *une* in the feminine. Thus,

J'ai acheté un manteau, un manchon, une voilette, une paire de bottines, et un éventail, *I have bought a cloak, a muff, a veil, a pair of boots, and a fan.*

Used with *tel*, or *si*, meaning *such*, the indefinite article is placed before these words. Thus,

un si bel homme, *such a handsome man*
une telle peur, *such a fright*

49. **Indefinite Article Before Nouns of Profession or Nationality.** — The indefinite article is suppressed before a noun denoting nationality, state, or profession, after the verb *être* and other verbs expressing existence; as, for example, *naître*, *mourir*, *devenir*, *paraître*. Thus,

Est-il soldat? *Is he a soldier?*
Il est né poête, *He was born a poet.*
Ils sont devenus médecins, *They became doctors.*
Ce monsieur est-il Français? *Is this gentleman a Frenchman?*

But if the noun denoting nationality or profession is qualified by an adjective, or if we desire to distinguish it from other nouns of the same class, the indefinite article is retained. Thus,

Son oncle est un riche Français, *His uncle is a rich Frenchman.*
L'autruche est un oiseau, *The ostrich is a bird.*
Vous êtes un bon avocat, *You are a good lawyer.*

50. **Indefinite Article After C'est and Ce Sont.** The attribute, after the impersonal expressions *c'est* and *ce sont*, ordinarily takes the indefinite article. Thus,

C'est un Français, un peintre, *He is a Frenchman, a painter.*
Ce sont des Allemandes, *They are German* (fem.).

The indefinite article after *c'est* may, however, be suppressed before the name of a thing; and is usually expressed before abstract nouns that are to be emphasized. Thus,

C'est folie, c'est sottise, c'est cruauté que d'agir ainsi, *It is folly, it is nonsense, it is cruelty to act thus.*

55—23

51. **Indefinite Article After Sans.** — The indefinite article is not used after the preposition *sans*, before a noun. Thus,

Il était sans feu quand je suis arrivé, *He was without a fire when I arrived.*

Je puis traduire sans dictionnaire, *I can translate without a dictionary.*

52. **Indefinite Article Omitted in Explanatory Sentences.** — Contrary to English custom, the indefinite article is omitted in French in exclamatory sentences. Thus,

Quelle belle voiture! *What a beautiful carriage!*

Quel homme généreux vous êtes! *What a generous man you are!*

La belle ville que Paris! *What a fine city Paris is!*

53. **Indefinite Article Omitted Before Nouns of Measure.** — The definite article *le* is used instead of the indefinite article *un* before nouns of measure or weight. Thus,

Ce drap vaut deux francs le mètre, *This cloth is worth two francs a meter.*

Je l'ai payé cinq francs la bouteille, *I paid five francs a bottle for it.*

Nous achetons du café à trois francs la livre, *We buy coffee at three francs a pound.*

When speaking of time, *par*, by, is used as the indefinite article is used in English. Thus,

Cet ouvrier gagne six francs par jour, *This workman earns six francs a day.*

Je paie cent francs de pension par mois, *My board is a hundred francs a month.*

SYNTAX OF THE NOUN

FUNCTIONS OF THE NOUN

CASE IN NOUNS

54. Meaning of Case. — A noun may be related in a number of different ways to other words in a sentence; that is, it may fill various uses or functions. For example; a noun may be the subject, the attribute, or the object of a verb, and it may fill other offices. These several uses of nouns in helping to express thought make up the **cases** in grammar.

In Latin, the various cases were indicated by changes in the form of nouns; but French nouns have no such inflection, case being denoted by the position of the noun in the sentence, or by the use of prepositions, especially *à* and *de*.

55. Relations of the Noun in the Sentence. — The following are the chief functions performed by the noun:

1. *Noun as Subject.* — A noun may be the subject of a finite verb; it is then said to be in the **nominative case.** Thus,

Le maître est malade, *The teacher is ill.*
Charles est parti ce matin pour la campagne, *Charles went to the country this morning.*

2. *Noun as Attribute.* — An attributive noun always denotes the same person or thing as the subject; it is, therefore, in the nominative case. Thus,

Le diamant est une **pierre** précieuse, *The diamond is a precious stone.*
Louis est l'**ami** de Charles, *Louis is the friend of Charles.*

3. *Noun in Apposition.*—A noun may be in apposition with another nominative. In such cases its function is similar to that of an adjective—explanatory and modifying. Thus,

Grant, le **général,** termina la guerre, *Grant, the general, ended the war.*

This is equivalent to *Le général Grant termina la guerre*, in which *général* is a modifier of Grant.

4. *Noun Independent.*—In this construction the nominative fills the office for which it is named—its nominating or naming function. A word so used has no grammatical relation to other words. It stands in an independent relation and has no other use than merely to name some person or thing. This independent use may assume one of three forms:

(*a*) By address. Thus,

Enfants, étudiez vos leçons, *Children, study your lessons.*

(*b*) By exclamation. Thus,

Amitié! La chose n'existe pas, *Friendship! There is no such thing.*

(*c*) By pleonasm. Strictly speaking, any noun or pronoun that adds unnecessarily to a construction is pleonastic; for this is what the word means. But pleonasm is the mere mention of a noun or a pronoun, not in the way of address or exclamation, but as suggesting that about which the sentence more fully treats. It is used for emphasis; the noun or pronoun is not the subject or object of a verb. Thus,

Je vous connais, je sais **qui vous êtes,** *I know thee, who thou art.*

Puissé-je, **de mes yeux,** y voir tomber la foudre! *May I with my own eyes see lightning strike it.*

5. *Noun as Object of a Verb.*—There are several varieties of the object complements of verbs:

(*a*)   Direct object.   Thus,

Il a acheté **un livre,** *He bought a book.*
Nous avons vendu **notre maison,** *We sold our house.*

(*b*)   Indirect object.   Thus,

J'ai acheté un chapeau **à Louis,** *I bought a hat for Louis.*
Il a donné une récompense à cet **enfant,** *He gave a reward to that child.*

6.   *Noun Complement of Another Noun.* — When so used, the second noun denotes possession, composition, etc., and is joined to the preceding noun by a preposition.   Thus,

La maison de **Henri** est bien jolie, *Henry's house is very pretty.*
Comment trouvez-vous cette table de **bois?** *How do you like this wooden table?*

NOUN COMPLEMENT OF ANOTHER NOUN

56.   **Possessive Case.** — To express possession, the name of object possessed is placed first, and is separated from the noun denoting the possessor by the preposition *de* with the article *le*, *la*, or *les*, contracted when necessary.   Thus,

le cheval du boucher, *the butcher's horse*
l'amie de la dame, *the lady's friend*
le livre de l'enfant, *the child's book*
les progrès des élèves, *the pupils' progress*

57.   **Material.** — The French language having no adjectives formed from nouns or adverbs denoting material, time, or place, such as woolen, straw, silk, etc., these adjectives are replaced by the noun or adverb denoting material, time, or place, and separated from the first noun by the preposition *de* without the article.   Thus,

une montre d'or, *a gold watch*
une maison de bois, *a wooden house*
le journal d'hier, d'aujourd'hui, *today's, yesterday's paper*
la guerre de Sept ans, *the seven-years' war*

The preposition *en* may also be used to express of what a thing is made. Thus,

Cette montre est en or, *This watch is of gold.*
Ce chapeau est en paille, *This hat is made of straw.*

In the first case, when *de* is used, the descriptive adjective furnishes the most exact English translation. In the second, when *en* is used, the meaning is best expressed by *made of* with the noun. Thus,

J'ai un chapeau de paille, *I have a straw hat.*
Mon chapeau est en paille, *My hat is made of straw.*

58. Dimensions. — There are several methods of expressing dimensions in French:

1. The verb *avoir* is generally used with a noun. Thus,

Combien la tour Eiffel a-t-elle de hauteur? *How high is the Eiffel tower?*
Elle a trois cents mètres de hauteur (*or*, de haut), *It is three hundred meters high.*

2. The following construction also may be used:

Quelle est la hauteur de la tour Eiffel? *What is the height of the Eiffel tower?*
La hauteur de la tour Eiffel est de trois cents mètres, *The height of the Eiffel tower is three hundred meters.*
La tour Eiffel est haute de trois cents mètres, *The Eiffel tower is three hundred meters high.*

NOTE. — Nouns expressing dimensions are formed by adding *ur* to the feminine form of the corresponding adjective of dimension. They are feminine.

ADJECTIVES (FEM.)	NOUNS
longue, *long*	la longueur, *the length*
haute, *high*	la hauteur, *the height*
épaisse, *thick*	l'épaisseur, *the thickness*
large, *wide*	la largeur, *the width*

59. Measure of Quantity. — Nouns expressing measure of quantity, of weight, of number, also adverbs of quantity, are joined to the noun by the preposition *de* without the article. Thus,

une bouteille de vin, *a bottle of wine*
un verre de lait, *a glass of milk*
un morceau de pain, *a piece of bread*
une livre de café, *a pound of coffee*
assez de viande, *enough meat*

EXCEPTIONS. — After *bien*, much, many, and *la plupart*, the greater part, the article is used with *de*. Thus,

bien des hommes, *many men*
la plupart des enfants, *most children*

60. **Du and De.** — Distinction between the contracted article (*du*, *de la*, *de l'*, *des*) and the simple preposition *de* must also be made, for these phrases do not express the same idea. Take for example the two phrases:

C'est un palais de roi, *It is a royal palace*.
C'est le palais du roi, *It is the king's palace*.

The first sentence is general, and qualifies *un palais*, showing the kind of palace; the second, on the contrary, indicates whose palace it is.

61. **Complement of the Noun With Preposition à.** The preposition *à* is put before a noun used as the complement of another noun in the following cases:

1. When the second noun is descriptive of the object it limits. Thus,

une voiture à quatre roues, *a four-wheeled carriage*
un vieillard à cheveux blancs, *an old man with white hair*
une maison à deux étages, *a two-story house*

2. When the second noun shows the use or purpose of the first. Thus,

la salle à manger, *dining-room*
une cuillère à café, *a coffee-spoon*
la brosse à dents, *the tooth-brush*

Note the difference between *à* and *de* used in the following expressions:

une tasse **à** café, *a coffee-cup*
une tasse **de** café, *a cup of coffee*

3. When the second noun indicates the means by which the first operates. Thus,

une machine à vapeur, *a steam-engine*
un fourneau à gaz, *a gas-stove*
une arme à feu, *a fire-arm*

4. In cooking terms, the second noun is preceded by *à* with the article contracted, if necessary, to designate the ingredient of the component parts of the first. Thus,

du café au lait, *coffee with milk*
potage au vermicelle, *vermicelli soup*
une tourte à la crème, *q cream-tart*

GENDER OF NAMES OF CITIES

62. General Rule. — In general, all names of cities are masculine; but the following names of cities, coming from Latin feminines, have retained their genders, namely: *Rome, Carthage, Athènes, Jerusalem, Lacédémone, Sparte, Syracuse, Florence, Venise, Lutèce, Thèbes, Grenade.* When the name of a city is used by address, it is generally feminine. Thus,

Tyr! dans quelles mains es-tu tombée? *Tyrus! into what hands hast thou fallen?* — FÉNELON.

Chante, heureuse Orléans, les vengeurs de la France, *Sing, happy Orleans, the avengers of France.* — C. DELAVIGNE.

63. Countries and Nationalities. — The names of the principal countries and the corresponding names of their inhabitants and languages are given below:

L'Afrique, *Africa*
L'Angleterre, *England*
L'Algérie, *Algeria*
L'Allemagne, *Germany*

L'Amérique, *America*
L'Asie, *Asia*
L'Australie, *Australia*
L'Autriche, *Austria*

La Bavière, *Bavaria*
La Belgique, *Belgium*
La Chine, *China*
Le Danemark, *Denmark*
L'Ecosse, *Scotland*
L'Espagne, *Spain*
La France, *France*
La Grèce, *Greece*
Le Hanovre, *Hanover*
La Hollande, *Holland*
L'Inde, *India*
L'Irlande, *Ireland*
L'Italie, *Italy*
Le Japon, *Japan*
Le Mexique, *Mexico*
La Norvège, *Norway*
La Prusse, *Prussia*
La Russie, *Russia*
La Saxe, *Saxony*
La Sicile, *Sicily*
La Suède, *Sweden*
La Suisse, *Switzerland*
La Turquie, *Turkey*
Africain, *African*
Anglais, *English*
Algérien, *Algerian*
Allemand, *German*

Américain, *American*
Asiatique, *Asiatic*
Australien, *Australian*
Autrichien, *Austrian*
Bavarois, *Bavarian*
Belge, *Belgian*
Chinois, *Chinese*
Danois, *Dane*
Ecossais, *Scotch*
Espagnol, *Spanish*
Français, *French*
Grec, *Greek*
Hanovrien, *Hanoverian*
Hollandais, *Dutch*
Indien, *Indian*
Irlandais, *Irish*
Italien, *Italian*
Japonais, *Japanese*
Mexicain, *Mexican*
Norvégien, *Norwegian*
Prussien, *Prussian*
Russe, *Russian*
Saxon, *Saxon*
Sicilien, *Sicilian*
Suédois, *Swede*
Suisse, *Swiss*
Turc, *Turk*

The names of countries, when ending in *e* without an accent, are feminine; except *le Mexique*, *le Maine*, *le Hanovre*.

FRENCH GRAMMAR

(PART 10)

SYNTAX OF THE ADJECTIVE

QUALIFYING ADJECTIVES

1. Relations Between the Noun and the Adjective.
A French noun becomes an adjective when it qualifies
another noun. Thus,

Lord Bacon n'est pas auteur du théâtre de Shakespeare,
Lord Bacon is not the author of Shakespeare's plays.
Napoléon fut à la fois général et législateur, *Napoleon was
at the same time general and legislator.*

Here the words *auteur*, *général*, and *législateur*, usually
nouns, must be regarded as adjectives, for their functions
are to qualify the nouns Lord Bacon and Napoleon.

Just as nouns may become adjectives, an adjective may
become a noun. When used in this sense, adjectives no
longer merely represent qualities, but, like nouns, they both
name and personify the qualities they ordinarily represent.
Thus,

Victor Cousin est l'auteur de "Le Vrai, le Beau, et le
Bien," *Victor Cousin is the author of "The True, the Beautiful,
and the Good."*

Adjectives may also be used to designate a class, or
an individual. They then acquire all the properties and

perform all the functions of true nouns. Such are adjectives like *malade, ambitieux, méchants,* etc. Thus,

Comment va votre malade? *How is your patient?*

L'avare n'amasse que pour amasser, *The miser accumulates solely for the purpose of accumulating.*

Les méchants ne sont jamais heureux, *The wicked are never happy.*

As has already been explained, a noun with a preposition before it is often placed after another noun to qualify its meaning. Such a construction is most nearly represented in English by a noun with adjectival functions before another noun, or by a mere adjective. Thus,

une robe de laine, *a woolen dress*
une machine à vapeur, *a steam engine*
le couteau à découper, *the carving knife*
le journal du soir, *the evening paper*
une mine de charbon, *a coal mine*
une femme de chambre, *a chambermaid*

When an adjective is thus used as a noun, its meaning may, like that of a noun, be modified by another adjective; but it nevertheless still retains something of the nature of an adjective, for it may also be modified by a pure adverb. Thus,

le vrai beau, *the truth beautiful*
les infiniment petits, *the infinitely small*
J'ai vu de pauvres aveugles, *I saw poor blind men.*

2. How to Avoid Ambiguity. — A qualifying adjective must always clearly refer to the noun or pronoun it qualifies. For example, the following sentence is ambiguous and consequently incorrect:

Riche et puissant, vous m'avez toujours été fidèle, *Rich and powerful, you have always been faithful to me.*

To whom *riche* and *puissant* refer is not clear. Is it to *me* or to *you?* The sentence does not clearly indicate. To avoid this ambiguity, the sentence should be either,

Vous m'avez toujours été fidèle, même quand vous étiez riche et puissant, *You have always been faithful to me, even when you were rich and powerful;* or,

Vous m'avez toujours été fidèle quand j'étais riche et puissant, *You were always faithful to me when I was rich and powerful.*

AGREEMENT OF ADJECTIVES

3. General Rule. — An adjective agrees in gender and number with the noun or pronoun it qualifies. Thus,

un homme charmant, *a charming man*
une femme charmante, *a charming woman*
des hommes charmants, *charming men*
des femmes charmantes, *charming women*

4. Adjective Qualifying Several Nouns or Pronouns. — When an adjective qualifies several nouns or pronouns, the adjective is put in the plural. As to its gender, three cases are to be considered:

(*a*) When the nouns or pronouns are masculine, the adjective takes the masculine form. Thus,

Louis et Charles sont contents, *Louis and Charles are glad.*

Mon ami et mon frère sont prêts, *My friend and my brother are ready.*

(*b*) When the nouns or pronouns are feminine, the adjective becomes feminine. Thus,

Louise et Marie sont contentes, *Louise and Mary are glad.*
Mon amie et ma sœur sont prêtes, *My friend and my sister are ready.*

(*c*) When the nouns or pronouns are of different genders, the adjective takes the masculine form. Thus,

Louise et Charles sont contents, *Louise and Charles are contented.*

Mon amie et mon frère sont prêts, *My friend and my brother are ready.*

NOTE. — When two nouns, one masculine and the other feminine, are used with the same qualifying adjective, the masculine noun is put last if the pronunciation of the adjective differs in its masculine and feminine genders. This rule is carefully observed in order to prevent a feminine noun from falling close to a masculine adjective. Thus,

Louise et Charles sont contents, not *Charles et Louise sont contents.* If, however, the adjective has the same pronunciation in both genders, the order of the nouns is immaterial. Either of these forms is consequently correct: *Louise et Charles sont dociles*, or, *Charles et Louise sont dociles.*

5. Synonymous Nouns. — An adjective placed after several synonymous nouns agrees with the last noun only. It may be said also that such synonymous nouns can never be joined by the conjunction *et*, the sign of addition. Thus,

Toute sa vie n'a été qu'un travail, qu'une occupation continuelle, *His whole life has been a continual endeavor, an enduring occupation.* — MASSILLON.

6. Nouns United by Ou. — An adjective placed after nouns joined by the conjunction *ou* agrees with the last noun only. Thus,

Ils obtinrent l'estime ou la confiance publique, *They won public esteem or confidence.*

7. Adjective After a Collective. — When used with a collective noun, an adjective agrees according to the sense of the sentence either with the collective noun or with its complement. But after the following expressions, an adjective always agrees with the complement of the collective: namely, *beaucoup de*, *peu de*, *bien des*, *la plus grande partie de.* Thus,

une quantité de cerises considérable, *a considerable quantity of cherries*
une quantité de cerises douces, *a quantity of sweet cherries*

8. Adjective After Two Nouns Separated by De. When an adjective is placed after two nouns, the second being a complement of the first, it may agree with either of the nouns it qualifies. Thus,

un morceau de viande trop **gros,** *a too large piece of meat*
un morceau de viande **crue,** *a piece of raw meat*
une corbeille de fruits bien **pleine,** *a very full basket of fruit*
une corbeille de fruits bien **mûrs,** *a basket of very ripe fruit*

9. Adjective Used With Avoir l'Air. — The expression *avoir l'air* has two meanings. In the first instance *air* may be a noun, meaning the air, carriage, exterior or manner of a person; in the second, it may form a compound expression having the sense of *to appear, to seem.* In the first case, the adjective agrees with the word *air;* in the second, with the subject of the verb. Thus,

Elles ont l'air hautain, mais l'accueil familier, *They have a haughty appearance, but a familiar welcome.* — VOLTAIRE.
Elle a l'air toute troublée, *She appears quite troubled.*

AGREEMENT OF CERTAIN ADJECTIVES

10. The following adjectives present certain peculiarities in their agreement with nouns:

Nu. — The adjective *nu*, naked, joined to *cou, tête, jambes, bras, pieds* is invariable, for it forms with them a kind of adverbial expression. Thus,

Il va nu-tête, nu-pieds, nu-jambes, etc., *He goes bareheaded, barefooted, barelegged,* etc.

In all other cases, *nu* agrees with its noun. Thus,

Il va toujours pieds nus, *He always goes barefooted.*
Toute nue, la vérite risque de déplaire, *Naked truth is likely to displease.*

Demi. — This adjective when standing before a noun is invariable; after a noun, it agrees with that noun in gender only. Thus,

Nous avons une demi-heure, *We have half an hour.*
Il est une heure et demie, *It is half-past one.*

Feu. — The adjective *feu*, meaning *late*, *deceased*, agrees with a noun only when put immediately before the noun it qualifies. It is invariable when separated from the noun by an article or a possessive adjective. Thus,

la feue reine, *the late queen*
feu la reine, feu ma sœur, *the deceased queen, my deceased sister*

Ci-joint, Ci-inclus. — These two expressions are invariable both at the beginning of a sentence, and in the midst of a sentence when placed before a noun not preceded by an article or determinative adjective. Thus,

Ci-joint, or ci-inclus la copie des articles de la société, *Enclosed the copy of the articles of the partnership.*

Vous trouverez ci-joint copie de ces articles, *You will find enclosed the copy of these articles.*

Franc de Port. — In this expression the adjective *franc* is invariable before a noun; but it agrees when the noun precedes. Thus,

Vous recevrez franc de port les marchandises suivantes, *You will receive prepaid the following merchandise.*

Ces marchandises sont franches de port, *These goods are prepaid.*

Proche. — *Proche*, when followed by *de*, is an adjective and agrees with its noun; or it is an invariable preposition. Thus,

Ces maisons sont proches l'une de l'autre, *These houses are near to one another.*

Les maisons que l'on construit proche de la rivière ne sont pas terminées, *The houses they are building near the river are not finished.*

Possible. — When *possible* refers to a noun, it agrees with that noun; but when it refers to a verb, expressed or understood, it is invariable in form. Thus,

J'ai employé tous les moyens possibles, *I employed all possible means.*

Le conquérant extermine le plus d'hommes possible, *The conqueror exterminates the most men he can.*

Attendu, Excepté, Non compris, Y compris, Sauf, Supposé, Vu. — These words are either variable adjectives following the noun with which they are associated, or they are prepositions and invariable when they precede it. Thus,

Cela vous coûtera cent francs, non-compris les dépenses, *That will cost you one hundred francs, not including expenses.*
Cela vous coûtera cent francs, les dépenses non-comprises.

11. Adjectives Used Adverbially. — When an adjective is used adverbially to modify a verb, it becomes a real adverb in nature and in function, and consequently remains invariable in form. Thus,

Ces livres coûtent cher, *These books cost much.*
Ces fleurs ne sentent pas bon, *These flowers do not smell good.*
Ils marchent vite, *They are walking rapidly.*

COMPOUND ADJECTIVES

12. Two Adjectives. — When a compound adjective is formed of two adjectives, both parts of the compound agree with the noun with which it is associated. Thus,

des hommes ivres-morts, *dead-drunk men*

But if the first of these adjectives modifies the second, the first is used adverbially, and is consequently then invariable. Thus,

Légère et court-vêtue, elle allait à grands pas, *Light and clad in short dresses, she was going with long steps.*
des enfants nouveau-nés, *new-born children*

EXCEPTIONS. — The adjectives *frais-cuilli, frais-éclos*, and *tout-puissant* have, for euphony, the feminine forms, *fraiche-cueillie, fraîche-éclose, toute-puissante;* but *tout* does not change in *tout-puissants*, the plural masculine of *tout-puissant*.

13. An Invariable Word and an Adjective. — When a compound adjective is formed of an invariable word (an adverb or a preposition) and an adjective, the adjective alone agrees with the noun with which the compound is used. Thus,

mes bien-aimés, *my dear beloved*
les avant-derniers évènements, *the next to the last events*

ADJECTIVES OF COLOR

14. General Rule. — Adjectives of color agree with the noun they qualify. Thus,

des robes blanches, *white dresses*
des livres rouges, *red books*

Nouns, however, are often used in French with a partial adjectival sense to denote color, and in such cases the noun is invariable. Thus,

des robes ponceau, *red-poppy dresses*
des drap marron, *chestnut-colored cloths*

NOTE. — The French words *cramoisi*, crimson; *écarlate*, scarlet; *rose*, pink; *violette*, violet, may be used as adjectives, and when so used they follow the general rules governing the agreement of adjectives.

15. Compound Adjectives of Color. — When two adjectives, the one modifying the other, form a compound adjective of color, both adjectives are invariable. Thus,

Il a les cheveux châtain clair, *He has light auburn hair.*
J'aime beaucoup les étoffes bleu foncé, *I like dark blue goods very much.*
J'ai acheté des rubans rose tendre, *I bought some light pink ribbons.*

16. Noun Not Repeated. — A noun that has once been expressed need not be repeated before a subsequent modifying adjective. Thus,

Avez-vous du papier blanc ou du bleu? *Have you white paper or blue?*

Avez-vous le vieux cheval ou le jeune? — J'ai le vieux; vous avez le jeune, *Have you the old horse or the young? — I have the old; you have the young.*

But if the modified noun is partitive in the first sentence, it must be represented in the second by the pronoun *en.* Thus,

Vous avez acheté du drap noir; j'en ai acheté du bleu, *You bought black cloth; I bought blue.*

Vous avez un vieux parapluie, et j'en ai un neuf, *You have an old umbrella, and I have a new one.*

17. An Adjective Represented by Le. — If an adjective is required by the sense of the sentence, but is not expressed, it is always represented by *le*, which has in this case the sense of *so.* Thus,

Etes-vous attentive? — Je le suis, *Are you attentive? — I am (so).*

Etes-vous mariée? — Je le suis, *Are you married? — I am (so).*

PLACE OF ADJECTIVES

18. Adjectives After Nouns. — French adjectives, especially those denoting form, shape, or color, those derived from proper names, and past participles used as adjectives, and adjectives denoting mental or physical qualities, generally follow the nouns they modify. Thus,

un champ rectangulaire, *a rectangular field*
une robe noire, *a black dress*
la langue allemande, *German language*
un enfant appliqué, *a studious child*
un homme intelligent, *an intelligent man*
une femme aveugle, *a blind woman*

It is impossible to give a general rule covering all cases to indicate the place of the adjective in the sentence. The latitude permitted the taste of the writer is great, and in many cases adjectives may be put before or after nouns at will. In many cases also, an adjective ordinarily placed after a noun is, in order to make it prominent in the sentence, placed before its noun. Sentential euphony demands also that a short adjective should precede a longer noun; and reciprocally, a long adjective ordinarily follows a shorter noun. Thus,

une longue promenade, *a long walk*
une somme considérable, *a considerable sum*

Several adjectives qualifying the same substantive are ordinarily placed after the substantive. So also an adjective modified by an adverb of appreciable length, ordinarily follows its noun; but the adverbs *si*, *très*, *bien*, *fort*, *plus*, have no effect on the position of the adjective. Thus,

Savez-vous que je suis le tuteur d'une fille assez jeune et passablement belle? *Do you know that I am the guardian of a girl, quite young and passably fair.* — MOLIÈRE.

Il possède un style rapide, concis, et nerveux, *He possesses a rapid, concise, and vigorous style.*

19. Adjectives Before Nouns. — Monosyllabic adjectives are usually placed before their nouns. Other short adjectives that generally precede the nouns with which they are used are:

beau, *beautiful*	jeune, *young*	petit, *small*
bon, *good*	joli, *pretty*	sot, *foolish*
grand, *large*	long, *long*	vaste, *vast*
gros, *big*	mauvais, *bad*	vieux, *old*
haut, *high*	méchant, *wicked*	vilain, *ugly*

When two of these adjectives qualify the same noun, they precede it, providing one of them forms with the noun but one idea. Thus,

une jolie petite fille, *a pretty little girl*
un beau jeune homme, *a handsome young man*
une très belle maison, *such a beautiful house*
un très joli chien, *a very pretty dog*

20. **Adjectives Whose Meanings Vary According to Their Relative Position in the Sentence.** — Certain adjectives differ in meaning according as they are placed before or after the noun. In general, the adjective retains its natural meaning when placed after the noun, while it has a figurative sense when placed before. Thus,

un bon homme, *a simple man*
un homme bon, *a good man*

le bon air, *good manners*
l'air bon, *a kind look*

un mauvais air, *a vulgar appearance*
l'air mauvais, *an ill-natured look*

un brave homme, *an honest man*
un homme brave, *a brave man*

le grand air, *noble manners*
l'air grand, *a noble look*

mon cher ami, *my dear friend*
une robe chère, *a dear dress*

un certain jour, *a certain day*
une chose certaine, *a sure thing*

un cruel enfant, *a teasing child*
un enfant cruel, *a cruel child*

une commune voix, *an unanimous voice*
une voix commune, *a common voice*

différentes choses, *sundry things.*
des choses différentes, *different things*

la dernière année, *last year (of all)*
l'année dernière, *the preceding year*

un furieux menteur, *an excessive liar*
un animal furieux, *a furious animal*

le haut ton, *the arrogant manner*
le ton haut, *a loud tone of voice*

une fausse clef, *a skeleton key*
une clef fausse, *a wrong key (in music.)*

une fausse porte, *a private door*
une porte fausse, *a false door*

un galant homme, *a gentleman*
un homme galant, *a courteous man*

un grand homme, *a great man*
un homme grand, *a tall man*

une grosse femme, *a stout woman*
une femme grosse, *a pregnant woman*

une sage-femme, *a midwife*
une femme sage, *a wise woman*

un honnête homme, *an honest man*
un homme honnête, *a civil man*

des honnêtes gens, *respectable people*
des gens honnêtes, *polite people*

un malhonnête homme, *a dishonest man*
un homme malhonnête, *a rude man*

un maigre dîner, *a poor dinner*
un dîner maigre, *a fish dinner*

un méchant livre, *a worthless book*
un livre méchant, *a caustic book*

le nouveau vin, *fresh wine*
le vin nouveau, *newly-made wine*

un pauvre homme, *a man of little merit*
un homme pauvre, *a poor man*

un plaisant homme, *a ridiculous man*
un homme plaisant, *a facetious man*
un petit homme, *a small man*
un homme petit, *a mean man*
les propres termes, *exact words*
le terme propre, *correct expression*
ma propre main, *my own hand*
les mains propres, *clean hands*
un seul homme, *a single man*
un homme seul, *a man alone*
un triste homme, *a pitiful man*
un homme triste, *a sorrowful man*
un unique tableau, *a single picture*
un tableau unique, *a matchless picture*

une véritable histoire, *a real story*
une histoire véritable, *a true story*
un vilain homme, *an ugly man*
un homme vilain, *a mean man*

THE COMPLEMENT OF AN ADJECTIVE

21. The **complement of an adjective** may be a noun or an infinitive joined to the adjective by a preposition. The connecting preposition is generally either *à* or *de*. One of the most difficult features of the French language is the use of the correct preposition after an adjective; for, in such constructions, French prepositions are not always correlative with their English equivalents.

22. Adjectives After the Impersonal Verb Etre. An adjective used with the impersonal form of *être* requires the preposition *de* before a following infinitive. Thus,

Il est utile de faire cela, *It is useful to do that.*

Il est nécessaire de travailler, *It is necessary to work.*

Il est difficile de faire des progrès sans travailler, *It is difficult to make progress without work.*

Il est temps de partir, *It is time to go.*

23. Adjectives That Require the Preposition À. It may be laid down as a general law that all adjectives denoting *inclination*, *habit*, *aptness*, *fitness*, require the preposition *à* before a complementary noun or infinitive, except when the adjective is construed with an impersonal form of the verb *être*. The following are the most important adjectives that require the preposition *à:*

adroit à, *dexterous in*	nécessaire à, *necessary to*
antérieur à, *prior to*	nuisible à, *hurtful to*
ardent à, *ardent in*	pareil à, *like*
attentif à, *attentive to*	prêt à, *ready to*
bon à, *good for*	prompt à, *quick at*
cher à, *dear to*	propre à, *fit for*
comparable à, *comparable to*	semblable à, *similar to*
conforme à, *conformable to*	sensible à, *sensible of*
egal à, *equal to*	sourd à, *deaf to*
enclin à, *inclined to*	sujet à, *subject to*
lent à, *slow to*	utile à, *useful to*

Il est très attentif à son travail, *He is very attentive to his work.*

Ceci n'est bon à rien, *This is good for nothing.*

Il fait cher à vivre, *Living is very expensive.*

C'est conforme à mes désirs, *This is conformable to my wishes.*

Il est enclin à la paresse, *He is inclined to be lazy.*

Ils sont toujours prêts à vous rendre service, *They are always ready to render you a service.*

Vous avez été sourd à mes appels, *You have been deaf to my appeals.*

24. Adjectives That Take the Preposition De. — It is also a general law that adjectives requiring in English the prepositions *of, from, with,* or *by;* adjectives denoting *plenty, scarcity,* or *want,* and adjectives expressing feeling or emotion, usually take the preposition *de* in French before their complementary noun or infinitive. The following list contains the most important of these adjectives:

agréable de, *agreeable to*	coupable de, *guilty of*
aise de, *glad to*	curieux de, *curious to*
avide de, *greedy of*	digne de, *worthy of*
capable de, *able to*	enchanté de, *delighted with*
chargé de, *loaded with*	ennuyé de, *weary of*
charmé de, *charmed with*	exempt de, *exempt from*
chéri de, *beloved by*	fâché de, *sorry for*
complice de, *accessory to*	fatigué de, *fatigued with*
content de, *pleased with*	fou de, *doting on*
connu de, *known to*	furieux de, *enraged at*

heureux de, *happy to*
inconsolable de, *inconsolable at*
inquiet de, *uneasy about*
libre de, *free from*
mécontent de, *dissatisfied with*
offensé de, *offended at*

plein de, *full of*
reconnaissant de, *grateful for*
satisfait de, *satisfied with*
sûr de, *sure of*
voisin de, *neighbor to*

Je suis bien aise de vous voir, *I am very glad to see you.*

Je suis charmé de faire votre connaissance, *I am delighted to make your acquaintance.*

Il est coupable de négligence, *He is guilty of neglect.*

Elle est fatiguée d'attendre, *She is tired of waiting.*

Nous sommes très mécontents de votre conduite, *We are much dissatisfied with your behavior.*

25. Complements of Adjectives With Other Prepositions. — Some adjectives require one preposition before the name of a person and another before the name of a thing, or before an infinitive. Thus,

Il est assidu à son travail, *He is assiduous in his work.*

Il est assidu auprès de sa mère, *He is attentive to his mother.*

Ce ruisseau est dangereux à traverser, *This brook is dangerous to cross.*

Ceci est dangereux pour la santé, *This is dangerous for one's health.*

Nous sommes endurcis
{
au travail, *We are inured to labor.*
contre l'adversité, *We are hardened to adversity.*
dans le crime, *We are hardened in crime.*
}

L'air est nécessaire
{
à la vie,
pour vivre,
}
Air is necessary to life.

The adjectives *affable, bon, complaisant, cruel, généreux, indulgent,* or any other adjective expressing kindliness or unkindliness of feeling toward individuals, ordinarily take the preposition *envers*. Thus,

Vous devez être poli envers tout le monde, *You must be polite to everybody.*

Cet enfant est cruel envers les animaux, *This child is cruel to animals.*

26. Several Adjectives Having the Same Complement. — When several adjectives have the same complement, the complement is expressed but once if the adjectives require the same preposition. Thus,

Ce fils est utile et cher à sa mère, *This son is dear and useful to his mother.*

In this case, *cher* and *utile* requiring the same preposition *à*, the common complement *à sa mère* is expressed only once. But, it would be incorrect to say: *Ce fils est utile et chéri de sa mère*, because *utile* requires the preposition *à*, while *chéri* requires *de*. The correct expression with these adjectives is: *Ce fils est utile à sa mère, et il en est chéri.*

POSSESSIVE ADJECTIVE

27. The Article Instead of the Possessive Adjective. — (*a*) The article is used instead of the **possessive adjective** when the sense clearly points out who is the possessor. Thus,

J'ai mal à la tête, *I have a pain in my head.*
Vous avez les mains enflées, *Your hands are swollen.*

Since there can be no doubt as to whose head is aching or whose hands are swollen, the article is deemed sufficient in French.

(*b*) In the case of a reflexive verb, there can be no ambiguity as to who is the possessor, and consequently the article is then always used instead of the possessive adjective. Thus,

Je me suis blessé à la main, *I have hurt my hand.*
Il se lave les mains, *He is washing his hands.*

By long usage, the two following familiar expressions are exceptions to the preceding rule:

Je me suis tenu sur mes jambes toute la journée, *I have been standing on my legs the whole day long.*
Il se tient ferme sur ses pieds, *He stands firmly on his feet.*

(*c*) The article is used for the English possessive pronoun before a noun construed as the direct object of a verb, when that article will sufficiently fill the place of the possessive. Thus,

Il m'a cassé le bras, *He broke my arm.*
Vous lui blessez la main, *You hurt his hand.*

28. When the Possessive Adjective Is Used. — The French possessive adjective is used instead of the article, when the article would make the sentence ambiguous. Thus,

Je vois que votre bras enfle, *I see your arm is swelling.*
Mon frère a perdu sa montre, *My brother lost his watch.*

If these two sentences were: *Je vois que* le *bras enfle*, and *Mon frère a perdu* la *montre*, it would be impossible to tell whether it were *your arm* or another's that I see swelling, or whose watch it was that my brother lost.

The possessive adjective is also used in speaking of a chronic complaint. Thus,

Ma migraine m'a repris, *My headache has returned.*
Sa goutte le tourmente, *His gout torments him.*

The possessive adjective is also used when we wish to emphasize the part spoken of. Thus,

Je l'ai vu de mes yeux, *I saw it with my own eyes.*
Il arrêta ses yeux sur lui, *He fixed his eyes upon him.*

Sometimes the two forms of expression, one with the article, the other with the possessive adjective, have different meanings. Thus,

Je lui ai offert la main, *I offered her my hand* (*to assist her*).
Je lui ai offert ma main, *I proposed to her* (*offered my hand in marriage*).

29. Number of Possessive Adjectives. — The possessive adjectives *notre, votre, leur*, placed before a noun standing in relation to another plural noun previously expressed, are put in the singular number when the sense of the sentence or clause is general or distributive; in other words, when the persons or objects are considered indi-vidually. Thus,

La plupart des hommes emploient la première partie de leur vie à rendre l'autre misérable, *Most men employ the first part of their life to render the other part miserable.*

But the plural of *notre, votre,* or *leur* is used when the following noun represents several objects taken collectively. Thus,

Ces dames avaient des fleurs sur leurs chapeaux, *These ladies had flowers on their hats.*
Tous ces messieurs étaient au bal avec leurs femmes, *All these gentlemen were at the ball with their wives.*

Notre, votre, and *leur,* although representing a collective idea, are always in the singular when placed before a noun not used in the plural; such as, for instance, *faim, soif, santé, humanité.* Thus,

Nous sommes mécontents de notre santé, *We are dissatisfied with our health.*
Je plains leur sort, *I pity their fate.*

30. Possessive Adjectives in Relation to the Names of Things. — The possessives *son, sa, ses, leur,* or *leurs,* are used when the notion of possession belongs to the name of a person or of a personified object. Thus,

Soyons ses ennemis, et non ses assassins, *Let us be his enemies, and not his assassins.*

In speaking of things, the possessive adjectives *son, sa, ses, leur,* or *leurs* are also used when the possessor and the object possessed occur in the same proposition. Thus,

Paris a ses maisons très hautes, *Paris has very high houses.*
Chaque âge a ses plaisirs, son esprit, et ses moeurs, *Each age has its pleasures, its ways, and its customs.*

These possessive adjectives are also used when preceded by a preposition. Thus,

Paris est une belle ville, j'admire la largeur de ses rues, *Paris is a beautiful city; I admire the width of its streets.*

In other cases, the English *its* or *their* is translated by the pronoun *en* with the article. Thus,

Ces langues sont riches, j'en admire les beautés, *These languages are rich; I admire their beauties.*

Il nous raconta ses malheurs; l'histoire en est longue, *He told us his misfortunes; their history is long.*

31. Remarks Concerning Possessive Adjectives. Note the following differences in the translation of possessive adjectives:

1. *A friend of mine, a book of yours.* In French, such expressions are translated *un de mes amis, un de vos livres,* literally, one of my friends, one of your books; so with all other phrases of the same nature.

2. *Mine, thine,* etc., with the verb *to be.* When the English verb *to be* is used with a possessive in the sense of *to belong,* it is translated in French by *être* with one of the disjunctive personal pronouns—*à moi, à toi, à·lui,* or *à elle,* etc. Thus,

Ce livre est à moi, *This book is mine.*
Cette montre n'est pas à lui, *This watch is not his.*

3. The forms *my brother's, my mother's* and the like, are translated in French by *à mon frère, à ma mère,* etc.

DEMONSTRATIVE ADJECTIVES

32. Uses of Ci and Là. — French **demonstrative adjectives** do not point out the relative positions of persons or things, as *this* and *that* do in English. It has been explained that *ci* and *là* may be joined to nouns or other substantives for that purpose. Their use, however, is resorted to only when this distinction is imperative. Thus,

Ce livre n'est pas à toi, *This* (or *that*) *book does not belong to thee.*

Cette table coûte cher, *This* (or *that*) *table is expensive.*

Although not necessary, *ci* and *là* are sometimes added for emphasis. Thus,

Ce jour-là, je pensai mourir, *That day, I thought I should die.*

Ce livre-là? mais c'est à moi, *That book? why, it is mine.*

NUMERAL ADJECTIVES

33. Unième. — *Unième*, first, is used after *vingt*, *trente*, *quarante*, *cinquante*, *soixante*, *quatre-vingt*, *cent*, and *mille*. In other cases, *premier* is used. Thus,

Je suis le premier, *I am the first.*

C'est la vingt-et-unième fois, *It is the twenty-first time.*

34. Elision With Numerals. — The words *onze, onzième*, and sometimes *une* are pronounced as if beginning with an aspirated *h*; that is, elision is not made before them. Thus,

Nous sommes le onze, *We are the eleventh.*

le onzième, *the eleventh*

au onze, *at the eleventh*

vers les onze heures, *toward eleven o'clock*

vers les une heure, sur les une heure, *about one o'clock*

INDEFINITE ADJECTIVES

35. Chaque. — *Chaque*, each, is an adjective, and should never be used without a noun. When the noun is not expressed, the pronoun *chacun*, each, should be employed. Thus,

Chaque livre me coûte cinq francs, *Each book cost me five francs.*

Ces livres me coûtent cinq francs chacun, *These books cost me five francs each.*

Chaque is invariable in form.

36. Tout. — *Tout*, every, any, may be used in the same sense as *chaque*, without the article before a noun in the singular. Thus,

Tout citoyen doit être prêt à donner sa vie pour sa patrie, *Every citizen must be ready to give his life for his country.*

Toute puissance est faible à moins que d'être unie, *Any power is feeble unless united.*

Tout, used as an adjective with inflections for gender and number, has the sense of *all*, *every*, *whole*, if placed before a noun preceded by the article or a determinative adjective. Thus,

toute une semaine, *a whole week*
tous les jours, *every day*
tout le monde, *everybody*
toutes les fois, *every time*

Tout may also be a noun meaning *the whole*. Thus,

Je vous laisse le tout à dix francs, *I will let you have the whole for ten francs.*

37. Tout Autre. — In this expression, *tout* is an adjective when it has the sense of *any*. Thus,

Toute autre position ne me conviendrait pas, *Any other position would not suit me.*

38. Quelque. — *Quelque* is an adjective when it modifies a noun. Thus,

Pouvez-vous me prêter quelques bons livres? *Can you lend me some good books?*

J'ai acheté quelques plumes, *I bought some pens.*

39. Même. — *Même* is an adjective when it precedes a noun or limits a pronoun. Thus,

Les même vertus qui servent à fonder un empire servent aussi à le conserver, *The same virtues that serve to found an empire serve also to preserve it.*

Nous nous sommes servis nous-mêmes, *We helped ourselves.*

SYNTAX OF THE PRONOUN

PERSONAL PRONOUNS

PERSONAL PRONOUNS USED AS SUBJECTS

40. Disjunctive Pronouns Used as Subjects. — In the following cases, disjunctive pronouns are used in French instead of the conjunctives employed in English:

1. In an answer to a question, when the verb is not expressed. Thus,

Qui a fait cela? — Lui, *Who did that? — He.*
Qui est là? — Moi, *Who is there? — I.*

2. When the pronoun is joined by a conjunction to a noun or another pronoun, or when two or more pronouns are used as the subjects of a verb. Thus,

Mon frère et moi partirons demain, *My brother and I will start tomorrow.*
Lui et moi étions absents, *He and I were absent.*

3. When the pronouns follow a comparative. Thus,

Il est plus âgé que moi, *He is older than I.*
Il est beaucoup plus riche que vous, *He is much richer than you.*

4. When the pronouns are followed by a relative pronoun, by the adjective *seul*, or by a present participle. Thus,

Eux que j'aimais tant, *They, whom I loved so much.*
Elle seule sait organiser cela, *She alone knows how to organize that.*
Eux voyant qu'il se fâchait se retirèrent, *They, seeing he was getting angry, left the place.*

But in old style and official speech this last rule is not always observed, and the pronoun subjects are not used in their disjunctive forms, although separated from their verb by an intervening word. Thus,

Je soussigné Louis Durand, reconnais devoir à M. Paul Duruy la somme de mille francs valeur reçue en espèces, *I, the undersigned, Louis Durand, acknowledge that I owe Mr. Paul Duruy the sum of one thousand francs for value received in cash.*

5.   After tenses of the verb *être*, whether in the affirmative, negative, or interrogative form. Thus,

C'est moi, *It is I.*
Ce n'était pas lui que je cherchais, *It was not he that I was looking for.*
Ne serait-ce pas elles?   *Would it not be they?*

41.   **Repetition of Personal Pronoun Subjects.** — Personal pronouns having the function of subjects must be repeated in the following cases:

1.   In changing the form of discourse from negation to affirmation; except that when the first verb is in the affirmative and the second in the negative, the pronoun is not repeated. Thus,

Je ne dors pas et je pense, *I do not sleep, and I think.*
Je pense et ne dors pas, *I think and do not sleep.*

2.   When several verbs having the same subjects follow in succession, the pronoun subject is repeated if the verbs are connected by conjunctions other than *et*, *ni*, *ou*, *mais*.   Thus,

Je vais à la campagne parce qu'il fait beau, *I am going to the country because it is beautiful weather.*

3.   The repetition of the pronoun generally renders the style more solemn and energetic, while its omission gives more rapidity to the discourse. Thus,

Je suis venu, j'ai vu, j'ai vaincu, *I came, I saw, I conquered.*
Elle va, vient, fait l'empressée, *She goes, comes back, feigns to be in a hurry.*

If a pronoun subject is to be made very emphatic, it is usually repeated in its disjunctive form, either before the verb or after it. Thus,

Je l'ai vu, moi, *I saw it myself.*

Lui, il n'a pas seulement un sou vaillant, *He (himself), he has not a single penny.*

Sometimes the proper subject is omitted, and the emphatic disjunctive stands alone as the subject. Thus,

Lui n'a eu qu'un ami, *He* (emphatic) *had only one friend.*

PERSONAL PRONOUNS USED AS OBJECTS

42. Conjunctive and Disjunctive Personal Pronouns. —As has been explained, the conjunctive pronouns are those that are used without a preposition or with the preposition *à*. They are:

SINGULAR	PLURAL
First person: me, *me*, or *to me*	nous, *us*, or *to us*
Second person: te, *thee*, or *to thee*	vous, *you*, or *to you*
Third person: le, *him;* la, *her;* lui, *to him*, or *her*	les, *them;* leur, *to them*

As has been explained, the conjunctive personal pronouns are generally placed after the pronoun subject, or after the negation in a negative sentence. Thus,

Il me voit, *He sees me.*

Je ne lui parle pas, *I do not speak to him.*

The disjunctive pronouns are used with any preposition other than *à*, such as *pour, dans, de, avec,* etc. They always follow the verb, and are:

SINGULAR	PLURAL
First person: moi, *me*	nous, *us*
Second person: toi, *thee*	vous, *you*
Third person: lui, *him;* elle, *her*	eux (*masc.*), elles (*fem.*), *them*

55—25

43. Disjunctive Pronouns With the Preposition À.
Sometimes, however, although used with the preposition *à*, the disjunctive pronouns may be employed; they are then placed after the verb. The following are the only cases in which they may be so used:

1. After a verb having two or more indirect objects; also with reflexive verbs. Thus,

Je parle à lui et à elle, *I speak to him and to her.*
Je me présente à vous, *I present myself to you.*
Il s'adressa à moi, *He applied to me.*
Il se montra à nous, *He showed himself to us.*

2. *A* is also used after the following verbs with the disjunctive pronoun: *aller, en appeler, courir, accourir, marcher, penser, songer, venir, viser, être* (in the sense of to belong), and after *avoir* used with the words *affaire, égard, rapport*, and *recours*. Thus,

Il vint à moi et me salua, *He came to me and saluted me.*
J'ai souvent pensé à lui, *I often thought of him.*
Pourquoi n'avez-vous pas recours à eux? *Why do you not have recourse to them?*

44. En and Y.—These two pronouns have many and important functions in French sentential structure. They are used with reference to things, and are to be found in both genders and numbers. *En* stands for a noun used with *de*, and translates the English phrases *some, some of it, of it, of them, from there; y* stands for the noun with the preposition *à*, and translates the English *there, here, to it, at it.* The following examples illustrate the uses of *en* and *y*:

Avez-vous de l'eau, de la bière, du vin, des liqueurs?— J'en ai, *Have you water, beer, wine, liquors?—I have* (*some*).
Avez-vous cinq livres?—J'en ai cinq, *Have you five books?— I have five* (*of them*).
Combien de livres avez-vous?—J'en ai cinq, *How many books have you?—I have five* (*of them*).

Venez-vous de Paris?—J'en viens, *Do you come from Paris?
I come from there.*

Etes-vous là?—J'y suis, *Are you there?—I am (there).*

Venez-vous ici?—J'y viens, *Do you come here?—I do
(come here).*

Avez-vous répondu à vos lettres?—J'y ai répondu, *Have
you answered (to) your letters?—I have (answered to them).*

Allez-vous à Paris?—J'y vais, *Are you going to Paris?—I
am going there.*

**45. Y Suppressed in the Future and Conditional
of Aller.**—Because the future and the conditional of *aller*
begin with the same sound as *y*, the word *y* is omitted with
those tenses. Thus,

Irez-vous à Paris?—Je n'irai pas, *Shall you go to Paris?—I
shall not go there.*

Irez-vous au bal? — J'irais si j'avais quelqu'un pour
m'accompagner, *Shall you go to the ball?—I would go
there if I had some one to accompany me.*

46. Repetition of the Pronoun Object.—Personal
pronouns used as the objects of several verbs are repeated
with each verb when those verbs are in a simple tense.
Thus,

Il vous estime et vous honore, *He esteems and honors you.*

Il nous ennuie et nous tourmente sans cesse, *He wearies
and torments us incessantly.*

But when the verbs are in a compound tense, and have the
same subject, object, and auxiliary verb, the subject, object,
and even the auxiliary may not be repeated, providing, however, that all the verbs govern their objects with the same
preposition. Thus,

Ils nous ont attaqués et ils nous
ont vaincus,
Ils nous ont attaqués et vaincus, } *They attacked and defeated
us.*

When the objects are not of the same nature, or when they are governed by different prepositions, their repetition, as well as that of the auxiliary verb, is imperative. Thus,

Voilà sa lettre: je l'ai lue et j'y ai répondu, *There is his letter, I read and answered it* (literally, *I read it and answered to it*).

J'y ai pensé, et j'en ai parlé, *I thought of it and spoke about it* (literally, *I thought to it and spoke of it*).

POSSESSIVE PRONOUNS

47. **Possessive Pronouns Used Absolutely.** — Possessive pronouns usually refer to an antecedent noun and agree with it in gender and number. However, they may be used absolutely in the singular to designate a person's property. Thus,

Le mien et le tien sont la source de toutes les querelles, *Mine and thine are the cause of all quarrels.*

They may also be used in the plural to designate a person's relatives, friends, or adherents. Thus,

Les vôtres se sont bien battus, *Your partisans fought well.*
Nous irons à la campagne l'été prochain, moi et les miens, *We shall go to the country next summer, I and my folks.*

48. **Commercial Terms.** — Contrary to the grammatical rule that a relative pronoun must refer to an antecedent noun, it is not uncommon in business correspondence to use such forms as follows:

En réponse à la vôtre du 22 avril, j'ai l'honneur de . . . *In answer to yours of April 22, I have the honor to . . .*

In this case *la vôtre* stands for *votre lettre*, but since the word *lettre* has not already been expressed, this form is grammatically incorrect, and it is much better to say: *En réponse à votre lettre du 22 avril, j'ai l'honneur de . . .*

DEMONSTRATIVE PRONOUNS

49. Uses of the Pronoun Ce. — The pronoun *ce* is used instead of the personal pronouns *il*, *elle*, *ils*, *elles*, as the subject of a proposition whose predicate attribute is a noun or pronoun. Thus,

J'aime Corneille; c'est mon auteur favori, *I like Corneille; he is my favorite author.*

A qui est ce livre? — C'est le mien, *Whose book is that? It is mine.*

Prenez ce cheval; c'est le meilleur, *Take this horse; it is the best.*

In this last example, the noun *cheval* is understood after *meilleur*.

When the predicate is an adjective, the personal pronoun is used instead of *ce*. Thus,

Prenez ce cheval; il est bon, *Take this horse; it is a good one.*

Mangez ce bouillon; il est excellent, *Eat that broth; it is excellent.*

In an interrogation, *ce* is more precise than *il*. Thus,

Quelle heure est-il? *What time is it?*

Quelle heure est-ce? *What hour is that (just striking)?*

50. Ce Used for Cela. — *Ce*, with *être* or before *devoir*, is often used in French for *cela* to introduce an attributive clause referring to a preceding sentence. Thus,

Il a fait cela, c'est bien, *He has done that; it is well.*

Vous n'avez pas réussi; ce n'est rien, *You did not succeed; that is nothing.*

Vous en avez trois; c'est assez, *You have three of them; that is enough.*

J'ai compris ce que vous m'avez dit; est-ce tout? *I understood what you told me; is that all?*

Tout le monde le dit; ce doit être vrai, *Everybody says so; it must be true.*

51. **Pleonastic Uses of Ce.** — The pronoun *ce* with the verb *être* may be pleonastically used in the following cases:

1. When the verb *être* is placed between two expressions, one of which may be the predicate of the other, a pleonastic *ce* may or may not be included, according to the taste of the speaker. Its use, however, adds vivacity, precision, and energy to the sentence. Thus,

La vertu la plus agréable à Dieu, c'est la charité, *The virtue most agreeable to God is charity*.

Ma mère, c'était ma seule amie, *My mother was my only friend*.

Le plus grand plaisir d'un avare, c'est de contempler son trésor, *The greatest pleasure of a miser is to contemplate his treasure*.

2. When the verb *être* is placed between two infinitives, *ce* must be used with it. Thus,

Déchoir du premier rang, c'est tomber au dernier, *To lose the first rank, is to fall to the last*.

Vivre content de peu, c'est être vraiment riche, *To live content with little is to be truly rich*.

In cases of this kind, however, *ce* is generally suppressed in a proverbial sentence when the verb is accompanied by a negation, or when the first infinitive is not followed by a second. Thus,

Abuser n'est pas user, *To abuse is not to use*.

Promettre et tenir sont deux, *To promise and to keep promises are different things*.

3. *Ce* with the verb *être* is used for emphasis. Thus,

C'est à Paris que nous allons demain,

C'est demain que nous allons à Paris,

C'est nous qui allons à Paris demain,

} *We are going to Paris tomorrow.*

4. When a sentence begins with *ce* followed by one of the relative pronouns *qui*, *que*, *quoi*, or *dont*, and a verb, any

following form of the verb *être* is generally preceded by *ce*. It is almost always so preceded when être is in turn followed by an infinitive or a noun. Thus,

Ce qui est certain, c'est que le monde est méchant, *What is certain is that the world is wicked.*

Ce que j'aime le mieux, c'est une promenade en voiture, *What I like best is a ride.*

When, however, *être* is followed by an adjective, *ce* is not used before it. Thus,

Ce que vous dites est intéressant, *What you say is interesting.*

Ce que je vous dis est la vérité (est vrai), *What I tell you is the truth.*

52. Ce as the Antecedent of a Relative Pronoun. The demonstrative pronoun *ce* is used as the antecedent of a relative pronoun when a relative clause modifies a proposition; *ce* must also be used after *tout* modified by a relative clause. Thus,

Je ne sais pas ce que vous voulez dire, *I do not know what you mean.*

J'achète ce qui me plaît, *I buy what pleases me.*

J'ai tout ce qu'il me faut, *I have all I want.*

53. C'est . . . Que. — To render the subject of a sentence very prominent, it is sometimes put last and preceded by *que*, in which case the predicate is written before the *que* and preceded by *ce* and a form of the verb *être*. Thus,

C'est une belle ville que Paris, *Paris is a beautiful city.*

C'était un grand homme que Napoléon, *Napoleon was a great man.*

Such constructions as these add vastly to the energy and vivacity of the sentence.

54. Ceci and Cela. — These two words are used absolutely to designate objects without naming them. Thus,

Ceci n'est pas à moi, *This does not belong to me.*

Cela est pour vous, *That is for you.*

Ceci is used in reference to a thought about to be expressed, while *cela* refers to a thought already known. Thus,

Retenez bien ceci: Il ne faut pas juger sur l'apparence, *Remember this: you must not judge according to appearances.*

L'orgueil est un grand défaut; n'oubliez jamais cela, *Pride is a great fault; never forget that.*

55. Celui, Celle, Ceux, and Celles. — These pronouns may represent either persons or things indifferently. Their sense is generally determined by an indirect object preceded by the preposition *de* or by a relative proposition. Thus,

J'ai mon livre et celui de mon frère, *I have my book and my brother's.*

J'ai loué ma maison et celle de ma sœur, *I rented my house and my sister's.*

These pronouns, if followed by a relative, may represent persons not previously introduced. In such cases, they are generally equivalent to *he who, she who, they who.* Thus,

Celui qui étudie fait des progrès, *He* } *who studies makes*
Celle qui étudie fait des progrès, *She* } *progress.*
Ceux qui étudient font des progrès, } *They who study make*
Celles qui étudient font des progrès, } *progress.*

56. Celui-ci and Celui-là. — When two persons or things have been introduced, *celui-ci* is used to translate *the latter* (the last named) and *celui-là, the former* (the first named). Thus,

On disait de Fénelon en le comparant à Bossuet, que celui-ci prouvait la religion, et que celui-là la faisait aimer, *It was said of Fenelon in comparing him to Bossuet, that the latter proved religion, and the former made us love it.*

INTERROGATIVE PRONOUNS

57. Difference Between Interrogative and Relative Pronouns. — Interrogative and relative pronouns differ chiefly in that **interrogative pronouns** are generally placed first in a sentence, and refer, not to an antecedent noun or pronoun, but to something unknown to the speaker which is to be expressed in answer to his question. The relative pronoun, on the contrary, always refers to an antecedent noun, pronoun, or phrase previously expressed. Thus,

INTERROGATIVE

Qui est là?—Moi, *Who is there?—I.*

Qui demandez-vous?—Je demande votre frère, *Whom are you asking for?—I am asking for your brother.*

RELATIVE

Cet homme que vous voyez là est mon oncle, *This man that you see there is my uncle.*

Lisez-nous quelque chose qui nous fasse rire, *Read something that will make us laugh.*

58. Qui.—The interrogative pronoun *qui* is almost exclusively used for persons only. It may be used as subject, object, predicate, or after a preposition. It has no inflection for gender or number. Thus,

Qui est arrivé? *Who has arrived?*

Qui cherchez-vous? *Whom are you looking for?*

Qui est-il? *Who is he?*

A qui appartient ce livre? *To whom does this book belong?*

Pour qui achetez-vous cela? *For whom are you buying that?*

De qui parlez-vous? *About whom are you speaking?*

For purposes of emphasis, *qui* is sometimes rendered by the phrase *qui est-ce qui* (*literally*, who is it who) as subject, and by *qui est-ce que* (*literally*, who is it that), as object. Thus,

Qui est-ce qui vient là bas? *Who is coming yonder?*

Qui est-ce que vous grondez? *Whom are you scolding?*

When used for things, *qui* is used in the form of *qu'est-ce qui*. Thus,

Qu'est-ce qui vous amène? *What brings you?*

Qu'est-ce qui vous ennuie? *What annoys you?*

Note the following fine distinctions in the use of *qui:*

Qui est-ce?—C'est un médecin, *Who is it?—It is a doctor.*
Qui est-il?—C'est M. Loubet, *Who is he?—It is Mr. Loubet.*
Qu'est-il?—Il est médecin, *What is he?—He is a doctor.*
Qui est, *or* quel est ce monsieur?—C'est le maître de
musique, *Who is that gentleman?—He is the music teacher.*

59.   Que and Quoi.—These two interrogative pronouns
are used of things only; they have no inflection for gender or
number.   *Que* is only the object of a verb, or predicate of an
intransitive verb.   *Quoi* is used with a preposition.   Thus,

Que désirez-vous?   *What do you desire?*
Que deviendra-t-elle?   *What will become of her?*
A quoi pensez-vous?   *What are you thinking of?*
De quoi parle-t-il?   *Of what does he speak?*

Que and *quoi* may be used in exclamations.   Thus,

Que vous êtes grande!   *How tall you are!*
Quoi! vous n'avez pas fini, *What! you have not finished.*

When *que* and *quoi* are followed by an adjective, the preposition *de* is required before the adjective.   Thus,

Quoi de nouveau?   *What news?*
Qu'avez-vous vu de beau?   *What did you see beautiful?*

60.   Lequel.—The interrogatives *lequel*, *laquelle*, etc.
are used for persons and things, but only when they are
determined by a following expression or by something preceding.   Thus,

Lequel de ces hommes vous a reconnu?   *Which of these
men recognized you?*
Laquelle de ces dames est la plus jeune?   *Which of these
ladies is the youngest?*
J'ai acheté des livres.—Lesquels?   *I have bought some
books.—Which?*

RELATIVE PRONOUNS

61. Relative Pronouns Never Omitted. — A **relative pronoun** must always be expressed in French, although it is often omitted in English. Thus,

Où sont les marchandises que j'ai achetées? *Where are the goods I bought?*

Voilà la dame dont vous parlez, *There is the lady you are speaking of.*

62. Place of the Relative Pronoun. — To avoid ambiguity, the French relative pronoun must be placed as near its antecedent as possible. Thus,

J'ai fait dans toute la Suisse un voyage qui m'a beaucoup plu, *I made a journey through Switzerland that pleased me very much.*

It would be incorrect to say, *J'ai fait un voyage dans toute la Suisse qui m'a plu beaucoup*, because the sentence would then be ambiguous, for it would not be clear whether it was *la Suisse*, or *le voyage* that pleased me very much.

63. Qui and Que. — When the pronouns *qui* and *que* refer to a determined antecedent, *qui* is the form used in the subject and *que* that used in the object. They have no inflection for gender or number, and may represent either persons or things.

To give rapidity and precision to style, the antecedent of a relative pronoun is often understood, especially in proverbs. Thus,

A qui venge son père, il n'est rien d'impossible, *To him who avenges his father, nothing is impossible.* — CORNEILLE.

Qui sert bien son pays n'a pas besoin d'aïeux, *He who serves his country well, has no need of ancestors.* — VOLTAIRE.

64. The Differences Between Qui and Lequel or Auquel. — *Qui*, preceded by a preposition, is used only in reference to persons, or personified things; but, when the relative pronoun used refers to things, the forms *lequel*, *auquel*, etc. must be employed. Thus,

Le monsieur avec qui vous êtes venu est mon ami, *The gentleman with whom you came is my friend.*

O rochers escarpés, je n'ai que vous à qui je puisse me plaindre! *O rugged rocks, I have none but you to whom I can complain!*

La maison dans laquelle vous demeurez vous appartient-elle? *Does the house in which you live belong to you?*

Le cheval sur lequel j'étais monté, était jeune et vigoureux, *The horse I was riding was young and vigorous.*

The pronoun *lequel* is also used when the pronoun *qui* would be ambiguous. This is especially likely to occur when it is impossible to place the relative near the antecedent, or when the relative refers to several antecedents. Thus,

Le père de la jeune fille, lequel nous a écrit . . . , *the young lady's father, who wrote to us* . . .

If *qui* were used here instead of *lequel*, the sentence would be ambiguous. It would not be clear whether it was the young lady or the father that wrote.

65. Dont and De Qui.—*Qui* preceded by the preposition *de* can refer to persons only; *dont* can refer either to persons or to things; it must be used when the reference is to things. Thus,

Voilà l'homme dont (or de qui) vous parlez, *There is the man of whom you are speaking.*

Il y a des animaux dont l'instinct approche de l'intelligence, *There are some animals whose instinct approaches intelligence.*

The order of French sentential construction differs from the English order when the relative *whose* is followed by the object of a verb, for in French *dont* and the subject of the relative clause cannot be separated. Thus,

Voilà le monsieur dont j'ai connu la sœur à Paris, *There is the gentleman whose sister I knew in Paris.*

INDEFINITE PRONOUNS

66. On. — The pronoun *on* is sometimes used for euphony, with the *l'* before it, after the words *et*, *si*, *ou*, *où*, and *que*. But even after these words it is often suppressed. It can never be used if the following word begins with *l*.

The pronoun *on* always takes the singular form of the verb, but a following adjective relating to *on* agrees in gender and number with the noun that *on* represents. Thus,

Quand on est **jeunes, riches,** et **jolies,** mesdames, on n'est pas **réduites** à l'artifice, *When one is young, rich, and pretty, ladies, one is not driven to deceit.*

Ici, on est égaux, *Here, people are equal.*

Nous or *vous* may be used after *on* as the object of a verb. Thus,

Aussi longtemps qu'**on** est riche, qu'**on** donne des dîners, ces parasites **vous** flattent, **vous** cajolent, s'empressent autour de **vous;** quand **on** n'a plus rien, ils font semblant de ne pas **vous** connaître, *As long as you are rich and give dinners, these parasites flatter you, fawn upon you, swarm around you; when nothing is left, they feign not to know you.*

The pronoun *on* is often used instead of the personal pronoun either to avoid designating persons directly, or to express a kind of contempt. Thus,

On se doute de quelque chose, *They are suspicious about something.*

On me surveille, *I am watched.*

On n'a pas voulu me laisser entrer, *They would not let me in.*

67. Chacun. — *Chacun* may be used absolutely in the sense of *every one;* it is then invariable. Thus,

Chacun veut être heureux, *Everybody wishes to be happy.*

Chacun vit à sa guise, *Every one lives as he likes.*

Chacun may vary in gender when limited by a complement. Thus,

Chacun de ces livres coûte dix francs, *Each of these books costs ten francs.*

Chacune de ces tables coûte dix dollars, *Each of these tables costs ten dollars.*

When *chacun* follows the direct object of a verb, or when the neuter verb by itself expresses complete sense, *son, sa,* or *ses,* is used, and *leur* or *leurs* in other cases. Thus,

Le ministre a reçu les visiteurs, chacun à son tour, *The minister received the callers, each in his turn.*

Ils ont apporté chacun leurs offrandes, *Each brought his offerings.*

68. Combinations With Autre. — The word *autre* enters the following combinations:

1. *L'un l'autre, l'une l'autre, les uns les autres, les unes les autres.* — These expressions, meaning *each other, the one the other, one another,* are used with reflexive verbs to mark reciprocity of action and to distinguish that reciprocity from reflexive action. Thus,

L'égoïsme et l'amitié s'excluent l'un l'autre, *Egotism and friendship do not go together* (literally, *exclude each other*).

Dans ce monde, il se faut l'un l'autre secourir, *In this world, we must help each other.*

In these cases, *l'un* appears in the role of the subject and *l'autre* in that of the object of a verb. The two preceding examples may also be expressed as follows:

L'egoïsme et l'amitié s'excluent: **l'un** *exclut* **l'autre;** or *Dans ce monde, il faut que* **l'un** *secoure* **l'autre.**

L'un—l'autre may also be used disjunctively in the sense of the former—the latter; some—some; some—others. Thus,

L'un travaille, l'autre s'amuse, *The former works, the latter amuses himself.*

Les uns chantent, les autres pleurent, *Some sing, some weep.*

Les uns sont généreux, les autres sont avares, *Some are generous, others are misers.*

When the object is indirect, *l'un* and *l'autre* are separated by a preposition governed by the verb. Thus,

La nature les a faits l'un pour l'autre, *Nature created them, one for the other.*

Ils se sont battus les uns contre les autres, *They fought, party against party,* (literally, *the one with the other*).

Un lien de malheur nous unit l'un à l'autre, *A tie of misfortune unites us to one another.*

In thus denoting reciprocity of action and having different grammatical functions, *l'un* and *l'autre* are never joined by the conjunction *et*, for this conjunction can only connect two words having the same function. When *l'un* and *l'autre* are joined by *et* the idea of reciprocity is transformed into an idea of simultaneity of action, as explained in the following paragraph.

2. *L'un et l'autre, les uns et les autres, l'une et l'autre, les unes et les autres.* — These expressions, meaning *both*, refer to antecedent nouns with which they agree in gender and in number. When the phrase *l'un et l'autre* is the object of a verb, a personal pronoun also is ordinarily used before the verb. Thus,

Je les ai suivis l'un et l'autre, *I followed them both.*

J'ai voulu leur parler, à l'un et à l'autre, *I wished to speak to both.*

3. *Either* is translated by *l'un ou l'autre, l'une ou l'autre,* etc., and the verb agrees with the last one. Thus,

Ils me l'ont promis l'un ou l'autre viendra, *They promised me that the one or the other will come.*

4. *Neither the one nor the other* is rendered by *ni l'un ni l'autre.* In this case, the verb is put in the plural when the action may be affirmed of both parties, it is put in the singular when the affirmation can be made of one of the two only. Thus,

Ni l'un ni l'autre ne seront ici, *Neither will be here.*

Ni l'une ni l'autre n'est ma mère, *Neither is my mother.*

69. Tout. — *Tout* may sometimes be used as an indefinite pronoun. Thus,

Dieu a créé tout, *God has created all.*
Nous sommes tous mortels, *We are all mortal.*

70. Quelqu'un. — This indefinite pronoun may be used absolutely, and when so used is invariable. Thus,

M. Colin, quelqu'un vous demande, *Mr. Colin, someone is inquiring for you.*
Avez-vous vu quelqu'un? *Have you seen anyone?*

But if *quelqu'un* becomes definite by means of a complement, it takes the gender of the complement. Thus,

Si quelqu'une de ces demoiselles désire chanter, accompagnez-la au piano, *If any of these young ladies wishes to sing, accompany her at the piano.*

A past participle referring to *quelqu'un* is preceded by the preposition *de.* Thus,

Y a-t-il quelqu'un d'arrivé? *Has any one arrived?*

71. Personne. — The pronoun *quelqu'un* is used in a sentence when the sense is positive, while *personne* is used when the sense is negative. When standing as the subject of a verb, *personne* is followed by the negative *ne;* when standing as the object, it is preceded by *ne*, and the respective positions of *personne* and *ne* are the same as those of *ne* and *pas* when the negative *ne* and *pas* is used. Thus,

Je ne vois personne, *I see no one.*
Personne ne me voit, *No one sees me.*

When, in an ellipsis, the verb is understood, the negative *ne* cannot be used, but the negative sense of *personne* remains unchanged. Thus,

Qui avez-vous rencontré? — Personne, *Whom did you meet? No one.*

Again, *personne* is used alone in place of *quelqu'un* in sentences implying doubt, or containing other negative words; also after a comparative adverb. Thus,

Y a-t-il personne qui en doute? *Is there any one who doubts it?*

Elle est partie sans voir personne, *She went away without seeing any one.*

Il fait cela mieux que personne, *He does that better than any one.*

72. Quelque Chose and Rien. — *Quelque chose*, something, and *rien*, nothing, are used in the same way, and follow the same rules as *quelqu'un* and *personne*. Thus,

Je ne dis rien, *I say nothing.*
Que dites-vous? — Rien, *What do you say? — Nothing.*

FRENCH GRAMMAR

(PART 11)

SYNTAX OF THE ADVERB

PLACE OF ADVERBS

1. General Rule. — The adverb in a simple tense is placed after the verb in French; as, *Je parle* **bien,** *J'étudie* **seulement** *le français, Je parlerai* **peu;** but in a compound tense, the adverb follows the auxiliary; as, *J'ai* **bien** *parlé, Il a* **très peu** *étudié.* Adverbs of several syllables, however, and adverbial phrases, are placed after the past participle in a compound tense. Thus,

J'y suis allé quelquefois, *I sometimes went there.*
Il est venu auparavant, *He came earlier.*
Nous sommes partis à la hâte, *We departed hastily.*

2. Adverbs Modifying Adjectives or Other Adverbs. Adverbs used to modify adjectives or other adverbs are placed before the words they modify. Thus,

Cette dame est très aimable, *This lady is very amiable.*
Il a très peu parlé, *He talked very little.*

3. Adverbs of Time and Place. — Adverbs of time and place are generally put after the verb, although for purposes of emphasis they are often placed first. Thus,

Jamais je n'oublierai cela, *I shall never forget that.*
Hier, je suis sorti de bonne heure, *I went out early yesterday.*
Ici je serai bien, *I shall be all right here.*

4. Interrogative Adverbs. — Interrogative adverbs regularly begin a sentence. Thus,

Où avez-vous été?   *Where have you been?*
Pourquoi n'arrive-t-il pas?   *Why does he not come?*

ADVERBS OF AFFIRMATION AND NEGATION

5. Adverbs of Affirmation. — The two adverbs of affirmation, *oui* and *si*, are often reinforced by *si fait*, yes indeed. *Si* is a more emphatic affirmative than *oui*, and is frequently used in answer to a negative question when the answer is expected to be in the affirmative; but *pardon* is much used in place of *si* and is considered to be a more polite answer.

Mais and *que* may be used before *oui* or *si*. Thus,

Je crois que oui, *I think so* (literally, *I think yes*).

Vous n'allez donc pas dîner? — Mais oui, j'y vais de ce pas, *You are not going to dinner, then? — Yes indeed, I am going presently.*

6. The Negative Non. — This adverb may be used in any of these various ways:

1. As a responsive — translating the English adverb *no.* Thus,

Cela sera, ma fille. — Non. — Si. — Non, vous dis-je. — Si, vous dis-je, *It shall be so, daughter. — No. — Yes. — No, I say. — Yes, I tell you.*

Les uns disent que non, les autres disent que oui, et moi je dis que oui et non, *Some say no, others say yes, and I say yes and no.*

Mais oui, cousine, on se marie, *Why yes, cousin, we are going to be married.*

2. Like the English not, *non* may be used elliptically to express a complete negative sentence. Thus,

Que m'importe à moi si Rome souffre ou non! *What is it to me whether or not Rome suffers?*

Frequently *non* is followed by *que* and then has the meaning of *ce n'est pas que*, it is not that; or *non* may sometimes be strengthened by the addition of *pas*. Thus,

Non que votre colère ou la mort m'intimide, *Neither your anger nor death intimidates me.*

C'est la loi, et non pas l'homme qui doit régner, *It is the law and not the man that must reign.*

3. *Non* is used to nullify any word other than a verb or a phrase. Thus,

Immolez, non à moi, mais à votre couronne, *Sacrifice, not to me, but to your crown.*

4. *Non* is also used in the idiomatic phrase *non plus*, no more. Thus,

Je ne le veux pas ni vous non plus, *I do not want it, neither do you.*

Elle n'est pas venue, ni lui non plus, *She did not come, neither did he.*

USES OF THE DOUBLE NEGATIVE

7. Compound Negatives. — The most important compound negatives are *ne . . . pas* and *ne . . . point*. Of the three negatives *ne, ne . . . pas*, and *ne . . . point, ne* is the weakest, *ne . . . point* the strongest, and *ne . . . pas* is intermediate. The only original negatives in French are *ne* and *non*, which latter word may be regarded as an elliptical negative sentence. *Ne* is invariably placed after the subject immediately before the verb or auxiliary in declarative sentences. It cannot be separated from the verb with which it is used except by a conjunctive personal pronoun.

Originally *ne* was a negative complete in itself, but gradually other words were associated with it for purposes of discriminating emphasis. Among these words are *pas*, step; *point*, point; *goutte*, drop; *mie*, bit; *brin*, mote. As a result of being constantly used with *ne*, their original sense became more and more obscure and feeble until, in course of time, they came to be regarded as mere complements of the negative. Thus, the literal translation of *je n'irai pas*, I shall not go there, is *je ne ferai même un pas pour y aller*, I shall not even make a step to go there.

Words are added to *ne* to form compound negatives, as follows:

ne . . . pas, *not*   ne . . . point, *not* (emphatic)

NOTE. — These two negatives may be strengthened by adding *du tout*, at all.

ne . . . guère, *but little*

ne . . . mot, in the expressions *ne dire mot*, not to say a word; *n'entendre mot*, not to hear

ne . . . goutte, in the expressions *ne voir goutte*, not to see at all; *n'entendre goutte*, not to hear at all

ne . . . jamais, *never*

ne . . . plus, *no more, no longer*

ne . . . nullement, *by no means*

ne . . . aucunement, *in no wise*

ne . . . rien, *nothing*

ne . . . personne, *nobody*

ne . . . aucun, *none*

ne . . . que, *only*

ne . . . nul, *not one*

ne . . . ni . . . ni, *neither . . . nor*

8. Place of the Second Part of the Compound Negative. — The second part of the negative is usually put immediately after the verb in a simple tense, or after the auxiliary in a compound tense. Thus,

Je ne vois pas Charles, *I do not see Charles.*
Je n'ai jamais menti, *I have never lied.*
Il n'a rien mangé, *He has eaten nothing.*
Vous ne voyez personne, *You see no one.*
Je n'y pensais plus, *I was no longer thinking of it.*

But for emphasis *jamais* is often placed at the beginning of a sentence. Thus,

Jamais je n'oublierai cela, *I shall never forget that.*
Jamais nous n'avons rencontré votre ami, *We have never met your friend.*

In these sentences the more usual order would have been:

Je n'oublierai jamais cela.
Nous n'avons jamais rencontré votre ami.

When a compound negative falls directly before an infinitive, the two parts of the negative are written together immediately before the verb. Thus,

J'aime mieux ne pas le faire, *I prefer not to do it.*
Je vous aime trop, ma chère nièce, pour ne pas vous dire vos vérités, *I love you too much, my dear niece, not to tell you the truth about yourself.*
C'est parler pour ne rien dire, *This is idle talk* (literally, *this is to speak to say nothing*).
Je quitte ce pays pour ne jamais revenir, *I leave this country never to return.*

When any of these negative expressions is used as the subject of a verb, the second part of the negative is written before the first. Thus,

Personne ne me voit, *No one sees me.*
Pas n'est besoin de vous dire combien j'étais heureux, *There is no need of telling you how happy I was.*
Nul n'est prophète en son pays, *No one is a prophet in his own country.*

9. Suppression of Ne. — Since the particle *ne* is so closely linked with the verb to which it is intended to impart the negative idea, it follows that *ne* can never be used in elliptical phrases in which the verb is missing. In such elliptical phrases the second part of the negative is used and it then has in itself the full negative sense of the compound. Thus, *jamais* used in a fully expressed sentence has the meaning of *ever* (or *never*, when employed with *ne*), but in elliptical expressions it acquires the complete meaning and force of *ne . . . jamais.* Thus,

Ferez-vous cela?—Jamais, *Will you do that?—Never.*

Similarly:

Qui avez-vous vu?—Personne, *Whom have you seen?—No one.*

Qu'avez-vous là?—Rien, *What have you there?—Nothing.*

Je suis donc libre!—Pas du tout, *I am free, then!—Not at all.*

Qu'est-ce qu'ils faisaient?—Rien du tout, *What were they doing?—Nothing at all.*

Ferez-vous cela?—Du tout, *Will you do that?—Not at all.*

10. **Differences Between Pas and Point.**—The following differences are to be observed between the uses of *ne . . . pas* and *ne . . . point:*

1. In declarative sentences *pas* is naturally less emphatic than *point,* for it is evident that *pas,* a step, is greater than *point,* a point, and consequently weaker when used to complete a negative idea. *Pas* designates something accidental or not permanent. Thus,

Il ne voit pas, il n'entend pas, *He does not see, he does not hear.*

In this sentence the meaning is that at this moment he neither sees nor hears. If, however, the sentences read: *Il ne voit point, il n'entend point,* the meaning conveyed would be that he never sees or hears.

Pas is used before comparative terms like *plus, moins, si, autant;* also before numerals. Thus,

Mon nom n'est pas plus à vendre qu'à louer, *My name is no more for sale than for rent.*

Il n'a pas autant d'argent que vous, *He has not so much money as you.*

Elle n'a pas vingt ans, *She is not twenty years old.*

2. In an interrogative proposition, *point* denotes a doubt in the mind of the speaker, while *pas* denotes that the speaker has no such doubt in mind. Thus,

Tout le monde rit: n'ai-je point dit quelque sottise? *Every-body is laughing: have I not said some foolish thing?*

Pourquoi me blamez-vous? N'ai-je pas dit la vérité? *Why do you blame me?—Have I not spoken the truth?*

11. Omission of Pas and Point.—The second part of the negative *ne . . . pas* or *ne . . . point*, may be suppressed in the following cases:

1. With the verbs *oser, pouvoir, cesser, savoir,* and *bouger,* the suppression of *pas* or *point* adds to the elegance of the sentence, but their suppression is not imperative. Thus,

Je n'ose vous dire cela, *I do not dare tell you that.*
Je ne puis marcher, *I cannot walk.*
Je ne cesse de vous répéter cela, *I do not cease to repeat that.*

2. *Pas* or *point* are never used when the sentence contains any other negative complement; as, *jamais, nul, personne, rien, plus,* etc.; nor any other equivalent expression; as, *âme qui vive,* living soul (for *personne*), *de ma vie,* in my life (for *never*). Thus,

Je n'ai parlé à âme qui vive, *I never told any one.*
Nous n'avons parlé à qui que ce soit, *We did not speak to any one this evening.*
Je ne la verrai de ma vie, *I shall never see her again.*
Il n'y voit goutte, *He sees nothing at all.*

3. Neither *pas* nor *point* can be used with *ni* to express the English *neither . . . nor.* So,

Ni loups ni renards n'épiaient
La douce et l'innocente proie,

Neither wolves nor foxes spied the sweet and innocent prey.

Ils n'étaient ni payés, ni habillés, ni nourris, *They were neither paid, nor clad, nor fed.*

4. In exclamations expressed in the interrogative form, especially after *qui* or *que, pas* and *point* are suppressed. Thus,

Il se tue à rimer, que n'écrit-il en prose? *He is killing himself by writing verses; why does he not write in prose?*
Qui de nous n'a ses défauts! *Who among us has no faults!*

5. After *depuis que* or *il y a*, *ne* without *pas* or *point* is used when these expressions are followed by a verb in a compound tense, but *pas* is used when the verb is in a simple tense. Thus,

Il s'est passé bien des choses depuis que je ne vous ai vu, *Many things have happened since I saw you.*

Il y a six mois que je ne lui ai parlé, *I have not spoken to him for six months.*

Il y a deux nuits que je ne dors pas, *I have not slept for two nights.*

6. In hypothetical phrases, the suppression of the second negation is permissible, but not always essential. It is, however, generally suppressed after *si*. Thus,

Si ce n'est toi, c'est donc ton frère, *If it be not thee, it is thy brother then.*

Si je n'étais dans cette prison, je serais dans une autre, *If I were not in this prison, I would be in another.*

Cette vie m'eût paru douce, si la douleur ne m'eût accablé, *This life would have been sweet to me, had not grief overwhelmed me.*

7. Sometimes, however, the introduction or suppression of *pas* materially alters the sense of the sentence. Thus,

Il ne sait ce qu'il dit, *He does not know what he said.*

Il ne sait pas ce qu'il dit, *He does not know the value of what he says.*

8. In elliptical sentences, *pas* or *point* is sometimes used without *ne*. Thus,

Pas de bonheur sans vertu, *No happiness without virtue.*

THE EXPLETIVE USES OF NE

12. **Ne After a Comparative.** — *Ne* is used expletively after a comparative of inequality followed by *que* and a complementary proposition. Thus,

Vous écrivez mieux que vous ne parlez, *You write better than you speak.*

Il est plus riche qu'il ne l'était, *He is richer than he was.*

Here *ne* is a true expletive; in other words, *ne* has no material value and does no essential work in the sentence. Its function in such constructions is merely to indicate that the second part of the sentence really involves a negative idea. The two preceding examples might correctly have had either of the following forms:

Vous ne parlez pas aussi bien que vous écrivez.

Il n'était pas aussi riche autrefois qu'il l'est aujourd'hui.

When, however, the first part of the comparative of inequality is negative, the expletive *ne* is not expressed. Thus,

Vous n'écrivez pas mieux que vous parlez, *You write no better than you speak*.

Il n'est pas plus riche qu'il l'était, *He is no richer than he was*.

In these examples the second part of the comparative has no negative sense, for these sentences really mean:

Vous avez pour parler le même talent que pour écrire.

Il est riche à un certain degré, il était aussi riche autrefois.

13. Ne After Verbs Expressing Fear.—After verbs expressing fear, such as *craindre, avoir peur, trembler, appréhender, prendre garde, redouter*, etc., an expletive *ne* is generally used with the dependent verb. Thus,

Je tremble qu'il ne nous surprenne, *I tremble lest he may surprise us*.

Prends garde qu'on ne te voie, *Take care not to be seen*.

When, however, the second verb is in the indicative or conditional mode, *ne* is not used. Thus,

J'ai peur qu'il sera blamé, *I fear he will be blamed*.

14. Ne After Verbs of Doubt.—After verbs expressing doubt, denial, or despair (as *nier, désespérer, douter, disconvenir*), an expletive *ne* is generally used when these verbs are in the negative or interrogative form. Thus,

Il ne douta pas qu'elle ne vînt se venger, *He did not doubt that she would come to avenge herself*.

Je ne doute pas que la vraie dévotion ne soit la source du repos, *I do not doubt that true devotion is the source of peace*.

15. **Ne After Certain Conjunctive Phrases.** — The conjunctive phrases *à moins que, de peur que, de crainte que*, and the verb *empêcher* always require *ne* in the subordinate proposition. Thus,

Je ne ferai pas cela, à moins que vous ne l'exigiez, *I shall not do this, unless you exact it.*

La pluie empêcha qu'on ne se promenât dans le jardin, *The rain prevented us from walking in the garden.*

16. **Ne After Certain Impersonal Verbs.** — When the expressions *il s'en faut que, il tient à moi que* are used negatively or interrogatively, an expletive *ne* is placed in the subordinate proposition. Thus,

Il ne s'en faut pas de beaucoup que la somme **n'y** soit, *It does not lack much for the sum to be there.*

Il ne tient pas à moi que cela ne soit, *It is not in my power that that be.*

_____

SPECIAL NOTES ON PARTICULAR ADVERBS

17. **Autour, Alentour.** — *Autour* is a preposition and as such requires an object, but *alentour* is an adverb and cannot have one. Thus, ·

Je l'ai vu autour de la maison, *I saw him around the house.*

Le roi était sur son trône, ses courtisans étaient alentour, *The king was on his throne, his courtiers were around.*

Autour may also be used adverbially, and of course cannot then have an object; in such cases, it is generally modified by another adverb. Thus,

Il regardait tout autour si on le suivait, *He was looking all around to see if he was followed.*

18. **Auparavant, Avant.** — As in the preceding case, *auparavant* is an adverb, but *avant* a preposition, that may sometimes be used adverbially. Thus,

Il était marchand auparavant, *He was formerly a merchant.*
Ne marchez pas avant lui, *Do not walk before he does.*
Je l'ai vu le jour d'avant, *I saw him the day before.*
N'allez pas si avant, *Do not go so far.*

19. Dessus, Dessous, Dedans, Dehors. — These words are adverbs and do not require an object. When it is necessary to attach the sense of one of these adverbs to a noun object, one of the prepositions *sur, sous, dans, hors* must be used instead. Thus,

Pourquoi l'avez-vous laissé dehors? *Why did you leave it outside?*
J'ai mis votre livre sur la table, *I placed your book on the table.*

When two of these words are used in opposition, they are prepositions and may take objects. Thus,

Votre livre n'est ni dessus ni dessous la table, *Your book is neither on nor under the table.*

When the above words are preceded by a preposition, they form a compound preposition, that regularly requires an object. Thus,

Il a sauté par-dessus les murs, *He jumped over the walls.*
Otez cela de dessus la table, *Take that away from the top of the table.*

20. Tôt and Its Compounds. — The meaning of *tôt* is *soon* or *shortly*. *Bientôt*, however, is now generally used to express *soon*. *Tôt* enters into the following expressions: *trop tôt*, too soon; *tôt ou tard*, sooner or later; *au plus tôt*, at the soonest; *tôt* enters also into the following compounds:

1. *Aussitôt*, as soon as, being an adverb, cannot, therefore, have an object. It is, then, incorrect to say: *aussitôt mon arrivée, aussitôt mon dîner. Aussitôt* is ordinarily followed by *après* as in the following expressions: *aussitôt après mon arrivée, aussitôt après mon dîner.*

2. *Plus tôt, plutôt.* — The adverb *plus tôt*, earlier, sooner, relating to comparative time, is the contrary of *plus tard*. *Plutôt* denotes preference and means *rather*, or sometimes *hardly.* Thus,

Je viendrai le plus tôt possible, *I shall come as soon as I can.*
Il était plutôt fait pour commander que pour obéir, *He was made to command rather than to obey.*
Il n'eut pas plutôt fait cela qu'il s'en repentit, *He had hardly done that when he repented.*

21. Tantôt, Tout à l'heure. — The adverbs *tantôt, tout à l'heure,* may refer to either a past or a future time. Thus,

Je le verrai tout à l'heure, *I shall see him presently.*
Je l'ai vu tout à l'heure, *I saw him just now.*
Je vous verrai tantôt, *I shall see you by and by.*
Je vous ai vu tantôt, *I saw you a little while ago.*

22. Davantage, Plus. — The adverbs *davantage, plus,* both mean *more. Plus,* however, can precede a noun, an adjective, or an adverb. *Davantage,* on the contrary, is ordinarily used absolutely, and is always employed at the end of a sentence instead of *plus.* Thus,

Je n'en dirai pas davantage, *I shall tell no more.*
J'aime la campagne plus que la ville, *I like the country better than the city.*

Davantage can never be used as the equivalent of *le plus.* It would be incorrect to say: *De toutes les fleurs, la rose est celle qui me plaît davantage.* The correct form is: *De toutes les fleurs, la rose est celle qui me plaît le plus.*

23. Même. — In the sense of *even though, also,* or *likewise, même* is an adverb and may modify either an adjective, a verb, or an adverb. It is an adverb:

1. When followed by an article or a possessive adjective. Thus,

Même ses ennemis lui rendent justice, *Even his enemies render him justice.*

2. When placed after several substantives or pronouns. Thus,

J'ai tout à craindre de leurs soupirs, de leurs larmes, de leurs plaisirs même, *I have everything to fear from their sighs, their tears, and their pleasures likewise.*

3. When modifying a word other than a noun. Thus,

Tout citoyen doit obéir aux lois même injustes, *Every citizen must obey even unjust laws.*

24. Plus, Moins. — These adverbs may be repeated, or they may be put in opposition.

Plus il est malheureux, plus il est redoutable, *The more unfortunate he is, the more he is to be feared.*

Plus il est riche, moins il est content, *The richer he is, the less he is satisfied.*

25. Si, Aussi. — These two adverbs are used in comparisons, *aussi* being used in affirmative or negative sentences, but *si* in negative sentences only. Thus,

Il est aussi âgé que vous, *He is as old as you.*

Il n'est pas si (*or*, aussi) âgé que vous, *He is not so old as you.*

Si but not *aussi*, may also be used to intensify. Thus,

Il est si bon, si honnête, *He is so kind, so honest.*

26. Aussi, Non plus. — *Aussi* in the sense of also has for its corresponding negative *non plus*, not . . . either. Thus,

Ils iront et moi aussi, *They will go and I also.*

Ils n'iront pas, ni moi non plus, *They will not go, neither shall I.*

27. De suite, Tout de suite. — *De suite* means *successively, without interruption*, while *tout de suite* means *right away, immediately*. Thus,

Il ne peut pas dire deux mots de suite, *He cannot speak two words in succession.*

Venez tout de suite, *Come immediately.*

28. **Tout à coup, Tout d'un coup.** — *Tout à coup* means *suddenly*, but *tout d'un coup* has the sense of *in one stroke.* Thus,

Tout à coup, on entendit un grand cri, *Suddenly a great cry was heard.*

J'ai perdu ma fortune tout d'un coup, *I lost my fortune in one stroke.*

29. **Comme, Comment.** — *Comme* expresses the effect of an action, and has the meaning of *as, like, to what degree. Comment*, on the contrary, has the sense of *how, in what manner.* Thus,

Voyez comme je travaille, *See how I work.*

Il a fait comme moi, *He did as I did.*

Il ne m'a pas dit comment il ferait, *He did not tell me how he would act.*

30. **Moins.** — *Moins* after a negation means *nevertheless, notwithstanding*, and the pronoun *en* is used with it. Thus,

Il ne vous a pas parlé anglais; il n'en est pas moins vrai qu'il peut le faire, *He did not speak English to you; nevertheless it is true that he may do so.*

31. **Beaucoup, Bien.** — When *beaucoup* is joined to a verb, it expresses intensity or prolongation of an action; but *bien* marks the quality, the degree of perfection of an action. Thus,

Si j'espère beaucoup, je crains beaucoup aussi, *If I hope much, I fear much also.*

Ce n'est que dans les siècles éclairés que l'on a bien écrit et bien parlé, *It is only in enlightened centuries that people have written and spoken well.*

Bien, never *beaucoup*, is employed before adjectives. Thus,

Il est bien heureux, *He is very happy.*

Before the comparatives *plus*, *mieux*, *moins*, either *bien* or *beaucoup* may be used. Thus,

Vous êtes bien (*or*, beaucoup) plus riche que moi, *You are much richer than I.*

32. **Tout.** — *Tout* is an adverb when it modifies an adjective or another adverb. Thus,

Vos habits sont tout déchirés, *Your clothes are badly torn.*
Ma mère est tout heureuse, *My mother is quite happy.*

Tout, although an adverb, varies its form for euphonic purposes before a feminine adjective beginning with a consonant or an aspirated *h*. Thus,

Le maison est toute pleine, *The house is quite full.*
Cette jeune fille était toute désolée, *This young girl was very desolate.*

Tout followed by *autre*, is an adverb when meaning *quite*, *other*, or *very differeut*, and is then preceded by *un*, *une*, or *de*. Thus,

Il a raconté une tout autre histoire, *He told quite another story.*
Je vous avais demandé de tout autres choses, *I asked very different things of you.*

33. **Quelque.** — *Quelque* is an adverb when modifying an adjective or another adverb. Thus,

Quelque grands que soient les rois, ils sont ce que nous sommes, *However great kings may be, they are such as we are.*
Quelque riches que vous soyez, ne méprisez personne, *However rich you may be, do not despise any one.*

34. **Toujours, Encore.** — *Toujours*, always, may be used in the sense of *encore*, still, to denote permanency of action. Thus,

Demeurez-vous toujours à la même place? *Are you still living in the same place?*
Il est toujours professeur à Lyon, *He is still a professor at Lyons.*

The negative answer to *encore*, still, more, is *ne* . . . *plus*, no more, no longer. Thus,

Voulez-vous encore du pain?—Merci, je n'en veux plus, *Do you want more bread?—Thank you, I do not want any more.*

Demeurez-vous encore à Paris?—Je n'y demeure plus, *Do you still live in Paris?—I no longer live there.*

SYNTAX OF THE PREPOSITION

35. General Remarks.—French prepositions are always placed before their complements; except *durant*, during, which may be placed either before or after the word it governs, as in the phrase *durant sa vie*, or *sa vie durant*, during his lifetime.

All French prepositions require a following verb to be in the infinitive; except only *en*, which requires the present participle. Thus,

Je viens d'arriver, *I have just arrived.*

Il faut manger pour vivre, et non vivre pour manger, *One must eat to live, and not live to eat.*

J'ai lu votre lettre en marchant, *I read your letter when I was out walking.*

36. Prepositions Used Before Names of Cities and Countries.—The prepositions *to, at, in*, are translated in French:

1. By *à* before the names of cities, or *au* before names of cities beginning with *le*. Thus,

Je vais à Paris, à Londres, à Bruxelles, *I am going to Paris, to London, to Brussels.*

Votre père est-il à Paris? *Is your father in Paris?*

2. By *en* before the feminine name of a country. Thus,

Je vais en Amérique, en France, en Chine, *I am going to America, to France, to China.*

Il est en France maintenant, *He is in France now.*

NOTE.—Names of countries ending in *e* without an accent are feminine; except *le Mexique* and *le Maine*.

3.   By *au* before the masculine name of a country, and by *aux* before the plural name of a country. Thus,

Nous allons au Canada, aux Etats-Unis, *We are going to Canada, to the United States*.

Il est arrivé au Mexique la semaine dernière, *He arrived in Mexico last week*.

4.   By *dans* with the article before the name of a country preceded by an adjective or followed by a determinative object. Thus,

Il est allé dans l'Amérique du Sud, *He went to South America*.

Et moi je vais dans la Nouvelle Zélande, *As for me, I am going to New Zealand*.

The preposition *from* is translated in French:

1.   By *de* before names of cities, and before feminine names of countries. Thus,

Nous sommes partis de France pour le Canada, *We started from France for Canada*.

Il est parti de Lyon à six heures, *He started from Lyons at six o'clock*.

2.   By *de* before masculine names of countries, whether or not modified by an article or an adjective; also before names of cities preceded by the article alone. Thus,

Notre oncle est arrivé du Danemark, *My uncle has arrived from Denmark*.

Nous partîmes du Hâvre à midi, *We departed from Hâvre at noon*.

PECULIARITIES OF CERTAIN PREPOSITIONS

37. The Preposition À. — The preposition *à* usually marks direction or movement toward a place. Thus,

J'irai à mon bureau ce matin, *I shall go to my office this morning.*

Remettons cela à demain, *Let us put that off until tomorrow.*

The preposition *à* expresses many relations that have been studied in connection with the government of verbs and adjectives.

38. The Preposition De. — The preposition *de* marks the starting point, generally expresses separation, and is used with reference to place, time, cause, or manner. Thus,

Venez de ce côté-ci, *Come on this side.*

Il est allé de porte en porte, *He went from door to door.*

J'y vais de temps en temps, *I go there from time to time.*

39. En, Dans, and À. — The preposition *à* points toward a place, *dans* points to the inside of a place, and *en* has a vague, indefinite sense, often forming with its associated noun a kind of adverbial phrase. Thus,

Mon père est au magasin, *My father is at the store.*

Mon père est dans ce magasin, *My father is in that store.*

Le café est en magasin, *The coffee is stored.*

En is generally placed before indeterminate nouns; as, *en mer*, *en colère*, *en voyage*, *en voiture*, etc. *Dans* is generally placed before nouns accompanied with the definite article or a determinative adjective; as, *dans la mer*, *dans sa colère*, *dans votre voyage*, *dans la voiture*, etc.

En used with reference to time, expresses longer or shorter duration while *dans* points to a definite moment when something will have taken place. Thus,

Il arrivera en trois jours, *He will arrive in three days.*

Il arrivera dans trois jours, *He will arrive within three days.*

40. Avant, Devant.—The prepositions *avant* and *devant* are both translated by *before*. The first refers to time or rank; the latter to place. Thus,

Venez avant lundi, *Come before Monday.*
Février est avant mars, *February precedes March.*
Il est devant la maison, *He is (in front of) before the house.*

The antonyms or opposites of these two prepositions have very different meanings in English. The antonym of *avant*, before, is *après*, after; but that of *devant*, before, is *derrière*, behind.

Avant, in French, placed before a noun or pronoun, is not followed by *de*. Thus,

Venez avant le dîner, *Come before dinner.*
Il est arrivé avant vous, *He arrived before you.*

Before an infinitive, the phrase *avant de* is used instead of the simple preposition. Thus,

Prenez une tasse de café avant de partir, *Take a cup of coffee before going.*
Pourquoi êtes-vous parti avant de m'écrire? *Why did you go before writing to me?*

41. Chez.—The preposition *chez*, with, from or at the house of, refers to persons, to professions, or one's home or country. Thus,

Vous êtes allé chez M. Bernard hier, *You went to Mr. Bernard's yesterday.*
J'ai acheté cela chez le libraire, *I bought that at the bookseller's.*
Pourquoi ne venez-vous pas chez nous? *Why do you not come to our house?*
Chez les Romains, l'autorité paternelle était excessive, *Among the Romans, paternal authority was severe.*

De chez, from the house of, should be distinguished from

de la part de. The first means from the person's house; the second, from the person. Thus,

Nous venons de chez M. Martin, *We come from Mr. Martin's.*

Nous venons de la part de M. Martin, *We come from Mr. Martin* (*Mr. Martin sent us here*).

42. Durant, Pendant.—The preposition *durant* embraces the entire extent of a period of time, while *pendant* may be used to indicate either the whole or a part of a period. Thus,

Durant le siège de Paris, la famine était terrible, *During the siege of Paris, the famine was terrible.*

J'ai été là pendant la guerre, *I went there during the war.*

43. Entre, Parmi.—*Entre* is generally used to express relation between two persons or two things only; it also expresses reciprocity in the sense of *among.* *Parmi* is used to express the similar relation of more than two objects, and is generally followed by an indefinite plural noun or a collective. Thus,

Il était assis entre vous et moi, *He was seated between you and me.*

Etampes est entre Paris et Orléans, *Etampes is between Paris and Orleans.*

Il fut trouvé parmi les morts, *He was found among the dead.*

De tout temps, on a vu des fripons se glisser parmi d'honnêtes gens, *In all time, rascals have been seen to steal in among honest people.*

44. Pour, Afin de.—These two prepositions have the sense of *in order to*, but *pour* is used when the accomplishment of a purpose is within reach; *afin de* when success is not assured. Thus,

Je vous ai fait venir pour vous dire cela, *I summoned you to tell you that.*

Nous lui avons montré cette lettre afin de le décider à partir, *We showed him this letter in order to induce him to go.*

45. Voici, Voilà. — *Voici* refers to what follows; *voilà* to what precedes. Thus,

> Voici trois médecins qui ne se trompent pas:
> Gaîté, doux exercice et modeste repas.

Here are three doctors who are never mistaken: gaiety, gentle exercise, and moderate eating.

Aimer et s'occuper; voilà le secret du bonheur, *To love and to be busy; there is the secret of happiness.*

When no opposition is to be marked, *voilà* is used in preference to *voici*. Thus,

Voilà une entreprise qui ne réussira pas, *That is an enterprise that will not succeed.*

Voici and *voilà* may be used with the conjunction *que* or with the relative pronoun *qui*. Thus,

Tiens! Voilà qu'on sonne, *Hark! There is some one ringing the bell.*
Le voici qui arrive, *Here he comes.*

46. De by Gallicism. — The preposition *de* is still employed in the following ancient Gallic constructions:

1. After superlatives, and after *le seul*, *l'unique*, *le premier*, *le dernier*, as *in* is often used in English. Thus,

Cette maison est la plus grande de la ville, *This house is the largest in the city.*
Londres est la plus grande de toutes les villes de l'Europe, *London is the largest of all the cities of Europe.*
Charles est le premier de sa classe, *Charles is the first in his class.*

2. After a noun preceded by a number before an adjective or a past participle. Thus,

Il y en eut cent de tués, *One hundred were killed.*
Il y eut trois cents hommes de proscrits, *Three hundred men were exiled.*

3. In familiar language, *de* is often used to unite a noun to a preceding modifier. Thus,

C'était un saint homme de chat, *He was a saint of a cat.*
Quel fripon d'enfant, *What a little rascal of a child.*

4. In interrogative sentences expressing a comparison, the preposition *de* is used before each term of the comparison. Thus,

Qui des deux fut le plus grand, de César ou d'Alexandre? *Who was the greater, Cæsar or Alexander?*
Il est difficile de décider laquelle on devrait le plus encourager, de l'agriculture ou de l'industrie, *It is difficult to decide which should be more encouraged, agriculture or manufacture.*

47. A travers, Au travers. — These two prepositions mean *across*, through, but *au travers* indicates that there may be obstacles in the way. Moreover, *au travers* requires the preposition *de* after it, while *à travers* takes no preposition. Thus,

Il a passé au travers d'un buisson, *He passed through a thicket.*
Nous sommes venus à travers les champs, *We came across the fields.*

48. Par terre, À terre. — *Tomber par terre*, to fall to the ground, is said of things already standing or resting upon the ground, as a man or a tree, for example. *Tomber à terre* is said of things that fall from an elevation to the ground. Thus,

Cet arbre est tombé par terre, *That tree fell to the ground.*
Une pomme tomba à terre, *An apple fell to the ground.*

49. À la campagne, En campagne. — *Etre à la campagne*, to be in the country, is to be in the country for some time; while *être en campagne*, is to be temporarily in the country — as for business purposes. This last expression applies particularly to the movements of soldiers in the field. Thus,

Je vais à la campagne tous les étés, *I go to the country every summer*.

Les armées sont en campagne, *The armies have taken the field*.

Il a mis ses amis en campagne, *He set his friends to work.*

50. Vis-à-vis de, Envers, À l'égard de. — The prepositional phrase *vis-à-vis de* is only used to denote opposition of place, and means *opposite, face to face;* as, *Il demeure vis-à-vis du Louvre*, He lives opposite the Louvre. This expression should never be used in the sense of toward, to express moral feeling. It would be incorrect to say, *Il est ingrat vis-à-vis de ses bienfaiteurs*, He is ungrateful toward his benefactors. Instead of *vis-à-vis* in such expressions, *envers* or *à l'égard de* are used. Thus, the correct ways of expressing the preceding sentence are:

Il est ingrat envers ses bienfaiteurs,   ⎫ *He is ungrateful*
Il est ingrat à l'égard de ses bienfaiteurs, ⎬ *toward his*
                                      ⎭ *benefactors.*

51. Près de, Prêt à. — These two expressions should be carefully distinguished. *Près de* is a preposition and means *near, by; prêt à* is a phrase formed with the adjective *prêt* and has the sense of *ready to;* the adjective agrees with its associated noun. Thus,

Les beaux jours sont près de finir, *Beautiful days are near an end.*

L'ignorance est toujours prête à s'admirer, *Ignorance is always ready to admire itself.*

52. Près de, Auprès de, À côté de. — These three prepositional expressions mark different degrees of proximity. *Auprès de* expresses a closer degree of proximity than *près de*, while *à côté de* means *next to*. Thus,

Asseyez-vous à côté de moi, *Sit next to me.*

Il demeure près de l'église, *He lives near the church.*

Il demeure auprès de l'église, *He lives close to the church.*

53. Jusque, Depuis. — *Jusque* marks the end while *depuis* marks the beginning of a movement, of a distance, or of a period of time. Thus,

Depuis quand est-il ici? *How long has he been here?*
Jusqu'à quand restera-t-il? *How long will he stay?*

REPETITION OF PREPOSITIONS

54. Monosyllabic Prepositions. — Monosyllabic prepositions are usually repeated before every complement, whether ⁓noun, verb, or pronoun, but need not be repeated before a succession of numeral adjectives. This rule is particularly pertinent to the prepositions *à*, *de*, *en*, and *sans*. The other monosyllabic prepositions need be repeated only when their complements are very unlike in meaning. Thus,

Il tâche de mériter et d'obtenir votre confiance, *He is endeavoring to merit and obtain your confidence.*

J'ai été en France et en Suisse, *I have been in France and Switzerland.*

Remplissez vos devoirs envers Dieu, envers vos parents et envers la patrie, *Fulfil your duties toward God, toward your parents, and toward your country.*

Elle charme tout le monde par sa bonté et sa douceur, *She charms everybody with her kindness and gentleness.*

55. Preposition Not Repeated. — No preposition is repeated before two nouns forming one and the same expression, as in the title of a book or literary selection. Thus,

Cette citation a été prise dans Paul et Virginie, *This quotation has been taken from Paul and Virginia.*

Dans la fable du Corbeau et le Renard, La Fontaine montre le danger d'écouter les flatteurs, *In his fable of The Crow and the Fox, La Fontaine shows the danger of listening to flatterers.*

56. Sans Not Repeated. — *Sans* is not repeated when the last complement is preceded by *ni*. Thus,

Il est sans feu ni lieu, *He is without fire or home.*

Il passa trois jours sans boire ni manger, *He spent three days without drinking or eating.*

COMPLEMENTS OF PREPOSITIONS

57. Several Prepositions With One Complement. Two prepositions may have only one complement. Thus,

Il a parlé pour vous et contre vous, } *He spoke for and against*
Il a parlé pour et contre vous,   } *you.*

After compound prepositions having the same final component part, the complement need not be repeated. Thus,

Il est près et autour de la ville, *He is near and around the city.*

This sentence is correct, because *près* and *autour* have both the preposition *de* after them. It would be incorrect to say, *Un magistrat doit toujours punir suivant et conformément aux lois,* because *suivant* does not require a preposition, and *conformément* requires *à*. To be correct, the sentence must be as follows:

Un magistrat doit toujours punir suivant les lois et conformément à ce qu'elles prescrivent, *A magistrate must always punish according to the law, and conformably with its prescriptions.*

SYNTAX OF THE CONJUNCTION

58. **Place of Conjunctions.** — Conjunctions serving to unite two propositions, are ordinarily placed in the body of the sentence. This is obligatory with the coordinating conjunctions *or, mais, et, car, pourtant, donc, toutefois*, etc. Thus,

Les hommes sont quelquefois habiles, mais ils sont rarement sages, *Men are sometimes clever, but they are seldom wise.*

On aime à deviner les autres, mais on n'aime pas à être deviné, *We like to unriddle others, but we do not like to be unriddled ourselves.*

Subordinate propositions beginning with *que* are generally placed after the principal proposition. Thus,

Je crois que la paresse est le plus grand de tous les vices, *I think idleness is the greatest of vices.*

Je ne pense pas qu'il viendra ce soir, *I think that he will not come tonight.*

It may also be remarked here that *que* is never omitted in French, as is so often done with *that* in English. When several subordinate propositions follow one another, *que* is repeated before each of them. Thus,

Je crois que Dieu est juste, qu'il récompense les bons et qu'il punit les méchants, *I believe that God is just, that He rewards the good, and punishes the bad.*

A clause beginning with *comme* usually has the first place in a sentence. Thus,

Comme ses raisons paraissaient bonnes, on s'y rendit, *As his arguments appeared good, they agreed.*

59. **Concerning a Few Conjunctions.** — When a subordinate proposition begins with the conjunctions *quand*, *lorsque*, *quoique*, *si*, as well as with compound conjunctions formed with *que*, like *pendant que*, *afin que*, etc., such a proposition may begin the sentence, especially when it is shorter than the principal proposition. Thus,

Pendant que vous dormiez, je travaillais à mon bureau, *While you were sleeping, I was working in my office.*

Quand il arrivera, tout sera prêt pour le recevoir, *When he arrives, everything will be ready to receive him.*

Si cela est possible, je vous promets de le faire, *If that is possible, I promise you to do it.*

Quoiqu'il soit riche, les pauvres n'en sont pas moins ses amis, *Although he is rich, the poor are nevertheless his friends.*

REMARKS ON CERTAIN CONJUNCTIONS

60. Et. — The conjunction *et* is a sign of addition. It adds to the thought, uniting affirmatives, negatives, or both. It is used in the following cases:

1. *Et* may unite principal propositions, either affirmative or negative. Thus,

Il a marché toute la nuit, et il doit repartir ce matin, *He walked all night, and he must start again this morning.*

Il n'a pas travaillé hier, et ne travaillera probablement pas aujourd'hui, *He did not work yesterday, and will probably not work today.*

2. *Et* may also unite principal propositions, affirmative or negative. Thus,

Je plie et ne romps pas, *I bend and do not break.*
Je ne plie pas et je romps, *I do not bend and break.*

3. *Et* may also unite subordinate propositions depending on the same principal proposition. Thus,

On n'a pas toujours cru que la terre est une planète et qu'elle tourne autour du soleil, *It was not always believed that the earth is a planet and that it turns around the sun.*

4. *Et* may also connect similar parts of a proposition, nouns with nouns, adjectives with adjectives, verbs with verbs, etc. Thus,

Il cultive les lettres et les sciences, *He cultivates letters and sciences.*

Son fils est studieux et intelligent, *His son is industrious and intelligent.*

Agissez lentement et prudemment, *Act slowly and prudently.*

Il parle et écrit très bien le français, *He speaks and writes French very well.*

61. **Repetition of the Conjunction Et.** — In order to render the style more forceful, the conjunction *et* is sometimes repeated before each term of an enumeration. Thus,

Et le riche, et le pauvre, et le faible, et le fort,
Vont tous également des douleurs à la mort.

The rich and the poor, the feeble and the strong, all alike pass from sorrow to death. — Voltaire.

On égorge à la fois les enfants, les vieillards,
Et la sœur et le frère,
Et la fille et la mère,
Le fils dans les bras de son père.

At the same time they slaughter children, old men, the sister and the brother, the daughter and the mother, the son in his father's arms. — Voltaire.

In ordinary style, however, *et* is placed only before the last term of an enumeration. Thus,

Les plaintes, les regrets et les pleurs sont superflus, *Complaints, regrets, and tears are superfluous.*

62. **Suppression of the Conjunction Et.** — 1. To give the style more rapidity and conciseness, the conjunction *et* is omitted in an enumeration. Thus,

Femmes, moines, vieillards, tout était descendu, *Women, monks, old men, all had alighted.* — LA FONTAINE.

Le lion a la figure imposante, le regard assuré, la démarche fière, la voix terrible, *The lion has an imposing figure, a confident look, a defiant stride, a terrible voice.* — BUFFON.

2. The conjunction *et* is not used in an enumeration whose parts are composed of synonymous expressions or are placed in gradation, nor if the last word of the enumeration sums up all others.   Thus,

Toute sa vie n'a été qu'un travail, qu'une occupation continuelle, *All his life has been only toil, ceaseless occupation.*

Son courage, son intrépidité étonne les plus braves, *His courage, his intrepidity astonishes the brave.*

Ce sacrifice, votre intérêt, votre honneur, Dieu vous le commande, *Your interest, your honor, God command this sacrifice.*

3. *Et* is generally omitted when two propositions begin with *plus*, *mieux*, *moins*, *autant*.   Neither can *et* be used between propositions expressing opposition.   Thus,

Mieux vous écouterez, mieux vous comprendrez, *The better you listen, the better you will understand.*

Plus on a, plus on veut avoir, *The more one has, the more one wants.*

Le chagrin compte les minutes; le bonheur oublie les heures, *Sorrow counts the minutes; happiness forgets the hours.*

This rule was not always followed, especially by French authors of the 17th century, as the following examples will show:

Plus l'offenseur est cher, et plus grande est l'offense, *The dearer the offender, the greater is the offense.* — CORNEILLE.

Plus les hommes seront éclairés, et plus ils seront libres, *The more enlightened men become, the freer they will be.* — VOLTAIRE.

Plus la fortune rit, et plus on doit trembler, *The more fortune smiles on us, the more we should tremble.*

4. When two verbs in the imperative mode are connected by *and* in English, the second being a complement of the first, the conjunction *et* is not used in French, and the second verb is put in the infinitive. Thus,

Venez me voir, *Come and see me.*
Allons le faire, *Let us go and do it.*

63. **Ni.** — *Ni* also is a sign of addition; but it adds negatively to the thought.
Ni is used:

1. To unite two coordinate principal negative propositions, if the second is elliptical. Thus,

Il ne boit ni ne mange, *He does not drink or eat.*
La boussole n'a pas été trouvée par un marin, ni le télescope par un astronome, *The marine compass was not invented by a sailor, nor the telescope by an astronomer.*

2. To unite two subordinate propositions coming after a negative principal proposition. Thus,

Je ne crois pas qu'il vienne ni qu'il pense à venir, *I do not believe he will come or that he is thinking of coming.*
Il ne croit pas que la terre soit une planète, ni qu'elle tourne autour du soleil, *He does not believe that the earth is a planet nor that it turns around the sun.*

3. To unite similar parts of a negative proposition. In such cases, *pas* may be replaced by a second *ni.* Thus,

Elle n'est pas belle ni riche, ⎱ *She is neither beautiful nor*
Elle n'est ni belle ni riche, ⎰ *rich.*

Vous ne devez pas le dire ni l'écrire, ⎱ *You should neither*
Vous ne devez ni le dire ni l'écrire, ⎰ *speak it nor write it.*

The similar parts of a negative proposition are sometimes regarded as synonymous or as being inseparable; in this case, *et* may be used instead of *ni.* Thus,

Les animaux n'inventent et ne perfectionnent rien, *Animals do not invent or perfect anything.*

Le savoir-faire et l'habileté ne mènent pas toujours à la fortune, *The knowing how to do and the power to execute do not always lead to fortune.*

4. Instead of *sans*, when that word should be repeated. If *sans* is repeated, *et* must be used instead of *ni*. Thus,

Il est sans père ni mère, ⎫ *He has neither father nor*
Il est sans père et sans mère,⎭ *mother.*

64. Ou. — *Ou* is used to join similar parts of a proposition to express an alternative. Thus,

Si ce n'est pas vous, c'est lui ou moi, *If it is not you, it is he or I.*
Qui est le plus intelligent, mon frère ou ma sœur? *Who is the more intelligent, my brother or my sister?*

To give more energy to a sentence, *ou* may be repeated before each subject, each complement, or each proposition. Thus,

Selon qu'il vous menace ou bien qu'il vous caresse,
La cour, autour de vous, ou s'éloigne ou s'empresse.

As he menaces or fondles you, the court recedes from you or approaches. — RACINE.

Plus de raison: il faut ou le perdre ou mourir, *No more arguments: you must either lose him or die.* — RACINE.

65. Mais. — When the conjunction *mais* unites two propositions, the first negative, the second affirmative, the verb may be understood in the second. Thus,

Je ne parle pas à Louis mais à vous, *I am not speaking to Louis, but to you.*
L'harmonie ne frappe pas seulement l'oreille mais l'esprit, *Harmony strikes not only the ear, but the mind.*

If, on the contrary, the first proposition is affirmative and the second negative, the verb must be repeated or *mais* must be followed by *non*. Thus,

Il aime bien son frère, mais il n'aime⎫ *He loves his brother,*
pas sa sœur, ⎬ *but not his sister.*
Il aime bien son frère, mais non sa sœur,⎭

66. **Soit, Soit que.** — *Soit* may be repeated before each term of a proposition or may be replaced by the conjunction *ou.* Before a verb, *soit* is followed by *que.* Thus,

soit bonté, soit faiblesse, }
soit bonté ou faiblesse, } *whether kindness or feebleness*

soit qu'il vienne, soit qu'il vous écrive, } *whether he comes*
soit qu'il vienne ou qu'il vous écrive, } *or writes you*

67. **Parce que, Par ce que.** — *Parce que* spelled in two words, is translated because, while *par ce que*, in three words, is translated *from what, by that which.* This last expression is formed of *par*, a preposition and the two pronouns *ce* and *que.* Thus,

Par ce que vous faites, je vois que vous n'y connaissez rien, *By that which you do, I see you know nothing about it.*

Parce qu'elle meurt, faut-il que vous mouriez? *Because she dies, should you die?*

68. **Parce que and Car.** — Both conjunctions mean *because;* but *car* is used when the speaker gives his own reasons for what precedes, while *parce que* emphasizes or introduces the cause itself. Thus,

Je ne vais pas avec vous car je suis fatigué, *I am not going with you for I am tired.*

Ce cheval ne me plaît pas parce qu'il est trop vieux, *This horse does not please me; it is too old.*

69. **Parce que, Puisque.** — The first of these expressions introduces a cause for the action that precedes, while the second introduces a consequence. Thus,

Pourquoi ne le payez-vous? — Parce que je n'ai pas d'argent, *Why do you not pay him? — Because I have no money.*

Donnez-lui au moins un à-compte. — Mais puisque je vous dis que je n'ai pas d'argent, *Give him a bill at least. — Why, I told you I have no money.*

Je ne suis pas venu chez vous parce que je ne croyais pas vous rencontrer, *I did not call on you because I did not believe I should find you.*

Je ne suis pas venu chez vous puisque vous aviez à sortir, *I did not call on you for you had to go out.*

70. Si, Quand, Lorsque. — The conjunction *si*, if, introduces conditional clauses not denoting time. *Quand* marks a condition depending on time, but *lorsque*, while also marking time, supposes the realization of the condition. Thus,

$$\text{Apportez-moi mon livre} \begin{cases} \text{si vous venez,} \\ \text{quand vous viendrez,} \\ \text{lorsque vous viendrez,} \end{cases}$$

$$\text{\textit{Bring me my book}} \begin{cases} \textit{if you come.} \\ \textit{when you come.} \\ \textit{as you come.} \end{cases}$$

In these sentences, the conjunction *si* leaves some doubt as to whether or not you will come; *quand* gives an idea of probability, but *lorsque* assumes the coming as a future fact already established. As may be seen, the difference is great between *si* on one side and *quand* and *lorsque* on the other. But the difference between *quand* and *lorsque* is very subtle, and the two are often treated as being synonymous.

71. Quoique and Quoi que. — *Quoique*, spelled in one word, is a conjunction and means *although*. Spelled in two words, the expression is formed of two pronouns *quoi* and *que*, and means *whatever*. Thus,

Quoiqu'il soit malade, il m'a promis qu'il viendrait, *Although he is ill, he promised me he would come.*

Quoi que vous lui disiez, il ne vous écoutera pas, *Whatever you may tell him, he will not listen to you.*

USES OF THE CONJUNCTION QUE

72. To Unite Propositions. — The conjunction *que* is used to unite subordinate propositions to a principal proposition. Thus,

Je crois que l'âme est immortelle, *I believe that the soul is immortal.*

J'admets qu'il a raison, *I agree that he is right.*

73. To Unite Terms of Comparison. — The conjunction *que* is used to unite the terms of a comparison. Thus,

Il est $\begin{cases} \text{aussi} \\ \text{plus} \\ \text{moins} \end{cases}$ âgé que moi, *He is* $\begin{cases} \textit{as old as I.} \\ \textit{older than I.} \\ \textit{less old than I.} \end{cases}$

Cet homme est plus éloquent que brave, *This man is more eloquent than courageous.*

74. Ne . . . que. — *Que* forms with *ne* a compound expression equivalent to *seulement*, only, and the two words are placed in the sentence as are *ne . . . pas.* Thus,

Il n'a que dix ans, *He is only ten years old.*

Je ne parle que français à la maison, *I speak French only at home.*

75. Que for Other Conjunctions. — *Que* may be used for other conjunctions as follows:

1. For *comme* after adjectives or adverbs of time. Thus,

Malade qu'il est, il veut sortir,
Malade comme il est, il veut sortir, } *Ill as he is, he wishes to go out.*

Maintenant que vous êtes riche, vous ne me parlez plus,
    Maintenant, comme vous êtes riche, vous ne me parlez plus, } *Now that you are rich, you no longer speak to me.*

2. For *combien* or *comme* in exclamatory sentences. Thus,

Que vous êtes riche!
Comme vous êtes riche! } *How rich you are!*
Combien vous êtes riche!

3. For *parce que* after *c'est*. Thus,

Si je ne mange pas, c'est que je n'ai pas faim, *If I am not eating, it is because I am not hungry.*

S'il ne se lève pas, c'est qu'il est fatigué, *If he does not get up, it is because he is tired.*

4. For *pourquoi* in interrogations. Thus,

Que ne me disiez-vous cela plus tôt? } *Why did you not tell me that sooner?*
Pourquoi ne me disiez-vous pas cela plus tôt?

5. For *quand* or *lorsque* after the expression *à peine.* Thus,

A peine avais-je douze ans que je quittai l'école, } *I was scarcely twelve when I left school.*
J'avais à peine douze ans quand je quittai l'école,

6. For *si, comme, puisque, quoique* to avoid repetition. Thus,

Puisqu'on plaide, et qu'on meurt, et qu'on devient malade,
        Il faut des médecins, il faut des avocats.

Since one sues, and one dies, and one becomes ill, one must have lawyers and doctors. — La Fontaine.

Comme il est malade, et qu'il a mal à la tête, il ne viendra pas, *Since he is ill and has a headache, he will not come.*

7. For certain compound conjunctions; as, *à moins que, afin que, depuis que,* etc. Thus,

Je ne lui écrirai plus qu'il ne m'ait répondu, *I shall write to him no more until he has answered me.*

Approchez que je vous parle, *Come nearer that I may speak to you.*

76. Que in Gallicisms. — *Que* is still used in a number of ancient Gallic expressions, as follows:

1. *Que* is used before a noun subject when the attribute is introduced by *c'est* and placed before the subject. This

construction has the effect of emphasizing that subject. Thus,

C'est une belle ville que Bruxelles, *Brussels is a beautiful city*.

Without emphasis, the preceding sentence would be:

Bruxelles est une belle ville.

If the subject of a sentence as above is an infinitive, *que* must be followed by *de*. Thus,

C'est un devoir que d'obliger ses amis, *It is a duty to oblige one's friends*.

C'est être sage que de se défier des méchants, *It is wise to mistrust the wicked*.

2. *Que* is used in exclamatory sentences when the exclamative attribute precedes the subject, and the verb is omitted. Thus,

Quel bonheur que de revoir sa patrie! *What a pleasure to see one's country again!*

Quel riche pays que les Etats-Unis! *What a rich country the United States is!*

3. *Que* is used in connection with *si*, *oui*, or *non* in sentences similar to the following:

Je pense que oui, *I think so*.
Je pense que non, *I think not*.
Je crois que si, *I believe so*.

4. *Que* is also used after *c'est-à-dire*, that is to say, to introduce an explanatory clause; also after *peut-être*, *voilà*. Thus,

Voilà qu'il pleut, *There, it is raining*.

Il m'a dit cela, peut-être que ce n'est pas vrai, *He told me that; it may not be true*.

Je l'ai payé; c'est-à-dire que je ne lui dois rien, *I paid him; that is to say, I owe him nothing*.

SYNTAX OF THE INTERJECTION

77. Two Kinds of Interjections. — There are two kinds of interjections: (1) such words as *ah! oh! hélas!* etc. are real cries thrown into the speech to mark feeling or emotion, and are thus real interjections; (2) such exclamation as *courage! silence! patience!* etc. are only elliptical propositions. It is as if one said (*prenez*) *courage*, take courage; (*faites*) *silence*, keep silence; (*ayez*) *patience*, have patience.

REMARKS ON INTERJECTIONS

78. Ah! Ha! — The interjection *ah!* expresses joy, pain, deep emotion, and is pronounced long; the interjection *ha!* expresses sudden surprise or fear. Thus,

Ah! que cela est beau!   *Ah! how beautiful that is!*
Ah! que je souffre!   *Ah! how I suffer!*
Ha! Ha! vous voilà!   *Ha! ha! there you are!*

79. Oh! Ho! Ô! — *Oh!* expresses admiration, exaltation; it is also sometimes used for mere emphasis. Thus,

Oh! qu'il est cruel d'être trompé par un ami!   *Oh! how cruel it is to be deceived by a friend!*
Oh! que c'est beau!   *Oh! how beautiful that is!*
Oh! je le ferai comme je vous l'ai promis!   *Oh! I will do it as I promised you!*

Ho marks astonishment. It is also used alone or in the compound expression *holà*, to call. Thus,

Ho! que me dites-vous là?   *Ho! what are you telling me there?*
Ho! *or* Holà, venez ici, *Hello! come here.*

Ô is used in simple exhortation. Thus,

O mon fils, adorez Dieu!   *O my son, adore God.*
O temps, Ô moeurs!   *O the times! O the customs !*

80. The imperative forms of the verbs *aller* and *tenir* are used as interjections. Thus,

Allons! mes amis, en route!   *Come, my friends, let us go!*
Va! tu es un bon garçon, *Come now! thou art a good boy.*
Tiens! c'est toi!   *What!   It is you!*
Tenez! ne m'en parlez plus!   *Hold! do not say any more about it!*

81. Interjectional Phrases. — Many words and phrases may be used as interjections. The most important are:

A la bonne heure! ⎫ *Well and good!* A merveille! ⎭	Eh bien! *Well!*
Bravo! *Bravo!*	Grand Dieu! ⎫
Tout beau! *Gently!*	Dieu de bonté! ⎬ *Heavens!*
Ma foi! *Upon my faith!*	Juste Ciel! ⎭

FRENCH GRAMMAR

(PART 12)

PROSODY

1. The Field of Prosody. — The word **prosody** comes from two Greek words meaning accent. Strictly speaking, prosody denotes merely that musical tone or melody which accompanies utterance, but the word is used both by classical and modern grammarians to include not only the doctrines of accent and quantity, but also the laws governing metrical composition and versification. In this wider sense, prosody treats of punctuation, utterance, the figures of speech, and versification. But the field of prosody is so vast and of so varied a character that just as orthography, or the grammar of letters, now finds its proper place in the dictionary, so the practice of late writers has been to treat of utterance under elocution, of the figures of speech under rhetoric, of punctuation and capitalization (which are mere devices to indicate the relations of words in written speech) under grammar, while versification has been reserved as the proper subject matter of prosody.

Prosody treats of the laws governing metrical construction and the art of poetical composition.

2. Prose and Poetry. — In every language, methods of thought and expression naturally fall into two great classes — *prose* and *poetry*. In **prose**, thought is expressed under the form or guise of ordinary discourse or composition, without special reference to rhythmic movement or metrical construction; but in **poetry**, thought is couched in language that is at once melodious and rhythmical and of imaginative and artistic form. In all good prose there is a certain rhythmical flow, but the movement is less obtrusive and far more difficult of analysis than is the rhythm of poetry. Of poetry there are two distinct classes: *poetic prose* and *verse*. In English, John Ruskin is, by the common consent of critics, the first master of poetic prose; in French, there are many passages of striking poetical beauty in the writings of Victor Hugo, Madame de Stael, Chateaubriand, and others. Perhaps one of the best known of these passages is the description of the battle of Waterloo in Hugo's *Les Miserables*.

Verse is but a special form of poetry. It is characterized by hard and fast rules governing its melody and rhythm. While all highly imaginative and artistic prose may properly be termed poetry, the popular conception of the word *poetry* restricts its meaning and identifies it with verse.

3. Technical Terms. — Verse is language arranged in metrical lines of determined length and rhythm. Each line is termed a **verse**. **Versification** is the making of that kind of literary composition known as verse. The **rhythm** of verse is the regular recurrence of long or short, or of accented or unaccented syllables. **Quantity** is the relative portion of time occupied in uttering a syllable. In classical verse, rhythm was determined by the succession and relation of long or short syllables; but in English verse, it is determined by the succession of accented or unaccented syllables. Rime, or rhyme, is a correspondence of the same sounds in two or more words, especially at the end of verses. In **blank verse,** the syllables at the end of the different verses do not rime. A **stanza** is a group of two or more rimed lines. A **poem** is the sum of the stanzas forming a literary composition. The **cesura** is the break or pause occurring after any word in the utterance of a line of verse; the **main cesura** is determined by the sense of the line. A **foot,** or **meter,** is a subdivision of a verse, containing a definite number of long, short, accented, or unaccented, syllables.

4. **Difference Between French and English Verse.**
It has already been explained that English verse depends on
the number of accented syllables. But since there are no
accented syllables in the French language, a verse depends
simply on the number of syllables. Verse dependent on the
number of long and short, or accented and unaccented
syllables, is called **metric** verse; while that dependent
simply on the number of syllables in a given line, is known as
syllabic verse. All French verse is necessarily syllabic.

5. **Importance of the Cesura and Rime in French
Verse.** — Since French verse is merely dependent on the
number of syllables in a line, the place of the cesura is of
the utmost importance in French poetry. For without a
skilful distribution of the cesural pauses, the general
character of French verse would not differ much from
French prose. The character and distribution of rime is also
of greater moment in French verse than in that of any other
language. Upon the rime and the cesura depend the melody
and the beauty of all French poetry.

6. **Points to Be Considered in Versification.** — The
following points must be given special consideration in
French versification: (1) *nature des syllabes*, nature of syllables; (2) *mesure*, foot; (3) *césure*, cesura; (4) *rime*, rime;
(5) *licences poétiques*, poetical licenses; (6) *enjambement*,
enjambement; (7) *hiatus*, hiatus.

NATURE OF SYLLABLES

7. **How to Count Syllables in Versification.** — Syllables are not counted in the same way in poetry as in grammar. The value of the syllables in a verse is dependent upon
the following rules:

1. *A mute syllable has no value at the end of a verse.* A
syllable is mute when it ends (*a*) in an unaccented *e*; as,
*par*le, *chan*te, *don*ne, *pom*me;

(*b*) in *es;* as, *tu par*les, *les pom*mes, except in such mono-
syllabics as *les, des, ses,* etc.;

(*c*) in *ent*, the third person plural of a verb; as, *ils parlent, ils chantent, elles donnent.*

The following verses, each ending in a mute syllable, contain twelve syllables of poetic value:

1 2 3 4 5 6 7 8 9 10 11 12
Il faut au tant qu'on peut o bli ger tout le mon de.

We must, as much as possible, oblige everybody. — LA FONTAINE.

1 2 3 4 5 6 7 8 9 10 11 12
J'ai ré vé lé mon cœur au Dieu de l'in no cence.

I have revealed my heart to the God of innocence.

1 2 3 4 5 6 7 8 9 10 11 12
Il gué rit mes re mords, il m'ar me de cons tance.

He assuages my remorse, he fortifies me with constancy. — GILBERT.

2. *A mute syllable in a verse has no poetic value when followed by a vowel or h mute.* The following verse contains twelve poetic syllables:

1 2 3 4 5 6 7 8 9 10 11 12
Le sa ge est mé na ger du temps et des pa ro les.

The wise man is saving of time and words.

The last syllable *ge* of *sage*, being mute and preceding a vowel, has no value as a syllable in the verse, but with *est* forms one syllable.

3. *A mute syllable in the body of a verse has the value of one, that is, of an ordinary syllable, when preceding a consonant or an aspirated h.* Thus,

1 2 3 4 5 6 7 8
Le mas que tom be, l'hom me res te

1 2 3 4 5 6 7 8
Et le hé ros s'é va nou it.

The mask falls, the man remains, and the hero vanishes.

The mute syllables *que* of *masque*, *be* of *tombe*, *me* of *homme*, and *le* have each the value of one syllable, because they precede a consonant.

4. *The mute syllables es and ent always have the value of one syllable in the body of a verse, even though placed before a vowel, because of the liaison.*

 1   2   3   4   5   6   7   8   9   10   11   12
Ni l'or, ni la gran deur ne nous ren dent heur eux.

Neither wealth nor greatness makes us happy.

 1   2   3   4   5   6   7   8   9   10   11   12
Crai gnez d'un vain plai sir les trom peu ses a mor ces.

Fear the deceiving attractions attendant on a vain pleasure.

8. Number of Syllables in Combinations of Letters. — When several vowels come together in a word, it is important to know how syllables are divided. The following rules cover most cases:

1. All the following combinations are monosyllabic: *ai, ain, an, eai, eau, ei, ein, eo, eoi, eon, eu, eui, ey, ied, ieu, oi, oin, ou, ouin, uin.* Thus the following words form one syllable only: *lait, pain, geai, beau, rein, pied, loin, crois, bout,* etc.

2. The diphthong *ia* generally makes two syllables; as in *di-amant, étudi-a, vi-ager.* But *ai* is monosyllabic in the following words: *diable, diacre, fiacre, liard.*

3. *Iai* is always dissyllabic; as in *je ni-ai, ni-ais, mari-ai.* The only exception is *bréviaire,* where *iai* is monosyllabic.

4. *Ian* and *ien* also generally make two syllables; except in *viande* and in short words like *bien, chien, mien,* etc.

5. *Iau* forms two syllables: *mi-au-ler, bes-ti-aux.*

6. *Ié* is ordinarily monosyllabic: *pitié, amitié.* But it is dissyllabic in *pi-été, sa-ti-é-té,* and in past participles of the verbs ending in *ier: mari-é, humili-é.*

7. *Iè* is always monosyllabic: *siège, liège, chaumière;* except in *quatri-ème* and *inqui-ète,* where it is dissyllabic.

8. *Ier* is dissyllabic: in verbs *humili-er, justifi-er, appréci-er.* Also in the body of a word when preceded by a double consonant; as, *marbri-er, meurtri-er, ta-blier.* But when, in the

body of a word, *ier* is preceded by a simple consonant, it is monosyllabic: *papier, premier, meunier.*

9.   *Hier* may be taken to form either one or two syllables at the pleasure of the writer.   Thus,

(*a*)   *Two syllables:*

1   2 3 4 5   6 7   8   9   10 11   12
Mais hi-er il m′ aborde et me prenant la main:
"Ah! monsieur, m'a-t-il dit, je vous attends demain."

(*b*)   *One syllable:*

1   2   3   4   5   6   7   8   9 10 11 12
Le bruit court qu'avant-hier on vous assassina.

10.   *Ierre* is always monosyllabic; as, *lierre, pierre.*

11.   *Ieu* is monosyllabic in nouns: *Dieu, milieu,* etc., but dissyllabic in adjectives; as, *séri-eux, audaci-eux, ambiti-eux.* The two words *mieux* and *vieux,* however, are monosyllabic.

12.   *Io* is monosyllabic in *fiole* and *pio-che,* but dissyllabic in other words; as, *di-ocèse, vi-olon, vi-olence.*

13.   *Ion* is dissyllabic in all nouns; as, *religi-on, nati-on, créati-on;* also in the verbs ending in *ier;* as, *nous étudi-ons, nous fortifi-ons;* but in all other cases, it is monosyllabic; as, *nous étions, nous aimions.*

14.   *Ui* is usually monosyllabic; as, *construire, fuir,* etc. But it is dissyllabic in the following words: *su-icide, ru-ine, flu-ide, bru-ine.*

15.   The affirmative *oui* is generally monosyllabic; but *oui* is dissyllabic when a diphthong in the midst of a word; as, *jou-ir, éblou-ir, inou-ï.*

16.   *Ieur* is always dissyllabic: *antéri-eur, ingéni-eur.*

17.   Several vowels grouped together are always dissyllabic when the first vowel is *é;* as, *agré-able, pé-age.*

FOOT

9. Different Kinds of Verses. — A foot in French verse is a syllable having poetic value; that is, it is a syllable which must be counted in determining the number of syllables in a line of French verse. Lines of French verse may contain any number of syllables from one to twelve; consequently, there are twelve different kinds of French verse. The most common verses, however, are those containing twelve, ten, eight, seven, or six poetic syllables. Verses of nine and eleven syllables are very rarely employed. In poetical phraseology the term *foot* is used instead of the word syllable. Thus, *un vers de dix pieds* is a verse of ten syllables.

10. Verses of Twelve Syllables. — The verse of twelve syllables is often called *Alexandrine*, because it is supposed to have been used for the first time by Alexandre de Bernay, in a poem on Alexander the Great.

  1   2   3   4   5   6 7 8 9 10 11 12
Ce lui qui met un frein à la fu reur des flots

  1   2   3   4   5   6   7 8 9 10 11   12
Sait aus si des mé chants ar rê ter les com plots

  1   2   3   4   5   6 7 8 9 10 11   12
Sou mis a vec res pect à sa vo lon té sainte

  1   2   3   4   5   6   7   8   9 10 11   12
Je crains Dieu, cher Ab ner, et n'ai pas d'au tre crainte

He who puts a brake to the fury of the waves, knows also how to stop the plots of the wicked. Submitting with respect to His holy will, I fear God, dear Abner, and have no other fear. — RACINE, *Athalie*

  1   2   3   4   5   6   7   8   9 10 11 12
Don nez, ri ches, l'au mô ne est sœur de la pri ère

  1 2   3   4   5   6   7 8 9   10 11 12
Hé las! quand un vieil lard sur vo tre seuil de pierre

  1   2 3   4   5   6   7   8   9   10 11 12
Tout rai di par l'hi ver, en vain tom be à ge noux

   1   2 3   4   5   6   7   8   9 10   11 12
Quand les pe tits en fants, les mains de froid rou gies

<pre>
1   2   3   4   5   6   7   8   9   10 11 12
Ra mas sent à vos pieds les mi et tes des or gies,
</pre>

<pre>
1   2   3   4   5   6   7   8   9   10 11 12
La fa ce du Sei gneur se dé tour ne de vous.
</pre>

Give, abundant alms are sisters of prayers. Alas! when an old man on your threshold of stone, all stiffened with cold, falls in vain upon his knees; when little children with their hands red with cold pick the crumbs of your feasts at your feet, the face of the Lord turns away from you.—VICTOR HUGO

The verse of twelve syllables is chiefly used in epic poetry, in tragedy and comedy, and in didactic poems.

11.   Verses of Ten Syllables.—This verse being more lively and rapid than the verse of twelve feet, is mainly employed in satire, epigram, and epistle.   The verse of ten feet was the only one used in old French poetry.   It was first employed in the old *Chansons de Geste*, the first epic poems of French literature.

<pre>
1   2   3   4   5   6   7   8   9   10
Rei-ne du mon-de, ô Fran-ce! ô ma pa-trie!
</pre>

<pre>
1   2   3   4   5   6   7   8 9 10
Sou-lè-ve en-fin ton front ci-ca-tri-sé;
</pre>

<pre>
1   2   3   4   5   6   7   8   9 10
Sans qu'à tes yeux leur gloi-re en soit flét trie
</pre>

<pre>
1   2   3   4   5   6   7   8   9 10
De tes en-fants l'é-ten-dard s'est bri-sé.
</pre>

Queen of the world, O, France! O, my country! Raise at last thy mended brow; the standard of thy children has been broken, but in thy sight their glory has not been tarnished.—DE BERANGER

<pre>
1   2 3   4   5   6   7   8   9   10
J'ai vu la Paix des-cen-dre sur la terre
</pre>
Semant de l'or, des fleurs et des épis;
L'air était calme, et du dieu de la guerre
Elle étouffait les foudres assoupis.
"Ah!" disait-elle, "égaux par la vaillance,
Français, Anglais, Belge, Russe ou Germain,
Peuples, formez une sainte alliance."

I saw Peace come down on the earth, sowing gold, flowers, and harvests; the air was calm, and she was stifling the slumbering thunder of the God of war. "Ah!" said she, "equal in valor, Frenchmen, Englishmen, Belgians, Russians, or Germans, do you people all form a sacred alliance." — DE BÉRANGER

12. Verses of Eight Syllables. — The following are examples of the verse of eight feet:

<pre>
 1   2   3   4   5   6   7   8
El le͜é tait pâ le͜et pour tant rose
Petite avec de grands cheveux
Elle disait souvent, "Je n'ose,"
Et ne disait jamais, "Je veux."
</pre>

She was pale with a suggestion of rose, small and had long hair. She often said, "I do not dare," and never said, "I want." — V. HUGO

<pre>
 1 2 3   4 5 6 7   8
De la dé-pouil-le de nos bois
L'automne avait jonché la terre;
Le bocage était sans mystère,
Le rossignol était sans voix.
</pre>

Autumn had covered the ground with the spoils of the trees; the grove was devoid of mystery, the nightingale was voiceless. — MILLEVOYE

13. Verses of Seven Syllables. — The verse of seven feet, although not so often used as the verse of eight syllables, is exceedingly melodious.

<pre>
 1 2 3   4 5 6   7
Ju-pi-ter, voy ant nos fautes
Dit un jour, du haut des airs:
"Remplissons de nouveaux hôtes
Les cantons de l'univers,
Habités par cette race
Qui m'importune et me lasse."
</pre>

Jupiter, observing our faults from the heights of the air, said

one day: Let us fill with new guests the districts of the universe
inhabited by that race which so importunes and wearies me. —
LA FONTAINE

　　　1　2　3　　4　　5　6　　7
　　De ta ti-ge dé-ta-chée,
　　Pauvre feuille desséchée,
　　Où vas-tu? — Je n'en sais rien:
　　L'orage a brisé le chêne
　　Qui seul était mon soutien.

Torn from the branch, whither away, poor dried leaf? — I know
not; the storm has broken the oak which was my only sup-
port. — ARNAULT

14. Verses of Six Syllables. — This verse, sometimes
called the *semi-Alexandrine*, seldom stands alone, but is
frequently combined with the verse of twelve feet.　Thus,

　1　　2　　3　4　　5　　6　　　7　8　　9　　10　11　　12
　Mais elle‿était du monde‿où les plus bel-les choses

　　　　　　1　2　3　4　　5　6
　　　　　Ont le pi-re des-tin;

　1　　2　　3　　4　5　6　7　　8　　9　10　　11　　12
　Et rose‿elle‿a vé-cu ce que vi-vent les roses,

　　　　　　1　2　3　4　　5　　6
　　　　　L'es-pa-ce d'un ma-tin.

But she belonged to that world in which the most beautiful
things inherit the most wretched destiny; and like a rose, she
lived as roses live, the length of a single morning. — MALHERBE

　　　　1　2　3　4　5　　6
　　Sur sa tige pen-dante
　　Voyez la rose thé
　　Etaler sa beauté
　　Lascive et languissante.

On pendant stem, watch the tea rose display its lascivious and
languishing beauty. — TARDIEU

15. Verses of Five Syllables. — The verse of five
syllables is one of the most melodious and sweetest of
French verses.

<pre>
  1   2   3   4   5
Dors entre mes bras
Enfant plein de charmes.
Tu ne connais pas
Les soucis, les larmes.
Tu ris en dormant;
A ton doux sourire,
Mon cœur se déchire.
Dors, ô mon enfant!
</pre>

Sleep in my arms, child of all charms. Knowing neither cares nor tears, thou laughest while sleeping. With thy sweet smile, my heart is outworn. Sleep on, O, my child!

<pre>
Que Dieu montre ou voile
Les astres des cieux,
La plus pure étoile
Brille dans tes yeux.
</pre>

Whether God displays or veils the stars of heaven, the purest star shines in thine eyes. — VICTOR HUGO

16. **Verses of Four, Three, Two, or One Syllable.**
Verses of one, two, three, and four feet are ordinarily used in combination with longer verses. Thus,

<pre>
  1   2   3   4 5   6 7   8
Sous ce champêtre monument
Repose une fille encore chère;
Elle n'a vé cu qu'un moment:
</pre>

<pre>
  1   2   3   4
Plai-gnez sa mère!
</pre>

Under this rural tombstone lies a daughter still beloved; she lived but a moment — pity her mother! — MILLEVOYE

<pre>
  1   2   3   4 5 6   7   8 9   10   11 12
Même il m'est arrivé quelquefois de manger
</pre>

<pre>
   1   2   3
Le berger.
</pre>

It has sometimes been my lot even to eat the shepherd.

1 2 3 4 5 6 7 8 9 10 11 12
C'est promettre beaucoup: mais qu'en sort-il souvent?

1 2
Du vent.

This is promising much: but what often comes out of it? Wind.

On y (in Paris) voit des commis
Mis
Comme des princes,
Après être venus
Nus
De leurs provinces.

There we see clerks who have come in threadbare from the country, clad as princes.

The following stanzas are curious examples of verses of one, two, three, and four syllables:

1 2 3 4
Le chèvrefeuille
Mêle sa feuille
Au blanc jasmin;
Et l'églantine
Plie et s'incline
Sur le chemin.

The honeysuckle mingles its leaves with the white jasmine; and the wild rose bends toward the road.

1 2 3 4
La vie est vaine:
Un peu d'amour,
Un peu de haine,
Et puis, bonjour,

La vie est brève:
Un peu d'espoir,
Un peu de rêve,
Et puis, bonsoir.

Life is vain: a little love, a little hatred, and then, good day. Life is brief; a little hope, a little dream, and then, good by.

1   2

Tout passe.

L'espace

Efface

Le bruit.

Everything passes.   Space erases the noise.

Fort

Belle

Elle

Dort!

Most beautiful, she sleeps.

CESURA

17. Definition of Cesura. — There is a pause in the midst of every French verse, whether or not so indicated by punctuation marks, which must be observed in reading. This pause is called the cesura, and divides the verse into two parts, each of which is known as the *hémistiche*, hemistich or half, verse.

18. Uses of the Cesura. — In the verse of twelve feet, the cesura is ordinarily placed at the end of the sixth syllable, and thus divides the verse into two equal parts.

Aux petits des oiseaux ‖ Dieu donne leur pâture.

To the little birds, God gives food.

Pour grands que soient les rois ‖ ils sont ce que nous sommes.
Ils peuvent se tromper ‖ comme les autres hommes;
Et ce choix sert de preuve ‖ à tous les courtisans,
Qu'ils savent mal payer ‖ les services présents.

However great kings may be, they are what we are. They may be mistaken like other men; and this right of choice is a proof to all courtiers that they are paying badly for my present services. — CORNEILLE, *Le Cid*

In the verse of ten syllables, the cesura is ordinarily placed after the fourth syllable.

Sur le coteau‖là-bas où sont les tombes,
Un beau palmier‖comme un panache vert,
Dresse sa tête‖où le soir les colombes
Viennent nicher‖et se mettre à couvert.

On yonder hill, where the tombs are, a beautiful palm tree raises its head like a green plumet, and there in the evening the doves fly to roost and shelter. — TH. GAUTHIER

The poets of the 19th century often divided the verse of ten syllables into two equal parts, by placing the cesura after the fifth syllable, as in the following verses:

Enfant, tu grandis:‖que ton cœur soit fort!
Lutte pour le bien:‖la défaite est sainte.
Si tu dois souffrir,‖accorde à ton sort.
Un regret parfois,‖jamais une plainte.

Child, thou art growing, let thy heart be strong! Fight for the good, defeat is holy. If thou must suffer, breathe for thy lot sometimes a sigh of regret, but never a complaint.

Verses, shorter than ten syllables, have no regular cesura; the pause may be established at will.

19. Exceptions to the Preceding Rules. — Rigorous conformation to these laws would render the reading of verses very monotonous. Indeed this is the reproach that strangers have often cast upon Alexandrine verse. But the rules just given are those of very pure classics only, and the best French authors have often introduced various other cesuras in order to avoid monotony, or to produce some striking effect peculiar to the sentiment or image expressed. In the following from Racine, for example, notice the great variety of pauses:

Oui, je viens‖dans son temple adorer l'Eternel.
Je viens‖selon l'usage antique et solennel
Célébrer avec vous‖la célèbre journée,
Où sur le mont Sina‖la loi nous fut donnée.

Que les temps sont changés! ‖ Sitôt que de ce jour
La trompette sacrée ‖ annonçait le retour,
Du temple ‖ orné partout de festons magnifiques,
Le peuple saint ‖ en foule inondait les portiques.

Yes; I am come to his temple to adore the Eternal; I am come, according to solemn and ancient usage to celebrate with you the famous day when the law was given us on Mount Sinai. How the times have changed! Formerly, as soon as the sacred trumpet had announced the return of this day, crowds of holy people filled the porticos of the temple which were decorated with magnificent festoons. — RACINE, *Athalie*

Note that in four of the preceding verses the regular cesura at the end of the sixth syllable almost disappears to be replaced by other pauses necessary to the sense of the sentence.

Early in the last century, the romantic school suppressed the regular cesura of the Alexandrine verse, thus reducing the monotony of the line and giving more latitude to the imagination and skill of the author. The romantic verse has consequently been more popular in recent years than the classical verse. In it Victor Hugo, Lamartine, A. de Vigny, Alfred de Musset, and others have composed their beautiful lines.

20. Rules Governing the Cesura. — While the position of the cesura may be varied more or less in the line, such variation is limited by the following laws:

1. The first hemistich can never end in one of the monosyllables *le, la, les, de, du, des, au, aux, que, ne*, nor in any possessive or demonstrative adjective, nor in a conjunctive personal pronoun.

2. The cesura is defective if it cuts a word in two. So, the following verse is wrong:

Que peuvent tous les fai ‖ bles humains devant Dieu?
What can all feeble human beings avail before God?

3. The cesura can never be put after a mute syllable, because the voice would then have to accent a sound that should be mute. The following lines are consequently not verses:

> Je viens dans son temp*le*—vénérer le Seigneur;
> Bons, méchants, lui rend*ent*—un honneur mérité.

I come in his temple to venerate the Lord; the good, the wicked, let them render him fitting honor.

When the first hemistich ends in *e* mute, it then really contains seven syllables, consequently the first word of the second hemistich must then begin with a vowel or *h* mute in order to provide for the elision of the mute *e*. Thus,

Un bruit assez étrang*e*—*est* venu jusqu'à moi, *A very strange noise has come to my ears.*

RIME

21. Definition of Rime. — Rime is uniformity of sound in the endings of two or more verses. Rime is the greatest charm of French poetry; it is the only resource left French poets for supplying the harmony of the long and short syllables of ancient and foreign poetry. So, in French versification rime acquires a value quite out of proportion to its importance in other languages. Several French authors have attempted the composition of unrimed poetry, but without much success. Such poetry is termed *vers blancs*, blank verse. Apparently the French language is not well adapted to it.

22. Nature of Rimes. — According to the endings of the last syllables or words of verses, two kinds of rime are to be distinguished: (*a*) *la rime masculine*, masculine rime; (*b*) *la rime féminine*, feminine rime.

Rime is **masculine** when it ends in a sonorous syllable; as, *Dieu, humain;* it is **feminine** when it ends in an *e* mute, *es,* or *ent* (of the third person plural of a verb); as, *faiblesse, rendent, aimées.*

Note that verses ending with a feminine rime actually contain one more syllable than those ending with a masculine rime; but the syllable is purely grammatical and has no poetic value.

Here the words *masculine* and *feminine* are not used in their grammatical sense. They are not applied to the gender of words, but simply to the manner in which they end. Thus,

> J'attendais de son fils encor plus de bonté;
> Pardonne, cher Hector, à ma crédulité.

I was expecting from his son still more kindness; pardon, dear Hector, my credulity. — RACINE

In this sentence the rime is masculine, although the words *bonté* and *crédulité* are grammatically feminine.

23. Quality of Rimes. — Rimes have been classified as follows, according to the more or less perfect resemblance of the last words or syllables of a verse:

1. *Rime Riche.* — A rime is *rich* when it is formed by several identical syllables; as, *naissance* and con*naissance;* évan*ouit* and ébl*ouit.*

2. *Rime Suffisante.* — A rime is *sufficient* when the final syllable is identical in the two words; as, ar*deur* and can*deur;* aff*ront* and f*ront.*

3. *Rime Pauvre.* — A rime is *poor* when the last syllables of each verse are the same except in their initial consonants; as, *guerriers,* and *prisonniers; accord* and *bord.*

4. *Rime Insuffisante.* — Rime is *insufficient* when the last letter only is the same; as, *parti* and *fini; aima* and *donna.*

24. Rules Governing Rime. — Rime, being designed for the ear rather than for the eye, must be judged by the sound of a word and not by its spelling. Thus, *arts* may rime with *hasards; voix* with *bois; assez* with *lancer,* although the spelling of these words is very unlike.

Two words having the same spelling do not necessarily rime. *Mer* does not rime with *aimer,* nor *fiers* with *altiers.* The following rules govern particular cases. There is no rime:

1. Between a noun and a verb derived from it; as, *flamme* and *enflamme; mettre* and *remettre; faire* and *défaire.*

2. Between a word and its compound; as, *poli* and *impoli; docile* and *indocile.*

3. Between a singular and a plural; as, *ami* and *ennemis; bâteau* and *châteaux; larme* and *alarmes.*

4. Between a long and a short vowel as, *âme* and *dame.*

5. Between the final letters *é, er, a, i, u,* etc., unless the preceding consonant is the same in both cases. Thus, *tomber* and *chanter* do not rime, nor *fini* and *bâti;* but *chanter* and *planter* will rime.

6. Between a syllable masculine and a syllable feminine having same sound. Thus, *détail* and *bataille* do not rime.

25.   Succession of Rimes. — In the great poetry of the Alexandrine verse, two masculine rimes are always followed by two feminine, and vice versa. They are called *rimes plates*, flat rimes. Thus,

> Celui qui met un frein à la fureur des *flots*⎫
> Sait aussi des méchants arrêter les com*plots*⎭   masculine

> Soumis avec respect à sa volonté *sainte*,
> Je crains Dieu, cher Abner, et n'ai point
> d'autre *crainte*   feminine

> Cependant, je rends grâce au zèle offi*cieux*
> Qui sur tous nos périls vous fait ouvrir les *yeux*   masculine

> Je vois que l'injustice en secret vous irrite,
> Que vous avez encor le cœur israélite.
>   — RACINE   feminine

The rimes are called *croisées*, crossed, in the following cases:

(*a*)   When a masculine rime alternates with a feminine; as,

> Dans la foule secrète*ment*
> Dieu parfois prend une âme **neuve**
> Qu'il veut amener lente*ment*
> Jusqu'à lui, d'épreuve en épreuve. — EUG. MANUEL

(*b*) When two feminine rimes are placed between two masculines; as,

> Toute haleine s'évan*ouit*
> La terre brûle et voudrait **boire,**
> L'ombre est courte, immobile et **noire**
> Et la grande route ébl*ouit*.—Sully-Prudhomme

(*c*) When two masculine rimes are placed between two feminines; as,

> Une hirondelle en ses voy*ages*
> Avait beaucoup appris.   Quiconque a beaucoup **vu**
> Peut avoir beaucoup rete**nu.**
> Celle-ci prévoyait jusqu'aux moindres or*ages.*

POETICAL LICENSES

26. Different Kinds of Licenses.—While poetry, being restricted by the foot and the rime, has not the same wide freedom belonging to prose, it has nevertheless certain privileges, certain licenses, not permitted in prose.   These licenses are of three kinds: *spelling, grammatical construction,* and *arrangement of words.*

27. Licenses in Spelling.—Licenses in spelling are explained by the necessities of the foot and the rime.   The principal are:

1. To write *encore* with or without an *e* according to the demand for one more or one less syllable in a verse.   Thus,

> *Encor* si vous naissiez à l' abri du feuillage
> Dont je couvre le voisinage.—La Fontaine

Here the first verse contains twelve syllables.   If *encor* had been written with an *e*, that *e* coming before a consonant would have made another syllable, and the line would have contained thirteen feet—an impossible verse.

2. To write with or without *s* the words *jusque, certe, naguère, guère, grâce à*, and certain proper nouns as *Londres, Versailles, Charles*, etc.   When these words are written without an *s* and placed before a vowel, they form one syllable

with that vowel; but when ending in *s*, their lost syllables cannot be elided before the vowel.

> Lion, *jusques* au ciel élevée autrefois,
> *Jusqu'*aux enfers maintenant abaissée. — RACINE

Et l'on insulte au dieu que Thèbe entière adore. — DESAINTANGE

Thèbes à cet arrêt n'a point voulu se rendre. — RACINE

3. To suppress *s* of the first person of certain verbs; as, *j'aperçoi*, *je voi*, *je croi*, *je doi*, etc.

Portez à votre père un cœur où j'*entrevoi*.

Moins de respect pour lui que de haine pour moi. — RACINE

28. Licenses in Grammar. — There are but few grammatical licenses; they authorize the use of certain words in the sense of other words; as, *dans* or *en* for *à* before the names of cities; etc.

29. Licenses in Arrangement of Words. — These licenses authorize several kinds of inversions that do not alter or make ambiguous the sense of the sentence. The most frequent are:

1. The inversion of the subject.

> Détestables flatteurs! présent le plus funeste
> Qu'ait jamais fait aux rois *la colère céleste*. — RACINE

2. The inversion of the complement of a noun.

> Dieu combla *du chaos* les abîmes funèbres.
> *D'une prison* sur moi, les murs pèsent en vain.

3. The inversion of the indirect object of a verb.

> *Aux petits* des oiseaux, Dieu donne leur pâture.

4. The inversion of circumstantial objects.

> *Vers la ville* à l'instant ils trottent côte à côte.
> *De sa tremblante main* sont tombés les fuseaux.

5. Inversion of a pronoun used with the imperative.

> Va, cours, vole et *nous* venge.

30. **Poetical Words.** — The literary style of poetry must be of a higher character than is essential in prose. Thus, the common expressions and vulgar terms sometimes admitted in prose can never be employed in poetry. On the other hand, certain archaic, curious, or unusual expressions and words that would be out of place in prose can often be used in poetry. Some of these expressions are:

PROSE	POETRY	PROSE	POETRY
amour	flamme	enfer	Achéron
ancien	antique	épee	glaive
boyaux	entrailles	femme	épouse
crime	forfait	mariage	hymen, hyménée
canon	airain	mer	amphitrite
cloche	bronze	poignard	acier
cheval	coursier	travail	labeur
colère	courroux	mari	époux

ENJAMBEMENT

31. **Definition of Enjambement.** — Enjambement is the continuation of the sense and construction of one line through one or more succeeding lines. Enjambement was much used in the 15th and 16th centuries, but largely fell into disuse in the 17th century. The Romantic school, however, revived enjambement, and their verses abound with many examples of its happy use. Its proper use adds much to the vividness of imagery and the sweetness of melody. The following verses are examples of enjambement:

J'ai quatorze bouteilles
D'un vin vieux . . . Boucingo n'en a pas de pareilles.
— BOILEAU

L'Evangile au chrétien ne dit en aucun lieu:
Sois dévot; il dit: sois simple, juste, équitable.
— BOILEAU

Je ne demande à Dieu rien de trop, car je n'ai
Pas grande ambition, et pourvu que j'atteigne
Jusqu'à la branche où pend la mûre ou la châtaigne,
Il est content de moi, je suis content de lui.
— VICTOR HUGO

HIATUS

32. Definition of Hiatus. — Hiatus is the strained pause arising from the meeting of two vowels that cannot be elided; as between a final and an initial vowel. Thus, t*u a*imes, il *a a*massé. The hiatus is a serious fault in poetry. Such expressions as the following should be carefully avoided: *loi éternelle, charité évangélique*, etc. The conjunction *et* before a vowel forms a hiatus, for the *t* can never make a liaison with that vowel. It would be very bad taste to use such an expression as *sage et aimable* in poetry.

A SERIES OF QUESTIONS

RELATING TO THE SUBJECTS
TREATED OF IN THIS VOLUME.

It will be noticed that the questions contained in the following pages are divided into sections corresponding to the sections of the text of the preceding pages, so that each section has a headline that is the same as the headline of the section to which the questions refer. No attempt should be made to answer any of the questions until the corresponding part of the text has been carefully studied.

FRENCH GRAMMAR
(PART 1)

EXAMINATION QUESTIONS

(1) Distinguish between language in its *widest sense* and *language as treated in grammar*.

(2) Explain why words pass out of use and new words appear in a language.

(3) (*a*) From what language is French derived? (*b*) What influences has it received?

(4) What is the difference between a *dialect* and a *patois?*

(5) How is grammar divided in this work?

(6) Give French equivalents for the following English sounds: *a* as found in *hat; a*, in *fate; ei*, in *their; o*, in *note; oo*, in *poor; i*, in *sir*. When there are several equivalents, give all.

(7) Explain the two kinds of *h* and their effects.

(8) (*a*) What are the sounds called that appear in *fin* and *bon?* (*b*) What happens to these sounds when the feminine ending is attached?

(9) When is the sound of *m* or *n* nasal in French?

(10) (*a*) What is the use of the *dieresis?* (*b*) of the *cedilla?*

(11) What is the use of the apostrophe?

(12) What are the different kinds of *e* in French and how are they pronounced?

§ 16

(13)   Give three cases where liaisons should be avoided.

(14)   How many parts of speech do we distinguish?

(15)   What is the difference between a conjunction and a preposition?

(16)   In what order do we study the parts of speech?

(17)   Why is the verb studied first?

(18)   How are *f*, *g*, and *x* final pronounced when followed by a word beginning with *h*?

(19)   How is *th* pronounced in French?

(20)   How is *eu* pronounced as a form of the verb *avoir?*

FRENCH GRAMMAR

(PART 2)

EXAMINATION QUESTIONS

(1) Give the feminine third person singular and the masculine third person plural of the past indefinite, pluperfect subjunctive, and past conditional of *donner, tomber, aimer, arriver, entrer, aller,* and *parler.*

(2) Give all the interrogative-negative forms of the future of *avoir* and *être.*

(3) Conjugate: Should I not have given? Interrogative-negative past conditional of *donner.*

(4) Give the first persons, singular and plural, past definite of *publier, arrêter, apercevoir, dormir, choisir, vendre, devoir.*

(5) Why is *j'appelle* spelled with *ll* and *nous appelons* with one *l*?

(6) Give the second persons, singular and plural, of the present subjunctive of *acheter, partir, rendre, percevoir, mentir, menacer,* in the negative form.

(7) Give the first persons imperative plural of *attendre, recevoir, sortir, chérir.*

(8) Give the infinitive, and name the tense and mode of *choisissions, dormais, aperçu, rende, arriverait, entrâmes, parleront, donnât, appelleraient.*

(9) Conjugate: Shall I not enter? Future of *entrer* interrogative-negative.

(10) Give the first persons, singular and plural, of the imperfect subjunctive of *appeler, descendre, concevoir, servir, fournir, remplir.*

(11) (*a*) Why do we spell *nous mangeons* with an *e* after the *g*? (*b*) Why do we not spell *nous mangions* with an *e*?

(12) Give the first persons, singular and plural, of the interrogative-negative imperfect-indicative forms of *décevoir, défendre, menacer, changer, bâtir,* and *réussir.*

(13) What are the orthographic irregularities of *acheter* in the present and future indicative?

(14) Give, in full, the negative pluperfect indicative forms of *oublier* and *aller.*

(15) Conjugate the future anterior of *penser* and *rester* in the interrogative-negative form.

FRENCH GRAMMAR
(PART 3)

EXAMINATION QUESTIONS

(1) Conjugate: *Should I not admire?* conditional of *admirer*, interrogative, with pronoun and negative.

(2) Give first persons, singular and plural, past definite of *vouloir, voir, devoir, donner, finir, rompre*.

(3) Why is *préférer* spelled with an acute accent over the second *e* and *je préfère* with a grave accent?

(4) Give second person, singular and plural, negatively of the past indefinite, of *aller, se coucher, se lever, connaître*.

(5) Give the principal parts of the following verbs: *venir, savoir, dire, mourir, envoyer*.

(6) What are the distinguishing characteristics of the regular conjugations?

(7) Give the third person, singular and plural, present subjunctive of *pouvoir, recevoir, tenir, résoudre, coudre, boire, croître, aller, écrire*.

(8) (*a*) What is an auxiliary verb? (*b*) How many are there in French?

(9) Give the second person singular of the imperative of *aller, donner, venir, faire, avoir*.

(10) Give the infinitive, and name the tense and mode of *vont, cousu, craignisses, crû, dissent, puissent, meut, écrive, née, parte.*

(11) Conjugate: *Shall I not come?* future of *venir*, interrogative with pronoun and negative.

(12) How many kinds of verbs are there in French?

(13) Give the principal parts of *faire, pouvoir, aller, sortir, détenir.*

(14) Give the first person, singular and plural, of the imperfect subjunctive of *appeler, ouvrir, dire, mettre.*

(15) What are the inflections of a verb?

(16) Give the principal parts of *venait, rendre, promis, aller, puissiez, voir, surprendre, fit, voulu, plaire.* Name also the tense and mode of these verbs.

(17) (*a*) Why do we spell *nous menaçons* with a cedilla under the *c*? (*b*) Why do we not spell *je menace* with the cedilla?

(18) Give the first person, singular and plural, of present indicative, in the interrogative-negative form, of *croire, mourir, prendre, haïr, faire.*

(19) What are the orthographic irregularities of *mener* and *jeter* in the present indicative and in the future?

(20) Give first and second persons singular of the future; the second person plural of the conditional; and the third person singular of the pluperfect subjunctive of *aller, voir, faire, appeler.*

(21) Give the second person plural imperative of *se plaindre, apporter, se lever, se promener, boire, sortir.*

(22) Write the principal parts of *arranger, rougir, apercevoir, rompre.*

(23) Give in full the pluperfect indicative of *s'asseoir*.

(24) Give in full the past conditional of *partir*.

(25) How are *avoir* and *être* used in the conjugation of French verbs?

(26) How does the past participle agree when conjugated with *être?*

(27) Translate: *There was, There would be, There has been, Here is, There should have been, That there may be.*

(28) How is the future tense formed?

(29) What tenses are formed from the infinitive?

(30) Conjugate in the past indefinite the phrase: *Se promener en voiture*, to drive.

FRENCH GRAMMAR
(PART 4)

EXAMINATION QUESTIONS

(1) When do we translate *here is* and *there is* (*a*) by *voici* and *voilà?* (*b*) when by *il y a?* Give two examples.

(2) How is the comparative denoted in French before: (*a*) substantives? (*b*) adjectives? Give examples of both cases.

(3) Translate the following sentences: (*a*) You have more books than John. (*b*) He is older than he seems. (*c*) She is more attentive and diligent than her sister. (*d*) The weather is becoming colder. (*e*) The richer he becomes, the less generous he is. (*f*) This book is cheaper than that one. (*g*) I am three years older than you.

(4) How is the passive voice avoided in French?

(5) State the gender and form the plural of *genou, travail, ciel, œil, cheval, chef-d'œuvre, école, matin, clou, jeu, tuyau, bal*.

(6) Write the feminines of *époux, trompeur, gouverneur, acteur, auteur, doux, faux*.

(7) Give exceptions to the general rule for forming the comparative of adjectives in French. Give examples.

(8) Translate: (*a*) My books are prettier than yours. (*b*) Your house is larger than mine; (*c*) than theirs; than his; than hers.

§ 19

(9)   What are the compound forms of the preposition *à* with the articles *le* and *les?*

(10)   Give the feminines of *grand, bon, riche, nouveau, vieux.*

(11)   Write the ordinals from 83rd to 92d.

(12)   Compare *studieux, mauvais, bon.*

(13)   Give the feminines of *aisé, bas, net, facile, frais, public, mou, sec, long.*

(14)   Give the rule governing the use of numerals (*a*) with days of the month; (*b*) with the names of princes.

(15)   Give the rule for the formation of the plural of proper nouns.   Give examples.

(16)   Give four sentences in French illustrating the inflections of the indefinite adjective *tout.*

(17)   Give examples illustrating the different ways of spelling *vingt, cent, mille.*

FRENCH GRAMMAR

(PART 5)

EXAMINATION QUESTIONS

(1) Compare *bon, mauvais, petit, bien, peu, studieux*.

(2) What do you know about the demonstrative pronouns and adjectives *this* and *that?* Give examples.

(3) (*a*) How is the comparative of adjectives and adverbs formed in French? (*b*) Are there any exceptions to the general rule? Give examples.

(4) Form adverbs from *prudent, fier, méchant, poli, aveugle, doux, bon, cruel, lent, bref*.

(5) What is the difference between *a* and *à?*

(6) What is the difference between *des* and *dès?*

(7) Give an example in which *y* is an adverb, and another where it is a pronoun.

(8) Give the class of words to which every word in the following sentence belongs:

"Quand on veut essayer de peindre Bonaparte, il faudrait, en suivant les formes analytiques pour lesquelles il a tant de goût, pouvoir séparer en trois parts fort distinctes son âme, son cœur et son esprit qui ne se fondaient presque jamais les unes avec les autres."

(9) Give the principal parts of all verbs contained in the above sentence.

(10) Write the third person plural, present indicative, present subjunctive, past definite, and future of the following verbs: *avoir, être, aller, courir, recevoir, devoir, faire, dire, prendre*.

§ 20

FRENCH GRAMMAR
(PART 6)

EXAMINATION QUESTIONS

(1) State and illustrate the three uses, or purposes, served by sentences. Give your examples in French.

(2) Write, in French, two sentences of each of the following kinds: (*a*) exclamatory-declarative, (*b*) exclamatory-interrogative, and (*c*) exclamatory-imperative.

(3) Analyze, grammatically, the following sentences: *Un coup de vent a emporté son chapeau*, A gust of wind carried his hat away. *Lisez-vous le journal français tous les jours?* Do you read the French paper every day?

(4) Give the first persons plural of the past definite of the following verbs: *voir, vivre, valoir, vaincre, taire, savoir, résoudre, pouvoir, naître, moudre, fuir, cueillir, coudre, asseoir, acquérir*.

(5) Write, in French, five declarative sentences, and then make them interrogative.

(6) Analyze, logically, by the French and English methods the following sentences: *Je suis, quoiqu'elle ne me connaisse pas, un ami de son mari*, I am, although she does not know me, her husband's friend. *Un jeune homme apparut, et s'arrêta sur le seuil*, A young man appeared, and stopped at the threshold. *Un dimanche, comme elle était ellée faire un tour aux Champs-Elysées, elle aperçut tout à coup une femme qui*

promenait un enfant, One Sunday, while she had gone for a walk in Champs-Elysées, she suddenly saw a woman, who was walking with a child.

(7) Give the past participles of *atteindre, faire, naître, apprendre, retenir.*

(8) Give the present participles of *savoir, falloir, sortir, devoir, vouloir.*

(9) Give the genders and form the plurals of *clou, chou, genou, travail, ciel, œil, chacal, animal, chef-d'œuvre, école, cheveu.*

(10) Give three French sentences in which you use the comma.

(11) Give three French sentences in which you use the semicolon.

(12) Give three French sentences in which you use the colon.

FRENCH GRAMMAR

(PART 7)

EXAMINATION QUESTIONS

(1)   Translate into French (see Arts. **3** to **15**):

Have you studied well?   Have they had much pleasure? Does your uncle speak French?   Will your friends arrive tonight?   Do I speak French well?   Who came to see me? What is this lady doing?   How are your friends?   Where do these gentlemen live?   When will your friend go to Paris?   Where does this gentleman take his meals?   In what country do they speak French?   "I shall not study," he said to me, "I am too busy."   May you come back soon! She was hardly twelve when she left school.   My sister had hardly left the house when your friend came in.   I am not speaking to him.   Do you speak to them?   Do you not see them?

(2)   Translate into French (see agreement of the verb in gender and number, Arts. **15** to **30**):

Your cousin, my uncle, and I will go to Paris next year. Your father and mine will start tomorrow.   Neither he nor I will go to Paris.   Reasoning, prayers, supplications, nothing prevented him from departing.   You and I will read this story.   It is you and your friend who said that.   He is the only one who has succeeded.   My father or I will go with you.   You and I have arrived the first.   You and your friend, who have been in Paris so long, will relate your adventures.   It is I who brought it.   It is they who arrived this morning.   They are two Germans.

222

(3)   Translate into French (see use of auxiliaries, Arts. **35** to **39**):

I took a walk this morning.   I went out with my mother. This gentleman sang last night.   Your uncle wounded himself; he fell.   I came in at half-past three.   Victor Hugo died in eighteen hundred and eighty-five.   I was born in America.   He disappeared suddenly.   Your friend passed in front of your house this morning at a quarter to ten.   This house would have suited you very well.   They agreed to the price.

(4)   Translate into French (see remarks on *être* and *avoir*, Arts. **39** to **57**):

Is your house for rent?   I have been delighted to make his acquaintance.   He is not satisfied with your work.   I am sorry to see you ill.   They are glad to see their parents.   It is now ten minutes to twelve.   He is right, that is sure. Let us do that; it is an excellent exercise.   Does he feel better?   You would come with me if you had time, would you not?   He is very sorry to leave you.   Why is he angry with me?   He is not very rich, is he?   I am always early; I am never late.   We always come home late at night.   She is late.   It is not late yet.   If I were in his place, I would buy that house.   It is I who spoke.   Whose turn is it to speak?   I am on bad terms with him.   To whom does this house belong?   You are always cross.   She is not attentive to what you say.   Such is their present situation.   Have you time to do this for me?   I had not the patience to listen to him.   Have you nothing to tell me?   What has he to do? I have two exercises to write.   Are you not thirsty or hungry?   He is sleepy.   How old is your father?   He is sixty-five years old today.   This child has sore eyes.   He has no reason for complaining.   When will your dinner take place?   I shall procure you a place.   I must speak to him. He listens in vain; he understands nothing.   He came to see me three weeks ago.   How far is it from New York to Chicago?   Is it long since you saw her?   It is not far from here to the park.

(5) Translate into French (see remarks on verbs, Arts. **57** to **98**):

Will you go on foot?   I do not answer for her.   Do not puzzle your brains.   This photograph is not at all like her. This coat fits you very well.   What is the meaning of this word in French?   He went to meet his father.   According to you, I am wrong.   Bring him his breakfast.   He was in business, but he failed.   He has brought his wife with him. Take this glass away.   He said it in a jest.   Were you present at his lesson?   He only waits for that.   You like to give assistance to the poor.   What do you think of my new dress?   **Whom** are you waiting for this morning?   Do you expect to see your friend in Paris?   Who broke this glass? I know how to count in French.   Can he rely on you?   We took the shortest way.   He has spread reports.   Run as fast as possible.   They have forbidden him to smoke.   Did you ask your father to come with me?   Wanted, a female French cook, speaking also English.   You are quite willing, are you not?   How much do you owe him?   She must be mistaken. You should work.   Do you blame him?   He appointed a meeting place here.   Where does this window open?   He does not take the trouble to do well.   Do you always listen to your teacher?   Did you try on your coat this morning? How cold it is.   Where do you have your clothes made? Mary, did you clean the room?   Do you know how to cook? Cook this meat for our breakfast.   He shammed illness. Remind me of that.   Did you pack your trunks?   He is studying law in Paris.   How much are you short?   He came near falling.   Did you lay the cloth?   At what time do you sit at the table?   He has instituted an inquiry.   They received us heartily.   He is exhausted.   He assured everything.   Mr. X begs me to answer your letter of the twelfth instant.   Are you acquainted with this lady that we just met?   I long to see France again.   He has been a father to him.   That is not worth speaking about.   He has just received a letter from his cousin.   Send for a good lawyer. How is it that you are here yet?   I do not know why he has a grudge against me.   What does he mean by that?

FRENCH GRAMMAR
(PART 8)

EXAMINATION QUESTIONS

(1) Translate into French (see Arts. **1** and **2**):

I am working hard now. Are you not studying French at present? I do believe that he is here. He is working to earn his living. My sister is in her room, where she is reading a very interesting book. Everybody thinks that both your brother and yourself are working too hard. How much is seven and eight? Seven and eight is fifteen. The earth is revolving around the sun in a little more than three hundred and sixty-five days. I leave tomorrow. I set out tomorrow for the country. I shall go to England next month, if I have enough money. Will you also go to France if you have (the) time? He does not know yet whether he will come or not. How long has he been here? How long have you been in America? I have been here ten years. I have just learned that he is ill.

(2) Translate into French (see Arts. **3** to **8**):

I was thinking of you when you entered. When I was in Paris, I generally walked in the Champs-Elysées. I often met Englishmen there. I wrote to Bordeaux yesterday. We met last year at Geneva. He used to live in this street. I was dressing when he came in. We had been two years in America when our brother arrived. I had been reading an hour when I was called. He received your letter the day before you left. I was just told that you were sick. I have been waiting for you a long time; what has delayed you?

He received a letter from his friend. Did you not answer the letter you received yesterday? In 1789 the people of Paris took the Bastile, and thus began a revolution. I should be delighted to go to France, if only I had (the) time. He would render you that service with pleasure if he could. Formerly I studied ten hours a day. If you would permit me, I would come to see you. We traveled through Italy and visited Rome. I met my best friend this morning. My sister-in-law has been ill this week. I slept badly last night, and I dreamed.

(3)   Translate into French (see Arts. **8** to **17**):

They had finished their work when we arrived. Were you up when I knocked at the door? Had he not sold his house before leaving the country? I would certainly have come sooner, if I had known that your friends were here. When they had received their money they started for France. Thou shalt not steal. Come to see us when they go away. He will tell what he pleases. Will you have finished before our return? Why is she not here? She has probably lost her way. What would you do if you had much money? I would study French if I had (the) time. She did not tell me whether she would study French or not. Were you told she would be here? He cannot tell you what he feels. Could he tell you her name? Why should he not put it on? Even though he should be poor, he would be satisfied. He would rather die than tell her name. They would have written to us if they had known we were here. Let them be angry. I had finished when you entered. The rain had ceased when the train arrived. As soon as we had received some money, we departed for Europe. Will you give me some hot water? I will give you some hot water every morning. I should be happy if you would permit me to stay. Even though he were a king, he would complain. When I had seen my error, I was ashamed of it. I was at your house this morning; I saw your brother and spoke to him. I shall wait for you until six o'clock. When I have done, I shall go out. I will call on you as soon as I have dined. If he should come, what should I say to him? Scarcely had I risen when he entered. I shall leave when I have finished my business. He would have come if he had been able. I shall follow him wherever he goes. Would you go there if they invited you? I don't know whether I would. I wish I knew why he does not come. You would regret it as long as you lived. I should rather remain here than go to the ball. Let me see what I have to do.

(4) Translate into French (see Arts. **17** to **30**):

Do you think he will come? I do not think he will come. I wish you may succeed. I did not think you would come. Do you doubt that I am your friend? He will wait until you are ready. I shall wait to hear from you. You deserve to be punished. I wish you to be happy. I doubt if you will say that before him. He fears that you may not arrive. It is necessary for me to work in the evening. Do you think he is as rich as they say? I do not think he has much money. I do not wish you to sing here. Give us the best wine you have. Are you not very glad that holidays come? I will speak, unless you object. However rich you may be, do not despise any one. You must come. It would be necessary for you to read. I wished you to be admitted. You must have finished before we return. We regret that you lose your time. I am astonished that we have not heard from aunt. Though you are rich and have talents, do not rely too much on those advantages. I am astonished that he does not see us. I fear he will not come. It is important that he be here before four o'clock. She wanted to buy a present that was pretty and did not cost much. I insist that you go away immediately. In case he tells me interesting news, I shall write you everything. Whatever riches he may possess, however learned he may be, whatever he may have done, it is character that makes the man.

FRENCH GRAMMAR

(PART 9)

EXAMINATION QUESTIONS

(1) Translate into French (see Arts. **1** to **14**):

He desires very much to see you. He does not know yet how to make an addition in French. She came to see me yesterday afternoon. I learned how to swim in my childhood. They seem to know you. He does not dare speak to you. We expect to see your father when we are in Europe. She seeks to sell her house. We were beginning to believe that he would not come. He fears to be recognized. He hastened to come to see me. You do not cease to complain. I thank you for having done that for me. He requested me to call at his house. He came in order to compliment me. He is getting ready to go to the ball. We did not want to disturb him. When did she come to see you? If it happens to rain, I shall stay here. They have just gone to the market. I have something to tell you. I authorize you to go with him. He expects to leave very soon. You will seek to know. They did not succeed in deceiving me.

(2) Translate into French (see Arts. **14** to **29**):

David is often represented playing on the harp. She is a woman of good disposition; always obliging her friends. Those foreseeing men have perceived the danger. Your sister is charming; how obliging she is! That letter is well written. Here are the letters that I have received. Here is the answer that I have received. They have deceived us. I have received no answer. They have spoken to one another. That song is charming; I heard it sung. Have you finished the letter that I gave you to write? What a beautiful rose you have given him! They (*fem.*) arrived day before yesterday. All those whom I loved are dead. We have taken a walk. Every Saturday evening I brought my mother the fifty francs I had earned during the week. Your mother admired her very much. The purse was there, where they had left it. She has cut her finger. What beautiful horses you have bought! How many pens have you bought? I have bought five. Did these boys wash themselves this morning? The few apples I ate made me ill. He gave them as he said he would. She took with her all the books she could. They begged her to write to them. The houses that I have seen sold were very cheap. There are the ladies I saw passing before your house. They dressed themselves before the dinner. Your children have worked very well. They did not play enough. The trees he planted last fall are all alive. The lady you met coming here is my aunt. Have you not found my pencil?

(3) Translate into French (see Arts. **29** to **54**):

Do you not like wine? I like wine very much, but I prefer cider. I like chocolate better than coffee. Have you not time to go with me to the store? I shall find time to go with you. Who started first? I do not understand German. He cannot keep silence. I have sore eyes. This coffee is worth forty cents a pound. Do you know France? I met Dr. Durand. I gave him full power. Do you not pity him? He brings good luck to us. Cheer up, my dear friend. Did you pay him a visit? This gentleman has neither a knife nor a fork. He became a soldier. Is this lady French? He is a good doctor. Can you translate this letter without a dictionary? How much does she earn a day?

(4) Translate into French (see Arts. **54** to **63**):

Have you seen Henry's knife? Here is our neighbor's house. There is the dining room and here is the bedroom. Have you a match box? I bought a gold watch the other day. Did you read yesterday's paper? How high is this mountain? It is one thousand feet high. The height of this mountain is one thousand feet. He was so thirsty that he drank two glasses of water. Many men are wicked. I rented a three-story house. Bring two coffee spoons. I cooked the dinner on my gas stove. Do you wish some vegetable soup?

(5) Give a general rule with examples for the agreement of the past participle (*a*) with *être*, (*b*) with *avoir*.

(6) How is the possessive case expressed in French? Give examples.

(7) When is the definite article omitted in the partitive construction?

(8) Explain the idioms formed with *venir* to express past action, with examples.

(9) What are the compound forms of the preposition *à* with the article?

(10) Give the first person plural of the simple tenses, interrogative, of *s'en aller*.

FRENCH GRAMMAR

(PART 10)

EXAMINATION QUESTIONS

(1) Translate into French (see Arts. **1** to **18**):

Her mother has bought a cotton dress for her. This man and this woman are very happy; their sons and daughters are very good. Louisa and Mrs. Loubet are ready. Why do you always go barefooted? It is now half-past three. They always go barefooted. Violets smell very good. Why do they walk so quickly? Has he bought the old horse or the young one? Mary bought a black dress and Louisa a white one. An Irishman said to a Scotchman: "Lend me three guineas" (guinée, *f*). "That is impossible, for I only possess half a guinea." "Well, lend it to me, and you will owe me two guineas and a half." They spoke loud. The rich and the poor are equal before God.

(2) Translate into French (see Arts. **18** to **27**):

You have a pretty little child. We spoke about different things. I do not like a fish dinner. He assured us it was a true story. It is necessary to go early. He is good for nothing. He was deaf to my request. He likes to be useful to men. Be attentive to what I say. She is not able to work. He is known to everybody. Am I not free in my actions? I am not sure to succeed. That is an amusing book. Are you ready to go out? He is slow to punish and prompt to reward. Your dress is like mine. I am glad to see you in good health. I am tired of running after him. He is very grateful for the services you have rendered him. We must be charitable to the poor.

(3)   Translate into French (see Arts. **27** to **49**):

His hands are swollen. I have a toothache. We are washing our hands. About eleven o'clock. He is not sending you to them. He has given them to us. He has not seen him. Does he give them to him? Has he not given it (*f*) to them? Does he not give me some of them? Do we not love him? Will you not lend it to him? Has he not seen them. Charles and I have gone to the country. You are older than he. He alone knows how to organize a family ball. He presented himself to me. I am always thinking of you. How many letters did you receive? I received five. I shall go there tomorrow. She is a friend of mine.

(4)   Translate into French (see Arts. **49** to **72**):

He had five of them; that was enough. If she has done that, it is well. He does not know what he wants. Have you all you want? Has he brought his trunk and his sister's? They who are never satisfied are never happy. Of whom are you thinking? What are you thinking of? Which of these ladies recognized me? Do you not speak to her when you meet her? He speaks to you and to him. Are you Dr. Loubet's daughter?—Yes; I am. His mother is an old acquaintance of ours. A sister of hers is dead. Is this house yours or his?—It is not mine. These keys are not mine, they are my father's or my mother's.

(5)   What is the difference between *qui* and *que* (1) as a relative pronoun; (2) as an interrogative pronoun?

(6)   What is the difference between *notre* and *le nôtre?* Give the plurals of the two.

(7)   When does *on* become *l'on?*

(8)   Write out the affirmative and negative imperatives of *se souvenir, jeter, se rappeler.*

(9)   When is *lequel* used instead of *qui* or *que?*

(10)   Give three meanings for *si*, and write three examples illustrating each case.

FRENCH GRAMMAR

(PART 11)

EXAMINATION QUESTIONS

The following Examination Questions, as well as those at the end of Part 12, are a general review of all the subjects treated in the Grammar.

(1) Write the plural of *feu, hibou, émail, bétail, pou, clou, paix, trésor, vœu, carnaval, contre-amiral.*

(2) Give the feminine of *sec, faux, mineur, vrai, furieux, caduc, cruel, complet, traître, instituteur, fier, épais, fort, loup, pécheur, malin, frais, indien.*

(3) Give principal parts of *mourir, craindre, tenir, faire, prendre, savoir, pouvoir, appeler, achever, devoir.*

(4) Name five adjectives that have two masculine forms; what is the rule for using these forms?

(5) Give the first person singular and plural present subjunctive of *aller, avertir, faire,* and *savoir.*

(6) What is the difference between *avant* and *devant, plutôt* and *plus tôt, tard* and *en retard?* Give examples.

(7) Form adverbs from *nouveau, doux, puissant, prudent, sec, vif, lent, hardi.*

(8) Give the masculine and feminine plural of *beau, juste, ce, celui, quel, lequel, tout, menteur, exquis, oisif, faux.*

(9) Translate into French:

He told me to wait here for him. I congratulate you on having succeeded. I hasten to answer your letter that I received four days ago. It is useless for you to speak to him; he will not obey you. He has a grudge against me because I did not lend him my French book. He takes after his mother; don't you think so? I fear it will rain this evening. Take care that he does not go out. I understand better than I speak. I have studied for eight months. I leave for eight months. How long have you been here? Here is the book of which you have spoken. She will never return it to you. Do not give it to her; give it to me. Have you much bread? Yes; I have some. Some books have been given me. Do you think that my brother is ill? I fear that he is ill. I am delighted to see you, sir; I have not seen you for a long time.

(10) Translate into French:

You have more books than John. He is older than he seems. She is more diligent and attentive than her sister. The weather is becoming colder and colder. The richer he becomes, the less generous he is. This book is cheaper than that one. I am three years older than you. I will give them back to you, be sure of it. I think of it. Give them back to me. Do not give them back to me. Take us there. Give them some of them. Do not go there. Do not go away. The whole class is punished. She is quite amiable. She is quite pale. Both have come. She is almighty. He comes to town every other day. I cannot love him however good he is.

(11) Translate into French:

The clock has just struck nine. The family are rising from the breakfast table. A ring at the door bell! The servant enters. Sir, a young man, Mr. A's clerk, has called,

and hopes you will not be offended, but he would feel particularly obliged if you would settle his account. He called
twice last week. He would not trouble you if it were not a
case of necessity.

(12) Translate into French:

What is there on the table? What do you see on the
table? Of what are you speaking? Of what are you thinking? What books are you reading? Our books are interesting. Are yours also interesting? Who is coming? Nobody
is coming. I see the man who is coming. Whom do you
see? Nobody. The man whom I see looks very old. The
book I am reading is not interesting. Which of these two
pencils do you wish? I don't know. Of whom are you
speaking? To whom are you speaking? The books of which
I spoke to you have arrived. The book of which you were
speaking to me has arrived. I speak to him, to her, to
them. I speak of him, of her, of them. I see him, her,
them, some one. I give it to him, to her, to them. I give
them to him, to her, to them. I think of him, of her, of
them. Give it to him, to her, them. See him, her, them.
I see him, her, them. Do not speak to him, to her, to them.

(13) When can *pas* and *point* be suppressed? Give four
examples.

(14) Translate into French:

SPEEDY PROMOTION.—One day, on the field, Napoleon's
hat having fallen off, a young lieutenant stepped forwards,
picked it up, and presented it to him. "Thank you, cap-
tain," said the emperor inadvertently. "In what regi-
ment, sire?" inquired the lieutenant, quick as lightning.
Napoleon smiled, and forthwith promoted the witty youth
to a captaincy.

(15) Translate into French:

THE LITTLE RED MAN.—The legend relates that when
the French monarchy is in danger, a little man clothed in
red wanders around the halls of the palace. One evening on

55—32

arriving at the Tuileries, Marie Antoinette and one of her maids of honor went together through the halls. Finally they stopped; the maid heard a noise, and turning around she saw a strange form clad in the manner of a man of the 15th century; he was dressed in red. The ladies could not restrain a cry, and hearing this, the form disappeared all of a sudden. They remained motionless for several minutes. Then the queen said: "Heaven wanted to warn me of the danger that threatens the monarchy. Let us go."

(16)   Translate into French:

I have been here two weeks. I enjoy myself very much when I am in the country. Poor John has no knife. He has lost it. Have you one for him? I arose early this morning (I will not tell you the hour) and went to the station. My sister arrived at half-past four. He has ceased singing. I am going to get some pens. It is cold tonight. I think it will freeze. Tomorrow we will take a sleigh ride. A little bird knocked at my window and said: "Open to me, I pray you; the snow is falling and I am cold and hungry." The bird flew into the room and picked up some bread that was on the table. In the spring time we opened the window. The bird flew away (*s'envoler*) into the neighboring woods, where he built his nest. What day of the month is it today? It is the sixteenth of December. They came on Monday morning. How old are you, Peter? I am twenty years old.

FRENCH GRAMMAR

(PART 12)

EXAMINATION QUESTIONS

(1) *Questions relating to French versification* (answer in French):   Quels sont les élements essentiels du vers syllabique?—Qu'appelle-t-on le vers alexandrin?—Donnez le nombre de syllabes de chacun des vers suivants, la place de la césure, la sorte de rimes (masculine ou féminine), et leurs qualités;

> Le renard sera bien habile
> S'il ne m'en laisse assez pour avoir un cochon.
> — La Fontaine

Demain, c'est le cheval qui s'abat blanc d'écume.
Demain, ô conquérant, c'est Moscou qui s'allume,
   La nuit comme un flambeau;
C'est votre vieille garde au loin jonchant la plaine.
Demain, c'est Waterloo, demain, c'est Sainte-Hélène!
   Demain, c'est le tombeau!   — Victor Hugo

(2)   Translate into French:

Character of Richard I

This renowned prince was tall, strong, straight, and well proportioned.   His arms were remarkably long, his eyes blue, and full of vivacity; his hair was of a yellowish color; his complexion fair, his countenance comely, and his air majestic. He was endowed with a good natural understanding; his penetration was uncommon; he possessed a fund of manly eloquence; his conversation was spirited, and he was admired for his talents; as for his courage and ability in war, both Europe and Asia resound with his praise.

(3) Translate into French: I can easily imagine that a Parisian ought to envy the happiness of those who live in small country towns. One needs not to go out of the noisy capital to know this. In Paris everybody is in haste, nobody can be quiet. But in a smaller town there is no anxiety. Nobody is obliged to run because there is time to walk. In the capital time is money. In the country everything is quite different. You find there different men. The streets seem wider, because there are few people in them, although they are in fact much smaller than those of Paris. The houses themselves are quite small, but you think that you could live in them more comfortably, because they are not all crowded together.

(4) Give the principal parts, also the third person plural of the future indicative, and the second person singular of the present subjunctive of the verbs represented by the following verb forms: *faille, vît, irions, craintes, firent, veniez, jetions, espérais.*

(5) Translate: Of what were you thinking when I spoke to you of the books that you had lost? Tell him what I was doing for her and tell it to them, but do not deceive yourself by thinking that you are the only man who knows it.

(6) Translate into French: The metric system is the system of weights and measures employed in France. Its establishment is one of the consequences of the French revolution, which began in the year seventeen hundred and eighty nine. Do not speak so fast; I cannot understand you. If you had taken better care of your books, you would not have lost them. If you do not respect yourself nobody will respect you. I have no money today. If I had any I would not lend you what you ask me, because I know that you would never return it to me. It is easier to correct your faults than to hide them. I have just seen your brother, and I am going to see your father. Gratitude is one of the noblest emotions of the human heart. In order to understand what I am writing to you, you must first remember the last words

I said to you when we left each other two months ago.
You were then very sad and disheartened. I spoke to
you of my old German friend and of the way in which he
had triumphed over all difficulties. I think it is possible
for you to follow his example, and I shall explain to you
how it can be done. Do not answer me that what was possible for him is impossible for you, or I shall think that you
have no courage at all.

INDEX

All items in this index refer first to the section number,—which is printed on the inside edges of the headlines and is preceded by the printers' section mark §,—and then to the page number. Thus ace, Suffix 20 39, means find the paper having § 20 on the headlines and then find page 39.

vii

INDEX

INDEX

INDEX

INDEX

xi

INDEX

xii

INDEX

INDEX

xiv

INDEX

INDEX

INDEX

xvii

INDEX

INDEX

xix

INDEX

INDEX

INDEX

INDEX

xxiii

INDEX

INDEX

XXV

INDEX

INDEX

xxvii

INDEX

INDEX

INDEX

INDEX

xxxi

INDEX

INDEX

INDEX

INDEX